ENCOUNTERS IN THE ARTS, LITERATURE,
AND PHILOSOPHY

Also Available from Bloomsbury

Philosophy, Literature and Understanding, Jukka Mikkonen (forthcoming)
Proust, Photography, and the Time of Life, Suzanne Guerlac
Henri Bergson and Visual Culture, Paul Atkinson
Erotic Love in Sociology, Philosophy and Literature, Finn Bowring
Deleuze and the Schizoanalysis of Literature, ed. Ian Buchanan,
Tim Matts, and Aidan Tynan

ENCOUNTERS IN THE ARTS, LITERATURE, AND PHILOSOPHY

Chance and Choice

Edited by
Jérôme Brillaud and Virginie Greene

BLOOMSBURY ACADEMIC
LONDON • NEW YORK • OXFORD • NEW DELHI • SYDNEY

BLOOMSBURY ACADEMIC
Bloomsbury Publishing Plc
50 Bedford Square, London, WC1B 3DP, UK
1385 Broadway, New York, NY 10018, USA
29 Earlsfort Terrace, Dublin 2, Ireland

BLOOMSBURY, BLOOMSBURY ACADEMIC and the Diana logo are trademarks of
Bloomsbury Publishing Plc

First published in Great Britain 2021
This paperback edition published in 2022

Copyright © Jérôme Brillaud, Virginie Greene, and Contributors, 2021

Jérôme Brillaud and Virginie Greene have asserted their right under the Copyright,
Designs and Patents Act, 1988, to be identified as Editors of this work.

For legal purposes the Acknowledgements on p. xv constitute an extension
of this copyright page.

Cover design by Charlotte Daniels
Cover image: Charlotte du Val d'Ognes by Marie-Denise Villers, 1801
(© FineArt / Alamy Stock Photo)

All rights reserved. No part of this publication may be reproduced or transmitted
in any form or by any means, electronic or mechanical, including photocopying,
recording, or any information storage or retrieval system, without prior
permission in writing from the publishers.

Bloomsbury Publishing Plc does not have any control over, or responsibility for, any
third-party websites referred to or in this book. All internet addresses given in
this book were correct at the time of going to press. The author and publisher
regret any inconvenience caused if addresses have changed or sites have
ceased to exist, but can accept no responsibility for any such changes.

A catalogue record for this book is available from the British Library.

Library of Congress Cataloging-in-Publication Data

Names: Brillaud, Jérôme, editor. | Greene, Virginie Elisabeth,
1959-editor. | McDonald, Christie, 1942- dedicatee.
Title: Encounters in the arts, literature, and philosophy: chance and
choice / edited by Jérôme Brillaud and Virginie Greene.
Description: London; New York: Bloomsbury Academic, 2021. |
Includes bibliographical references and index. |
Identifiers: LCCN 2020050385 (print) | LCCN 2020050386 (ebook) |
ISBN 9781350160903 (hardback) | ISBN 9781350160910 (ebook) |
ISBN 9781350160927 (epub)
Subjects: LCSH: Chance. | Meetings. | Arts.
Classification: LCC BD595.E53 2021 (print) |
LCC BD595 (ebook) | DDC 123/.3–dc23
LC record available at https://lccn.loc.gov/2020050385
LC ebook record available at https://lccn.loc.gov/2020050386

ISBN: HB: 978-1-3501-6090-3
PB: 978-1-3502-2518-3
ePDF: 978-1-3501-6091-0
eBook: 978-1-3501-6092-7

Typeset by RefineCatch Limited, Bungay, Suffolk

To find out more about our authors and books visit www.bloomsbury.com
and sign up for our newsletters.

For Christie McDonald

CONTENTS

List of Figures   x
Notes on Contributors   xi
Acknowledgments   xv

INTRODUCTION   1

Chapter 1
ENCOUNTERING THE DIVINE: ON THE COGNITION OF
GOD IN EARLY FRENCH CHRISTIAN HUMANISM   21
    Jacob Vance

Chapter 2
EVENT AND INVENTION: READING MONTAIGNE AND
ROUSSEAU THROUGH DELEUZE   35
    Tom Conley

Chapter 3
ENCOUNTERING VENTURE: DISSONANCE, DECEIT,
AUTOBIOGRAPHY   47
    Pierre Saint-Amand

Chapter 4
COLONIAL ENCOUNTERS OF "LA BELLE ET LA BETE"   59
    Kylie Sago

Chapter 5
MISSED CONNECTIONS: LITERARY HISTORY AND
SAINT-AUBIN'S *LE DANGER DES LIAISONS*   71
    Sanam Nader-Esfahani

Chapter 6
REJECTED ENCOUNTERS WITH WOMEN WRITERS: THE CASE
OF *LES PENSEES ERRANTES*   81
    Caleb Shelburne

Chapter 7
ENCOUNTERING WOMEN WRITERS AND THEIR TEXTS: LOUISE DE
KERALIO'S PIONEERING ANTHOLOGY   93
   Vicki Mistacco

Chapter 8
CHÂTELET, LAVOISIER, CHARRIÈRE: NEGOTIATING
THE BORDERLANDS OF THE REPUBLIC OF LETTERS   107
   Ian Van Wye

Chapter 9
WOMEN'S FICTIONS AND TRANSLATIONS IN SUPPORT OF
ENLIGHTENMENT VALUES   117
   Monique Moser-Verrey

Chapter 10
STOWE MEETS THOMAS: WHAT IS LITERARY PROPERTY?   135
   Gary Wihl

Chapter 11
FORM ENCOUNTERS SENSE: THE SEMIOLOGICAL DIMENSIONS OF
WAGNERIAN ANTI-SEMITISM   147
   Jean-Jacques Nattiez

Chapter 12
"UN AUTRE MOI-MÊME": BETWEEN THE SELF AND THE
OTHER IN PROUST'S CORRESPONDENCE   153
   François Proulx

Chapter 13
EKPHRASING AS ENCOUNTER: "TRY SAY" WITH GEORGES
DIDI-HUBERMAN AND HÉLÈNE CIXOUS   165
   Ginette Michaud

Chapter 14
CARING FOR ENCOUNTERS   179
   Verena Andermatt Conley

Chapter 15
PRIVATE LIVES, PUBLIC HISTORY: ENCOUNTERING
THE FILMMAKER ISTVÁN SZABÓ   191
   Susan Rubin Suleiman

Chapter 16
CREATION AND RE-CREATION ACROSS CULTURES
AND DISCIPLINES: TAHITIAN ENCOUNTERS FROM
BOUGAINVILLE TO GAUGUIN AND BEYOND 201
   Christie McDonald

Bibliography 215
Index 237

FIGURES

7.1 Frontispiece, *Collection des meilleurs ouvrages français composés par des femmes*, vol. I. FC7.R5406.786c, Houghton Library, Harvard University. 100
7.2 Victory, Trajan's Column, Rome (© J.C.N. Coulston.) 101
7.3 Cesare Ripa, *Iconologia, or Moral Emblems*, 1709. Image by Vicki Mistacco. GEN (MS Eng 1188), Houghton Library, Harvard University. 102
9.1 D'Ussieux's Fleuron. Designed by F. Clerc and etched by E. Fessard, 1772. Title page to Louis d'Ussieux, *Le Décaméron françois*, vol. 1 (Paris: Costard, 1772). Image courtesy of the *Bibliothèque des livres rares et collections spéciales*. Direction des bibliothèques, Université de Montréal. 124
9.2 D'Ussieux's Fleuron. Anonymous. Title page to Louis d'Ussieux, *Le Décaméron françois*, vol. 2 (Paris: Dufour, 1774). Image courtesy of the *Bibliothèque des livres rares et collections spéciales*. Direction des bibliothèques, Université de Montréal. 125
9.3 Frontispiece to *Dubois et Gioconda: Nouvelle corse* (Paris: Brunet, 1781). Designed by Desmaisons and etched by Madame Ponce. In Louis d'Ussieux, *Nouvelles françaises*, vol. 3 (Paris: Nyon l'aîné, Belin, 1784), 5–61. Image courtesy of the *Bibliothèque des livres rares et collections spéciales*. Direction des bibliothèques, Université de Montréal. 127
9.4 Vignette to *Dubois et Gioconda: Nouvelle corse* (Paris: Brunet, 1781). Designed by Desmaisons and etched by Madame Ponce. In Louis d'Ussieux, *Nouvelles françaises*, vol. 3 (Paris: Nyon l'aîné, Belin, 1783), 5–61. Image courtesy of the *Bibliothèque des livres rares et collections spéciales*. Direction des bibliothèques, Université de Montréal. 127
14.1 Jan Van der Straet, "Amerigo Vespucci Discovers America" (c. 1587–9). Reproduced in accordance with the Metropolitan Museum of Art's Creative Commons Zero (CC0) policy. 180

NOTES ON CONTRIBUTORS

Jérôme Brillaud is the author of *Sombres Lumières* (2011) and *A Philosophy of Simple Living* (2020, translated into German as *Der Philosophie der Einfachheit*). He has co-edited a volume on life in the seventeenth century and has written articles on early modern philosophy and literature. He teaches at the University of Manchester.

Verena Andermatt Conley teaches in Comparative Literature and in Romance Languages and Literature at Harvard University. She is currently writing on the notion of care in relation to ecology. Recent publications include *Spatial Ecologies* (2013) and *Cree: To Believe in the World* (2015).

Tom Conley is the Abbott Lawrence Lowell Professor of Visual and Environmental Studies and of Romance Languages and Literatures at Harvard University. He is author of *À fleur de page: Voir et lire le texte de la Renaissance* (2016), co-editor with Hunter Vaughan of the *Anthem Anthology of Screen Theory* (2018) and with T. J. Kline, of *The Wylie-Blackwell Companion to Jean-Luc Godard* (2014). A sequel to his *Errant Eye: Poetry and Topography in Early Modern France* (2011) is forthcoming.

Virginie Greene is the author of *Un petit rouage dans la grande machine: Thomas Rodman Plummer 1862–1918* (2018); *Logical Fictions in Medieval Literature and Philosophy* (2014), and *Cent vues de John Harvard* (2011). She has edited a volume of essays, *The Medieval Author in Medieval French Literature* (2006). She is Professor of French literature at Harvard University.

Christie McDonald is the Smith Research Professor of French Language and Literature in the Department of Romance Languages and Literatures, and Research Professor of Comparative Literature at Harvard University. Recent publications include co-edited works: *Proust and the Arts* (2015) with François Proulx; *Rousseau and Freedom* (2010) with Stanley Hofmann; *French Global: A New Approach to French Literary History* (with Susan Suleiman, 2010). She is the author of *The Extravagant Shepherd* (1973, 2006) on Rousseau; *The Dialogue of Writing* (1985) on Rousseau, Derrida, and Diderot; *Dispositions* (1986) between music and text; *The Proustian Fabric* (1991); "Le dix-huitième siècle," in *Femmes et littérature: Une histoire culturelle* (2020), and *The Life and Art of Anne Eisner (1911–1967): An American Artist Between Cultures* (2020).

Ginette Michaud is Professor of French-Language Literature at the Université de Montréal. A member of the international editorial committee responsible for Jacques Derrida's seminars, she has coedited *The Beast and the Sovereign* (2009; 2011) and *Le parjure et le pardon* (2019; 2020), and has dedicated several essays to Derrida, Cixous and Nancy. She is especially interested in the question of art from deconstruction's point of view and has co-edited a collection of Derrida's writings on art, *Thinking Out of Sight* (forthcoming 2020), and architecture, *Les arts de l'espace* (2015), as well as an issue of *Études françaises* on ekphrasis (2015).

Vicki Mistacco is Professor *Emerita* of French at Wellesley College. She is the author of *Les femmes et la tradition littéraire: Anthologie du Moyen Age à nos jours* (two vols, 2006–7). Her research focuses on French women's literature and women's literary history across the centuries, with emphasis on female-authored anthologies and other compendia of women writers, 1750–1970, and the writings of Louise de Keralio. Her recent publications include essays on Genlis, Louise d'Alq, Keralio, Riccoboni, and Sand, and the entry "La femme auteur" for the *Dictionnaire des femmes des Lumières*. She is currently writing a book on Keralio as an Enlightenment intellectual.

Monique Moser-Verrey is honorary professor and member of the Canadian Center for German and European Studies at the University of Montreal. Holding a PhD in Comparative Literature (University of Zurich), she taught French and German literatures at Laval University and was the editor of *Études littéraires*. Her research focuses on illustrated tales and novels of the long eighteenth century: *Le corps Romanesque: images et usages topiques sous l'Ancien Régime* (with L. Desjardins and C. Turbide, Quebec 2009, Paris 2015), *The Visual Culture of Print, Eighteenth-Century Fiction* 23:4 (2011), *Isabelle de Charrière: salonnière virtuelle* (2013).

Sanam Nader-Esfahani is Assistant Professor of French at Amherst College. At the intersection of the French and Italian traditions of the sixteenth and seventeenth centuries, her work focuses on literature, science and technology. Her current book project examines the dialogue between literature and visual theories and technologies in the early modern period.

Jean-Jacques Nattiez is Professor *Emeritus* of musicology at the Faculty of Music of the University of Montreal. He is author of numerous books and articles on musical semiotics, Wagner, Boulez, the relationships between music and literature, and various musics of oral tradition. His works have been translated into Albanian, English, Italian, Japanese, Portuguese, Spanish, and Romanian. He is editor of a five-volume music Encyclopedia published in Italian (Einaudi) and French (Actes Sud), as well as lecturer and guest Professor in around twenty countries, including at the Collège de France, Paris. A synthetic book on Inuit music, and a *Traité de musicologie générale* are under preparation.

François Proulx is Associate Professor of French at the University of Illinois at Urbana-Champaign. He is the author of *Victims of the Book: Reading and Masculinity in Fin-de-Siècle France* (2019) and co-editor of *Proust and the Arts* (with Christie McDonald, 2015).

Kylie Sago is a PhD candidate in the Department of Romance Languages and Literatures at Harvard University. Her current research examines the intersections of French literature and empire in the eighteenth and nineteenth centuries. She has previously written on cultural and postcolonial studies and served as assistant editor to Andrew Sobanet for the volume, *Revisioning French Culture* (2019).

Pierre Saint-Amand teaches the literature and philosophy of the French Enlightenment at Yale University where he is the Benjamin F. Barge Professor of French. His books include *Diderot: Le Labyrinthe de la relation* (1984), *The Libertine's Progress: Seduction in the Eighteenth-Century Novel* (1994), *The Laws of Hostility: Politics, Violence, and the Enlightenment* (1996) and more recently, *The Pursuit of Laziness: An Idle Interpretation of the Enlightenment* (2011).

Caleb Shelburne is a doctoral student in the History of Science at Harvard University. His current research examines nineteenth- and twentieth-century histories of technology and the social sciences in the Ottoman Empire.

Susan Rubin Suleiman is the C. Douglas Dillon Professor of the Civilization of France *Emerita* and Professor of Comparative Literature *Emerita* at Harvard University. Her books include *The Némirovsky Question: The Life, Death, and Legacy of a Jewish Writer in 20th-Century France* (2016), *Crises of Memory and the Second World War (2006)*, *Risking Who One Is: Encounters with Contemporary Art and Literature* (1994), and the memoir *Budapest Diary: In Search of the Motherbook* (1996). Among collective volumes she has edited are *Exile and Creativity* (1998) and *French Global: A New Approach to Literary History* (with Christie McDonald, 2010).

Jacob Vance holds a BA in English Literature and Liberal Arts from Concordia University, an MA in Comparative Literature from the University of Washington, a DEA (or MA) in Early Modern European Culture and Civilization from the University of Geneva, and a PhD in Romance Languages and Literature from Johns Hopkins University.

Ian Van Wye works at Farrar, Straus and Giroux in New York. He graduated summa cum laude from Harvard College in 2017 with an AB in History and Literature.

Gary Wihl is the Hortense and Tobias Lewin Distinguished Professor of the Humanities at Washington University in St. Louis. He is the author of books on John Ruskin and on literary theory published by Yale UP. His current research consists of a series of essays on law and literature. In recent years he served as Dean of Humanities at Rice University and Dean of the Faculty of Arts and Sciences at Washington University. In 1994 he coedited a volume of essays with Christie McDonald, *Transformations in Personhood and Culture After Theory* (Penn State Press).

ACKNOWLEDGMENTS

On April 29, 2017, a group of scholars from the USA, Canada, the UK, and France met to thank Professor Christie McDonald for her friendship, mentorship, and her intellectual generosity as she was about to retire from Harvard University. On that day, we knew full well that we were not parting ways—that we would meet again. With this book, we indeed do so. The co-editors of the volume would also like to thank, as a way of keeping them close to the intellectual project started in 2017, all those who contributed to the conference—Diane Berrett Brown, Sylvaine Guyot, Alice Jardine, Natasha Lee, Éric Méchoulan, Richard Moran, Martine Reid, Kay Shelemay, Susan R. Stebbins and Tali Zechory—as well as those who contributed to the present volume. Our deep gratitude goes to Anne Ratnoff and Emma Zitzow-Childs for their precise and dedicated editorial work. We owe a special thank you to Michael Rosengarten for his support and hospitality all throughout the process. At Bloomsbury, we would like to thank our editors, Liza Thompson, Lisa Goodrum, and Lucy Russell for their support and suggestions throughout the publication process. Finally, we would like to recognize the financial support of the Harvard Provostial Fund for the Arts and Humanities and the Murray Anthony Potter Fund for Publication in the Department of Romance Languages and Literatures at Harvard.

INTRODUCTION

Jérôme Brillaud and Virginie Greene

Errant Knights and Bedazzled Philosophers

Neither Greek nor Latin has a term corresponding to "encounter," "*rencontre*," or "*Begegnung*," expressing a move against, toward, and forward, and the result of this move. When, around 1132, Peter Abelard looked back at his life experience, he wrote it down as a history of his disasters, rather than as a history of his encounters with remarkable people.[1] He was following the Augustinian model, in which all encounters are subsumed by the ultimate encounter of a creature with its creator. As an aspiring neo-Greek philosopher, Abelard thought of encounter as a kind of "accident."[2] As a Christian theologian, he confessed it as a cause for sin or as an occasion for conversion. As a man, he experienced it through the filters of his time and with the intensity of his temper. There is no doubt that his encounters with his masters, his students, and his lover, wife, and colleague, Heloise, left enduring traces in our history and imagination, but they did not trigger a theoretical adjustment in the debates on universals, on faith and reason, on human intelligence, and on signification that subsequently occupied logicians, philosophers and theologians from Abelard to Descartes. But why would the accidents affecting the life of a philosopher affect an intellectual tradition defining itself as emotional asceticism?

At the same time, the Western philosophical tradition came into its pre- or early-modern form through a meeting of languages, cultures, and faiths across the Mediterranean area. Aristotle was progressively rediscovered in the West, throughout the twelfth and the thirteenth century, thanks to translations from Greek into Arabic, Hebrew and Latin.[3] This does not imply an intellectual move from categories toward events, or a professional turn from debating to encountering, but creates the conditions of historical events such as the condemnation of Averroism in Paris in 1270 and 1277, which inflected modes of thinking about the subject, the intellect, reason, and faith. In opposition to the Averroists' theory of a universal intelligence thinking through each individual intellect, Thomas Aquinas roots thinking in individual subjects.[4] This potentially gives encounters between subjects a more interesting role to play in the transmission of thoughts and ideas.

However, as long as philosophy remains more focused on categories than events, encounter remains an accident that can be folded in theories of change and movement without being foregrounded. It may be viewed as a slippery notion such as time, which Augustine described as known only when not thought about and escaping knowledge when focused upon.[5]

The roots of our own practice and theory of encounter do not come directly from Platonism, Aristotelianism, or Augustinianism, even given the eventful history of their developments. They are to be retraced along indirect itineraries, often in works at the border of Latinate and vernacular, clerkly and courtly, high and low cultures—in works that perform encounter in their form and style. Encounter has been told, sung and written before being conceptualized. The following examples isolate a few memorable encounters in pre-modern literature, without proposing an overview of encounter as a motif.

The sub-genre of the *pastorella* includes in its required features a chance encounter between a knight and a shepherdess. "The other day, in the morning, between a wood and an orchard, I found a shepherdess."[6] The charm of this limited but successful lyric niche has much to do with the various outcomes of the mandatory script.[7] The poet-knight is not always the winner, and gender reversal combined with class revenge may give a carnivalesque twist to the plot. The aristocratic *trouvère* may be defeated by the wit and eloquence of the *pastoure*, strengthened, if necessary, by the cudgels of her lover, brothers, and allied folks. Alternatively, a courtly beginning may be a prelude to rape, reaffirming male and aristocratic privilege, and a conception of desire going against the grain of courtly love. The simplicity of the *pastorella* structure underlines the potentialities of encountering as a poetic, erotic and narrative trope. The trouvère "*trouve*" (finds) a story and a song as he encounters a woman.

In courtly romances, a larger frame in verse or prose allows for more complex plots, interactions, and encounters. Adventure moves the story forward in a contradictory tension between contingent itinerary and manifest destiny. An errant knight is by definition a professional "encounterer" realizing his vocation through trying his luck. Grail stories push that tension to the extreme. What is encountered remains obscure, although it is shown in full light. Why this encounter happens, for what reason, and to whose benefit are subjects of speculation down to this day. The first quester, Perceval, fails to understand something is happening to him when he witnesses an apparition of the Grail.[8] His stupidity appears to be a pre-condition of his election as the knight of the Grail. Must we foster a certain kind of simplicity to expose ourselves to extraordinary encounters? What is the relation between encounter and knowledge?

Boethius was far from naïve when Philosophy appeared to him. At the beginning of *Consolation of Philosophy*, the philosopher, fallen out of imperial favor, is in jail, waiting for execution. Thus, he has met the conditions for happiness according to most philosophers—pagan and Christian—of his times: he has abandoned the illusory goods of this world and renounced human affections and ambitions. But Boethius is not happy at all. Philosophy in jail is a different story from philosophy in the comfort of one's study. Philosophical lessons authorized by big names in the pantheon of dead philosophers would have failed to meet Boethius' depressed state. Nothing less than an encounter of the most intense kind can shake him out of his un-philosophical mood. "While I silently pondered these things, and decided to write down my wretched complaint, there appeared standing above me a woman of majestic countenance whose flashing eyes seemed wise beyond the ordinary wisdom of men."[9]

The encounter of Boethius and Philosophy corresponds to the scene of the Annunciation, in which a woman encounters a male figure that is not a man but an angel. The possibility of a man encountering a woman at full intensity on all levels of human existence has been avoided by philosophers and theologians, left to the fantasies dreamt of by poets or lived by ordinary people. Tristan meets Iseult for a life full of lies ending in unheroic deaths. Nicolette meets Aucassin for a life full of adventures ending in a happy marriage. The philosophical poets tempted by the Boethian matrix and desirous to give a human name to their *donna* (whether it is Beatrice, Laura or Délie), could not avoid an allegorizing effect that, in the end, left them alone with an angel, a tree, or an idea. Encountering a woman turned out to be a more difficult problem than the quarrel of the universals.

Passages

To map encounter as a semantic and semiotic field, we can first distinguish between encounter as a falling-upon (indicated in Latin verbs such as *occurro* and *invenio*) and encounter as a convergence (indicated in Latin verbs such as *concurro* and *conjungo*).

Encounter as a falling-upon can be subdivided in two categories: at the high end, the epiphany (of the Philosophy-appears-to-Boethius type); at the low end, the opportunity (of the knight-meets-a-shepherdess type). Both epiphanic and opportunistic falling-upon encounters are asymmetric, and tend toward hierarchy and brevity. What suddenly appears suddenly disappears. One element transcends, dominates or takes advantage of the other. The outcome may be a conversion, a seduction, or a conquest, as well as the failure to convert, seduce, or conquer. In any case, the knowledge obtained is experiential and hard to share with those who were not there at the right time. To be part of such a happening, one needs to not seek it and to be open to opportunities—that is, to move outside one's usual social ground. If Boethius had not lost his high status, he would not have been open to listening to Philosophy as he never had before, when he was reading philosophers. The knight who takes his chance with a shepherdess strays from his aristocratic and military height toward the unknown ground that his horse treads. The *trouvère* who raises his eyes toward his lord's wife and ceremoniously courts her assumes a similar position of social dissonance.

Encounter as convergence relates two items on the same plane, in a dynamic exchange spatially organized according to notions and practices of territory. A medieval territory is a space delineated by clear landmarks such as city walls or milestones, or buffered by marches—that is, borderlands without clear delimitations. One can get across a territory and pass to another one by using passages, either punctual such as gates, passes, fords or bridges, or extended such as roads, streams, or bodies of water. This sense of space is reflected in the linguistic use of three Latin prepositions: *inter* (between), *trans* (through or across), and *cum* (with). Instead of someone falling upon something or somebody as happens in opportunist or epiphanist encounters, in convergent encounters, people meet between, through, or with.

In the mountainous marches between Spain and France, all paths lead to Roncevaux. Roland, count of the marches of Brittany, sets the trap into which he will fall by sending his stepfather Ganelon to the Saracens, on a suicide mission. But Ganelon and the Saracen King Marsile find common ground in their hatred of Roland. The strategy is simple: "If I manage to find him in a mountain pass or defile / I'll engage him in mortal combat."[10] In the Old French epic tradition, the legend of Roland may have reached fame precisely because it sets up encounters between Christians and Saracens in a space emblematizing medieval territoriality. Loyalty and treachery to one's god or one's lord are only different ways to cross bonds of fealty, and, in *The Song of Roland*, to cross the Pyrenees. Fame or shame, life or death, defeat or victory depend on the time and place of encounters between all those marching through a rugged landscape: "The mountains are high and the valleys are shadowy."[11]

It is in a similar landscape that Dante locates the beginning of his journey: "But when I reached the foot of a hill at the end of that valley, which had pierced my heart with fear, I looked up." Unwittingly, with a mind "full of sleep," he has found "the pass which never yet let any go alive."[12] On his own, he would not be able to overcome his fears, materializing in the guise of monstrous beasts. As he retreats, he becomes aware of a presence: "When I was rushing down to the place below there appeared before my eyes one whose voice seemed weak from long silence."[13] It is hardly an apparition, even less an epiphany: someone or something vague coming from below is ready to answer, if only someone coming from above dares to speak first. It takes most of the first and all of the second canto for Dante to negotiate this encounter through the kind of awkward conversation that may occur when one meets a celebrity in an incongruous place, and does not recognize the famous person at first sight. It is only once Virgil has revealed that their encounter was not pure chance, but due to a mutual acquaintance in a higher sphere, that Dante agrees to follow his appointed guide.

Such reluctance is not shown by the pilgrims hosted at the Tabard Inn of Southwark in Kent, an April night, when the inn-keeper appoints himself both their guide to Saint Thomas of Canterbury and the judge of a storytelling contest. About thirty pilgrims, who met at the inn "by aventure," decide to form a "felaweshipe."[14] Not only will they share their experience of religious fulfillment, but also stories "of aventures that whilom han befall."[15] In Chaucer's days, traveling together toward a common destination was a more realistic setting than the lonely journeys of errant knights, and the commingling of folks coming "from every shires end / Of Engleland to Caunterbury" was a mode of encounter with which people from all walks of life could identify.[16] However, the encounter that the narrator dreads is with his readers. "But first I pray yow, of your curteisye, / That ye n'arette it nat my vileinye / Thogh that I pleynly speke in this mateere / To telle yow hir wordes and hir cheer."[17] A knight, a miller, a cook, a prioress, a clerk, a merchant, etc., may meet, travel together and tell each other about their lives without much ado, but giving voice to each of them in writing was to open up new territories in reality and fiction for encountering across social classes, orders, and genders.

The Risks of Modernity

It is one thing to create territories of the imagination defined by encounters; it is another to create a self defined by encountering. In his life and works, Montaigne pushed the logic of the errant knight toward the psychology of the errant *moi*: "This book was written in good faith, reader. It warns you [*te*] from the outset that in it I have set myself no goal but a domestic and private one. I have had no thought of your [*ton*] service or my own glory."[18] In this encounter between author and reader, no concession is made to common rules of encounters among strangers. There are no greetings, no *vous* to soften the face to face. The first essay seems to start out of nowhere to go nowhere: "First Chapter. By diverse means we arrive at the same end."[19] The reader who manages to overcome his or her initial befuddlement is taken for a ride together at the slow pace that long travels require. While recognizing that "[t]he soul that has no fixed goal loses itself" and that the choice of retirement he made in 1571 had the effect of unleashing in his mind "so many chimeras and fantastic monsters, one after another, without order or purpose," Montaigne continues on the dangerous path of free wandering, letting his fantastic monsters and chimeras proliferate, with the only constraint being "to put them in writing, hoping in time to make my mind ashamed of itself."[20] Accepting the risk to meet unsettling or shameful aspects of himself, Montaigne finds out that it is the best way for him to put his mind to work: "This also happens to me: that I do not find myself in the place where I look; and I find myself more by chance encounter than by searching my judgment."[21] Montaigne might have been one of the very first tourists of Europe, if by tourism we mean a humanist way of traveling.[22] His *Essays* mark the moment when it becomes possible to adopt a way of life and a mode of thinking in which external encounters nourish the inner encounter with oneself, and vice versa. This does not go without risks.

Encounters mark departures from *loci communes* where habits of thought hamper the mind and constrain the body. Truths, according to Descartes, are encountered in the world. For the inquisitive and free mind traveling the world, unpredictable encounters test the resilience of the self, sharpen a moral sense, and exercise reason. "Reason is a universal instrument which can be used in all kinds of situations"—or in all kinds of "rencontres," as per the French text.[23] Only encounters with a consequence matter, as only they can lead to the truths about oneself and about the workings of the world. Itinerant philosophers seek in worldly encounters the ferment of systems where truths are deployed if only to be tested again and to be encountered anew.

Others flee encounters altogether, "trembling at being met again," confesses Rousseau's student Émile.[24] "But where to flee"? he asks.[25] Where to escape others who see you for who they think you are? The flight from the omnipresent gaze and judgment of the other lies in a philosophy of life rooted in the absolute isolation in the present moment severed from the passing of time and the society of others: "I said to myself that in fact we are never doing anything but beginning, and that there is no connection in our existence other than a succession of present moments, the first of which is always the one that is happening. We die and we are born every instant of our lives."[26] Published four years after his death in 1778, the *Confessions* testify to the many strategies—stylistic and existential—Rousseau devised to hide from others and often from himself. When hiding in the folds of family myths, when sheltering in the exclusivity of the moment, when coining new names for himself and running from place to place to escape enemies—real or imagined—the nomadic philosopher never established roots, as he was too busy evading others. Nonetheless, a world without encounters is but a hypothetical state predating all society, the kind of state philosophical dreams are made of.

In the primeval forest of the state of nature hypothesized by Rousseau in his *Discourse on the Origins of Inequality*, chance encounters between men and women are brief. Such encounters may guarantee the survival of the species, but they never stimulate parental instincts and children are auspiciously absent from this forest. In Rousseau's state of nature, Louis Althusser sees "individuals without encounters"; he reads the "radical absence of society" as the "essence of any possible society."[27] Society then emerges out of encounters provoked by natural catastrophes where men and women find themselves confined to territories such as islands after having roamed childless and free in the infinite forest. Althusser compares Rousseau's forest to the Epicurean void in which atoms rain down without encountering one another, except when one accidentally swerves. In the accident lies the first encounter, and from it emerges the possibility of a new society where subsequent encounters, some of them bellicose, are mitigated, and where interests are subsumed in the general will.

Two Rebellious Philosophies

Unlike many philosophers who sought shelter from the materialist rain, Louis Althusser and Gilles Deleuze saw in the *clinamen*, or encounter of atoms, the possibility of a new philosophy. In a series of essays he wrote later in his life, Althusser developed a philosophy of encounter. In "The Underground Current of the Materialism of the Encounter," he brings to light

> the existence of an almost completely unknown materialist tradition in the history of philosophy: the "materialism" (we shall have to have some word to distinguish it as a tendency) of the rain, the swerve, the encounter, the take [*prise*]. I shall develop all these concepts. To simplify matters, let us say, for now, a materialism of the encounter, and therefore of the aleatory and of contingency.[28]

Althusser differentiates his materialism of the encounter from other materialist traditions, Marxism for instance, on the basis that such materialisms are but forms of idealisms relying on rationalism, necessity, and teleology.[29] Following Epicurus, Althusser offers the vision of a world originating in an infinitesimally small swerve where an atom encounters another atom, where encounters leading to lasting encounters inaugurate a world. In the encounter, atoms emerge from their "*unreal existence*" to have their reality conferred upon them.[30] The atom is not origin; the encounter is.

For Althusser, the encounter is doubly aleatory: its origin is aleatory in that the encounter might not have taken place, but it did.[31] Its effects are aleatory in that nothing prior to the encounter itself presages the being that will come into existence from the association. Nothing guarantees the encounter and its lasting effects. Similarly, what has come into existence in the encounter does not acquire a permanent and stable existential significance just because it now is.[32] The materialism of the encounter combats the principles of reason, necessity and eschatology, as well as the quests for origins and ends. It posits that there is no eternity in any laws or any world, that any accomplished fact will be revoked by an unpredictable and undecipherable fact yet to be accomplished.[33] Althusser's materialism of the encounter is a philosophy of the void:

> Not only the philosophy which *says* that the void pre-exists the atoms that fall in it, but a philosophy which *creates the philosophical void* [*fait le vide philosophique*] in order to endow itself with existence: a philosophy which, rather than setting out from the famous "philosophical problems" (why is there something rather than nothing), *begins by evacuating all philosophical problems* hence by refusing to assign itself any "object" whatever ("philosophy has no object") in order to set out from *nothing*, and from the infinitesimal, aleatory variation of nothing constituted by the swerve of the fall. Is there a more radical critique of all philosophy, with its pretension to utter the truth about things? Is there a more striking way of saying that philosophy's "object" *par excellence* is nothingness, nothing, or the void?[34]

Althusser did not try to elaborate a new form of materialism which would overturn the old ones, but rather to expose "The Underground Current of the Materialism of the Encounter"—as his title indicates—if only so as to philosophize the void where swerves may happen, where rain, torrential or drizzling, may create new worlds.

While Althusser's materialism of encounter taps into Epicurean sources, Deleuze's theory of encounter departs from the idea of the *clinamen* and contingency of the present in which the accidental deviations of atoms happen. For Deleuze, the encounter occurs in a present which is not so aleatory as it is "fortuitous and inevitable"[35] and which contains the traces and the possibility of its own deciphering.[36] In *Proust and Signs*, Deleuze opposes encounters to recognition. He draws a line between the objects of recognition and the objects of encounters: "something in the world forces us to think. This something is an object not of recognition but of a fundamental *encounter*."³⁷ Objects of recognition leave the mind inactive or give it a false sense of activity.

> What forces us to think is the sign. The sign is the object of an encounter, but it is precisely the contingency of the encounter that guarantees the necessity of what it leads us to think. The act of thinking does not proceed from a simple natural possibility; on the contrary, it is the only true creation. Creation is the genesis of the act of thinking within thought itself.³⁸

The experience of the encounter is an experience of forces imposed by cosmic necessity while remaining only partially organized.³⁹ For Deleuze, an encounter resulting from the collision of forces always results in metamorphosis.⁴⁰ Contrary to representation and recognition which anchor and confirm thoughts, encounters—not without violence—cause a disruption which forces us to experience the world differently, no longer in a totalizing and hermeneutically organized way. Alain Beaulieu sees in Althusser's and Deleuze's philosophies of encounter propositions against hegemonical regimes which impose external modes of representations on all. Encounters, on the contrary, offer to individuals the opportunity to self-determine and self-constitute, and to travel.

New Worlds

Jacob Levy Moreno spent the first six years of his life in Bucharest before his family relocated in 1895 to Vienna, where he studied medicine, mathematics, and philosophy. There, in 1912, he met Sigmund Freud. In "Invitation to an Encounter" (1914), Moreno invited us to think beyond the dyadic Freudian therapeutic model. His theory of encounter, psychodrama, and sociodrama later developed into what is commonly known as group therapy. In educational environments, "encounter groups"—also called "sensitivity-training groups" as pioneered by Carl Rogers—are pedagogical situations where participants are divided into small groups. As they experience group dynamics, participants learn about themselves as individuals interacting within a group and as individuals interacting with a group as a whole.

The ramifications of Moreno's ideas on encounters go far and wide. Perhaps his most enduring legacy can be felt in Martin Buber's dialogical philosophy. Buber identified two broad types of encounters: the I-Thou and the I-It encounters. As Maurice Friedman has shown, the I-Thou relationship is one of "openness, directness, mutuality, and presence," and of recognized uniqueness.⁴¹ The encountered other may be an animal, a stone, or God. In the I-It encounter, the It does not exist before the I encounters it; its existence is fully predicated on the pre-existence of the I. Our lives are made, often enriched by these two kinds of encounters. Buber distilled his views in one line: "all real life is encounter" ("Alles wirkliche Leben ist Begegnung").⁴²

In Moreno's "Invitation to an Encounter" as in Buber's *I and Thou*, philosophy meets poetry to beget new ideas and ethical ways of life. Moreno's is a book that invites its reader to close it, to put it down, and to go out in the world to encounter real people, face to face.⁴³ In the "Invitation" one reads: "Then I will look at you with your eyes / And you will look at me with mine." In real-life encounters, even more so than in encounters on a page, existences and ideas travel from one to the other, from one another. Moreno's poetry and his contributions to the expressionist theater movement of early twentieth-century Vienna translated into social activism. In 1909 (or 1912), with a group of fellow students, he created "The House of Encounter" where new immigrants received legal and material assistance. A sign above the front door read: "Come to us from all nations. We will give you shelter."⁴⁴ Ethics of care, selflessness, and the anonymity of the giver were at the centre of a worldview that came to be known as "The Religion of Encounter."

Admittedly, Moreno's encounters, in his art, in his philosophy and in his life aimed at uniting people in mutual respect and assistance. But not all encounters are as mutualistic or pacifist as that of Moreno, who was acutely aware of the need for positive encounters to counter endemic violence, xenophobia, antisemitism, and exclusiveness. He left a definition that translates the complexity of encounters:

> "Encounter" is a rough translation of the German word "Begegnung." Actually, Begegnung is difficult to translate. It has attained many connotations which no single Anglo-Saxon word conveys; several English words must be used to express its atmosphere. It means meeting, contact of bodies, confrontation, countering and battling, seeing and perceiving, touching and entering into each other, sharing and loving, communication with each other in a primary, intuitive manner, by speech or gesture, by kiss and embrace, becoming one —*una cum uno*. It encompasses not only loving, but also hostile and threatening relationships. It is not only an emotional rapport, like the professional meeting of a physician or therapist and patient, or an intellectual rapport, like teacher and student, or a scientific rapport, like a participant observer and his subject. It is a meeting on the most intensive level of communication.⁴⁵

If an encounter is indeed a meeting "on the most intensive level of communication," then our enquiry does well to focus on the arts, philosophy, and literature, as all three forms of expression and thought emerge from and generate intense modes of communication, which in turn occasion new encounters. But the intensity of communication can also conceal messages.

Stephen Spielberg's script for *Close Encounters of the Third Kind* starts in the sound and the fury of a Mexican desert storm, in a Babelesque moment out of which rise the first intelligible words spoken in "high school Spanish": "Are we the first to arrive? . . . Are we the first here"?⁴⁶ The only interpreter available to translate to the French team is an amateur, a "map maker" by trade.⁴⁷ Out of the roaring storm, out of the cacophony of mispronounced names and words, and in the foreign terms inserted in Spielberg's English text, two questions surface: who was there first? And how can we understand each other? These questions, which underlie most encounters, particularly colonial encounters, initiated the science of interpretation. As Terry Eagleton points out, hermeneutics originates in Friedrich

Schleiermacher's translation of *An Account of the English Colony in New South Wales*. "It was from a colonial encounter that the art of interpretation was born," writes Eagleton.[48] Deciphering meaningful signals, translating cultural codes, and determining the rights of the first occupier lie behind many encounters, colonial and of the third kind. But in the fracas of encounters, what can we really hear?

Associations of Ideas

Taking, like Althusser, as a point of departure the conflicted writings of Rousseau, Christie McDonald followed another path toward thinking encountering. In her first book, she describes Rousseau's *La Nouvelle Héloïse* as an impossible site of encounter between imagination and reason, men and women, the individual and society, nature and culture: "At no stage has the dialogue with nature led to an equilibrium between man's mind and his environment ... Through a localized geography, Rousseau seeks to express the utopian ideal of infinite happiness in an enduring present. Julie's death reveals the impossibility of this endeavour."[49] But if the "sentimental geography" of the pastoral fails to produce equilibrium or happiness, in later works, Rousseau proposes botany as a "technical geography" able to comfort and appease: "In times of unhappiness botany becomes a crutch not only for the imagination but memory as well."[50] McDonald then cites a passage of the *Reveries of the Solitary Walker*: "I am attached to botany by the chain of accessory ideas."[51] It may have been a similar "chain of accessory ideas" that attached McDonald to literary criticism as a place where encounters between thinkers could lead to something else than a *dialogue de sourds*.

It is around the idea of an ear and a special way of hearing that Christie McDonald encountered Jacques Derrida in 1979 at a conference in Montreal. *L'oreille de l'autre* and its translation *The Ear of the Other*, published a few years later, contain both Derrida's lecture "Otobiographies" and the round tables and discussions that followed. It also contains a written exchange between McDonald and Derrida titled "Choreographies."[52] Today, reading these texts elaborated forty years ago, one cannot help to be struck by the desire to encounter one another across disciplines, languages, and borders that all participants express—and by the singular position Christie McDonald occupied as the only woman among the contributors present on stage at the conference.[53] She had to speak both as a woman (*the* woman) and not just as *a* woman. Hence the salt of her questions:

> My question: in the reading or readings that remain to be done of Nietzsche by this deciphering ear, and without letting oneself get caught in the trap of what you have called gynegogy, does the "I" have a gender [*genre*]?[54]
>
> [I]f the question of sexual difference is not a regional one (in the sense of subsidiary), if indeed "it may no longer even be a question," as you suggest, how would you describe "woman's place"?[55]

A philosopher met a woman who was not appearing to him from on high, but who instead addressed him at eye level—as a thinker with her own mind and not as an allegory reflecting his mind. The philosopher answered seriously and courteously. One may think that he shrewdly avoided the point, or that he avoided imposing his gendered opinion on a matter that was not only theoretical for his interlocutor: "Why must there be a place for woman? And why only one, a single, completely essential place?"[56] Instead of a "place," a space was opened by both interlocutors—a space for more dialogues, questions, and encounters.

In collaboration with Ginette Michaud, McDonald edited a special issue of *Études Françaises*, titled *Ça me fait penser* and dedicated to association as a mode of thinking, gathering studies by philosophers, psychoanalysts, and literary critics. McDonald's own essay presents a counterpart to Rousseau's pastoral utopia: Diderot's experimentation with a philosophy of the contingent and the accidental.[57] For Diderot, the association of ideas provides a way to resolve the tension between irrational and rational, and to create a maze of borrowings between arts and sciences: "To translate the sense of these chains of association becomes each time an operation bearing on particular, not on universal sense: to render the connection is to order while organizing the elements; which means that to invent through associating is 'nothing else but to think' if only one think differently."[58] Thinking differently or otherwise—through particulars instead of universals—bypasses the question of gender without erasing it and pursues the work of "deconstruction" without crystallizing it. In Diderot, McDonald found a nimbleness that allowed, in particular, musicality to play more than a metaphorical role in reading, thinking, and writing.

Proust, today, stands for "French literature." To write about Proust is to write about French literature at its most singular (and singularly French with its *madeleine,* its *clochers de Martinville,* its *bœuf à la gelée,* or its *sonate de Vinteuil*) and at its most philosophical.[59] In her book on Proust, McDonald, instead of opposing Proust the novelist to Proust the philosopher, examines first "the Project" and second "the Text," distinguishing an aspirational level from an operational one, but noting that "Proust enacted his writerly freedom by revising the novel until the time of his death."[60] The project evolving with the text can never be identified with a theory: "Music guides the artist away from the pitfalls of idolatry and intellectualism."[61] But it is choreography that realizes in Proust's novel the most memorable embodiment of "the problem of the one and the many" and "the relationship of the whole to the parts."[62] A band of five or six young girls appears to the narrator on the beach of Balbec as a "théorie" (theory), or a procession perfectly merging chance encounter and necessity.[63]

Christie McDonald's attention to encounters found another expression in a team project which started in 2015, when she accepted Martine Reid's invitation to write an essay on women writers in the eighteenth century for a book of cultural history on women and literature in French, from the Middle Ages to today. In order to give an accurate account of the French Enlightenment period for women writers, she gathered a research group including three undergraduates and three graduates, supported by Harvard curators and reference librarians, as well as input from other scholars. They created a database listing all women writers in French between 1715 and 1793 they could identify. A new picture is emerging from this work in progress, correcting the dominant Lansonian canon and the missed encounter between the French reading public and a large part of French literature.

Encounters in Literature, Philosophy and the Arts

Encounter does not fit in classical Western philosophies. Yet, it is built into philosophical genres (e.g., dialogue, debate, apothegm, aphorism, life of philosopher, example). It also shines through concepts such as "accident," "swerve," "existence," or "dialectics," but shining through is not enough to warrant philosophical legitimacy. Today we are witnessing an ongoing process of legitimization and recognition of encounter as a concept—a process which started about a century ago. This book is part of this process as it examines and questions encounters in and between philosophy, literature, and the arts. How can we isolate encountering while retaining its power of escaping categorization? How can we use our own interest in or even obsession about encounter to interpret philosophical, literary, or artistic productions that do not share or foreground it? How can we encounter encounter and present that encounter to readers?

Encounters are more than chance meetings: they are dynamic situations which may last and continue to generate further encounters. In April 2017, a group of scholars convened at Harvard University to honor and discuss the work of Christie McDonald in eighteenth- and twentieth-century French Studies, in Women's Studies, and in Critical Theory and Continental philosophy. The Harvard conference sparked further encounters and projects. This book is one of them. It is shaped by the choice of focusing on a scholar who works tirelessly between *(inter)* cultures, through or across *(trans)* fields, and with *(cum)* others. McDonald provided the theme of the conference as both a challenge and an invitation. The contributors of this book—some attended the conference while others joined the project later—responded with their own associations of ideas and preoccupations, and their own sense of encountering as a practice, an event, and a concept. The editors decided from the beginning that the book should balance choice and chance, constraint and freedom, convergence and divergence. The Table of Contents was formed at the end as a "falling into place," but even these places are not final because readers will make their own connections between essays, creating their own encounters of ideas, texts, and sources as they read. If this book was to be performed, it would be as a late medieval motet or a postmodern polyphony: everyone singing together a different lyric on a different tune and yet, somehow, somewhere all meeting as a chorus of singular voices.

The essays collected in this volume span the early sixteenth century to the late 2010s. It may seem paradoxical for humanists to focus on human encounters with God rather than among humans, but, as Jacob Vance demonstrates, studying theories of theophany allowed Catholic humanists Lefèvre d'Étaples and Josse

Clichtove to attempt reconciling faith and reason, theology and philosophy, and Greek and Latin Christianities. For Montaigne, a close brush with death results in a temporary loss of consciousness followed by an epiphany narrated as an encounter with oneself. Tom Conley shows how Rousseau, narrating a similar incident, uses Montaigne in a "creative plagiarism" folding together life and writing, in the one coming out of the many that Deleuze names "event." Rousseau, the solitary man *par excellence*, meets a surprising musician in Pierre Saint-Amand's contribution, and learns the hard way how imitation and imposture can lead to social and musical dissonance. At the very least, Rousseau did not fail to encounter the public of his times. Thanks to a group of scholars working with Christie McDonald and Martine Reid, we can meet again writers of fiction, of philosophy, of science, from the long Enlightenment—all of them women whose voices were muted in official motets and polyphonies. Sanam Nader-Esfahani brings to light Madame de Saint-Aubin's *The Danger of Liaisons* [*Le Danger des Liaisons*] as a novel worth encountering not only to redress an injustice, but above all to allow us to understand the whole literary landscape of Saint-Aubin's time. Kylie Sago, through her study of different versions of *The Beauty and the Beast* [*La Belle et la Bête*], shows that contextual and transversal reading revives literary and colonial encounters we may no longer ignore. Caleb Shelburne studies how anonymity was played by Henriette de Marans, in order to share her *Stray Thoughts* [*Pensées errantes*] and encounter readers "on her own terms." Vicki Mistacco presents the pioneering work of Louise de Keralio, who designed in the 1780s, ahead of her time, a vast editorial program integrating women authors in the French national canon and literary history. A common thread emerging in women's contributions to knowledge and art is translation. Ian Van Wye studies three women using translation as a way of negotiating their presence in the Republic of Letters and in the Sciences. Their tireless and rich contributions need to be reevaluated, in particular with regard to ethics and religion, as Monique Moser-Verrey argues in her study of literary women such as Isabelle de Charrières and Madame d'Ussieux. Gary Wihl takes the translation thread in a different direction in his study of the trial opposing Harriet Beecher Stowe to F. W. Thomas, who had translated *Uncle Tom's Cabin* into German without her authorization. From the nineteenth century to the present day, literary property and copyright laws have been regulating encounters between writers and readers. Jean-Jacques Nattiez studies in the music of Wagner the fear of encountering otherness close to oneself. Thus, he demonstrates that antisemitism can be expressed formally and semiologically through musical citations vilifying synagogue music while integrating it on the opera stage. François Proulx, reading Proust's correspondence, shows a mode of encounter where the other is seen as another self, in which "Jewish difference" can be reconciled with other identities. Seeing as encounter, and encounter as seeing, is central in the essays of Ginette Michaud and Susan Suleiman. Michaud reads Georges Didi-Huberman's and Hélène Cixous's texts on seeing and saying and on painting and writing as a negative phenomenology, pushing language to its limits to describe various epiphanies (aesthetic, aisthesic, erotic, and ethical). Suleiman's encounter with the filmmaker István Szabó and his œuvre remains within the boundaries of ordinary language (in their case, Hungarian and English), while it expands the scope of the private to coincide with a large historical panorama. Between cinema and reality, Suleiman and Szabó address the question of choice and chance in a human life as honestly as possible. Starting with the discovery of America seen from the perspective of the encounterer (Vespucci), Verena Conley reflects on encounters in a world in continuous vibration and ceaseless communication, in which the encountered may paint back, and in which philosophers, scientists, and environmentalists imagine an ethics preventing encounters from destroying what is encountered. Focusing on Tahiti instead of America, Christie McDonald asks how previous encounters bear on subsequent ones. From Bougainville to Gauguin, myths and fantasies of primitive femininity are repeated, but they are also questioned and exposed when someone takes the risk of meeting anew.

An Addendum Which is Also on How to Meet Anew

On March 11, 2020, the World Health Organization declared the new coronavirus a pandemic. By that time, thousands had already died and countless more had been infected. Governments have reacted with varying degrees of severity in their efforts to confine citizens to their houses—when they have one—and to limit social interactions with the implementation of so-called "social distancing" measures, the two-meter or six-foot separation which saves lives. At the time of our writing, the effects of the pandemic cannot be fully gauged. At the time of our writing, there is no cure or vaccine for COVID-19. We can observe that old ways of meeting people in the flesh, as the phrase goes, have changed or have been banned altogether. New ways of communicating and socializing are emerging sometimes in waves that sweep across several countries, such as the rainbow drawings hanging in many windows in the UK and in Europe repurposing a symbol of equality, diversity and pride into a message of hope drawn by children for the older generations. In devastated Italy, people sing from their balconies, their voices uniting in concerts of optimism and joy. There is hope, not for all, but for many. Our planet seems to breathe as we choke for air. In the Northern Hemisphere and the temperate zone, spring is blooming, undeterred.

The global propagation of the virus draws a map of our encountering patterns. The mode of transmission is not sexual encounters as in some previous epidemics, but the most banal social interactions. Greeting, shopping, traveling, partying, and crowding are such fundamental elements of our way of life that until now, we failed to see them as anthropologically significant and related. We now know that these activities turn every human body into a possible vector of transmissible diseases, such as in the three influenza pandemics of the twentieth century: the 1918 so-called "Spanish flu" caused by virus H1N1, the 1957 so-called "Asian flu" caused by virus H2N2, and the 1968 so-called "Hong-Kong flu" caused by virus H3N2.[64] The first two decades of the twenty-first century have already seen one influenza pandemic (2009–10, caused by virus H1N1)[65] and a global epidemic (the 2002 SARS, caused by virus SARS-CoV).[66] The current pandemic caused by virus

SARS-CoV-2 did not arrive unannounced or unprecedented. What makes it different is the rapidity and extent of its spread, as well as the panoply of measures taken to slow it down. Quarantine, self-isolation, confinement, and contact tracing are not new practices, but they are now applied on a scale that is unique in human history—and shall be for an unknown length of time.

We are now testing the capacity of societies to continue functioning while their economic systems are massively reorganized to avoid as much as possible physical contact and encounters, while one of the main engines of mass consumption—the desire to be with others and to be like or different from others—is thwarted. All of a sudden, a robotic future of distant labor looks more like a necessary adaptation than a technological dream (or nightmare, depending on what one thinks of robots replacing workers). The distinction between "essential" and "non-essential" businesses and workers redefine our sense of social value and usefulness. The new heroes are no longer the start-up entrepreneurs making money from any idea that may succeed on the market, whether leading to essential or non-essential products. The new heroes are health-workers, truck-drivers, tomato-pickers, waste-collectors, package-delivers, postal workers, and other laborers exposing themselves to contamination in order to feed, clean, and heal us. Other heroes are those maintaining and adapting the tools of communication allowing confined humans to remain social, and those practicing care beyond themselves and their closer circle. The notion of hero has exploded in a myriad of gestures and stories. Do we still have such a thirst to encounter celebrities and know about their lives?

As final goodbyes are said through Skype, families, friends, new and old, students and colleagues turn to social media and teleconferencing to meet. Even the government sends private messages in this medium.[67] Unannounced and uninvited—much like viruses—such governmental messages light up our screens to remind us that the best antidote to the novel virus is isolation: "stay at home." But we continue to socialize online. With every new day, TikTok has new users, new interactions, and new "safe" encounters.[68] In its short history, social media has rarely been more useful to connect or reconnect with family, friends, and sometimes strangers. Evidently, distant encounters have a long tradition. Cicero's letters testify to the complexity of epistolary relationships characterized by the palpable absence of the other: the addressee is generally absent as the letter is being written; the writer is often absent when the letter is read. Yet, letters, especially love or sentimental letters, offer the poignant illusion of presence, for epistolary art transforms the displeasure of absence into the pleasure of sublimated presence in the words on the page. As the pen lands on paper, as the fingertips press the keyword, the genie of the other appears. Or, in the words of Kafka, letters are but intercourses with ghosts, one's own ghost and the ghost of the other.[69] On December 27, 1852, Gustave Flaubert wrote to Louise Colet that letters were for him like a lamp one lights in the night when afraid to be alone in the dark.[70] Text messages, Tweets, Facebook posts, TikTok videoclips, and the many new forms of correspondence may be just that: absences sublimated into messages like a million lights in our darkest hours.

Ghostly encounters—whether couched on paper or written in the Cloud—will not replace physical encounters. As time passes, the absence of physical contact, in the flesh, with people out of our most immediate circles turns into longing. No kisses, no hugs, little intimacy. Will we hug more when we are told we again can? In private moments, it is perhaps less the virus and its deadly shadow than the internalized voice of Hippocrates that we heed. Never before have private and public encounters been medicalized to such a scale. We wash our hands of encounters. What will be the offspring of the union of medicine and politics? Will the recent bedrocks of our Western neoliberal cultures, science, and politics be further eroded as their fissures and internal contradictions show more blatantly every day? What is emerging as we are writing this introduction is the colonization of some terms like "pandemic"—etymologically pertaining to all people—by the medical sciences. Will the virus that many of us carry unknowingly give way to a pandemic of compassion, love, and encounters when we encounter in the flesh, anew?

Notes

1 In his autobiographical letter to an unnamed friend, Abelard defines his subject as "the history of my own misfortunes." Peter Abelard, *Letters*, trans. Betty Radice (London: Penguin, 2003), 57.
2 In his introduction to the logic of Aristotle, Porphyry gives this definition: "Accidents are items which come and go without the destruction of their subjects." Porphyry, *Introduction*, trans. Jonathan Barnes (Oxford: Oxford University Press, 2003), 12.
3 Bernard Dod, "Aristoteles Latinus," in *The Cambridge History of Later Medieval Philosophy*, eds. Norman Kretzman, et al. (Cambridge: Cambridge University Press, 1982), 45–79.
4 For an overview of the problem of the subject of thought, see Alain de Libera, *Archéologie du sujet III.1: la double révolution* (Paris: Vrin, 2014), 22–3. On Averroes and Averroism, see Libera, 165–244. For a brief introduction: Maurice-Ruben Hayoun and Alain de Libera, *Averroès et l'averroïsme* (Paris: Presses Universitaires de France, Que Sais-Je?, 1991).
5 Augustine, *Confessions*, trans. Frank J. Sheed (Indianapolis: Hackett, 2006), 242–3.
6 Thibaut de Champagne, "L'autrier par la matinee," in *Chansons des trouvères: Chanter m'estuet*, ed. and trans. Samuel N. Rosenberg, Hans Tischler, and Marie-Geneviève Grossel (Paris: Librairie générale française, 1995), 608–9. Translation ours.
7 Michel Zink, *La Pastourelle* (Paris: Bordas, 1972).
8 Chrétien de Troyes, "The Tale of the Grail," in *Arthurian* Romances, trans. William Kibler (London: Penguin, 1991), 419–21.
9 Boethius, *The Consolation of Philosophy*, trans. Richard Green (New York: Macmillan, 1962), 3.
10 *The Song of Roland*, ed. and trans. Gerard J. Brault (University Park: The Pennsylvania State University Press, 1978), 2:43 (st. 52, ll. 657–8).
11 *The Song of Roland*, 1:53 (st. 66, l. 814).
12 Dante. *The Divine Comedy: 1. Inferno*, trans. John D. Sinclair (New York: Oxford University Press, 1939), 23 (canto 1, l. 11–15 and 26–7).
13 Dante, 25 (canto 1, ll. 61–3).
14 Geoffrey Chaucer, "General Prologue" in *The Canterbury* Tales, ed. A. C. Cawley (New York: Everyman's Library, 1958), 2 (ll. 25–6).

15 Chaucer, 25 (l. 795).
16 Chaucer, 2 (ll. 15–16).
17 Chaucer, 22 (ll. 725–8).
18 Michel de Montaigne, "To the reader," *Essays*, in *The Complete Works of Montaigne*, trans. Donald Frame (Stanford: Stanford University Press, 1957), 2.
19 Montaigne, *Essays* I, 1, 11.
20 Montaigne, "Of Idleness," *Essays* I, 8, 21.
21 Montaigne, "Of Prompt or Slow Speech," *Essays* I, 10, 26–7.
22 See his *Travel Journal* in *The Complete Works*.
23 René Descartes, "Discourse on the Method," in *Descartes: Selected Philosophical Writings*, eds. John Cottingham, et al. (Cambridge: Cambridge University Press, 1988), 44.
24 Jean-Jacques Rousseau, "Émile," in *The Collected Writings of Rousseau*, eds. Christopher Kelly and Allan Bloom (Hanover: University Press of New England, 2009), 13:695.
25 Rousseau, 13:710.
26 Rousseau, 13:705.
27 Louis Althusser, *Philosophy of the Encounter, Later Writings, 1978–1987* (London: Verso, 2006), 184.
28 Althusser, 167.
29 Althusser, 167–8.
30 Althusser, 169–70.
31 Althusser, 193.
32 Jean-Claude Bourdin, "La recontre du matérialisme et de l'aléatoire chez Louis Althusser," *Multitudes* 21, no. 2 (2005): 145.
33 Althusser, *Philosophy of the Encounter*, 174.
34 Althusser, 174–5.
35 Gilles Deleuze, *Proust and Signs*, trans. Richard Howard (Minneapolis: University of Minnesota Press, 2000), 102. See also Alain Beaulieu, "La politique de Gilles Deleuze et le matérialisme aléatoire du dernier Althusser," *Actuel Marx* 34, no. 2 (2003): 169.
36 Deleuze, *Proust and Signs*, 97.
37 Gilles Deleuze, *Difference and Repetition*, trans. Paul Patton (London: Bloomsbury, 2006), 139.
38 Deleuze, *Proust and Signs*, 97.
39 Beaulieu, "La politique de Gilles Deleuze," 169.
40 Beaulieu, 169.
41 Martin Buber, *Between Man and Man* (London: Routledge, 2002), xii.
42 Martin Buber, *Ich und Du* (Gütersloh: Gütersloher Verlagshaus, 1997), 17. Translation ours.
43 John Nolte, *The Philosophy, Theory and Methods of J. L. Moreno: The Man Who Tried to Become God* (London: Routledge, 2014), 18.
44 Børge Kristoffersen, "Jacob Levy Moreno's encounter term: a part of a social drama," *Zeitschrift für Psychodrama und Soziometrie* 13 (June 2014): 59–71.
45 Quoted in Peter C. Howie, "Philosophy of Life: J. L. Moreno's Revolutionary Philosophical Underpinnings of Psychodrama and Group Psychotherapy," *Group: Philosophy and Group Psychotherapy* 36, no. 2 (Summer 2012): 139.
46 Stephen Spielberg, *Close Encounters of the Third Kind* (New York: Dell, 1977), 5.
47 Spielberg, 6.
48 Terry Eagleton, *After Theory* (New York: Basic Books, 2004), 23.
49 Chrstie McDonald, *The Extravagant Shepherd: A Study of the Pastoral Vision in Rousseau's* Nouvelle Héloïse, Studies on Voltaire and the Eighteenth Century, vol. 105,

ed. Theodore Besterman (Banbury: The Voltaire Foundation Thorpe Mandeville House, 1973), 171.
50 McDonald, 172.
51 Jean-Jacques Rousseau, "The Reveries of the Solitary Walker," in *The Collected Writings of Rousseau*, ed. Christopher Kelly (Hanover: University Press of New England, 2000), 8:67.
52 A first English translation was published in 1985 by Schocken Books, Inc., and a second one by University of Nebraska Press in 1988. The latter includes Jacques Derrida and Christie McDonald, "Choreographies: Interview," reprinted from *Diacritics* 12, no. 2 (Summer 1982): 66–76. Our citations come from the University of Nebraska Press edition.
53 Two other women, Monique Bosco and Nicole Bureau, asked questions "from the floor" in the roundtable on translation, but "on the stage," McDonald was the only one.
54 Christie McDonald, ed., *The Ear of the Other: Otobiography, Transference, Translation: Texts and Discussions with Jacques Derrida*, trans. Avital Ronnell and Peggy Kamuf (Lincoln: University of Nebraska Press, 1988), 49. Originally published as *L'oreille de l'autre: otobiographies, transferts, traductions: textes et débats avec Jacques Derrida* (Montréal: VLB, 1982).
55 McDonald, *Ear of the Other*, 164.
56 McDonald, 168.
57 Christie McDonald, "Résonnances associatives: La pensée analogique de Denis Diderot," in *Ça me fait penser*, ed. Christie McDonald and Ginette Michaud, special issue of *Études françaises* 22, no. 1 (Spring 1986): 12. Translation ours.
58 McDonald, 21. Translation ours.
59 Proust has been and is still a major site of encounters between philosophers and literary critics. To give only a few examples: Gilles Deleuze, *Proust and Signs*, trans. Richard Howard (Minneapolis: University of Minnesota Press, 2000); Vincent Descombes, *Proust: Philosophie du Roman* (Paris: Minuit, 1987); Julia Kristeva, *Time and Sense; Proust and the Experience of Literature*, trans. Ross Guberman (New York: Columbia University Press, 1996); Joshua Landy, *Philosophy as Fiction: Self, Deception, and Knowledge in Proust* (New York: Oxford University Press, 2004); Georges Poulet, "Proust," in *Studies in Human Time*, trans. Elliott Coleman (Baltimore: The Johns Hopkins University Press, 1956), 291–322.
60 Christie McDonald, *The Proustian Fabric: Associations of Memory* (Lincoln: University of Nebraska Press, 1991), 82.
61 McDonald, 56.
62 McDonald, 97.
63 McDonald, 100.
64 Edwin D. Kilbourne, "Influenza Pandemics of the 20th Century," *Emerging Infectious Diseases* 12, no. 1 (January 2006): 9–14, see www.ncbi.nlm.nih.gov/pmc/articles/PMC3291411/. Accessed April 4, 2020.
65 Nahoko Shindo and Sylvie Briand, "Influenza at the beginning of the 21st Century," *Bulletin of the World Health Organization* 90 (2012): 247–47A. See www.who.int/bulletin/volumes/90/4/12-104653/en/. Accessed April 4, 2020.
66 "SARS (Severe Acute Respiratory Syndrom)," World Health Organization disease information, see www.who.int/ith/diseases/sars/en/. Accessed April 4, 2020.
67 "GOV.UK ALERT CORONAVIRUS New rules in force now: you must stay at home. More info and exemptions at go.uk/coronavirus. Stay at home. Protect the NHS. Save lives." March 24, 2020. Interestingly, our citizen's duty is to protect an institution, the

National Health Service, which has been under attack by the government that sent the message.

68 See for instance Kari Paul, "'It's Corona time': TikTok helps teens cope with the coronavirus pandemic," *The Guardian*, March 12, 2020, see www.theguardian.com/world/2020/mar/12/coronavirus-outbreak-tik-tok-memes.
69 Franz Kafka, *Letters to Milena*, trans. Philip Boehm (New York: Schocken Books, 1990), 223.
70 Gustave Flaubert, *Correspondance*, eds. Danielle Girard and Yvan Leclerc, see https://flaubert.univ-rouen.fr/correspondance/edition/.

Chapter 1

ENCOUNTERING THE DIVINE: ON THE COGNITION OF GOD IN EARLY FRENCH CHRISTIAN HUMANISM

Jacob Vance

This essay is about the way early sixteenth-century French humanists theorized the mind's encounter with the divine through cognition. It addresses the relation between reason and faith in early French humanist discourse, and how humanists theorized the unity of faith and reason in articulating the soul's encounter with God. The early Renaissance humanists Jacques Lefèvre d'Étaples (1450–1536) and Josse Clichtove (1472–1543) formed an important part of the sixteenth-century Catholic Pre-Reformation movement.[1] The Pre-Reformation represents a brief period in the history of French Renaissance intellectual thought, but also a period of great humanist scholarly activity during which Catholic reformers sought to cultivate models for spiritual life and to theorize the soul's encounter with the divine in both philosophical and Scriptural terms.[2] By making available classical and medieval texts, along with new commentaries on those texts, Lefèvre and his associate Clichtove sought to renew both philosophical and spiritual models for the soul's encounter with God, in order to revitalize religious life and piety in France. They strove to reform educational and religious institutions, at a time when the French educational system and Church had fallen into disarray, and to cultivate devotional life by translating and publishing philosophical and spiritual texts. In their commentaries on these texts, they conceived of the soul's encounter with the divine in both philosophical—pertaining to rational cognition—and pietistic terms of the Christian faith. Their synthesis of faith and reason as alternative but complementary paths to encountering the divine represents one important chapter in the long history of speculation about the connections between philosophy and religion in Western Europe, from Late Antiquity to the early Renaissance.[3]

Lefèvre d'Étaples' travels to Italy to meet the great Italian humanists, and to assimilate their scholarly and historical methods, are now a story well known within Renaissance studies. Lefèvre actively sought to rediscover classical and medieval theories of the human soul's encounter with the divine through both reason and revelation, and to situate these theories within a broader Evangelical framework. Lefèvre led the early Pre-Reformation initiative in France, which spanned from approximately 1450 to 1536. He died in 1536, the same year that his great contemporary Northern humanist, Erasmus of Rotterdam (1466–1536), passed away on the eve of the French Protestant Reformation. The year 1536 marks an end to the Catholic Pre-Reformation in France, as it was the same year that John Calvin (1509–1564) published his *Institutes of the Christian Religion*.[4]

Lefèvre and Clichtove took a particular interest in classical philosophy, and in medieval theology and spirituality, reacting as other humanists did against the dominance of logic in late-medieval education and theology. Logic, they thought, could not account for the fullness of human religious experience. Instead, they turned to models of encountering the divine that integrated both reason and faith. They took a particular interest in medieval Greek theological texts, in part because medieval Greek theology represented an alternative to late scholastic theology and to the influence of Greco-Arab philosophical thought.[5] For Lefèvre and Clichtove, the tradition of medieval Greek theology represented a synthesis of philosophy and theology that could serve to remedy the degenerate state of medieval educational and religious life. Their editorial and commentarial activity served to put patristic texts into circulation in modernized editions—with new introductions, and new critical notes—as a way of promoting theological and spiritual models which integrate a strong cognitive component. This cognitive element, this emphasis on *gnosis*, was arguably vital to the way in which they understood the soul's encounter with God.

Two medieval Greek Christian thinkers—Pseudo-Dionysius the Areopagite (late fifth or early sixth century CE), and Saint John of Damascus (675–753 CE)—held a particularly important status for Lefèvre and Clichtove. Pseudo-Dionysius offered a theory of theophany in which the human soul encounters the divine through knowledge of its manifestations in nature and human tradition. Dionysius was (probably) a Syrian monk who synthesized Platonic philosophy with Christian thought in a manner that proved central to early French humanists. He offered a theory of the soul's encounter with the divine that combined Pagan philosophy and Christian theology.[6] Lefèvre and Clichtove joined Dionysius' theory of the soul's ascent to the divine with their humanist and Evangelical perspective, bringing together philosophy, theology, and Evangelical literature into a coherent, unified whole. However, Dionysius was a pseudonym: the author fictitiously presented himself as Dionysius the Areopagite, the Athenian judge at the Areopagus who was converted by Saint Paul in the first century CE. This pseudonymous authorship later contributed to the creation and circulation of a legend in France that this Dionysius was Denis, the third-century Christian martyr and saint who was believed to have become the first Bishop of Paris.[7]

Lefèvre's and Clichtove's interpretation of Pseudo-Dionysius' works was based on what could be described as an uncritical acceptance of the legend of Dionysius's fictitious identity as a disciple of Saint Paul. This legend had already been put into question by, among others, Nicholas of Cusa, Lorenzo Valla, and Erasmus of Rotterdam. Yet until 1522, Lefèvre held to the fictitious authority of Dionysius as a disciple of the Apostle.⁸ Lefèvre perhaps upheld the legend in part because it enabled him to theorize the unity of Christian piety and philosophical reasoning. We may speculate that Pseudo-Dionysian philosophy in general, and of the idea of theophany in particular, represented an important model for the encounter between the divine and the human soul.

Thus, while one could interpret Lefèvre's and Clichtove's acceptance of the legend of Pseudo-Dionysius as a lack of historical method and as an adherence to authority, and while they could be understood as having merely prolonged an error, there was arguably more at stake than mere adherence to the authority of a legend. Lefèvre and Clichtove possibly upheld the legend of Dionysius because his works offered a synthesis of Platonic and Aristotelian philosophy, and a way to conceive the unity of patristic and medieval spirituality. They developed an Evangelical interpretation of Dionysius in their commentaries by referencing the relevant passages of Scripture in the margins of Dionysius' text. In this way, they constructed an Evangelical lens through which to interpret Dionysius—a lens that harmonized Evangelical faith and theological reasoning. Lefèvre and Clichtove used the notion of theophany to unify various strands of Aristotelianism, Platonism and Evangelism. By maintaining the legend of Pseudo-Dionysius, they could conceive of theophany as an extension of Saint Paul's teachings. They appropriated the idea of theophany to situate philosophical, mystical, and theological texts within an Apostolic lineage. Moreover, the Pseudo-Dionysian notion of theophany involves the view that the cosmos is a hierarchical and rational order. Thus, by using Pseudo-Dionysian philosophy, Lefèvre and Clichtove embraced a theory of hierarchy that made reason and rational order central to their spirituality. They interpreted Pseudo-Dionysian theophany, and hierarchy, from their unique perspective in French religious history—that is, from the perspective of the first generation of early French Renaissance thinkers to combine philosophy and theology with Christian Evangelism.⁹

In *Celestial Hierarchy* and the *Ecclesiastical Hierarchy*, Pseudo-Dionysius theorizes a God that lies beyond all created beings; he also offers a Platonic theory of the way the multiplicity of entities in the created world relate, through a series of cosmic and institutional hierarchical structures, to the unknowable divine essence.¹⁰ For him, this unknowable divine essence is absolutely simple and unified, but it emanates, manifesting itself and making itself known as it descends through the rationally ordered hierarchy. The divine essence, though mysterious in and of itself, emanates through the order of the hierarchy, which enables the soul to return to divine unity and divine simplicity—and to thereby become deified.¹¹

For Pseudo-Dionysius, theophany is a kind of epiphany or mode of encountering the divine through order and structure in which cognition plays a vital role. In the Pseudo-Dionysian philosophical and theological model, the order and hierarchy of creation represents a theophanic revelation of the divine. God is conceived as transcending creation, but also as disclosing Himself in and through the order of the created world. In this perspective, creation is theophany, a rational and ordered manifestation of the divine, that deifies the soul. According to Pseudo-Dionysius, the soul encounters the divine through rational structure.¹²

Reason, which discerns the order of the universe, plays a vital part in the deification of the soul.

Dionysius' synthesis of Platonism and Christianity—specifically in terms of his theory of theophanic revelation—would provide Lefèvre and Clichtove a lens for interpreting John of Damascus' work. The latter was a monk and priest of Syrian origin who lived under Islamic rule during the period of the Umayyad caliphs and belonged to the Christian Melkite tradition. His *Fount of Knowledge* (c. 720–43) defined the Christian position on orthodoxy within the Islamic world.[13] The book has three parts, of which the third part, titled *On the Orthodox Faith*, consists of a compendium of Christian theological treatises. In this part, John of Damascus offers the Platonic and Christian idea, which we also find in Dionysius' works, that God is entirely unknowable in His essence. He is, however, knowable through His energies that manifest themselves in and through the created world. These energies can be known, in this Greek tradition of speculation, partly through human reason and cognition because the energies are themselves intelligible in nature.[14] While there are some traces of Dionysius' thought in John of Damascus' work, Lefèvre and Clichtove amplify those Dionysian elements, and they interpret the entirety of Damascus' work through a Dionysian lens.

For Pseudo-Dionysius and John of Damascus, reason has an important role to play in faith and theology, but it has limitations due to the absolute transcendence of the divine. In the medieval Greek tradition, inquiry into the nature of the three persons of the Holy Trinity—as united or separated—constitutes a form of positive or rational theology. In contrast, inquiry into divine essence must proceed by means of negative theology, which refers to the divine through negation and abstraction, rather than through positive affirmation. But despite the transcendent nature of the divine, both Dionysius and John of Damascus attribute an important role to rational philosophy in theology and faith. For them, although God is the source of being, and of knowledge, He is beyond being; God's essence lies beyond all creation and thus beyond cognition. However, His essence can be approached through his energies, which manifest themselves to human senses through reason and intellect.[15]

Drawing on Pseudo-Dionysian theories, Lefèvre and Clichtove adapted the idea of the universe as an ordered, hierarchical structure, in which reason can elevate the soul toward union with the divine. This allowed them to situate rational philosophy within a more general theory of the soul's encounter with the divine. Much of their commentaries consists of establishing connections—or a concordance—between Pseudo-Dionysian theories and Christian Evangelism. Lefèvre and Clichtove unified philosophy with an eclectic and inclusive form of Evangelism, integrating a strong rational component into their conception of Christian piety.

Lefèvre d'Étaples and Clichtove drew on Pseudo-Dionysius' works as a model for interpreting philosophical texts, which they viewed as repositories of Christian Apostolic wisdom. Their choice of Pseudo-Dionysian theology, as a broad paradigm for syncretizing Platonic and Aristotelian philosophy with Christian Evangelism, enabled them to harmonize philosophy and Christian piety in the soul's encounter with the divine. They chose Pseudo-Dionysian theophany as a model for understanding divine revelation, a choice that represents a Renaissance adaptation of medieval Greek Patristic thought in an early modern, Evangelical context. Pseudo-Dionysius had been important in the Latin west since Eriugena (*c.* 800–77 AD), who introduced Pseudo-Dionysius' works into the medieval Christian world in the ninth century.[16] However, medieval Greek theories of theophany also entered into the Latin west in the fifteenth century, as Byzantine scholars and thinkers emigrated to Italy after the Turkish conquest of Byzantium, bringing with them a knowledge of Greek, as well as Greek manuscripts, and a long history of close contact with Christian Platonism.[17] As knowledge of Byzantine sources extended north of the Alps into Northern Europe, it offered humanists such as Lefèvre and Clichtove a theory of faith and reason that, they maintained, originated in Saint Paul and reached Christian Platonism via Pseudo-Dionysius. We may speculate that, for Lefèvre and Clichtove, the Byzantine tradition remained closest and truest to its Platonic sources, and that their turn to the Byzantine tradition was also a turn away from the Greco-Arab Platonic and Aristotelian traditions, toward a Byzantine tradition that was believed to have derived from Apostles.

In 1499, Lefèvre published Pseudo-Dionysius's works in the *Corpus Dionysiacum*. In 1515, his associate Josse Clichtove published commentaries on the *Corpus Dionysiacum*, which he dedicated to Bishop Guillaume Briçonnet, who was Marguerite de Navarre's spiritual advisor and the head of the French Catholic Pre-Reformation.[18] Between 1499 and 1522, Lefèvre and his humanist entourage edited and commented Evangelical, ancient, late antique, and medieval, texts. They used Pseudo-Dionysian theories to unify these texts and their ideas into a coherent whole. The Pseudo-Dionysian notion of theophany allowed Lefèvre to elaborate different forms of philosophical and theological thinking as partial dispensations of divine truth, as partial manifestations of divine wisdom.

Although scholars have examined various strands of Renaissance religious and philosophical eclecticism, I argue that the importance of theophany as an organizing principle in Lefèvre's and Clichtove's commentaries deserves closer attention.[19] As stated before, for Lefèvre and his acolytes, reason and intellection as well as faith enable the encounter with the divine. While Lefèvre seized on Greek notions of God as beyond all being and human knowing (*incognitus, incomprehensibilis*), he was mainly concerned with understanding the ways in which God discloses Himself in and through nature and history.[20] Thus, while Lefèvre affirms that God is beyond all cognition, through theophany he emphasizes the human potential for deification (*deiformitas*) through the partial dispensations of divine truth. In his view, God's manifestations make themselves known in and through history in general, and in the history of philosophy in particular.[21]

For Pseudo-Dionysius, the idea of God's manifestations, or theophanies, relates to the ideas of hierarchy, and to role of analogy within hierarchy. Each created being in the hierarchy of creation receives divine grace to the extent it is capable of so doing. The place in the hierarchy that each being occupies determines its capacity for receiving divine grace.[22] Each created being within the hierarchy has a given capacity for receiving divine knowledge. Although the divine light is equally available to all levels of the hierarchy, each level of the hierarchy differs in its capacity to receive and transmit light. All creatures are capable of perfection, which is achieved in the final stage of a three-fold process of spiritual progress (purgation, illumination, and finally perfection).[23]

For Pseudo-Dionysius, the processions (*proodoi*) or emanations of the divine knowledge through the hierarchy enable God to appear in the whole of creation. While God remains secret in His essence, He is manifest through the hierarchy, in a manner that is proportionate to each level of the order. Divine being reveals itself through His manifestations but simultaneously remains hidden. To the extent that created beings disclose the divine, they are themselves partial manifestations of God; they are His energies, and to know these manifestations represents a form of spiritual cognition.[24]

In 1512, Lefèvre's associate Josse Clichtove (1472/73–1543) published his literal, or *ad litteram*, commentary on Lefèvre's edition of Saint John of Damascus' *On the Orthodox Faith*, which had been published without commentary in 1507. Damascus' *On the Orthodox Faith* was one of the most influential texts in medieval Greek patristic thought.[25] The marginal notes in Lefèvre's 1512 edition, like much of the commentary, serve to establish a concordance between the assertions made by John of Damascus and the New Testament. However, the commentary situates Damascus' work also in the context of Pseudo-Dionysian philosophy. The initiative of using Pseudo-Dionysius to explain *On the Orthodox Faith* stemmed, naturally, from their view that Pseudo-Dionysius was a disciple of Saint Paul. In the first chapter of his commentary, Clichtove refers his readers directly to the theory of theophany as stated in the fourth chapter of Pseudo-Dionysius *Celestial Hierarchy*.[26] This initial reference is a clear indication that theophany occupies a central place in Clichtove's interpretation of Damascus' text.

In his commentary, Clichtove, like his predecessors, uses the word apparition (*apparitio*) to refer to theophany.[27] He further refers to theophanies as signs (*signa*) and as visions (*visiones*). For him, theophanies are revelations accommodated to the limits of human capacity; they are, he writes, signs (*signa*) that serve to adapt divine revelations to finite creatures.[28] He describes the spiritual knowledge of these manifestations in terms of the dynamic between light and vision. Clichtove uses a host of terms including light (*lux, lumen*), brilliance (*splendor*), brightness (*fulgor*), illumination (*illuminatio*), and ray (*radius*) to refer to divine emanations through metaphors of light, which are metaphors for degrees of cognition, and which imply that the human faculties of reasoning and intellection apprehend these divine revelations.[29] These metaphors of light describe the communication of divine knowledge through the levels of the hierarchy of beings; all designate manifestations of the divine to human cognition.

Adapting medieval mystical vocabulary, Lefèvre and Clichtove frequently employ the term *acies mentis* (point of the mind) and related terms, such as *obtutus mentis* (mental gaze), to describe the faculty of the soul to which these theophanies or visions appear.[30] This faculty is both cognitive and spiritual in nature. Clichtove writes that such metaphorical spiritual vision lifts the veils (*velamina*) of corporeal things and leads the perceiver towards the hidden recesses (*occultus*) of the divine. For Lefèvre and for Clichtove, this form of spiritual vision is a cognition of God (*dei cognitio*).[31] He asserts that although the divine essence remains unknown (*incognitus*) and incomprehensible (*incomprehensibilis*), its apparitions accommodate human limitations through signs (*signa*). The purpose of the hierarchy of beings is to draw (*subvehere*) the soul toward similitude with the divine, or deiformity (*deiformitas*). This process of hierarchical emanations transforms the soul into a similitude of God (*similitudo*), deifying it and rendering it "deiform" (*deiformis*). All beings within creation, in this perspective, represent the "vestiges" (*vestigia*) of the divine archetype (*archetypus*), or exemplar.[32] Clichtove's interpretation emphasizes metaphors of light to articulate an image theology, according to which God discloses himself in order that humans become spiritually renovated. To recognize and experience the world as theophany takes place through a cognitive act that refers vestige within nature and human tradition to their principle of origin, or exemplar.

For Lefèvre and Clichtove, the notion that divine vestiges lie hidden in the created world plays a central role in their understanding of the way the human soul ascends to God. They consider that creation is itself a manifestation of divine energies, and that philosophical inquiry allows humans to refer the world of multiplicity to its simple, unified principle of origin. Clichtove draws on the idea of divine vestiges to explain what we may arguably understand as a theory of analogy.[33] For Lefèvre and Clicthove, vestiges are divine analogies, the recognition of which allows the soul to elevate itself to union with the divine through cognition. These analogies or vestiges manifest themselves throughout the history of philosophy, and Christian literature. This is evident in a preface Lefèvre wrote to his paraphrases of Aristotle's *Physics* (1492), in which he rehearses the idea that Aristotelian philosophy contains analogies. These analogies can be described as principles that, when known, elevate the soul toward the perfection of knowledge, and ultimately to union with the divine. Lefèvre refers to these principles as a "secret analogy" (*secretam analogiam*). Without analogy, he writes, philosophy would be lifeless.[34]

We find a similar reference to the idea of secret analogy in Clichtove's commentaries on Pseudo-Dionysius. As author of the commentary, he must uncover the hidden significance of the text for his readers. In his 1515 commentary on Pseudo-Dionysius' *Divine Names*, Clichtove also writes that the use of positive affirmations in referring to God involves secret analogies. He asserts that this is the method of Holy Scripture. Both Clichtove and Lefèvre interpret Scripture as positive affirmations about the nature of God which serve to elevate the believer toward the divine.[35] Later, in 1517, in a prefatory letter to an edition of Euclid's *Elements*, Lefèvre wrote that one truth shines through all things—a truth which inhabits an inaccessible light, towards which we may ascend step by step (*gradus*), and more specifically through analogy and what he calls assurection (*assurectio*), by which he means an ascent of the soul towards a perfecting encounter with the divine. Mathematics and geometry, for Lefèvre, raise the mind toward the divine because they are abstract and incorporeal. In his view, geometry contains analogies that exercise cognition. This is a form of spiritual cognition, a cognition of secret analogies, which raises the soul above the corporeal world, leading to union with the divine.[36] The cognitive and spiritual faculty of the soul (*acies mentis*) can perceive the unity of the divine in the world of created multiplicity—and it is drawn toward that unity by the divine analogies that it perceives both within nature and human tradition.

This line of thinking suggests that, for Lefèvre and Clichtove, the vestiges or analogies of the divine can be traced throughout different philosophical and religious traditions, which are in their view various emanations of a single source of intelligibility. Although one could interpret Lefèvre's and Clichtove's openness to different Western philosophical and religious traditions as a form of tolerant eclecticism, we must recall that the appeal to Greek patristic thought may have represented a turn away from the philosophical traditions that entered Western Europe through the mediation of translations and commentaries written by Islamic and Jewish commentators of the Middle Ages. Lefèvre's adherence to the authority of Pseudo-Dionysius' legend and theology as a "pure" Christian source can be explained by a wish to maintain the value of cognition in Evangelical Christianity and to synthesize a diversity of Western philosophical, theological, and spiritual traditions according to a principle of analogy.

Although Lefèvre—in his prefatory letter to his *Commentaries* on the Gospel of 1522—declares that belief must precede understanding, and although he thereby subordinates reason to faith, he does this precisely because of the need to clarify his understanding of the relation between philosophy and Scripture. He argues that one does not believe in order to understand Scripture.[37] He decisively subordinates the rational element of belief to Evangelical faith, but this represents a late development in his thought. Lefèvre had, until this point in 1522, harmonized reason and faith. Although in his philosophical commentaries Lefèvre uses Pseudo-Dionysian theology to situate discursive reasoning below cognition through intellect, Pseudo-Dionysius' theory of analogy enabled him to maintain the value of rational philosophy as a manifestation of truths that are also known to intellect. While he subordinates reason to belief in the *Preface* to the Commentaries of 1522, the very act of doing so indicates how important it was for him to maintain reason and understanding as values in Christian piety. Despite this subordination of reason to faith, he uses Pseudo-Dionysius theology to bridge rational philosophy and Scripture. For, in the same Preface of 1522, Lefèvre appeals to Pseudo-Dionysian theology to situate rational discourse and commentary in relation to Christian piety.[38] The purpose of writing commentaries, Lefèvre asserts, is to understand the Gospel and to disclose their hidden meaning. But, he continues, previous commentators have been blinded to the light of Scripture and unable to explain it. Lefèvre's purpose, therefore, is to guide the reader to what he calls the cognition of Evangelical truth.[39] He maintains that a proper understanding of Scripture is necessary for proper belief. His commentaries therefore aim at providing a correct literal interpretation of Scripture so as to avoid misguided beliefs. This might seem paradoxical, given that he uses the fictitious authority and Neo-Platonic theology of Pseudo-Dionysius to explain the method of significance of Scripture. Drawing on Pseudo-Dionysius, Lefèvre explains that his commentaries serve to purge the human mind of darkness and to prepare the reader for both illumination and perfection.[40] The role of commentary thus corresponds to the first of three parts in the Pseudo-Dionysian doctrine of spiritual ascent (of purgation, illumination and perfection), but it also implies illumination, and therefore the cognition of divine truths. For Lefèvre, then, the purpose of commentary and initiation into the literal meaning of sacred texts is to purge the mind and to prepare it for encountering the divine through illumination.

For Lefèvre and Clichtove, rational knowledge is a vital part of Christian piety. They were inspired by the notion that philosophical reasoning can be a spiritual practice.[41] While Augustine had provided a model for synthesizing faith and reason that held a position of great influence through the Middle Ages, these two humanists—though still inspired by Augustine and the Greco-Roman tradition extending from Late Antiquity to the time of Saint Anselm—turned to Byzantine models of spiritual experience. The Byzantine models that arrived in Europe at a time when humanists sought to restore the "pure" sources of Christian philosophy, over and against the tradition of scholastic reasoning that came to dominate the late-medieval educational institutions of Northern France. Lefèvre and Clichtove turned to the medieval Greek past and held to its fictitious historical ties with Saint Paul's teachings. They turned away from the Greco-Arab tradition and from the Latin scholastic philosophy that grew out of it.

Orienting themselves toward the influence of Byzantine translations and philosophy, Lefèvre and Clichtove were perhaps not trying to do something new. They valued the Greek tradition precisely because it represented a legacy of thought that remained closer to its roots in the Platonic tradition, which these French humanists interpreted as having taken root in Apostolic thought. What we consider to be new in the Renaissance must be understood in relative terms. We might speak more properly here of renewal, because Lefèvre and Clichtove understood their initiatives not so much as innovations as a return to pure sources of Christian thought—sources that are as much philosophical as pietistic. Far from being a mere matter of adherence to authority, their allegiance to the legend of Pseudo-Dionysius can be understood within the larger context of their wish to maintain the purity of Christian philosophy, and to advocate for the integration of philosophical reasoning with Christian piety. Their adherence to the legend can also be understood in terms of the broader significance of appropriating Greek patristic texts over and against sources influenced by the Greco-Arab tradition. The Greek theory of theophany enabled Lefèvre and Clichtove to interpret the history of philosophy and Christian theology as containing partial dispensations of divine truth. These dispensations can, they argued, be discovered through philosophical reasoning and inquiry, and thus help to elevate the soul through the hierarchy of the cosmos, drawing it toward union with the divine. Their theory of encountering the divine appeals to cognition as a form of spiritual exercise. The mind—and more generally, the human soul—cannot encounter God without training and exercise, and the practice of commenting texts serves this purpose.

Notes

1. For a historical study of the French Catholic Pre-Reformation, see Jonathan Reid, *King's Sister—Queen of Dissent: Marguerite of Navarre (1492–1549) and Her Evangelical Network*, Studies in Medieval and Reformation Traditions no. 139, 2 vols. (Leiden; Boston: Brill, 2009).
2. On the spirituality and literature of the French Catholic Pre-Reformation, see Jan Miernowski, *Signes dissimilaires: La quête des noms divins dans la poésie française de la Renaissance*, Travaux d'Humanisme et Renaissance no. 312 (Genève: Droz, 1997). See also Jan Miernowski, *Le Dieu Néant: Théologies négatives à l'aube des temps modernes*, Studies in the history of Christian thought, no. 82 (Leiden; New York: Brill, 1998).
3. While the relations between faith and reason in early French humanist literature have not, to my knowledge, been the focus of any monographs, one may read on the medieval background Alain de Libera, *Raison et foi: Archéologie d'une crise d'Albert le Grand à Jean-Paul II*, L'Ordre philosophique (Paris: Seuil, 2003).
4. In 1916, Augustin Renaudet published a foundational study for the French Catholic Pre-Reformation. See *Préréforme et humanisme à Paris pendant les premières guerres d'Italie (1494–1517)*, 2nd ed. (Paris: Librairie D'Argences, 1953).
5. For general orientation on the reception of the Church Fathers in the Renaissance, see Irena Backus, *The Reception of the Church Fathers in the West*, 2 vols. (Leiden: Brill, 1997). On Lefèvre d'Étaples and the Church Fathers, see Eugene Rice, "The Humanist Idea of Christian Antiquity and the Impact of Greek Patristic Work on Sixteenth-Century Thought," in *Classical Influences on European Culture A.D. 1500–1700*, ed. R. R. Bolgar (Cambridge: Cambridge University Press, 1976), 199–203 and the related essays cited in Irena Backus, *The Reception of the Church Fathers in the West*, 534.
6. For a now classic and still important study of Pseudo-Dionysian theology, see René Roque *L'Univers Dionysien: Structure hiérarchique du monde selon le Pseudo-Denys*, Théologie no. 29 (Lille: Aubier, 1954).
7. On Pseudo-Dionysius in particular, and the tradition of Byzantine theology in general, one may read Alain de Libera, *La philosophie médiévale*, 2nd ed., Quadriges manuels (Paris: Presses Universitaires de France, 2014), 9–52, particularly 22–5. See also 272–4.
8. On Lefèvre d'Étaples and Josse Clichtove's adherence to the legend of Dionysius' authority, see Jonathan Reid, *King's Sister*, 123, n. 25 and bibliography, as well as Colm Luibhéid and Paul Rorem, "Introductions," in *Pseudo-Dionysius: The Complete Works*, Classics of Western spirituality (New York: Paulist Press, 1988), 11–46, the bibliography on 37–8, and notes 16 and 17. In their "Introductions," Luibhéid and Rorem address the influence of Pseudo-Dionysius the Western Middle Ages, Renaissance and Reformation. Clichtove refuted the arguments against the authority of the legend of Lorenzo Valla and Erasmus of Rotterdam. On this, see Jean-Pierre Massaut, *Critique et tradition à la veille de la Réforme en France*, De Pétrarque à Descartes no. 39 (Paris: Vrin, 1974), 179–289. Cited in Reid, as well as in Luibhéid and Rorem.
9. On French Renaissance interpretations of the history of philosophy, see D. P. Walker, "The *Prisca Theologia* in France," *Journal of Warburg and Courtauld Institutes* 17, no. 3–4 (1954): 204–59.
10. On theophany in Pseudo-Dionysius, see Eric Perl, *Theophany: The Neoplatonic Philosophy of Dionysius the Areopagite*, SUNY series in ancient Greek philosophy (Albany: State University of New York Press, 2008). In *Celestial Hierarchy* I, creation is conceived as a manifestation, or as a theophany, of a hidden divine essence. The hierarchy consists of different orders of being, each of which has a prescribed capacity

for participation in the divine. These orders of being are arranged according to their capacity. Although the capacity for receiving divine knowledge varies, and although the limits are different for each level, the divine is nonetheless fully present to each level to the extent those levels are capable. God is manifest equally to each level, in proportion to their distance or proximity to God. While the divine transcends the hierarchy and lies beyond it, it is mysteriously manifest through the hierarchical structure that it causes. *The Celestial and Ecclesiastical Hierarchy of Dionysius the Areopagite*, translated by John Parker (London: Skeffington, 1894), 15–16. On analogy in Pseudo-Dionysius, one may read V. Lossky's "La notion des 'Analogies' chez Denys le Pseudo-Aréopagite," *Archives d'histoire doctrinale et littéraire du Moyen Âge* 5 (1930): 279–309.

11 Pseudo-Dionysius, *The Divine Names*. In *Dionysius the Areopagite: On the Divine Names and the Mystical Theology*. Translated C. E. Rolt (Grand Rapids, MI: Christian Classics Ethereal Library [undated reprint of the 1920 translation]), Chapter 1, 41–51; Chapter 2, 52–62; Chapter 4, 67–95.

12 For Pseudo-Dionysius, the capacity to receive grace is determined by ideas, or in other words, by rational principles. Manifestations of the divine that are rational in nature constitute the cosmic hierarchy. These diverse manifestations have a relation to divine unity and simplicity which can be discerned through reasoning. For an overview of the distinction between essence and energies in the Greek fathers and their later influences, one may read Alexis Torrance "Precedents for Palamas' Essence-Energies Theology in the Cappadocian Fathers," *Vigiliae Christianae* 63, no. 1 (2009): 47–70. On p. 62, Torrance writes that for the Greek father Gregory of Nazianzus, the theme of knowledge of God gives way to the theme of "encounter," in the sense that it is always bound to the idea of experiencing Him, which is articulated through metaphors of light.

13 On John of Damascus, see Alain de Libera's *La philosophie médiévale*, 68–9. De Libera notes that John of Damascus pursued philosophy in eighth-century Damascus, which had become the capital of the Umayyad Empire. John of Damascus represents a prolongation of the Greek philosophy practice in the Byzantine Empire of the sixth century, but in an Islamic context.

14 For Pseudo-Dionysius, the processions of the divine begin with the persons of the Trinity, whose relations are studied through logical method. Manifestations are the objects of rational discernment. On this, and what Perl calls the "continuum of cognition," see Perl, *Theophany*, Chapter 6, 83–100. The author explains that, for Pseudo-Dionysius, sense and intellect are mediated by discursive reason, and that these three faculties exist on a continuum of cognition ranked according to the multiplicity and unity that they can respectively perceive. While intellect perceives perfect unity, reason perceives the One through multiplicity, and sense perception perceives the One in greater multiplicity than reason. But all three faculties manifest a common activity; while reason is the proper cognitive activity for the human soul, the human soul can rise to angelic contemplation, because they are all the same manifestations of one consciousness. Both reason and intellect apprehend one same reality, and all three represent cognitions of a unified, intelligible reality. However, they perceive that reality through different modes of cognition. We could say these modes of cognition represent different modes of encountering one same reality through forms of consciousness that have different levels of capacity to perceive unity. While the One ultimately lies beyond all cognition, human cognition apprehends the One in its manifestations in the form of Being.

15 Pseudo-Dionysius brings an interpretation of Neo-Platonic philosophy to bear on Christian Scripture. He brings philosophy into the domain of faith. See *Divine Names*, 50–1.

16 On Eriugena's interpretation of theophany, see Emmanuel Falque, "Jean Scot Érigène: La théophanie comme mode de la phénoménalité," *Revue des sciences philosophiques et théologiques* 86, no. 3 (2002): 387–421. On divine nothingness and theophany in Eriugena, see Edouard Jeauneau, "Néant divin et théophanie (Érigène disciple de Denys)," in *Langages et philosophie: Hommage à Jean Jolivet*, ed. A. de Libera, A. Elamrani-Jamal and A. Galonnier, *Études de philosophie médiévale* 74 (Paris: Vrin, 1997): 331–7.

17 On Briçonnet and Pseudo-Dionysius, see Cathleen Eva Corrie, "'Sy excellente pasture': Guillaume Briçonnet's Mysticism and the Pseudo-Dionysius," *Renaissance Studies* 20, no. 1 (2006): 35–50.

18 Lefèvre d'Étaples, Jacques (ed.), *Theologia vivificans, cibus solidus. Dionysii Celestis hierarchia. Ecclesiastica hierarchia. Divina nomina. Mystica theologia. Undecim epistole. Ignatii Undecim epistole. Polycarpi epostola una* (Paris: Higman and Hopyl, 1499). On this, see Cavazza, Silvano, "Platonismo e riforma religiosa: La 'Theologia Vivificans' de Jacques Lèfevre d'Étaples," *Rinascimento* 22, no. 2 (January1982): 99–149. On the legend of Pseudo-Dionysius among early European humanists, cf. Irena Backus, "Renaissance Attitudes to New Testament Apocryphal Writings: Jacques Lefèvre d'Étaples and His Epigones," *Renaissance Quarterly* 51, no. 4 (Winter, 1998), 1169–98.

19 On Pseudo-Dionysius and negative theology in the French Renaissance, see Jan Miernowski, *Le Dieu Néant*.

20 This idea is indebted to Emmanuel Falque, who argues that Eriugena's translation and interpretation of Dionysius's works transformed the latter's thought by placing importance on the modes of God's manifestation over and above his unknowability in "Jean Scot Érigène: La théophanie comme mode de la phénoménalité."

21 The most important essay on French Renaissance syncretism is still D. P. Walker, "The *Prisca Theologi*a in France."

22 The notion that each being receives a determined measure divine light is known as analogy of reception. On this, see Jean-François Courtine, "Différence ontologique et analogie de l'être: le tournant suarézien," in *Bulletin de la Société française de philosophie* 83, no. 2 (April–June 1989): 163–79. Theories of analogy of reception can be considered a mode of encountering the divine.

23 Pseudo-Dionysius, *Celestial Hierarchy*, Chapter 3, 9–10.

24 For Pseudo-Dionysius, the celestial hierarchy allows the soul to move through the stages of purification, illumination and perfection, which is a movement of spiritual understanding and knowledge. Cf. Paul Rorem, *Pseudo-Dionysius: A Commentary on the Texts and an Introduction to Their Influence* (Oxford: Oxford University Press, 1993), 57–9. The ascensional movement of the soul through the hierarchy is a movement of spiritual cognition.

25 Lefèvre d'Étaples's translation of the *De fide orthodoxa [On Orthodox Faith]* is titled: *Contenta: Theologia Damasceni. I. De ineffabili diuinitate. II. De creaturarum genesi ordine Moseos. III. De iis que ab incarnatione vsque ad resurrectionem. IIII. De iis que post resurrectionem vsque ad vniuersalem Resurrectionem* (Paris: Henri Estienne, 1507). The same translation was published in 1512 with Clichtove's commentary under the title: *In hoc opere contenta: Theologia Damasceni quatuor libris explicata et adiecto ad litteram commentario elucidata . . .* (Paris: Henri Estienne, 1512) [hereafter referred to as *De fide orthodoxa*]. On Lefèvre's edition and its medieval precedents, see Irena Backus, "John of Damascus, De Fide Orthodoxa: Translations by Burgundio (1153/4), Grosseteste (1235/40) and Lefèvre d'Étaples (1507)," *Journal of the Warburg and Courtauld Institutes* 49 (1986): 211–17.

26 See Lefèvre, *De fide orthodoxa*, f. 3v.
27 Lefèvre, *De fide orthodoxa*, f. 3v-4r. Clichtove refers directly to Pseudo-Dionysius' *Celestial Hierarchy*, Chapter 4, when he explains divine apparitions, visions and signs. Clichtove uses the Latin verb *manifestare* to refer to God's theophanic revelation. For example, he explains that Saint Paul's epistles to the Corinthians and to the Romans describe God as revealing, or "manifesting" Himself through cognition. In his commentary on Chapter 4 of the *Celestial Hierarchy*, Lefèvre notes that the word apparition (*apparitio*) translates the Greek term for theophany. See Lefèvre, *Theologia vivificans*, f. 19v.
28 Lefèvre, *De fide orthodoxa*, f. 3v and *Theologia vivificans*, f. 19v.
29 Clichtove uses metaphors of light throughout his commentary to refer to spiritual understanding and knowledge, and to its unity despite the differences of receptivity different entities may have. We could say, following Alexis Torrance's suggestion, that these are metaphors for encountering the divine in human experience. See n. 13 above. On Plotinian and Pseudo-Dionysian metaphors of vision for intelligibility, see Perl, *Theophany*, 89–99, especially 97, where Perl argues that for Pseudo-Dionysius, intellection is comparable to vision, because vision extends its gaze outward to the world and allows for objects to enter awareness. This is for him comparable to the way intellection extends outward to assimilate the pure forms of corporeal reality. Pseudo-Dionysius' metaphors of light serve to describe the way in which created beings reveal the divine through both their very being, and through their modes of knowledge. See Lefèvre, *Theologia vivificans*, f. 20v. where these metaphors of vision refer to a cognition (*cognitio*) that goes beyond the veil (*velamen*) of corporeal existence. This vision contemplates the hierarchy of being, which elevates the soul to the contemplation of spiritual and intelligible reality.
30 Lefèvre writes that theophanies are apprehended through the soul's highest point (acies mentis) and spiritual gaze (obtutus mentis), which are both spiritual and cognitive faculties. See for example, Lefèvre, *Theologia vivificans*, fols. 9v, 20v, 79v, 108v, 175v.
31 On this expression, cf. Lefèvre, *Theologia vivificans*, fols. 39v, 92v, 108v.
32 These terms appear throughout Lefèvre's and Clichtove's writings in which they draw on Platonism. We find an important use of these terms in Lefèvre's 1522 *Commentaries on the Gospel according to Saint John*. In his commentary on the first chapter of the Gospel According to John, Lefèvre uses the verb *manifestare* to refer to the revelation of the divine Logos, and he is careful to distinguish his commentary from what he refers to as Platonism. This suggests that he understood the Gospel of Saint John in terms of theophanic revelation. He writes that the divine Logos or Verb is the "archetype" or "exemplar" of all things, which are the "vestiges" of the Logos. The Logos is, he writes, a "singular idea" (*unica idea*). He uses the term "proportion" or "ratio" synonymously with "idea," and argues that God, the Logos or Verb and the Holy Spirit contain all things in themselves in archetypal form, but not in in the way (he writes) Platonic authors conceive of archetypes. Lefèvre d'Étaples, *Commentarii*, fol. 260v–261r.
33 Both Lefèvre and Clichtove use the terms exemplar and archetype to refer to the way in which the divine contains within itself the forms of all created things. Created entities are vestiges of those intelligible forms, and they bear a relation of resemblance to the archetype. These vestiges participate in the divine through imitation. The human soul can ascend through the order of vestiges and become deiform.
34 Rice, *Epistles*, 6.
35 Lefèvre, *Theologia vivificans*, fol. 107r.
36 Rice, *Epistles*, 380.

37 Rice, 438.
38 Rice, 436.
39 Rice, 439.
40 Rice, 439–40.
41 On the idea of spiritual exercise, see Pierre Hadot, "Spiritual Exercises," in *Philosophy as a Way of Life,* ed. A. Davidson (Malden: Blackwell, 1995), 80–125. Lefèvre and Clichtove valued Neo-Platonism in part because of the notion of spiritual cognition that it enabled them to develop. The notion that we ought to exercise our rational capacities in the service of devotion was not new in the Renaissance, but it was revived by humanists in opposition to the domination of logic in the late-medieval educational system in Paris.

Chapter 2

EVENT AND INVENTION: READING MONTAIGNE AND ROUSSEAU THROUGH DELEUZE

Tom Conley

Admirers of Christie McDonald's magnificent studies of Rousseau wonder if and how the *Confessions* or *The Reveries of the Solitary Walker* relate to what she aptly calls the fabric, tissue, texture, or even the manufacture of literary objects. Working through *La Nouvelle Héloïse*, *À la recherche du temps perdu* and now, the labors of a panoply of women writers extending from the Enlightenment to our day, she studies areas where contradiction and paradox drive creative process. In the paragraphs that follow I would like to contend that in her patient and informative readings of Rousseau, an author who might qualify as a *compagnon de route*, McDonald discerns in the matter and manner of his writing that which philosophers of recent vintage call *events*. In McDonald's eyes, Rousseau—an architect and a chronicler of events—has much to say about the nature of cognition and what it means, by way of writing, firmly and intransitively, to "be" and to "become." Rousseau and the authors who inspire him deploy language to invent *experience*—to find ways and means to test and palpate the world. If tradition has it that experience is a relation with the unknown, we might say that they *apprehend* it through imaginative inquiry and creative doubt.[1] We obtain a breathtaking sense of the nature of experience through what Rousseau relates in his autobiographical writings about encounters and unforeseen events, and all the more when we see how he refashions a limit-experience Montaigne had long before related to his would-be-readers in the *Essais*.

The Reveries of the Solitary Walker is an enduring point of reference for any reflection on occasion, accident, or encounter: in the second promenade, Rousseau tells of an accident that befell him when he had been taking a delightful walk outside of Paris. Struck by a moving carriage, thrown topsy-turvy, he loses his senses, recovers consciousness, discovers himself battered and bruised, and soon after ambles home. Time and again, literary historians have shown that his account draws on what Montaigne had related of a harrowing moment in his later years when he was tossed from his horse, knocked unconscious, taken for dead, but later brought back to life.[2] In what follows, instead of examining—as might a source study—how Rousseau builds upon and deviates from Montaigne's tale of his brush with death, I would like to consider their accounts in a welter of broader issues in a sub-field of philosophy that, perhaps for political reasons, tends not to appeal to canons of early modern literature or founding works of autobiography.[3] At the same time, in view of a legacy that reaches back to the beginnings of deconstructive process, it will be argued that Montaigne's and Rousseau's depictions of their accidents can be seen as writing lessons or *scènes d'écriture*.

Prior to his description of the event in the second promenade, despondent about his declining faculties, Rousseau recalls joyously the "inner delights" that "loving and sweet souls" find in contemplation.[4] While walking (Rousseau seems to write when he is on foot), "those moments of rapture, those ecstasies, which I sometimes experienced in walking around alone" that counter disgruntling reminders of people whom he felt were his persecutors.[5] When finding delight in the landscape he feels compelled to commit his sensations to writing. He negotiates sensation and language: "In the midst of so many riches, how could a faithful record of them be kept? In wanting to recall so many sweet reveries, instead of describing them, I fell back into them."[6] Because they could not be translated into written or printed signs, or because, sublime and evanescent, they were beyond the pale of language, all of a sudden, they reminded him of what he had experienced on the heels of his "*plans to write* the sequel to my *Confessions*."[7] As if skittering away from the unwelcome feeling that, written, what he states is couched in an indifferent tongue, he defers addressing the event in question, "the one I am going to speak of and during which an unforeseen accident came to interrupt the thread of my ideas and give them another direction for some time."[8]

A feeling of blissful elevation prefaces the account of the "accident." In the vicinity of Ménilmontant (on Thursday, October 24, 1776), he reports a rush of pleasure in the sunshine, in this "cheerful countryside [*riant paysage*]," a landscape personified, that laughs with and at him, en route to Charonne, when he takes note of two plant species, uncommon around Paris, that he identifies as a *Picris Hieracioides* and a *Bupleurum falatum*.[9] Upon encountering these plants (or, in the text of the promenade, what seems to be the pleasure of noting their scientific names piquing his readers' curiosity, indulgence, or guilt for lack of Latin) he smiles when suddenly happening upon yet another species. Its name seems to percolate through the depths of his memory: "This discovery delighted and amused me for a very long time and ended in the discovery of an even rarer plant, especially in high places, namely, the *Cerastium acquaticum*."[10] He adds abruptly, in the breath of the same sentence, "in spite of the accident that befell me the same day, I have come across in a book I had with me and have now placed in my herbarium."[11]

At the risk of tautology, the scene could not be more "rousseauesque" or, more properly "roussellien": botanist that he is, everywhere Rousseau discerns nature as he moves through it, book or paper in hand or in mind, juggling the flora he sees with, as he goes, what he reads on a page or recalls on a memory-screen.[12] The contradiction is salient: "Finally, after having looked thoroughly at several other plants I saw still in bloom and which I was always pleased to see even though I was familiar with their aspects and name, I gradually turned away from these minute observations so as to give myself up to the no less charming, but more moving, impression which the scene as a whole made on me."[13] If the words betray an unconscious, a symptom would be the unsettling reference to printed writing: the French *parcourir* (look thoroughly) refers to passing over signs in a book, while the *énumération* (translated as "name" here) could belong to a declension, and the aim to "give himself up [*se livrer*]" to the "impression" left upon him carries echoes of print technology.[14] What produces a "mixed impression, sweet and sad," that could be both sentient and printed gives way to a melancholic reflection buoyed by recalling that once again he could give himself up to enjoy "these peaceful meditations"—but only when, "at the height of my reverie, I was dragged out of it by the *event* which remains for me to relate."[15]

The paragraphs that follow belong to a category of what might be called creative plagiarism. At their juncture in the *Essais,* at the moment when the self-portrait is first considered, Montaigne's reflections on his fall lead directly to the project that becomes a model for Rousseau's *Confessions*. From a binocular (and not a chronological) perspective, the relation that Rousseau's narrative holds with Montaigne's can be taken in the sense of a "stratigraphy." We are compelled to see the one with and through the other and, together, to determine how they consider the nature of what they report to be life-changing encounters. First, Montaigne: "Of practice" (II, vi) ["De l'exercitation"], one of the first essays to consider *experience* as practice, is tied to the theme of the *ars moriendi,* that had been broached in the deliberative style of "That to philosophize is to learn to die" (I, xx) ["Que philosopher, c'est apprendre à mourir"], in which death is "essayed," in a topical fashion, as it might in a forensics session. Forcibly having no idea about what it is or feels "like," never having died, a subject or a living being "prehends" death (*apprendre* in echo of *apprendere,* "to lay hold upon to seize, take hold of"),[16] through the force of imagination (the topic and title of "On the Strength of Imagination" [I, xxi] ["De la force de l'imagination"], the essay that follows). The event of death can only be experienced in the imagination or—as it becomes clear in the account that follows—what he *invents* through a narrative of collision and fall.

His memory fuzzy, Montaigne can't recall exactly *when,* in which of the civil wars the event took place, but he is aware of *where* and *how* it happened.

> During our third civil war [*troubles*] or the second (I do not quite remember which), I went riding [*promener*] one day about a league [about three miles] from my house, which is situated at the very hub [*moiau*] of all the turmoil of the civil wars of France. Thinking myself perfectly safe and so near my home that I needed no better equipage, I took a very easy but not very strong horse.[17]

Sudden mention of war draws attention to the title and its synonyms, to *exercitus* and *exercitatio,* cognates which lend a military inflection to the essay. Since (as he relates in detail in "On Physionomy" [III, xii] ["De la phisionomie"]) the "troubles" were especially devastating in his region, Montaigne would not have been taking a gentleman's ride far beyond his chateau. When an unstated occasion requires that he venture into territories in conflict, outside of the perimeters of his *habitus*, he rides the same horse, but he is accompanied by an armed escort:

> On my return, when a sudden occasion came up for me to use this horse for a service to which it was not accustomed, one of my men, big and strong, riding a powerful work horse who had a desperately hard [*désespérée*] mouth and was moreover fresh and vigorous—this man, in order to show his daring and get ahead of his companions, spurred his horse at full speed up the path behind me, came down like a colossus on the little man and little horse, and hit us like a thunderbolt with all its strength and weight, sending us both head over heels.[18]

It appears that the occasion or fall (from *occidere*) takes place in the discourse—in the signifying matter—before the narration relates or "represents" how the event took place. In this strange passage the reader wonders if, when describing how the "little man and little horse" are knocked head over heels, Montaigne puts himself in the third person so as to be seen outside of himself. The words indicate that in observing his own demise he identifies himself as *moy*, a *moy* other than itself, perhaps in recall of *moi-au*, the hub [*moiau*] of the ongoing wars and *moy-en*, a means [*moyen*] of mediating the personal situation in the context of the Wars of Religion:

> So that there lay the horse bowled over and stunned, and I [*moy*] ten or twelve steps beyond, dead, stretched on my back, my face all bruised and skinned, my sword [*mon espée*], which I [*je*] had had in my hand, more than ten paces away, my belt in pieces, having no more motion or feeling than a log. It is the only swoon that I have experienced to this day. Those who were with me, after having tried all the means they could to bring me round, thinking me dead, took me in their arms and were carrying me with great difficulty back to my house, which was about half a French league from there.[19]

In moving from the third person ("the little man and little horse") to *je* and then to the intermediate *moy*, the personal pronoun or *shifter* suggests that the narration is both inside and outside of its origin or invention. The event is described from a point of view that recalls it was experienced, but also, and no sooner from another angle, in what might be qualified as a "free indirect subjectivity."[20] In a tenor of writing close to Maurice Blanchot—twice repeating a formula, *pas au delà*, that can be taken as a "step (not) beyond"—Montaigne sees himself dead but not dead.[21] The *moy* becomes a particle iterated over and again, nestled into cognate figures—in the lexicon of philosophy—that de-territorialize or estrange the self from itself, and that eventually draw the episode away from the context of war, as it can be seen in the original passage:

> ... *moy* qui suis assis dans le *moiau* ... *moy* dix ou douze pas au-delà ... [c]eux qui estoient avec *moy*, après avoir essayé tous les *moyens* ... [j]e n'imagine aucune estant pour *moy* si insupportable et horrible que d'avoir l'ame vifve et

affligée, sans *moyen* de se declarer ... [ou] *moyen* quelconque d'expression ... [c]omme j'approchai de chez *moy* ... des pensemens vains ... ne venoyent pas de chez *moy*. Je ne sçavoy pourtant ny d'où je venoy, ny où j'aloy ... ce conte d'un évenement si legier est assez vain, n'estoit l'instruction que j'en ay tirez pour *moy* ...²²

The encounter with—or apprehension of—death galvanizes the greater project of self-study and, as the latter moves ahead, that of the self-portrait. In Montaigne's *Exemplaire de Bordeaux* (1588) that Rousseau would not have seen, the text of 1580 (or the "A stratum" of the *Essais*) ends when the essay looks back upon itself, declaring that after all, whatever its gravity, it is the tale of an ever-slight but highly instructive *event* that takes place on the surface of the printed page:

> This account of so trivial an event would be rather pointless, were it not for the instruction that I have derived from it for myself; for, in truth, in order to get used [*s'aprivoiser*] to the idea of death, I find there is nothing like coming close to it [*s'en avoisiner*]. Now as Pliny says [*comme dict Pline*], everyone is a very good discipline [*discipline*] to oneself, provided they have what they need to spy on themselves closely [*de s'espier de près*]. What I write here is not my teaching, but my study; it's not the lesson of others, it is mine alone.²³

In an untranslatable drift of the words, to domesticate oneself, *s'aprivoiser* slips into *s'avoisiner*, to approximate, to locate oneself in proximity to a given place or condition. No less, *Pline*, a "proper" noun, is echoed in a "common" counterpart, in *discipline*, that can be read as *dit-ci-pline*, "here says pline", but with the effect that a "fold", a *pli*, emerges from the play of signifiers. The mantra to study oneself alertly and intensely implies that, folded into and over one another, the letters, words and spacings that convey the self-description are also subject to close inspection: *s'espier de près*, to "spy" on oneself from close up, recalls the weapon he had lost upon being thrown from his horse: "my sword that I had in my hand, more than ten steps beyond [*mon espée que j'avoy à la main, à plus de dix pas au delà*]" was beyond his reach.²⁴ The turn of phrase may indeed be what prompts Montaigne to pen one of the longest *alongeails* or handwritten supplements in the margins of the *Exemplaire*, the edition of 1588 to which he added material, so it seems, in preparation of a later edition (published posthumously in 1595).²⁵ In this *alongeail*, he notes: "What is useful to me may also by accident be useful to another [*Ce qui me sert, peut aussi par accident servir à un autre*]."²⁶ The tale just told about the occasion, fortuitous encounter, mistake or "accident," which he avows he is relating with great pleasure, might be another "accident" serving the needs of others. Having just "essayed" death through writing he takes pride in noting that only "two or three" authors of the classical age have done as much, but by all means, in one of the most telling phrases of the *Essais*, that surely would have marked Rousseau, he adds, noting that the scene of the writing of the accident exceeds whatever it was in so-called reality:

It's a thorny undertaking [*une espineuse entreprinse*], and more so than it seems, to follow a movement so wandering as that of our mind [*esprit*], to penetrate the opaque depths of its innermost folds [*ses replis internes*], to pick out and immobilize the innumerable flutterings that agitate it.[27]

The *espineuse* or "spiny" enterprise of self-espionage could entail seeking the juncture of the body and the soul. It could also be related to an autopsy, to the examination of the spine or dorsal column as shown in anatomical "theaters" of the same vintage.[28] By all means, to study (hence alienate) oneself entails seeking where the breath or *esprit* is felt in words, notably, in the *espineuse entreprinse* that delves into the dark depths, the *replis internes*, or unknown regions of the body. Little wonder that in the *Exemplaire de Bordeaux* Montaigne notes how this essay and others can be appreciated as a public dissection: "I expose myself entire: my portrait is a cadaver [*skeletos*] on which the veins, the muscles, and the tendons appear at a glance, each part in its place."[29] In reflecting on what he has wrought, Montaigne corrects those who would condemn the project that covets self-description, "who call it daydreaming [*resverie*] and idleness to be concerned with oneself."[30] In the same passage, asserting (angrily, even defensively, so it seems), "it is not my deeds that I write down, it is *myself*, it is my essence [[*c*]*e ne sont mes gestes que j'escris, c'est moy, c'est mon essence*],"[31] Montaigne anticipates the sense that *je est un autre* (I is another) with the bonus that the correlative *moy* belongs to a webbing of words signaling mediation and alteration. Within the frame of "De l'exercitation" Montaigne's tale of his unsettling encounter with the unknown gives rise to the "enterprise" of the *Essais*.

In the spirit of what he recounts in the second promenade, Rousseau's confessions are said to be born of Montaigne's "exercitation." Rousseau's words are in dialogue with the essay at the moment it depicts the accident that precipitated Montaigne's fall from his horse.[32] He writes:

I saw a huge Great Dane rushing down upon me. Racing before a carriage, the dog had no time to check its pace or to turn aside when it noticed me. I judged that the only means I had to avoid being knocked to the ground was to make a great leap, so well-timed that the dog would pass under me while I was still in the air. This idea, quicker than a flash and which I had the time neither to think through nor carry out, was my last before my accident. I did not feel the blow, nor the fall, nor anything of what followed until the moment when I came to.[33]

Where, in the midst of war, Montaigne was armed, equipped, on horseback and in protective company on a military expedition, alone, on foot, observing flora, Rousseau enjoyed the pleasure of gathering plants on a sunny afternoon. Montaigne witnessed a livid horse that "came down like a colossus on the little man and little horse [*fondre comme un colosse sur le petit homme et petit cheval*]";[34] afterward, "when my memory came to open up and picture to me the state I had been in at the instant I had perceived that horse *bearing down* [*fondant*] on me ... it seemed to me that a flash of lightning was striking my soul with a violent shock, and that I was coming back from the other world."³⁵ In the blink of an eye, Rousseau recalls, "I saw a huge Great Dane rushing down upon me."³⁶ His decision to jump came fast, "quicker than a flash."³⁷ In concert with Montaigne's essay, the *Reveries* place emphasis on the *moi*, an agent both self and other that mediates the "impressions"—or, broadly, a welter of *ap-prehensions* felt, seen and "experienced" in the printed writing.

In both accounts we see the same words twice. Descriptions of encounters redound, and so also depictions of beatitude that follow. Like Montaigne who recalls the pleasure of slipping into sleep, into "an idea that was only floating on the surface of my soul, as delicate and feeble as all the rest, but indeed not only free from distress but mingled with that sweet feeling that people have who let themselves slide into sleep,"³⁸ Rousseau notes, "I felt a rapturous calm in my whole being; and each time I remember it, I find nothing comparable to it in all the activity of known pleasures."³⁹ Like Montaigne, who vomited a bucket of blood when he was carried "half a French league [*une demy lieuë Françoise*]"⁴⁰ from the site of the accident to his home, Rousseau, although returning on his own means, spit blood while walking the same distance, "the half-league from the Temple to the Rue Platrière."⁴¹ He recalls returning home without other accident until the sight of his battered body becomes the cause of his wife's alarm. After making an inventory of his ills (an upper lip split up to his nose, four loosened teeth, a swollen and bruised jaw, one thumb bent and the other wounded, the left arm sprained, the left knee swollen, a contusion stiffening the body), happy that nothing was broken, he sums up, "that, very faithfully, is the story of my accident."⁴² Equally or even more unsettling, he infers, was that when the news of the fall circulated in Paris, like the bruised face he saw in his mirror, it became "changed and disfigured" through gossip. No matter how Rousseau recoiled when he heard what was being made of his accident, or how, from another angle, it gave way to further turmoil in the social order (obsequious praise of his work on the part of a female novelist),⁴³ his tale becomes a point of reference not only in the *Reveries* but also for how writing and rewriting become events of a first kind.

In "Qu'est-ce qu'un événement ?" ("What is an event?"), a rich and dense chapter of *Le Pli: Leibniz et le baroque* (*The Fold: Leibniz and the Baroque*), Gilles Deleuze engages reflection in response to the question its title poses. What exactly *is* an event? *Is* it what philosophy *is* best equipped to consider? Is it what philosophy aims to create *tout court*? Threading a reading of Leibniz through Alfred North Whitehead, he contends that an event is more than—contrary to Montaigne and Rousseau—the report of a fall, collapse, or calamity such as "a man has been run over."⁴⁴ An event is not conveyed or experienced through the representation of a fall, a swoon, a ravishment, a syncope or even a mystical voyage. Rather, Deleuze imagines, as if thinking about how Napoleon's soldiers might have gazed upon the Great Pyramid while trudging across the desert in the Egyptian campaign (1798–1801), a shared sighting of the monument could qualify as an event. It would be felt in the recognition of its duration "during one hour, thirty minutes, five minutes . . ., a passage of Nature, or a passage of God, a view of God."⁴⁵ Implied is that an event could be anywhere and everywhere, and not be a unique occurrence but, in greater likelihood, a continuum or a process. Deleuze poses a second question: "What are the conditions of an event so that everything can be event [*soit événement*]?"⁴⁶ In its stenography, the question moves from *an* event to event *tout court* (event without article or particle). He adds: the event is produced in "*a* chaos, in *a* chaotic multiplicity, provided that *a sort of screen* [*une sorte de crible*] can intervene."[47] The play of articles is decisive for what he is getting at: at the core of the event, "chaos would be a pure *Many* [in English in the text], a pure disjunctive diversity, while something is a *One* [*un* One], not a unity already, but rather the indefinite article [of] some kind of singularity? How does the *Many* become [as] *One*?"[48] Emerging from chaos, *the* event would not exist without an amorphous elastic "membrane", comparable to the *chora* that Plato describes in the *Timaeus*, that brings it forward.[49] For Leibniz, chaos would be a world of "depthless shadows" through which a screen extracts a dark bottom, a *fuscum subnigrum* that makes it perceptible or even visible.[50] Once manifest, by virtue of the screen, chaos is felt as a "universal dizziness, the sum of all possible perceptions" otherwise infinitesimal or infinitely small, of an infinite totality beyond human measure.[51] The event would be something "one" that emerges from the "many" that remain in a background.[52] By way of the screen (which might be written language) an event could be one *and* many, both singular *and* plural, and given to iteration *and* a play (as shown by Montaigne and Rousseau) of difference *and* repetition.

Deleuze delineates three features or attributes of an event. A sense or intuition of *extension* is the first component, discerned when one element (a perception) stretches over those that follow, leading to connections of wholes and parts that form "an infinite series that contains neither a final term nor a limit (the limits of our sense being excepted). The event is a vibration with an infinity of harmonics or sub-multiples, such as an audible wave, a luminous wave, or even an increasingly smaller part of space over the course of an increasingly smaller duration."[53] Extension cannot be dissociated from a second component, designated as "*intensions, intensities, or degrees*. It is something rather than nothing, but also this rather than that: no longer the indefinite article, but the demonstrative pronoun."[54] And the third component— here Deleuze reads Leibniz through Whitehead—is the "individual," a "'concrescence' of elements" that comprises a "*prehension*: one element is the given, the 'datum' of another element that prehends it. Prehension is individual unity. Everything prehends its antecedents and its concomitants and, by degrees, prehends a world."[55] Living beings "prehend" water, earth, carbon, and salt. Returning to the beginning of the chapter, Deleuze adds that an event can take place at any time and anywhere. "At a given moment the pyramid prehends Bonaparte's soldiers (forty centuries are contemplating us) and inversely. We can say that 'echoes, reflections, traces, prismatic deformations, perspective, thresholds, folds' are prehensions that somehow anticipate psychic life."[56] A vector of prehension goes from the world to the prehending subject (say, from the pyramid to the soldier) and from whatever is prehended to the prehender (from the soldier to the pyramid that as he trudges along feels is taking ominous note of him). Summing up—and here Montaigne's and Rousseau's expression of *apprehension* becomes pertinent—Deleuze argues,

> the prehended, the datum, is itself a pre-existing or coexisting prehension, such that all prehension is a prehension of prehension, and the event thus a "nexus of

prehensions." Each new prehension becomes a datum. It becomes public, but for other prehensions that objectify it; the event is inseparably the objectification of one prehension and the subjectification of another; it is at once public and private, potential and real, participating in the becoming [*le devenir*] of another event and the subject of its own becoming. The event always includes something psychic.[57]

Three sub-categories follow. First, when a subject prehends a "datum" in a manner that is positive, it "folds" into itself what it feels worthy and pleasurable while it excludes data (perceptions) that would be of negative inflection. Second, these positive prehensions go from one to another "in a [state of] becoming, putting the past into a present that opens onto the future, leading finally [thirdly] to psychology of perception,"[58] a condition of "self-enjoyment" that makes things possible.

What Deleuze does with the event through *prehension* and *concrescence* offers a way to rethink and reterritorialize Montaigne's and Rousseau's narrations. Be it the encounter of a desperate horse or of a dog and a carriage, for the two authors, what spurs the events they describe is initially exceptional, unexpected, even uncanny. On protracted reading, Montaigne and Rousseau's descriptions indicate that anticipations, micro-perceptions as it were, are felt either before or co-extensively with the accidents themselves. At the beginning of "Of practice," anticipation of a deadly event is part and parcel of its apprehension:

> It is the approaches [*approches*] that we have to fear; and these may fall within our experience. Many things seem to us greater in imagination than in reality. I have spent a good part of my life in perfect and entire health: I mean not merely entire, but even blithe and ebullient. This state, full of verdure and cheer, made me find the thought of illnesses so horrible that when I came to experience them I found their pains mild and easy compared with my fears. Here is what I experience every day: if I am warmly sheltered in a nice room during a stormy and tempestuous night, I am appalled and distressed for those who are then in the open country; if I am myself outside, I do not even wish to be anywhere else.[59]

The event takes place in its "approaches," in its encounter or apprehension—which is not far from what Deleuze calls "perception in the folds,"[60] what Montaigne might describe as a flash or thunderbolt emanating from "opaque depths" and "inner pleats" of the mind (*esprit*).[61] Deleuze explains how "these tiny, obscure, confused perceptions"[62] operate in the experience of Leibniz's dog, that when its master either whips or feeds it, it feels pricklings of disquiet [*inquiétude*], synonymous with apprehension, whose counterpart is satisfaction.

> If I abruptly flog my dog who eats his meal, the animal will have experienced the minute perceptions of my stealthy arrival on tiptoes, my hostile odor, and my lifting of the rod that subtend the conversion of pleasure into pain. How could a feeling of hunger follow one of satisfaction if a thousand tiny, elementary forms of hunger (of salts, of butter, sugar, etc.) were not released at diverse and indiscernible rhythms? And inversely, if satisfaction follows hunger, it is through

the sating of all these particular and imperceptible hungers. Tiny perceptions are as much the passage from one perception to another as they are the components of each perception. They constitute the animal or animated state par excellence: disquiet.[63]

The scenario is familiar: when Montaigne's memory comes back to him, in recalling the horse (also) coming at him before the collision, the thought of what would happen had been so sudden that it seemed as if a lightning bolt were striking and shaking his soul; that he was coming out of death, what he calls "the other world," before or upon dying. When Rousseau glimpsed the dog galloping in front of the carriage, unable to change its course when it noticed him, instinct told him to jump in the air. The decision came so quickly that reason was useless. Because he felt neither the blow, the fall, "nor anything about what followed up to the moment," when he came back to his senses the event took place in recall of anxiety of anticipation. It can be said that as scenes of writing the unique episodes recounted in the *Essays* and the *Reveries* are inventions of experience, understood not as the cliché circulates nowadays, either in the singular ("the scholarly experience," the "Fenway Park experience," the "Air France experience," etc.) or plural ("I have had many experiences," "when he was overseas, the student I am recommending gained many valuable experiences," etc., *ad nauseam*), but as a relation or even an experiment with death. Iterated, printed, studied and analyzed over and again, their singularity becomes a commonality, and what we make of them as public objects acquire personal or private consequence. By all means, demonstrating in their style and manner how apprehension and prehension belong to a rich and enduring legacy of encounter- and event-theory, Montaigne and Rousseau belong to a field in which in her own writing Christie McDonald has made many inroads and, along the way, continues to open us onto new horizons of inquiry. It is up to us to follow her lead.

Notes

1 Clinical analyst Guy Rosolato maintains that our sentient lives cue on the presence of two types of "unknown": unknown known and unknown unknown (the experience of birth and death), in *La Relation d'inconnu* (Paris: Éditions Gallimard, 1978) and "L'Inconnu dans l'idéalisation du désir," reprinted in *La Portée du désir ou la psychanalyse même* (Paris: PUF, 1996), 135–52.
2 In "Of practice" ("*De l'exercitation*"), chapter 6 of the second volume. Reference will be made to: Michel de Montaigne, *Essays* and *Travel Journal* in *The Complete Works of Montaigne*, trans. Donald Frame (Stanford: Stanford University Press, 1957) and occasionally to the *Œuvres complètes*, ed. Albert Thibaudet and Maurice Rat (Paris: Gallimard/Pléiade, 1962).
3 Among others, Jonathan Bennett, *Events and their Name* (Indianapolis: Haggart, 1988); Donald Davidson, *Essays on Action and Events* (Oxford: Oxford University Press, 2001); Alain Badiou, *L'être et l'événement* (Paris: Éditions du Seuil, 1988); for the context of what follows, Alfred North Whitehead, *Process and Reality* (Cambridge: Cambridge University Press, 1929).

4   Jean-Jacques Rousseau, *The Reveries of the Solitary Walker* in *The Collected Writings of Rousseau*, ed. Christopher Kelly (Hanover: University Press of New England, 2000), 8:9.
5   Rousseau, 9.
6   Rousseau, 9–10.
7   Rousseau, 10. Emphasis added.
8   Rousseau, 10.
9   Rousseau, 10.
10 Rousseau, 10.
11 Rousseau, 10.
12 Famously, in 1753, while walking through the forest of Saint-Germain, meditating, Rousseau composes and writes his *Discours sur l'origine de l'inégalité parmi les hommes*. From the outset, the *Confessions* are rife with scenes where Rousseau moves through landscapes that he encounters because they come before his eyes in conjunction with writing or printed signs he either reads or recalls in the midst of his ambulations.
13 Rousseau, *The Reveries*, 10.
14 French editors Gagnebin and Raymond note that "*Parcourir en détail* immediately seems strange because *parcourir* is used only when speaking of books, works of the mind, papers glanced in passing." Translation mine. See Jean-Jacques Rousseau, *Les Rêveries du promeneur solitaire,* in *Œuvres complètes,* ed. Bernard Gagnebin, Robert Osmont, and Marcel Raymond (Paris: Éditions Gallimard/Pléiade, 1959), 1:1772, n. 9.
15 Rousseau, *The Reveries*, 11. Emphasis added.
16 For Montaigne, whose knowledge of Latin appears flawless, *apprendre* recalls *apprehendere*, to "take, to seize." The *Trésor de la langue française* [http://stella.atilf.fr/Dendien/scripts/tlfiv5/advanced.exe?8;s=2256125760] indicates that it is not far from *appréhender*, to apprehend. In his *Dictionarie of the French and English Tongues* (London: Adam Inslip, 1611), Randle Cotrave translates *apprehendre* thus: "*To apprehend, conceive, understand, perceive, discouer* [sic]" and, tellingly, "*to spie out.*" For *apprendre* he notes: "*To learne, comprehend, conne; also, to teach, or (as we say also) to learne one a thing, whence*; Apprendre aux poissons à nager. *To teach fishes to swimme; (an idle vaine, or needlesse labour) we say, to teach his grandame to grope ducks.*"
17 Montaigne, "Of practice," *Essays* II, 6, 268–9.
18 Montaigne, "Of practice," *Essays* II, 6, 269.
19 Montaigne, "Of practice," *Essays* II, 6, 269.
20 What is seen or shown through the text is both subjective *and* objective, "half-subjective, if one wishes, but this half-subjectivity indicates nothing that is at all variable or uncertain," notes Gilles Deleuze, in *Cinéma 1: L'Image-mouvement* (Paris: Éditions de Minuit, 1983) 110–11. The definition is close to what elsewhere he calls an "event," in *Le Pli: Leibniz et le baroque* (Paris: Éditions de Minuit, 1988), 105–6.
21 Maurice Blanchot, *Le Pas au-delà* (Paris: Éditions Gallimard, 1973). In several essays—including "Pas" (*Gramma* 3–4 (1975): 111–217, reprinted in *Parages* (the first syllable of the title being an echo of *pas*) (Paris: Éditions Galilée, 1986) and "Spéculer—sur Freud" Jacques Derrida ties the "step-not-beyond" principle to Freud's *Beyond the Pleasure Principle* (in French as *Au-delà du principe de plaisir*), in *La Carte postale* (Paris: Aubier-Flammarion, 1978).
22 Montaigne, *Œuvres complètes*, ref. already given n. 2 352–7.
23 Montaigne, "Of practice," *Essays* II, 6, 272. With my changes in the translation to keep it closer to the original.
24 Montaigne, "Of practice," *Essays* II, 6, 272; "De l'exercitation," *Essais* II, 6, 353.

25 This page of the Exemplaire de Bordeaux can be visited at the site of the *Montaigne Project*: see https://artflsrv03.uchicago.edu/philologic4/montessaisvilley/navigate/1/4/7/?byte=1126711&byte=1126713.
26 Montaigne, "Of practice," *Essays* II, 6, 272; "De l'exercitation," *Essais* II, 6, 353.
27 Montaigne, "Of practice," *Essays* II, 6, 273; "De l'exercitation," *Essais* II, 6, 358.
28 "Espineux: m. euse: f. thornie, brierie, full of brambles; also, belonging to the backbone; and hence; Muscle espineux. A certaine muscle which helps to stretch out the necke," notes Cotgrave in his *Dictionarie*, s.v. "Espineux", see https://archive.org/details/fre_b2062733/page/n11/mode/2up.
29 Montaigne, "Of practice," *Essays* II, 6, 274.
30 Montaigne, "Of practice," *Essays* II, 6, 274.
31 Montaigne, "Of practice," *Essays* II, 6, 274; "De l'exercitation," *Essais* II, 6, 359-60. Emphasis added.
32 Montaigne, "De l'exercitation," *Essais* II, 6 (352-3).
33 Rousseau, *The Reveries*, 11.
34 Montaigne, "Of practice," *Essays,* II, 6, 269.
35 Montaigne, "Of practice," *Essays,* II, 6, 272. Emphasis added.
36 Rousseau, *The Reveries* 11.
37 Rousseau, 11.
38 Montaigne, "Of practice," *Essays,* II, 6, 269-70.
39 Rousseau, *The Reveries*, 12.
40 Montaigne, "Of practice," *Essays,* II, 6, 269.
41 Rousseau, *The Reveries*, 12.
42 Rousseau, 13.
43 The novelist in question is Mme d'Ormoy. See Rousseau, *Œuvres complètes*, p. 1007 n3.
44 Gilles Deleuze, *The Fold: Leibniz and the Baroque*, trans. Tom Conley (Minneapolis: University of Minnesota Press, 1993), 76.
45 Deleuze, 76.
46 Deleuze, 76.
47 Deleuze, 76. Emphasis added and translation slightly modified.
48 Deleuze, 76.
49 Deleuze, 76.
50 Deleuze, 76.
51 Deleuze, 76.
52 Deleuze quotes a letter from Leibniz to Louis Bourguet (dated March 1714): "I do mean that whoever would have sensitive organs discerning enough to notice the smallest parts of things would find that everything is organized ... For it is impossible for a creature to be capable of delving at once into the smallest parcel of matter because the actual sub-divisions go up to infinity." Deleuze, 153-4, n. 4.
53 Deleuze, 76.
54 Deleuze, 77. Emphasis added.
55 Deleuze, 76.
56 Deleuze, 78.
57 Deleuze, 78.
58 Deleuze, 92.
59 Montaigne, "Of practice," *Essays,* II, 6, 268.
60 "Perception in the Folds" is chapter 7 of Deleuze, *The Fold*.
61 Montaigne, "Of practice," *Essays* II, 6, 273; "De l'exercitation," *Essais* II, 6, 358.
62 Deleuze, *The Fold,* 86.
63 Deleuze, 87.

Chapter 3

ENCOUNTERING VENTURE: DISSONANCE, DECEIT, AUTOBIOGRAPHY

Pierre Saint-Amand

I choose to present encounter as someone bursting into another person's life. This encounter causes an upheaval—a shock that alters the person in a decisive manner, transforming his fragile autonomy and causing a fundamental sense of alienation. For these reasons, this other can be painted with a cultural mask that depicts him with exotic features, with a sense of the *foreign*. Hence the anthropological contamination in the discourse bearing witness to the encounter. This is what I would like to foreground in an episode taken from Rousseau's *Confessions* (1782) as well as its critical commentary.

This episode from Book IV of Rousseau's *Confessions* continues to intrigue Rousseau's critics; it is a program of musical imposture associated with the name of Vaussore de Villeneuve, himself associated with another name, Venture de Villeneuve—the flamboyant character who makes his entrance in Book III of the *Confessions*. Christie McDonald reads this episode narrating Rousseau's improbable and unforgettable encounter with music within the larger context of Rousseau's musical theory and the way the question of music is associated with his name. Moreover and more precisely, McDonald seeks to juxtapose (or reconcile) the two images of Rousseau in his practice and theory of music: the theoretician of "new perspectives" on the art of music on the one hand, and a debased vision of the same character on the other, who, McDonald writes, "gave a performance in spite of his admitted musical ineptitude, 'with stupid shamelessness that he is the Author of things he cannot perform.'"[1] For McDonald, an emblematic scene frames this question—the scene in which Rousseau performs in public as an imitation of the infamous French musician, Venture de Villeneuve.

"A very pretty voice"

In the *Confessions*, the first meeting with Venture is narrated as an encounter that turned the young Jean-Jacques's head, leading him to commit, he writes, "some new follies."[2] And Venture quickly appears as someone encouraging Jean Jacques's "unruly head."³ It is worthwhile to go over the scene in its entirety, which takes place one evening in the month of February in Annecy. Here is the way the itinerant musician bursts into Rousseau's life, and here is the description of the musician who appears one cold evening, opening Rousseau's dazzled eyes and arriving there as if blown by the wind. For Alain Grosrichard, commenting on this passage and the name of Venture, the visitor is "he who is fated to come (*venturus*), to seduce the little boy (*Petit*), sitting like a good boy at Mama's side."⁴

> I examined him while he warmed himself up and chattered while waiting for supper. He was short of stature, but broad shouldered; he had an indefinable something malformed in his shape without any particular deformity; he was a hunchback with flat shoulders so to speak, but I believe he limped a little. He had a black coat more worn out than old, which was falling to pieces, a very fine and very dirty shirt, beautiful fringed ruffles, gaiters in each of which he could have put both his legs, and to protect himself from the snow a little hat to carry under his arm. Nevertheless, in this comic outfit he had something noble that his bearing did not belie; his physiognomy had something delicate and pleasing, he spoke easily and well, but not very modestly.⁵

This figure made an immediate impression on the young Rousseau, first for the well-known company he seemed to know and keep—"He knew all the great virtuosi, all the famous works, all the actors, all the actresses, all the pretty women, all the Great Lords"⁶—and later for the demonstration of his talents—"the next day there was music at the Cathedral; M. le Maître proposes that he sing there ... He sang his two solos with all the accuracy and all the taste imaginable, and what is more with a very pretty voice."⁷ The author of the *Confessions* does not hide his infatuation with Venture, nor his taste for him.⁸ We are privy to a thinly veiled love story directed at this singer, justified in the following manner: "I loved to see him, to listen to him; to me everything he did appeared charming, to me everything he said seemed to be oracles."⁹ Later, Rousseau tried to introduce the young man into his relationship with Madame de Warens, Rousseau's famous hostess and then lover, but he did not succeed, enduring instead the refusal of his patroness: "He found her affected; she found him to be a libertine, and being alarmed about such a bad acquaintance for me, not only did she forbid me to bring him back but she depicted to me the dangers I was running with this young man so strongly that I became a little more circumspect about abandoning myself to them."¹⁰

In Book IV of the *Confessions*, Rousseau nevertheless tells of his next meeting with the same Venture, with no hint of any lessening of his great infatuation, to the point that he becomes distracted from his first love: "I found M. Venture again ... I found him brilliant and celebrated throughout Annecy; he was all the rage among the Ladies. This success turned my head completely. I no longer saw anything but M. Venture, and he almost made me forget Mme de Warens ... I proposed that he share his lodging with me; he consented to do so."¹¹ It is this person, in any case, whom Rousseau imitates and on whom he bases his new future itinerant lifestyle:

> In this pedestrian pilgrimage I compared myself to my friend Venture arriving in Annecy. I warmed up so well from this idea, that, without thinking that I had neither his engaging manner nor his talents, I took it into my head to play the little Venture at Lausanne, to teach music which I did not know, and to say I was from Paris where I had never been.[12]

Lausanne would become the theater for the most grandiose imposture in the *Confessions*, the culmination of the episodes in which Rousseau shows his "unruly head"[13] had turned.[14] Once again, in narrating Venture's influence on him, Rousseau admits that "[his] head was tuned to the tone of a foreign instrument, it was out of its diapason."[15] He goes so far as to call himself "venturized" by the man he considers his "great model."[16] This is the word Rousseau chooses to describe the change in him under the musician's influence. But the term *engouement*, used by Rousseau to describe his infatuation as early as his first encounter with Venture, already contains this intrusive idea of "embodiment," since etymologically, the French verb "*s'engouer*" means to swallow. The word therefore spans and permeates a mimetic dimension: to swallow the other translates the ultimate desire of blending or extreme identification with the model. And Rousseau in the process layers contradiction on top of contradiction: "A Parisian from Geneva and a Catholic in a Protestant country, I believed I ought to change my name as well as my religion and my fatherland ... He had called himself Venture de Villeneuve; I made an anagram of the name Rousseau in that of Vaussore, and I called myself Vaussore de Villeneuve."[17]

Christie McDonald is particularly interested in this episode of alienation, of becoming the other. About this episode of advanced "duplicity," she writes that "[t]he imposture constitutes an identification aimed at changing Rousseau through and through."[18] Ultimately, McDonald is at a loss to know how to characterize this imposture. In the subtitle of the chapter where she analyzes this entire episode, she evokes the "vagabond's vodou,"[19] and we notice the sequence of contagion of the "v" in Venture's name. Is it the *venturization* of Rousseau that inspires her to use this ethnological reference, which is not developed in her text aside from the subtitle. Furthermore, she alludes to another anthropological scene in her analysis of the same episode in her reference to Jean Starobinski: "the scene ushers in a new and fictive identity, which must follow its course. This is why Jean Starobinski speaks of "magic," of an act which, in making Rousseau into a composer and a musician instantaneously, transforms his desire (for Venture, for music) into destiny."[20] Insisting on the depersonalization of Rousseau in the Venture episode, Starobinski indeed attempts to demonstrate that Rousseau felt himself to be possessed by someone else. Having first considered hypnosis, he proceeds to explain the reference to magic (by the passivity of the act of identification): "[it] entails, indeed, calling upon forces that one then allows to act upon him; these forces operate by themselves, beyond our control ..."[21] If we understand Christie McDonald, "vodou" is a theoretical, metaphorical shorthand for describing the complex episode of this fascinating duplicity sought by Rousseau. He becomes indeed as if "possessed" by his passion for Venture, inhabited by this character. What he describes in the *Confessions* evokes the intrusion of the other into his psyche and his person. In a note related to these pages, Starobinski gives an interesting explanation of the initial anagrammatic operation cited above, transforming Rousseau into Vaussore de Villeneuve. "It is," he writes, "the grafting of an altered self onto the name of an admired *other*."²² In any case, Rousseau himself admits to his Venture madness, his delirium, his dispossession, his loss of self, on paper: "I was no longer myself," he writes simply.²³

We can interpret this double madness from another perspective—that of mimetic desire as theorized by René Girard. The above-mentioned possession can also benefit from this interpretation. In *Violence and the Sacred*, Girard examines such pathological phenomena of identity, interpreting them through the lens of *mimesis*. He proposes the following analysis of possession, for him: "[it] is an extreme form of alienation in which the subject totally absorbs the desires of another."²⁴ As I have mentioned, Venture is the "great model" for Jean-Jacques. If Jean-Jacques desires Venture (and we note the eroticism in the relationship for the one who takes the place of Mme de Warens), Venture is also someone who embodies desire. He is, in fact, the master of erotic desire. Rousseau writes that all the women were sweet on him. Oddly enough, he personifies seduction, first and foremost with his voice. It is enough for him to sing and speak for everyone around him to be in agreement. Rousseau compares himself negatively to this worldly man living the true life, leaving him to his solitude and imperfections while he returns to his worldly pursuits: "Venture left to go into his social circles where he ate, and I went to walk alone, meditating upon his great merit, admiring, coveting his rare talents, and cursing my dull star which did not call me to that happy life."²⁵

But if Venture is the model of talent, he is also that of imposture.²⁶ When Rousseau encounters this person for the first time, he is struck both by his knowledge and ability to appear the opposite, a pretender not quite "with it" [*au fait*, as Rousseau puts it].²⁷ The author of the *Confessions* evokes his roguishness [*polissonnerie*],²⁸ his bragging [*gasconade*]²⁹ which work against him, and make one believe the opposite of what he is saying. Hence, when invited to perform at the cathedral by M. le Maître, Venture does not even glance at the piece he is supposed to sing, causing his host to expect the worst—that in reality he could not read a single note of music.³⁰ It is this hesitation with regard to the truth of this person that produces a particular effect on Rousseau. He tells us that his "heart beat with a terrible strength" at the concert, waiting for proof of Venture's talents.³¹ Venture gives no clue of his experience or his merits, obscuring the very truth of his person in boasting of things he knows nothing about, and remaining silent about those he does. "He waited," Rousseau explains, "for the occasion to show them."³² Hence a kind of suspense or suspension in the unveiling of his truth, which both excites and fascinates Rousseau. Venture appears as a veritable model of fraudulence and contradiction. In the portrait of him, he appears as an odd, double-faced fellow: noble and beggarly, talented and eccentric, polite and roguish, short and wide, "malformed in his shape" without being deformed.³³ And as Alain Grosrichard points out,³⁴ his name itself might be fake, a pseudonym, since Rousseau takes the trouble to write: "He had called himself Venture de Villeneuve."³⁵ Hunched and limping, he appears with his double infirmity, striking the author as an almost mythic character, a comic monster, a magnetic figure of desire, to whom Rousseau grants a sacred aura.[36] Let's remember that he writes of the young musician, that to him "everything he said seemed to be oracles."[37]

It is this type of vacillating model of truth that Rousseau will seek to imitate in the famous scene of the concert at the home of M. de Treytorens, in which imposture combines with plagiarism. The interloper in the concert is Venture himself, since it is after all a performance *à la Venture* that Rousseau is attempting, but it is also the piece added to the composition prompted by the musician, a minuet which Rousseau shamelessly plagiarizes:

> I began to compose a piece for his concert as brazenly as if I had known how to set about it. I had the steadfastness to work for fifteen days on this beautiful work, to make a fair copy of it, to write out the parts and to distribute them with as much self-assurance as if it had been a masterpiece of harmony. Finally, what will hardly be believed, and which is very true, to crown this sublime production worthily, at its conclusion I put a pretty minuet which was making the rounds, and which perhaps everyone still remembers ... Venture had taught me this tune along with the bass and using other, filthy words, with the aid of which I had retained it. Thus I put this Minuet and his bass at the end of my composition while suppressing the words, and I have it out as my own.[38]

We know the outcome of this duplicity. In the *Dialogues*, we find the same expressions as in "Rousseau's self-criticism of "Jean-Jacques"[39] (the revealing admission quoted earlier by Christie McDonald): "Even though he does not find himself learned enough for his chosen trade, that does not stop him from claiming with stupid shamelessness that he is the Author of things he cannot perform."[40] Nevertheless, the "masterpiece of harmony" written beforehand turns into a "din [*charivari*]."[41] Rousseau finds himself the butt of public ridicule, at the center of an uproar of humiliation. Here is the horrible scene of his debacle:

> The musicians stifled laughs; the listeners opened their eyes wide and would have very much liked to close their ears, but they had no way to do it. My torturers of musicians, who wanted to have some fun, scraped so as to rupture the eardrum of the patient at the *Quinze-Vingt*. I was steadfast enough to keep going at my pace, sweating big drops it is true, but held in place by shame, not daring to flee and entirely stuck here. For my consolation, around me I heard the audience speaking into each other's ears or rather into mine. One, "Nothing in it is bearable"; another, "What rabid music?" another, "What an infernal racket?"[42]

Vicissitudes of the charivari

The uproar or charivari becomes the expression of the crisis of the aspiring musician. Rousseau appears on stage as the parodic version of a music master.

While *charivari*, in French, means a raucous and discordant music, we must retain in this word the idea of a ritual deriding of someone. In Rousseau's *Dictionary of Music* (1764), Rousseau presents *charivari* as the music played by substitutes, the doubles, those who sing when they have to replace the original singers.[43] Everything becomes dissonant to Rousseau's ear. The score before his eyes, which he reads as if blind, becomes a cacophony. He further pays the price of this disgraceful concert in his body, in describing his loss of composure (sweating, shame). The plagiarized minuet mentioned earlier, on the other hand, the foreign composition, that is the exogenous graft, completes the immolation of Jean-Jacques. It is this tune (recognized by the public) that silences the chorus of critics, yet discloses Jean-Jacques's theft of property: "Everyone congratulated me on my pretty taste for a song; they assured me that this minuet would make me talked of, and that I deserved to be sung everywhere."[44] In this supplement to Rousseau's composition, it is the sexual residues associated with Venture that unconsciously come to manifest themselves.[45] Nonetheless, this unhappy episode makes a name for Rousseau throughout Lausanne.

And while Rousseau acknowledges his imposture, we note that in the end he blames others for the fiasco. It was the interpreters of his music, his "torturers of musicians,"[46] as he calls them, who made it impossible for him to follow the score. Returning to the infamous concert, he admits his handicap—that he was incapable of knowing whether they played well or not the score he had in front of him and which he himself had composed.[47] It is Rousseau's own ignorance that creates an alienation of his own making, but it was the musicians who were responsible for having dissociated Rousseau from his word. In any case, what he experiences and what reaches his ear is pure dissonance—a diabolical inversion of music. Theoretically it is a sort of non-work, a de-composition in which he cannot recognize himself.

Rousseau will contrast this musical fiasco to the performance of his opera *The Village Soothsayer* (1752) when his composition was played at Fontainebleau, before the King and Queen of France. This event reconciles Rousseau to himself and his creations. Book VIII of the *Confessions* tells the triumphant tale of this reconciliation of the execution with the text. Rousseau makes a point of noting that "the Piece was very poorly performed with regard to the Actors, but well sung and well executed with regard to the music."[48] Rousseau recounts how he wrote this work inspired by Italian opera in a single stroke. It was as if the work emerged from him fully fledged. The progression of the composition is dazzling, and almost natural: one night, six days, three weeks. In the end it is an innovative work, reconciling poetry and song, the written word and voice: "I finished it all with such rapidity that in three weeks my scenes were put in a fair copy and in condition to be performed."[49] When Rousseau compares it with the concert for M. de Treytorens, he finds everything in order here. And the event as a whole is experienced as a general rectification of things and a reconciliation—most of all, of Rousseau with himself. Just after the performance, the composer reassures himself with a list of reasons for this: "I told myself, 'I am in my place, since I am seeing my piece played, since I was invited, since that is the only reason I composed it, and since after all no one has more right than myself to enjoy the fruit of my labor and my talents.'"⁵⁰ The composer enjoys unanimous praise: the applause beginning in the boxes, and finally affecting "the whole assembly."⁵¹ Rousseau also experiences this triumph with an erotic voluptuousness: the musical pleasure is tinged with a sexual thrill. The laughter from the Lausanne concert with its degrading contagion, here is changed into tears. The author tells us that he "savored his glory" with pleasure: "The pleasure of giving some emotion to so many lovable persons moved me to the point of tears."⁵² Once more evoking the ordeal of the concert for M. de Treytorens in Lausanne, Rousseau was already comparing it with his triumph at Fontainebleau, and he expressed the meaning of the emotional verdict of others: "Poor Jean-Jacques; at that cruel moment you would hardly hope that one day in front of the King of France and all his court your sounds would excite murmurs of surprise and applause, and that in all the boxes around you the most lovable women would say to themselves in a low voice, 'What charming sounds! what enchanting music! all these songs go to the heart.'"⁵³ It is therefore the heart which mediates between the public and the composer. The emotional response of the public at Fontainebleau serves to confirm Rousseau's musical genius. The public and the musician together compose the success of the spectacle. The pleasure of others even ascends to the level of "intoxication," but this excitement is just as much an enjoyment experienced as if for the first time.⁵⁴

In two musical episodes recounted back to back in *Les Confessions*, Rousseau is confronted with shame, the suspicion of plagiarism and ignorance. In Book V, he recounts how, in Chambéry, in the context of a public concert, he offered a cantata of his own composition. But doubt is immediately cast on his talent, when he reads music so poorly.⁵⁵ M. de Nangis, as verification, he believes, asks him for a transcription of a bass part. Rousseau meets the challenge, and rises to the occasion in composing only "the bass part of the recitative," which succeeds in erasing any doubts about his knowledge. The other episode stems from a similar suspicion. We are still in Chambéry. This time, it is the marquis of Sennecterre who asks Rousseau to write down a song. After a difficult reading of a score, Rousseau confirms that "Monsieur de Sennecterre must have been tempted to believe that I did not know music."⁵⁶ Rousseau succeeds, admitting, "I wrote it, even without making him repeat very much. He read it next, and found, as was true, that it had been very correctly noted down."⁵⁷ The apprentice musician is rightly saved from shame. He succeeds in turning it into triumph, not only for himself, but into gratitude in front of others.

Let us conclude with one final scene. Many years later, in Book VIII of the *Confessions*, Rousseau will once again meet up with his "great model," his former hero Venture. But he sees him through different eyes. Gone is the infatuation of the days in Annecy. This time, in Paris, the musician lacks both youth and the grace of age; Rousseau thus contemplates the passing of time:

> How changed he appeared to me! Instead of his former graces I no longer found in him anything but a crapulous air, which kept me from opening up with him. Either my eyes were no longer the same, or debauchery had besotted his mind,

or all his first brightness depended on the youth that he no longer had. I saw him almost with indifference, and we separated rather coldly.[58]

Airs of Dissonance

In *Rameau's Nephew* written in early 1761–2 but published posthumously in 1805, Diderot presents an encounter between a philosopher and a musician, a meeting also occurring under the aegis of seduction and upheaval. As with Rousseau, it is an encounter with a most radical other. Diderot confronts the philosopher with a counterfeit artist, a magician of dissonance. Indeed, one rainy day, outside the Café de la Régence in Paris, the philosopher crosses paths with a comic monster, an unusual mixture of spectacular contradictions spanning the whole range of physiognomic oddities. Here is the portrait of this odd character:

> He's a mixture of the lofty and the sordid, of good sense and unreason ... Nothing is more unlike the man than he himself. Sometimes, he is as thin and pale as someone in the last stages of consumption and you can count his teeth through his cheeks—you'd think he'd not eaten for days or that he'd just come out of a Trappist monastery. A month later, he is as fleshy and replete as if he'd been at a banker's dinner table the whole time or been comfortably cloistered with the Bernardins. Today, skulking in dirty linen, with torn breeches, his coat in tatters, his shoes hanging off his feet, and his head held low, you'd be tempted to call him over and slip him a coin. Tomorrow, hair powdered and curled, well shod and well dressed, he goes about in public, his head held high, and you'd almost take him for a respectable man.[59]

Later, in keeping with his character, Jean-François Rameau, the titular Nephew of the famous Jean-Philippe, will play for the philosopher an impossible score, a palimpsest of the works of others, a truly occasional piece:

> He piled up and mixed together thirty tunes, Italian, French, tragic, comic, with lots of different characters; at points, he would descend into the depths of the underworld in a low baritone, at others, he would go right up high in a glass-shattering fake falsetto, mimicking the different singing roles in the way he walked, held himself, and gestured; by turns furious, soothed, imperious, sneering. Now he's a young girl weeping, and he acts out her every simpering move; now he's a priest, he's a king, he's a tyrant, he threatens, he commands, he loses his temper; he's a slave, he obeys. He calms down, he is sorry, he complains, he laughs; never a false note, never out of time, always capturing the meaning of the words and the character of the music.[60]

Diderot creates a character/orchestra whose music is like a collection of all airs, an encyclopedia of dissonant sounds:

But you would have roared with laughter at the way he impersonated the different instruments. The horns and bassoons, he did puffing his cheeks up like balloons, and making hoarse, low sounds; he made a piercing, nasal noise for the oboes; his voice catapulting up and down at incredible speed, he did as close an imitation of the strings as he could; he whistled the piccolos and cooed the flutes; shouting, singing, charging about like a madman, single-handedly doing the dancers, both male and female, the singers, both male and female, a whole orchestra, a whole opera company, dividing himself between twenty different roles; running around, suddenly stopping and looking like a man possessed, his eyes blazing, foaming at the mouth.[61]

Whereas for Rousseau, Venture's encounter was experienced as a rift, the breaking apart of personality under the weight of heterogeneity, for Diderot the paroxysms of imitation end in mutual pleasure, including the fact that the philosopher claims to have been "moved" by the performance of the failed composer. Nonetheless he confesses that his first impression was "tinged with ridicule."[62] But the crisis is sublimated in artistic creation and the Nephew's cacophony ends up offering Diderot a model of singing, a brilliant theory of the lyrical—as opposed to Rousseau's melodic vision, which is simplistic and calm. Diderot's theater is indeed marked by a turbulence of intensities, an exacerbation of passions: "We need exclamations, interjections, half-finished or broken-off phrases, affirmations, negations," in short a whole complex and provocative range of emotions.[63]

The encounter with the other is for Rousseau the source of an unbearable anxiety that culminates in a crisis of identity. While it began euphorically, it is quickly transformed into something he cannot assimilate and that he ends up rejecting and expulsing. The protagonist must recover the comfort of autonomy and transparency, to become to some extent re-possessed. We are not surprised to see that Diderot's text works in an opposite fashion. Contrariwise, it is open to difference, multiplicity, and volatility. After the crisis, Diderot's protagonist recomposes himself in a sort of *kairos* of creation. In Diderot's case, it is also a matter of a multiplicity reconciled with affect (which horrified Rousseau), a complexity embracing sensitivity.

Translated by Sophie Hawkes

Notes

1 Christie McDonald, *Dispositions* (La Salle: Hurtubise, 1986), 29. For the embedded citation: Jean-Jacques Rousseau, *Rousseau, Judge of Jean-Jacques*, in *The Collected Writings of Rousseau*, ed. Roger D. Masters and Christopher Kelly, trans. Judith R. Bush, Christopher Kelly and Roger D. Masters (Hanover: University Press of New England, 1990), 1:16
2 Jean-Jacques Rousseau, *The Confessions and Correspondence, Including Letters to Malesherbes*, in Christopher Kelly and Roger D. Masters, eds., *The Collected Writings of Rousseau*, vol. 5, trans. Christopher Kelly (Hanover: University Press of New England), 5:103.

3   Rousseau, *The Confessions*, 5:103.
4   In Jean-Jacques Rousseau, *Les Confessions*, ed. Alain Grosrichard (Paris: GF-Flammarion, 2002), 1:369. Translation mine.
5   Rousseau, *The Confessions*, 5:103–4.
6   Rousseau, 5:104.
7   Rousseau, 5:104.
8   Rousseau, 5:104–5.
9   Rousseau, 5:105.
10 Rousseau, 5:105.
11 Rousseau, 5:112.
12 Rousseau, 5:123.
13 Rousseau, 5:103.
14 Rousseau, 5:124.
15 Rousseau, 5:109.
16 Rousseau, 5:124.
17 Rousseau, 5:124. Geoffrey Bennington summarizes this encounter with this calligraphic tableau: "To give oneself a name for another, to make oneself a name that isn't Rousseau. Doubles and counterfeits: to counterfeit an original doubly counterfeit, to produce a counterfeit piece that is also a counterfeit." In *Dudding: Des noms de Rousseau* (Paris: Galilée, 1991), 54.
18 McDonald, *Dispositions*, 31.
19 McDonald, 28.
20 McDonald, 31–2.
21 Jean Starobinski, *La Transparence et l'obstacle* (Paris: Gallimard, 1971), 79. Translation mine.
22 Starobinski, 78. Translation mine.
23 Rousseau, *The Confessions*, 5:124.
24 René Girard, *Violence and the Sacred*, trans. Patrick Gregory (London: Continuum, 2005), 175.
25 Rousseau, *The Confessions*, 5:112.
26 This would apparently be a case of bad imitation, based on a bad model, of an unworthy fellow, condemned in Plato's *Republic*, and the ferment of imposture. See Christopher Miller, *Impostors: Literary Hoaxes and Cultural Authenticity* (Chicago: Chicago University Press), 4.
27 See Jean-Jacques Rousseau, *Les Confessions*, in *Œuvres complètes,* ed. Bernard Gagnebin and Marcel Raymond (Paris: Gallimard, 1959), 1:124.
28 Rousseau, 1:124.
29 Rousseau, 1:124.
30 Rousseau, *The Confessions*, 5:104.
31 Rousseau, 5:104.
32 Rousseau, 5:105.
33 Rousseau, 5:104.
34 See Grosrichard's notes to Rousseau, *Les Confessions*, ed. Alain Grosrichard, 1:368.
35 Rousseau, 5:124.
36 For the physical signs, see René Girard, *Des choses cachées depuis la fondation du monde* (Paris: Grasset, 1978). On monstrosity, see chapter 10 of his *Violence and the Sacred*, 264–88.
37 Rousseau, 5:105.
38 Rousseau, 5:124–25.

39 Jean-Jacques Rousseau, *Rousseau, Judge of Jean-Jacques*, in Christopher Kelly and Roger D. Masters, eds., *The Collected Writings of Rousseau*, 1:16.
40 McDonald, *Dispositions*, 29.
41 Rousseau, *The Confessions*, 5:125.
42 Rousseau, 5:125.
43 See the article "Doubles," in Jean-Jacques Rousseau, *Dictionnaire de musique*, in Gagnebin and Raymond, eds., *Œuvres complètes,* 5:785. For the victimizing scheme of cacophony (*charivari*), see the excellent essay by Éric Négrel "Politique du charivari," which analyzes it as a mythic-ritual scenario. He explains how cacophony derives from the enactment of "collective manifestations of racket, disorder and derision" (303). The victim of the cacophony is associated with the sacrificial goat, to the point of becoming a "human goat" ("*l'homme-bouc*") (310). Négrel takes the trouble to remind us that the universe of discordant sounds of the cacophonies are produced according to a "dissonant acoustic code" (308), a music of the underworld and the devil. In *Théâtre et charlatans dans l'Europe moderne*, ed. Beya Dhraïef, Eric Négrel, and Jennifer Ruimi (Paris: Presses Sorbonne Nouvelle, 2018). Translations mine.
44 Rousseau, *The Confessions*, 5:125.
45 Alain Grosrichard explains how this minuet taught to Rousseau by Venture is a parody, where innocent words are transformed intro salacious ones, thus degrading an original composition. Rousseau is a victim of *contre-sens*. See Grosrichard's notes to Rousseau, *Les Confessions*, ed. Alain Grosrichard, 1:375.
46 Rousseau, *The Confessions*, 5:125.
47 See Rousseau, 5:126.
48 Rousseau, 5:317
49 Rousseau, 5:315.
50 Rousseau, 5:317. In commenting on the catastrophe of "Venturization" from the perspective of a questionable authorship, Geoffrey Bennington recalls the rectification enacted by Rousseau in *The Village Soothsayer*. In the preface to the work, the philosopher in fact writes, giving the impression of a natural paternity: "because this opus bears my name, it must be mine . . ." quoted in Bennington, *Dudding*, 100.
51 Rousseau, *The Confessions*, 5:317.
52 Rousseau, 5:318.
53 Rousseau, 5:125.
54 Rousseau, 5:318.
55 Rousseau, 5:176.
56 Rousseau, 5:177.
57 Rousseau, 5:177.
58 Rousseau, 5:334. Finding Venture with "another man," Rousseau gazes severely at his former friend. Catriona Seth reads in this disappointment Rousseau's confrontation of his repressed homosexuality. See her "Rousseau et ses doubles dans les livres I à VI des *Confessions*," http://ceredi.labos.univ-rouen.fr/public/?rousseau-et-ses-doubles-dans-les.html.
59 Denis Diderot, *Rameau's Nephew – Le Neveu de Rameau: A Multi-media Bilingual Edition*, ed. Marian Hobson, trans. Kate E. Tunstall and Caroline Warman (Cambridge: Open Book Publishers, 2016), 16.
60 Diderot, 76–7.
61 Diderot, 77.
62 Diderot, 77.
63 Diderot, 79.

Chapter 4

COLONIAL ENCOUNTERS OF
"LA BELLE ET LA BÊTE"

Kylie Sago

In spite of the tale's renown, "La Belle et la Bête" ("Beauty and the Beast") has long been encountered out of context. Written by French women in the eighteenth century, the first two versions of this fairy tale were published in the form of a story within a story. Their frame narratives—that is, the stories in which the fairy tale was embedded—clearly set the scene of storytelling in the eighteenth-century Atlantic world. Gabrielle-Suzanne de Villeneuve (c. 1695–1755), an author of novels and short fiction, is most famous for penning the first known variant of the tale. In Villeneuve's *La Jeune Amériquaine et les Contes marins* (*The Young American and the Sea Tales*, 1740), "La Belle et la Bête" figures first in a series of stories traded by ship passengers during the weeks-long transatlantic journey from La Rochelle to Saint-Domingue (present-day Haïti). This text appeared anonymously during Villeneuve's lifetime, and "La Belle et la Bête" enjoyed immediate popularity.[1] Jeanne-Marie Leprince de Beaumont (1711–80), best known for her pedagogical texts for girls and young women, included a much-abridged and unattributed version of the tale in *Le Magasin des enfans* (*The Young Misses Magazine*, 1756).[2] In it, a French governess recounts the story to her young English wards, one of whom relates Belle's shifting perception of the Beast to her own experiences with a Black servant in her family's household. Leprince de Beaumont's iteration of the tale revived its popularity in the late eighteenth century and cemented its fame.[3]

As "La Belle et la Bête" was re-edited and translated, the fairy tale began to circulate independently of Villeneuve's and Leprince de Beaumont's frame narratives. The eighteenth-century Atlantic backdrops that had once been so explicit are absent from twentieth-century adaptations such as Jean Cocteau's oneiric film, *La Belle et la Bête* (1946), and Angela Carter's starkly violent short story, "The Tiger's Bride" (1979). Perhaps nothing has stripped the story of context quite like the refrain from the Disney animated feature musical (1991), proclaiming it to be a "tale as old as time."[4] Scholarship has focused on the content of the fairy tale and especially its portrayal of what Raymonde Robert calls "the monstrous marriage."[5] Psychoanalytic readings by Jacques Barchilon and Bruno Bettelheim suggest that "Beauty and the Beast" illustrates individual psychosexual dramas, such as a woman overcoming the repression of sex or transferring an infantile attachment to her father to an appropriate object of adult desire.[6] Other approaches historicize the story's depictions of marriage, sex, and family dynamics. Arguing that fairy tales socialize their eighteenth-century readers, Jack Zipes underscores the resonance of "La Belle et la Bête" for young women likely to have found themselves in advantageous matches with undesirable men.[7] To some scholars, the fairy tale serves less as a tool of socialization than as a vehicle for social critique. Tatiana Korneeva suggests it portrays the object-status of women whose value is determined in their exchange between men.[8] Marina Warner proposes that Villeneuve's version of the tale in particular critiques the powerlessness of young women in the face of what Elisa Biancardi calls "the tyrannical authority of parents."[9]

To fully understand "La Belle et la Bête" in context, however, it is necessary to attend to the global settings made explicit in Villeneuve's and Leprince de Beaumont's original frame narratives. This reading of the fairy tale thus responds to Christie McDonald's and Susan Rubin Suleiman's call in *French Global* to forge a new approach to literary history, one that reads "works in relation to the globe: as world, as sphere, as a space of encounter with others and with the very idea of otherness."[10] In *Strange Encounters*, Sara Ahmed suggests that reading is itself a kind of encounter, "a meeting between reader and text" in which the identities of both reader and text are constituted. To consider reading in this way, Ahmed proposes, is "not only to refuse to assume that the text or the reader have an independent existence, but also to suggest that it is through being read that the text comes to life as text, that the text comes to be thinkable as having an existence in the first place."[11] Ahmed goes on to argue that, as with reader and text, the identities of "the subject" and "the stranger" are constituted in the encounter.

This essay draws on Ahmed's argument that the encounter indelibly links reader and text, as well as subject and stranger, to resituate "La Belle et la Bête" within its global contexts. In the original versions of the story, the encounter between reader and text is not an implicit condition of the latter's existence. The frame narratives of Villeneuve's and Leprince de Beaumont's fairy tales explicitly depict the scenes of their respective storytelling, and situate the encounter with the tale on opposite sides of the Atlantic ocean: aboard a ship bound for Saint-Domingue, and in an English household that displays its wealth through the ostentatious use of a Black footman. Reading "La Belle et la Bête" alongside its frame narratives shows how this tale "comes to life as text" in the eighteenth-century Atlantic world and how its morals, in turn, come to bear on colonial encounters.

Villeneuve's Sea Tale

The frame narrative of Villeneuve's *La Jeune Amériquaine et les Contes marins* recounts the story of a lifelong friendship between Doriancourt and Robercourt, two young men from impoverished noble families in Picardie.[12] Robercourt travels to Léogâne, Saint-Domingue, to attempt to make his fortune in the colony. There, he is mentored by Monsieur du Charoy, a prosperous plantation owner. Less than six years later, the young man's wealth exceeds his wildest dreams. Robercourt marries Charoy's daughter, who gives birth to a girl: the titular Young American. Doriancourt sends his youngest son (aged seven) to learn plantation management from Robercourt in Saint-Domingue. In exchange, the Robercourt's three-year-old daughter is raised by the Doriancourt family in Picardie. After a decade of this arrangement, Mademoiselle de Robercourt and young Doriancourt are betrothed, and the young man travels to France to fetch his future bride. On the return voyage from La Rochelle to Léogâne, Mademoiselle de Robercourt asks her maid, Mademoiselle de Chon, to tell stories to break up the monotony of life at sea. The captain chances on one of the tales and asks the maid to share them with a wider audience. Each evening, when matters of navigation require the fewest hands on deck, passengers and members of the crew gather for one hour and take turns telling each other stories. "Beauty and the Beast," the first of these "sea tales," is recounted by Mademoiselle de Chon over five days.

Just as the maid is about to begin her tale, the reader is abruptly invited to take part in this nightly meeting of passengers. "[May the reader] be transported aboard *The ****. Imagine making the journey to Saint-Domingue. Know that after dinner, each person retires for a nap or performs the necessary tasks for navigation. And at a convenient hour for all, we gather on the upper deck or in the captain's chamber, where Mademoiselle de Chon thus begins her story."[13] A typographical *cul-de-lampe* at the close of this passage marks the meeting point of frame narrative and fairy tale, which begins directly on the next page. Until Chon finishes her story, the frame narrative fades away. Previously, the text specifies that readers on land should feel free to modulate their own reading rhythms. Regardless of the pace they choose, they are invited to imagine the transatlantic journey as the backdrop for their encounter with the story.[14] Transported onto *The ****, listening to the fairy tale alongside fellow passengers and the crew, readers may appreciate the extent to which "La Belle et la Bête" is itself a "sea tale."

Although the fairy tale's setting is vague, the presence of the Atlantic world is implied from the very outset of the story, when a merchant loses his fortune in a series of tragedies. A fire destroys his home, consuming "the magnificent furniture that filled it, the account books, bills, gold, silver, and all the precious merchandise that comprised the merchant's wealth."[15] Although the exact products are not specified, the immensity of his wealth and the value of the objects lost in the fire suggest that the merchant is involved in overseas trade. This is reinforced by the next misfortune to befall him: the loss of his ships "to either shipwrecks or privateers," the latter of which evokes Atlantic maritime conflicts.[16] Receiving word that one of his "richly laden" vessels may have returned to harbor with its cargo intact, the merchant hurries to an unnamed city in the hopes of recovering as much of his losses as possible.[17] After six months "of trouble and expense" engaged in vain attempts to salvage his fortune, he is obliged to return home. Caught in a sudden blizzard, the merchant seeks refuge in a seemingly enchanted castle, where orange trees flourish in a discordantly tropical climate. He plucks a rose to bring to his youngest daughter, known simply as "la Belle" (the Beauty). Suddenly, the enraged Bête (Beast) appears and dramatically threatens to kill the merchant for stealing the flower. The Beast offers to allow the merchant to go free if one of his daughters will sacrifice herself in her father's stead. Belle volunteers to return to the Beast's castle, where she fully expects to be eaten. Instead, she finds an opulent prison.

Although Belle is the sole human inhabitant of the Beast's castle, she discovers a menagerie of birds and primates that become her servants. In her dreams, Belle is visited by a man called the Bel Inconnu (Handsome Stranger) and a beautiful lady, who caution Belle not to be deceived by appearances. On her first night in the castle, she finds "a cup of hot chocolate" prepared for her to drink before bed. The source of the Beast's immense wealth is never specified in the text. This drink, however, brings explicit colonial associations to the Beast's life of luxury: another trace of eighteenth-century transatlantic trade in the world of the fairy tale. It hints, moreover, at the rise of sugar plantations in the Caribbean, where enslaved labor was exploited with deadly calculation. Sugar was in high demand to make products like chocolate more palatable.[18]

Villeneuve's tale makes clear that Belle's life of luxury is not without danger. Her captivity is blighted by the terrible Beast and the violence he threatens. Daily, he asks Belle, "do you want me to sleep with you?" Belle is initially terrified at the question, and her fear of sexual violence never fully dissipates. Eventually, Belle also grieves the separation from her family, and the Beast reluctantly permits her to visit them. Overstaying her leave, Belle returns to the enchanted castle and discovers the Beast slumped over, apparently dead. With the assistance of her primate servants, Belle succeeds in reviving him. The next time the Beast asks to sleep with her, Belle assents, on the condition that they exchange provisional marriage vows. They climb into bed, and to Belle's immense relief, the Beast instantly begins snoring. The next morning, she awakens to find herself next to the Bel Inconnu of her dreams. A fairy appears and reveals that he is a mortal prince who had been turned into the Beast by an evil fairy. Belle also learns that she is the daughter of a powerful fairy and a mortal king. As an infant, she had been secretly placed in the merchant's care to protect her from a curse that she would one day marry a beast.

That this story is recounted during a transatlantic journey towards France's richest colony invites readers to consider the resonances between the fairy tale and the frame narrative's depictions of colonial life. Time and again, Belle chooses duty over her own desires. Beyond sacrificing herself for her father and later agreeing to marry the Beast instead of her beloved Inconnu, Belle even offers to renounce her provisional marriage to the Prince in light of the apparent disparity in their social positions. By contrast, in the frame narrative, the sacrifice of inclination to duty is most frequently exemplified by male characters. Robercourt initially does not pursue the hand of Charoy's daughter in marriage: "He loved her, but gratitude seemed to forbid him from pursuing an inclination that he imagined would not entirely be to Charoy's liking. Ostensibly, his benefactor would have set his sights on more advantageous matches for his daughter."[19] In both fairy tale and frame narrative, these characters are richly rewarded—in emotional and material terms—for their willingness to let gratitude and duty, rather than desire, guide their choice of a partner. The final couple of the frame narrative—Mademoiselle de Robercourt and young Doriancourt—are lucky that their families take painstaking care to make the match seem as personally desirable as it is financially advantageous.

Even so, "La Belle et la Bête" makes clear that to sacrifice personal inclination to duty is to be willing to assume great risk. Belle's courage despite her fear of being consumed—first eaten by the Beast, then falling victim to his wolfish desire—echoes Robercourt's resolve as he ventures to the "Americas." Even as the frame narrative suggests that the perils of colonial life are exaggerated by popular opinion ("far from ports of embarkation, the dangers are believed to be much worse than they really are"), *Les Contes marins* catalogues these risks.[20] Wealth is not guaranteed: whereas Doriancourt successfully sends French goods to Robercourt in Saint-Domingue, the catastrophic losses sustained by the merchant in the fairy tale suggest the vulnerability of commerce to dangers lurking on the seas. At best, transatlantic travel is difficult for the uninitiated. Only young Doriancourt, seasoned by two previous Atlantic crossings, is spared the seasickness that afflicts Mesdemoiselles de Robercourt and de Chon for the first two days aboard the ship (an illness, the text adds, that will persist for less hardy passengers until they set foot once again on dry land).[21] The dangers will not cease once the ship arrives in port; in Saint-Domingue, Madame de Robercourt lays dying of "a malignant influence [that] corrupts the air of this rich climate."[22]

For every suggestion of the risks of colonial life, however, the text insists on the wealth of the Americas—exemplified by the generous hospitality of colonists like Charoy and the dizzying fortune that Robercourt accumulates. The text's explicit, though cursory nod to the source of this wealth merits careful consideration. When Charoy first asks Robercourt to stay on his plantation, the younger man misinterprets the invitation as a "proposition to be the overseer of his slaves [*son commandeur de nègres*] or his bookkeeper," occupations that Robercourt feels are beneath him.[23] This initial misunderstanding underscores the source of his future wealth: the plantation and the captive labor it exploits. Later on, Robercourt may oversee his enslaved workers from a genteel distance, but his hand in managing the plantation is undeniable. The text notes that Mademoiselle de Robercourt stands to inherit "the immense assets of the late Monsieur du Charoy [which] were considerably augmented by Robercourt's care and industry."[24]

Enslavement not only figures in the Charoy/Robercourt plantation of the frame narrative, but also in the fairy tale itself. When Belle enters the menagerie of animals in the Beast's castle, she wishes aloud that some of them might "keep her company"—a desire that is immediately realized. "Instantly, two large female apes in court dress entered and solemnly stood next to her, as if awaiting her orders. Two small spirited monkeys picked up her dress and served as pages. A pleasant macaque, styled as a *señor escudero*, presented her with a properly gloved paw. Accompanied by this singular entourage, Beauty went off to dine."[25] The characterization of the silent primates that serve Belle reads as a racist caricature of enslaved people working in the main house of a plantation. The Spanish phrase, "*señor escudero*" (mister squire), echoed in the next paragraph's reference to "these *señores* monkeys and *señoras* apes," evokes the linguistic world of the Caribbean, and especially the destination of the ship, *The ****: the island formerly called Hispaniola, divided between the French and Spanish in the 1697 Treaty of Ryswick.²⁶ Whereas statues adorning the grounds of the Beast's castle (later revealed to be servants turned to stone by a fairy) regain their human form once the curse is lifted, Belle's primate companions will neither change form nor be manumitted. In fact, Belle and the Prince request that these animals remain to serve them during future visits to the castle. Elsewhere in the tale, the merchant tells his daughter that with the money and jewels sent to him by the Beast, he purchased "slaves that spare [the family] from the toil to which necessity had subjected [them]."²⁷ Villeneuve's *Contes marins* thus makes clear that in enchanted and non-enchanted contexts alike, coming into wealth entails the acquisition of enslaved labor.

Villeneuve's frame narrative never mentions how the listeners aboard *The **** reacted to these references to enslavement, or if they appreciated the echoes between the fairytale and their own lives. After the second volume of Villeneuve's *La Jeune Amériquaine et les Contes marins* was published in 1741, the planned third and final volume never appeared. The frame narrative thus breaks off midway through the transatlantic voyage. Readers are left to surmise how the lessons of "La Belle et la Bête" may find application upon Mademoiselle de Robercourt's and young Doriancourt's arrival in Saint-Domingue. Leprince de Beaumont's adaptation of Villeneuve's fairy tale, by contrast, leaves no doubt as to the pertinence of "La Belle et la Bête" to colonial encounters in the Anglophone Atlantic world.

Beaumont's Imperial Education

The alternate title of Leprince de Beaumont's *Magasin des enfans—Dialogues between a governess and several young ladies of quality her scholars*—signals both the form and didactic function of this pedagogical manual.²⁸ The frame narrative centers on Mademoiselle Bonne (Mademoiselle Affable), a French woman working as a governess in England, who invites the young friends of her ward Lady Sensée (Lady Sensible, aged twelve) to gather daily to tell stories and recite their lessons. By portraying Bonne's careful guidance of the girls' discussions, the *Magasin des enfans* establishes a *mise en abyme* of reading and interpretation. "La Belle et la Bête" features as one of the "moral tales" that the governess recounts to the girls. It is an unattributed and dramatically abridged version of Villeneuve's text, slashed from over three hundred pages to a mere thirty-three.

Given the tender age of Mademoiselle Bonne's audience, the Beast is not so loathsome as in Villeneuve's text. His fearsome appearance notwithstanding, he retains human qualities like intelligence, generosity, and goodness of character. Gone too is the menace of sexual violence he represents, though Belle still fears being eaten; instead of asking to sleep with Belle, the Beast asks for her hand in marriage. The elimination of Belle's competing love interest shifts the tale's moral away from the sacrifice of personal inclination to duty and gratitude. Instead, Leprince de Beaumont stresses the priority of inner character over outer appearance. Although the *Magasin des enfans* eliminates Villeneuve's framing device of the sea voyage, colonial elements—the merchant's maritime losses, the consumption of chocolate—remain present in the fairy tale. Furthermore, the dialogue immediately following Mademoiselle Bonne's telling of "La Belle et la Bête" explicitly links its messages about appearance to skin color.

At first, the girls debate if they, like Belle, could have married the Beast despite his monstrous form and terrible manners. Their interpretation of the tale remains focused on marriage until Miss Molly (aged seven) offers a new application for its moral on physical appearance. Molly's reading relates Belle's experiences with the Beast to her own interactions with a Black servant in her family's household:

> Just like Beauty, I think I would have grown used to seeing [the Beast]. When Papa took a little black boy to be his lackey, I was afraid of him, and hid when he entered. He seemed to me uglier than a beast. But little by little I grew used to him. He helps me into the carriage, and I no longer think of his face.[29]

The lackey's skin color offers a historically specific marker of the global reaches of British imperialism, present in this domestic interior space in the English metropole. From the second half of the seventeenth century, increasing absenteeism among Caribbean plantation owners (who returned to England with enslaved workers) made it fashionable for well-to-do households to include Black servants.[30] That Molly's father "took a little black boy" gives little indication as to the child's status as a free or enslaved person. It does, however, suggest his deliberate placement in one of the most public-facing positions in the house. As a lackey—a footman, and most often a running footman who ran ahead of the carriage to announce its arrival—the young man's skin color and liveried dress would serve as conspicuous proof of the household's wealth.[31]

Save for his appearance and position, however, Leprince de Beaumont's text gives no further information regarding the child's identity.[32] Given the international circulation of the *Magasin des enfans*—printed in some forty-seven editions between 1756–80 and translated into twelve different languages[33]—the lackey's unspecified personal history would allow his skin color to flexibly conform to the different imperial contexts of the *Magasin*'s international readership. The interpretation of his skin color, however, is wholly determined by the text. Molly directly relates the lackey's Black skin to beastliness and finds the servant's Blackness "even uglier." In the parallel between the Black child and the Beast, Molly identifies with Belle; both the young girl and fairytale heroine experience time's softening effects on their initial aversion. For Belle, marriage to the Beast is made possible by focusing on his inner goodness. For Molly, however, the passage of time results in a further erasure of the footman into servile anonymity. If Molly no longer thinks of his face, she neither considers his life story nor imagines his experience of their interactions. Consigning him to invisibility allows her to be served without perturbation.

Mademoiselle Bonne concurs with Molly's racial application of the fairy tale's moral, even as she steers the girls' discussion back towards marriage. "*Miss Molly is right*," Bonne crisply confirms, "it is possible to grow accustomed to ugliness, but never to meanness. Rather than trouble ourselves over being ugly, we must try to be good, so that our face may be forgotten out of love of our heart."[34] Time permits a woman to grow accustomed to the appearance of others, whether that of her suitors or servants. Bonne adds that the girls can further use this lesson to their advantage by dissimulating their own ugliness beneath a virtuous character. "La Belle et la Bête" not only models how to tolerate a disappointing match, but also suggests strategies to attract a more desirable partner. Furthermore, the young readers' dialogue shows how a white woman's gendered vulnerability coexists with her ability to assert racial power, for instance, by wielding racialized people as proof of her wealth or class. By including different readings of the tale in the frame narrative itself, the *Magasin des enfans* demonstrates the wide potential relevance of "La Belle et la Bête" for a reader confronting her relative power in an imperial society.

*

McDonald and Suleiman suggest that a global approach to literary history demands an expansive conception of the globe: not only as geographical expanse and geopolitical sphere, but also "as a space of encounter with others and with the very idea of otherness."[35] Ahmed's definition of reading-as-encounter helps to underscore how, precisely, "La Belle et la Bête" "comes to life as text" in the eighteenth-century Atlantic world.[36] That the story is told against the backdrop of the French and English empires draws attention to markers of the colonial world in the fairy tale itself. Furthermore, Villeneuve's and Leprince de Beaumont's frame narratives indicate that readers do not encounter the tale in solitude. Instead, readers are in the imagined company of characters whose lives are structured by transatlantic interests: sailors who transport people and products across the sea; a plantation heiress and her fiancé educated in different parts of the French empire; and families who display their wealth through references to enslavement, if not its actual practice. Acknowledging that readers encounter the fairy tale alongside those who most benefit from colonial economic systems and social hierarchies invites a re-evaluation of how "La Belle et la Bête" presents an "encounter ... with the very idea of otherness" (to return once more to McDonald's and Suleiman's phrase). For so long, the "otherness" depicted in this particular fairy tale has been interpreted in terms of gender and sexuality. The Atlantic settings of these frame narratives, however, suggest the need to understand this "otherness" in terms of empire.

Leprince de Beaumont makes explicit what Villeneuve leaves implicit: it is possible to read "La Belle et la Bête" as depicting an encounter with a racialized "other." In order to understand Molly's racial reading of the fairy tale, it is useful to briefly consider Ahmed's argument that "acts of reading constitute 'the subject' in relation to 'the stranger.'"[37] Ahmed suggests that in such an encounter, a body is scrutinized for signs of difference, which are compared with recognized signs of "otherness." As Ahmed puts it, "the present encounter reopens past encounters."[38] When Molly draws on her acquaintance with a Black footman to understand the

Beast, she associates beastliness with Blackness. In this act of reading, Molly claims the identities of both reader and encountering subject for herself and fixes the footman as the racialized object of her encounter. As readers experience this story alongside Molly, their perspective implicitly aligns with hers as both fellow interpreters of the tale and, crucially, subjects of colonial encounters. When "La Belle et la Bête" circulates separate from Villeneuve's and Leprince de Beaumont's original frame narratives, it is therefore not only the global settings of storytelling that are forgotten. Reading "La Belle et la Bête" out of context obscures the fact that the reader's encounter with the tale was understood to be not only colonial, but colonialist.

Notes

I first encountered "La Belle et la Bête" as a research assistant to Christie McDonald. I am profoundly grateful for her generous mentorship throughout every stage of this research. I likewise thank Janet Beizer, Jérôme Brillaud, Sarah Grandin Virginie Greene, Sylvaine Guyot, and Françoise Lionnet for their invaluable feedback on different versions of this argument.

1. In a letter dated March 17, 1741, Françoise de Graffigny wrote, "All of Paris is crazy for it. I myself was quite amused...," quoted in Elisa Biancardi, ed., *La Jeune Américaine et les Contes marins (La Belle et la Bête). Les Belles Solitaires. [Suivi de] Magasin des enfants (La Belle et la Bête).* Bibliothèque des génies et des fées 15 (Paris: Champion, 2008), 51, translation mine. The year after its publication, Nivelle de la Chaussée loosely adapted the Villeneuve text for a play entitled *Amour pour Amour* (1741). See Sophie Allera and Denis Reynaud, eds., *La Belle et la Bête: quatre métamorphoses, 1742–1779* (Saint-Etienne: Publications de l'université de Saint-Etienne, 2002).
2. Leprince de Beaumont's other didactic texts include *Le Magasin des adolescentes* (*The Young Ladies' Magazine*, 1760) and *Instructions pour les jeunes Dames qui entrent dans le monde, se marient, leurs devoirs dans cet état et envers leurs enfans* (*Instructions for Young Ladies on their Entering into Life, their Duties in the Married State, and towards their Children*, 1764), a sequence that attests to the author's sensitivity to the gender, age, and marital status of her readers.
3. Marmontel and Grétry adapted the story for their opera, *Zémire et Azor* (1771), and Stéphanie-Félicité de Genlis rescripted it for her *Théâtre pour l'éducation des enfants* (1779). See Allera and Reynaud, eds., *La Belle et la Bête*. On the reach of Marmontel and Grétry's opera, see Mélanie Traversier, "1771: *La Belle et la Bête*, scène fantastique à la cour de France," in *Histoire mondiale de la France*, dir. Patrick Boucheron (Paris: Seuil, 2017), 380–4.
4. "Beauty and the Beast," by Howard Ashman and Alan Menken, track 9 on *Beauty and the Beast: Original Motion Picture Soundtrack*, Walt Disney Records, 1991, compact disc.
5. Raymonde Robert, *Le Conte de fées littéraire en France: de la fin du XVIIe à la fin du XVIIIe siècle* (Paris: Champion, 2002), 148.
6. Jacques Barchilon, "Beauty and the Beast: From Myth to Fairy Tale," *Psychoanalysis and the Psychoanalytic Review* 46, no. 4 (1959): 19–29; Bruno Bettelheim, *The Uses of Enchantment: The Meaning and Importance of Fairy Tales*, (New York: Knopf, 1976).

7   Jack Zipes, *Fairy Tales and the Art of Subversion: The Classical Genre for Children and the Process of Civilization*, 2nd ed. (London and New York: Routledge Classics, 2012), 47–56.
8   Tatiana Korneeva, "Desire and Desirability in Villeneuve and Leprince de Beaumont's 'Beauty and the Beast,'" *Marvels & Tales* 28, no. 2 (2014): 233–51.
9   Marina Warner, "Reluctant Brides: Beauty and the Beast I," in *From the Beast to the Blonde: On Fairy Tales and Their Tellers* (New York: Noonday Press, 1996), 272–97; Biancardi, ed., *La Jeune Américaine et les Contes marins*, 1447.
10 Christie McDonald and Susan Rubin Suleiman, eds., *French Global: A New Approach to Literary History* (New York: Columbia University Press, 2010), xvii.
11 Sara Ahmed, *Strange Encounters: Embodied Others in Postcoloniality* (London and New York: Routledge, 2000), 7. Ahmed suggests that "colonial encounters" collapse the distance between the distant and the local (associated with "the stranger" and "the subject," respectively), a spatial consideration that lies beyond the present essay's scope. *Strange Encounters*, 9–12.
12 Gabrielle-Suzanne de Villeneuve, *La Jeune Amériquaine et les Contes marins*, in Elisa Biancardi, ed., *La Jeune Américaine et les Contes marins*, 78. Translations mine unless otherwise noted.
13 Villeneuve, 94.
14 Villeneuve, 94.
15 Villeneuve, 95.
16 Villeneuve, 95–6.
17 Villeneuve, 99.
18 Villeneuve, 119; Marcy Norton, "Tasting Empire: Chocolate and the European Internalization of Mesoamerican Aesthetics," *The American Historical Review* 111, no. 3 (2006): 660–91. The first sugar plantation in Saint-Domingue's West Province was established in 1680 at Léogâne, and by the end of the eighteenth century, the region produced 75 percent of the colony's brut sugar exports. From 1697–1740, an estimated 119,010 captives were disembarked in French Saint-Domingue. The estimated population of enslaved people in the colony reached 465,000 by 1789. Jacques de Cauna, *Au temps des isles à sucre: histoire d'une plantation de Saint-Domingue au XVIIIème siècle* (Paris: Karthala, 2003), 14; *The Trans-Atlantic Slave Trade Database*, accessed September 21, 2018, see www.slavevoyages.org/estimates/rIuAF2im; Laurent Dubois, *A Colony of Citizens: Revolution and Slave Emancipation in the French Caribbean, 1787–1804* (Chapel Hill: University of North Carolina Press, 2004), 50.
19 Villeneuve, *La Jeune Amériquaine*, 82–3.
20 Villeneuve, 79–80.
21 Villeneuve, 91.
22 Villeneuve, 88.
23 Villeneuve, 81–2.
24 Villeneuve, 86–7.
25 Villeneuve, 127.
26 Villeneuve, 127.
27 Villeneuve, 142.
28 The English translation of the alternate title, as well as the character names of Lady Sensible and Mademoiselle Affable, are taken from Jeanne-Marie Leprince de Beaumont, *Magazin des enfans, or the Young Misses Magazine: Containing the Dialogues between a Governess and several Young Ladies of Quality her Scholars*, 4 vols. (London: Printed for S. Field, W. Ware, and T. Johnson, 1765).

29 Jeanne-Marie Leprince de Beaumont, *Le Magasin des enfants*, in Biancardi, ed., *La Jeune Américaine et les Contes marins*, 1031. Translations mine unless otherwise noted.
30 On absenteeism, see Peter Fryer, *Staying Power: The History of Black People in Britain* (London: Pluto Press, 1984) 14, 18–19. On the legal status of Black servants, see Kathleen Chater, *Untold Histories: Black People in England and Wales during the Period of the British Slave Trade, c. 1660-1807* (Manchester and New York: Manchester University Press, 2009), 77–101.
31 *Oxford English Dictionary Online*, s.v. "Lackey, n.," accessed September 20, 2018, see www.oed.com/view/Entry/104871; J. Jean Hecht, *The Domestic Servant Class in Eighteenth-Century England* (London: Routledge & Paul, 1956), 52–5.
32 Per Chater's research, the origins of 76 percent of Black people living in England between 1660–1812 are unknown. Of the remaining, 53 percent came from the Caribbean (in descending order, from Jamaica, Barbados, Bermuda, St. Kitts, Martinique, Nevis, and Santo Domingo); 34 percent came from Africa; 20 percent from the East Indies; and 16 percent from North America. *Untold Histories*, 62–6.
33 Biancardi, ed., *La Jeune Américaine et les Contes marins*, 935.
34 Leprince de Beaumont, *Le Magasin des enfants*, 1031, emphasis added.
35 McDonald and Suleiman, eds., *French Global*, xvii.
36 Ahmed, *Strange Encounters*, 7.
37 Ahmed, 7; see especially chapter 2, "Embodying strangers," in *Strange Encounters*, 38–54.
38 Ahmed, 53.

Chapter 5

MISSED CONNECTIONS:
LITERARY HISTORY AND SAINT-AUBIN'S
LE DANGER DES LIAISONS

Sanam Nader-Esfahani

Life is too short to read bad or mediocre books. "There are still books that are neither good nor bad, but if there exist some excellent books, why must one waste one's time reading the mediocre ones? Does life seem so long to you?"[1] This is the position that Friedrich Melchior Grimm adopts in a correspondence with a "woman of high intellect" regarding Madame de Saint-Aubin's *Le Danger des liaisons, ou Mémoires de la Baronne de Blémon* (*The Danger of Liaisons, or Memoirs of the Baroness of Blémon*), published in 1763.[2] In contrast to his female correspondent who defends the literary virtues of the novel, the critic, journalist, and contributor to Diderot and d'Alembert's *Encyclopédie* expresses his profound displeasure. He condemns Saint-Aubin's style for its lack of verisimilitude and objects to the endless chain of ill-fated events befalling its characters. The excess of heart-wrenching moments, in his mind, detracts from the work's affective impact. Thus, he finds *Le Danger des liaisons* to be significantly inferior to Samuel Richardson's epistolary novel *Clarissa* (1748). The anonymous "woman of high intellect" eventually convinces Grimm to distribute copies of *Le Danger des liaisons* to his friends, while keeping his opinions to himself so as not to dissuade other philosophers from reading the book. Given that neither Saint-Aubin nor *Le Danger des liaisons* resonates in the ears and minds of scholars and readers today, one may wonder if Grimm did in fact honor the promise he made to his addressee.

Though the name Marie-Françoise-Félicité Mauguet de Mézières (1717–90), marquise de Saint-Aubin and baronne d'Andlau bears little familiarity today, her home was frequented by ambassadors, musicians, artists, writers, and philosophers, including prominent figures like Rameau, d'Alembert, and Madame de Riccoboni.[3] It was entirely by chance, however, that she became a woman of society. Abandoned at a young age by a cruel and widowed mother,[4] she was to commit to a monastic life in a convent near Paris. Under the care of the nuns, she received a fine education in letters and music. Despite her refusal to take her vows—much to the chagrin of her mother—she remained at the convent until the age of twenty-six, when she crossed paths with and subsequently married Pierre-César Du Crest, marquis de Saint-Aubin, the relative of a widow who had retired to the convent.[5] A late-comer to the literary scene, she founded *Le Courier de la nouveauté* (1758), the first French fashion magazine, and authored two novels, *Le Danger des liaisons* at the age of forty-six, and *Mémoires, en forme de lettres, de deux jeunes personnes de qualité* (*Memoirs, in the Form of Letters, Between Two Young Persons of Quality*, 1765).

The three tomes of Saint-Aubin's debut novel, *Le Danger des liaisons*, use a frame narrative to coalesce the stories of various characters who, through their encounters with the protagonist Laure de Blémon, confide their misadventures in first-person accounts. Despite the multiplicity of perspectives, the tales told by Laure and her mostly female companions share a common denominator: they portray impressionable and virtuous characters compromised by their associations with predatory and morally corrupt acquaintances who ultimately lead them astray. Without the sequence of dubious events, however, these protagonists would have no regrets to bemoan, no tales to tell, and perhaps, no reason to find solace and forge meaningful friendships with those who console them. As such, the conniving secondary characters, who bring into being the tragic content of the tales, are at the origin of the act of storytelling, transforming the individual protagonists into narrators. If the title of Saint-Aubin's novel cautions its readers against the dangers of the connections one makes, the novel's legacy and its near effacement from literary history is instead suggestive of missed connections that are no less problematic. This essay will examine the significance of encounters and liaisons in Saint-Aubin's novel and lay bare the biases of a particular version of literary history which limits encounters with voices rarely heard, notably the voices of women writers.

Beyond the novel's mellifluous and melodramatic tone criticized by Grimm, and its depictions of dangerous associations and their moral and moralizing undertones, the reader discovers a rich representation of kinship. By privileging female narrators and a significant cast of female perpetrators, Saint-Aubin emphasizes the blessings and the perils of female friendships while addressing the implications of romantic entanglements.[6] Where the relationships between Laure, the main character, and her companions show the value of close female confidants, other liaisons between female characters lead to the demise of the innocent. In this way, Saint-Aubin's novel clearly explores the late seventeenth-century denotation of "liaison" as a bond or as a sentimental attachment that is not exclusive to an amorous relationship. The text also exemplifies the generally negative connotation of the plural form "liaisons" in the eighteenth century when we consider those people or intercessors who arrange encounters between protagonists and predators (male and female alike). "Alas! It is to my *liaison* with this dangerous friend that I owe my misfortune!"[7] Such words could very well be the novel's leitmotif. Betrayal, financial ruin, tarnished reputations are but some of the dangers of liaisons.

Neither dangerous liaisons nor the cautionary tales that emerge from them would have existed without encounters between seducers, victims, helpers, and confidants. Drawing on the two main types of encounters defined in the introduction of this volume—either as a "falling upon" or chance encounter, or as a convergence predicated on a spatial organization whereby "people meet between, through or with"[8]—we may identify two types of liaisons. The presence or absence of a liaison is the condition that differentiates between chance encounters that are fleeting and those that endure. The ephemeral encounter that does not extend in time is characterized by the absence of liaison, a non-bonding, a lack of connection. Conversely, the chance encounter that grows in emotional and affective depth over time occurs as a result of an affinity, however stable or volatile, that envelops the encountering bodies and holds them together, much like the chemical bond (or *liaison chimique* in French) that results from the attraction of atoms and molecules. When "encounter" is understood as convergence, the implications of liaison are no longer temporal—the condition required for the endurance of encounter in time— but spatial. Here, the liaison becomes synonymous with the site of encounter, the person, space, thing, or medium by or through which an encounter occurs, perhaps in a less aleatory fashion.

That Saint-Aubin's title warns not of "encounters" but of "liaisons" is also suggestive of the degree of vulnerability associated with each notion. Where liaison's spatial connotation is favored, the risk is one and the same for both terms. We may think of the novel's depictions of the duplicitous friend who acts as an intermediary between an innocent protagonist and other characters of questionable repute. Such a figure is an incarnation of a perilous link or site of encounter. A different dynamic emerges when we consider the relationship between liaison and fortuitous encounters. The meeting may indeed harbor potential for danger, but this potential is more likely to actualize when the encounter endures in time, when the relationship is sustained. Here, the real danger resides in the liaison—born out of choice, sheer naivety and inexperience, or other power differentials. The lasting bond enables and ensures the presence of the cunning characters within the intimate sphere of the novel's protagonists. This proximity in turn increases the opportunity for influence, manipulation, and exploitation, which ultimately leads to the downfall of the virtuous and vulnerable.

However arbitrary or calculated the liaisons may be in the world of Saint-Aubin's characters, they are, of course, the fruits of the author's pre-meditated plan. The connections that arise from "chance" encounters with unsavory characters, within the bustling streets and salons of Paris or through the malicious intermediaries, are all staged to generate the very content of the novel. Like variations on a single formula, the act of multiplying stories of victims and predators accentuates the prevalence of nefarious liaisons to more loudly sound the alarm that warns of their consequences. And yet, despite Saint-Aubin's emphasis on the destructive dimension of liaisons, one notable authorial decision, the structure of the novel as a polyphonic memoir, challenges—consciously or unconsciously—the negative connotation of the word. The fortuitous encounters between the various protagonists and Laure are in reality governed by the structure of a frame narrative. Even though Laure pens this text to divulge her own misfortunes, almost two-thirds of the novel foreground the stories of other characters. When the chance meetings between Laure and these other figures burgeon into meaningful friendships, Laure becomes a listener, ceding her own voice to that of another to mark the beginning of a framed narrative. Similarly, as a sympathetic and privileged interlocutor, Laure herself, like the convents or country homes where she and the other protagonists come into contact, becomes a site of encounter. For instance, the lives of Lucie and Adélaïde, a woman and the daughter she had given up for adoption, respectively, intertwine through the stories they each share with Laure;[9] it is also through Laure that one of the protagonists meets, falls in love with, and marries Laure's brother.

As Laure oscillates between past and present versions of herself, between her roles as impressionable protagonist and seasoned narrator, she offers the following reflections: "But how many women haven't had this happen to them, like it has to me, to make a mistake? And how many are there who, like me, have realized this mistake only when it has led them as far as they could have been led by love?"[10] Recognizing her own trajectory as one iteration among countless others ("how many women"), Laure highlights the affinity between her life and those of other women ("like me"), all victims of dangerous liaisons who later regret the moral boundaries they were driven to transgress. Through her personal tale, she embodies a collective experience, and as the point of convergence for the novel's other female protagonists, she illustrates that beneath the particularities of each story is a shared and universal narrative. In her capacity as confidant, Laure and the pages of the memoirs she "authors" become a connective node, linking together the novel's framed stories, their respective narrators, and the "many women" with whom these accounts resonate. If dangerous liaisons fuel the content of the protagonists' stories, it is through the conduit of genuine friendships and constructive liaisons that those stories find expression. If dangerous liaisons give the protagonists a story to tell, the status of these characters as storytellers is only legitimized when someone is willing to listen.

Although *Le Danger des liaisons* was received favorably by some contemporary readers,[11] even earning its author some laudatory lines by Voltaire,[12] literary history has sided with Grimm, relegating Saint-Aubin to the rank of *auctores minores*. She appears in Jacques Hébrail and Joseph de Laporte's 1769 *La France littéraire* (*Literary France*),[13] and gains a place among the illustrious female authors in Laporte's *Histoire littéraire des femmes françoises* (*Literary History of French Women*) published the same year.[14] But in the nineteenth century, literary anthologies which celebrated the talents of France's women relocate her to a more marginal place or efface her altogether.[15] Even her own daughter, Stéphanie Félicité de Genlis, ignores her mother's contributions to the world of French letters in her *De l'influence des femmes sur la littérature française* (*On the Influence of Women on French Literature*) published in 1811,[16] though she does briefly mention her mother's literary activity in her *Mémoires*.[17] Paradoxically, Genlis's fame has afforded Saint-Aubin recognition for her progeny of flesh and blood, though not for her literary offspring.[18] Where one nineteenth-century author flirts with the idea of Saint-Aubin exercising influence over Laclos, asking whether *Le Danger des liaisons* would have been on Laclos's mind when he composed his *Les Liaisons dangereuses* (*Dangerous Liaisons*) almost two decades later,[19] modern scholars dismiss any such correlation. Crushed beneath the weight of his-story—of Laclos's

Les Liaisons dangereuses and her own novel's misfortunes in the annals of literary history—Saint-Aubin's *Le Danger des liaisons* is silenced or pulverized to a mere iteration of a literary commonplace.

Laclos's celebrated epistolary novel would have shared the title of Saint-Aubin's work had its author not changed his mind. Whether he did so in order to distinguish his own text from Saint-Aubin's[20] or to mitigate the moralizing tenor of *Le Danger des liaisons* seems to matter little.[21] If the two writers gave their works a similar title, it is, critics suggest, because "*danger des liaisons*" was simply a theme or *topos*, and Saint-Aubin's characters were common types to be found in many novels of the period.[22] But why is it that Laclos's *Les Liaisons dangereuses* still touches the minds of specialists and non-specialists alike, its title resounding on paper, on the stage and on the screen, when Saint-Aubin's *Le Danger des liaisons* barely appears on the pages of academic publications? Perhaps, as Grimm suggests, the endless tales of victimhood and of pathetic narrators cease to be effective and engaging. It could also be argued that Laclos is the more skillful writer, or that *Les Liaisons dangereuses* is simply the more tantalizing of the two novels, the more pleasurable read as we are privy to the thoughts and machinations of the wicked, witnessing first-hand the orchestration of the victims' demise. Is it that Laclos's deliciously devious characters and the plots they concoct are more salient than the stirring and pitiable stories of misfortune and compromised virtue or the depictions of the financial realities governing the decisions and lives of women? Perhaps the answer resides in what Joan Hinde Stewart observes in her study on the place of eighteenth-century women writers. She suggests that if the novels of women are excluded from the literary canons established in the nineteenth century, it is because "the questions they raise—the passionate nature of women, the economic necessity and indeed the very possibility of marrying and remarrying, the livability of contemporary marriage, the significance of mothering and domesticity—as much as the way in which they raise them, didn't appear sufficiently important to the literary establishment."[23]

When we turn a blind eye to texts such as Saint-Aubin's, what are we excluding from our field of vision? What thoughts are we filtering out of our minds? What questions are we keeping ourselves from asking? What imaginative and intellectual worlds could be revealed in a more inclusive history of literature? What connections are we missing?

For instance, we might better understand how women lived by studying the many references to inheritance and financial blackmail in Saint-Aubin's novel. Adélaïde's story in the second and third volumes addresses the fate of her dowry and the disputes surrounding her inheritance. Mademoiselle de Chansai provides an account of her father's fortune. Laure's story of her own compromised reputation in the second part of the third volume opens with her travelling to Clermont to take care of her inheritance. In placing examples such as these from a work of fiction in dialogue with historical accounts of women and their finances (as daughters, as wives, as widows), we might better gauge how women sustained themselves in some milieus during the eighteenth century. By extension, we may explore the relationship between a woman's economic condition and the power dynamics that would have made her vulnerable to manipulation or exploitation. The nineteenth-century literary establishment may not have deemed these subjects worthy of serious inquiry, but the selections operated in anthologies and the complete dismissal of women authors from the literary canon denies us the opportunity to evaluate works that were once considered worthy of being read. It also impedes modern readers—who may be guided by different questions and priorities—from judging for themselves the merits as well as the shortcomings, the beauty, and the relevance of works like Le Danger des liaisons.

In a literary landscape where editorial practices still reflect the "gender biases in the conception of literary history,"[24] what do we make of minor writers who are further dismissed because of their gender? If even the most renowned eighteenth-century female writers have little visibility,[25] thus leading or rather, *mis*leading readers to equate invisibility with inactivity (or worst, with inability), what place might we grant a figure like Saint-Aubin? Is she deserving of a position in the distinguished company of a Genlis, an Isabelle de Charrière, or an Olympe de Gouges? Maybe, maybe not. The way in which literary history forms and informs our access to this text and our understanding of it prevents us from asking the very questions that would make such a debate possible, let alone fruitful.

Decisions about what constitutes "sufficiently important" content are not without consequences, and the literary history inherited from the nineteenth century is a limited and limiting site of encounter. Minds fettered by received ideas and biases come across certain narratives in confined or distorted forms—or miss them altogether. The possibility these minds have for new encounters and connections is restricted. These are the challenges facing the study of female authors, which Martine Reid so poignantly describes in her introduction to a recent volume on eighteenth-century women writers.[26] In her evaluation of the reception of works by women in contemporary scholarship in France and the English-speaking world, Reid foregrounds the obstacles a corpus of texts written by female authors continues to confront. Such obstacles include the lack of interest in women writers, the parochial ways in which they are studied, and the methodological problems of approaching "women's writing" as a theme or sub-genre. She denounces the "sexuation" or gendering of the literary field that isolates women as an object of analysis. Reid also questions the very category of "écriture feminine," interrogating the false homogeneity that the expression encapsulates, effacing not only stylistic but ideological diversities that inform the works of female authors.[27]

Obstacles may persist, but ongoing efforts are undoing the restrictive bonds of literary history, generating the connections by which and multiplying the spaces through which works by women can be encountered. Initiatives in scholarship, publishing, and teaching continue to excavate and give greater visibility to both known and lesser-known women writers of the eighteenth century.[28] Digital Humanities projects like SIEFAR (Société Internationale pour l'Étude des Femmes de l'Ancien Régime) and other databases are documenting works penned by women.[29] The recent *Femmes et littérature: Une histoire culturelle* (*Women and Literature: A Cultural History*) under Reid's aegis, whose fourth part on the eighteenth century is authored by Christie McDonald, similarly champions women as agents in the literary landscape.[30] By bringing women to the foreground, these endeavors are challenging and revising the history of literature so that we may think of literary works in different and more inclusive ways while allowing for new questions and connections to emerge. Much like the friendships in *Le Danger des liaisons*, literary history need not necessarily serve as the dangerous encounter that ultimately distorts our perception and leads us astray in our pursuit of texts and authors. Surely, there also exists a version of literary history that allows a formerly marginalized figure to become a storyteller and share *her* story. After all, what would have become of Lucie, Adélaïde, Mademoiselle de Chansai, and the many other characters-turned-narrators had Laure de Blémon, the principal narrator and the "author" of the memoirs, not added their voices to her own? The major events of Laure's own life are mostly limited to the beginning of the first book and the second half of the third. She, and the pages of her memoirs, exemplify the generative site of encounter and the expansive and creative potentials of liaisons. Both unite, frame, and tie together the stories of the women and men who are themselves shaped by encounters. Without Laure, those stories would fall into oblivion; without those stories, Laure's own story would be incomplete.

Notes

1 Friedrich Melchior Grimm, *Correspondance littéraire*, ed. Ulla Kölving (*Ferney-Voltaire: Centre International d'Étude du XVIIIe Siècle, 2016*), 10:49. Translation mine.
2 Marie-Françoise-Félicité Mauguet de Mézières, Marquise de Saint-Aubin, *Le Danger des liaisons, ou Mémoires de la Baronne de Blémon*, 3 vols. (Geneva: n.p., 1763). All translations are my own.
3 Stéphanie-Félicité de Genlis, *Mémoires inédits de Madame la comtesse de Genlis sur le dix-huitième siècle et la Révolution Française* (Paris: Ladvocat, 1825), 1:95–106. In her *Mémoires*, Genlis, who is Saint-Aubin's daughter, describes gatherings of musicians in the chapel of their home, where her mother would play the organ. Genlis, 95. In these pages, she also recalls other figures whom she met as a young woman living with her mother.
4 Genlis, 114. Genlis paints her grandmother through the eyes of her mother as a cruel and even "denatured" mother.
5 Genlis, 114, 119–25.
6 Laurent Versini, *Laclos et la tradition: Essai sur les sources et la technique des* Liaisons dangereuses (Paris: Klincksieck, 1968), 155.
7 Saint-Aubin, *Le Danger des liaisons*, 1:141.
8 See the Introduction to the present volume by Jérôme Brillaud and Virginie Greene, 4.
9 Lucie is the narrator of the second part of the first volume. Adélaïde's story appears in the end of volume two and at the beginning of volume three.
10 Saint-Aubin, *Le Danger des liaisons*, 3.2:131.
11 Catriona Seth, "La fortune des 'Liaisons dangereuses,'" in Pierre Choderlos de Laclos, *Les Liaisons dangereuses*, Bibliothèque de la Pléiade 6 (Paris: Gallimard, 2011), 797–8.

12 Voltaire, "Vers à Madame de C.***, auteur du Danger des liaisons," Œuvres complètes de Voltaire, Writings of 1763–1764, ed. Simon Davies, Graham Gargett et al. (Oxford: Voltaire Foundation, 2014), 57A:319.
13 Jacques Hébrail and Joseph de Laporte, La France littéraire, Les Académies établies à Paris & dans les différentes villes du royaume (Paris: La Veuve Duchesne, 1769), 1:396.
14 Joseph de Laporte, Histoire littéraire des femmes françoises ou lettres historiques et critiques (Paris: Lacombe, 1769), 5:412–32.
15 Fortunée B. Briquet, Dictionnaire historique, littéraire et bibliographique des Françaises, et des étrangères naturalisées en France (Paris: Gillé, 1804). Briquet praises the "gripping narrative, pleasurable style, and brilliant thoughts" of Le Danger des liaisons before applauding the moral quality of Saint-Aubin's epistolary novel. Briquet, 7. Translation mine.
16 Stéphanie-Félicité de Genlis, De l'influence des femmes sur la littérature française, comme protectrices des lettres et comme auteurs; ou précis de l'histoire des femmes françaises les plus célèbres (Paris: Mardan, 1811).
17 Genlis, Mémoires, 154–5. Genlis even cites Voltaire's poem in praise of Le Danger des liaisons.
18 See Julia Kavanagh, Women in France during the Eighteenth Century (London: Smith, Elder, and Co., 1850), 2:44–45; Marie Aurore Dupin, La France illustrée par ses femmes (Paris: Maumus, 1833). Dupin refers to the young Madame de Genlis as "Mademoiselle de Saint-Aubin." Dupin, 266. See also André Albert Delmas and Yvette Mialon Delmas, À la recherche des Liaisons dangereuses (Paris: Mercure de France, 1964), 32.
19 M. le C. d'I*** [Jules Gay], Bibliographie des ouvrages relatifs à l'amour, aux femmes, au mariage, et des livres facétieux, pantagruéliques, scatologiques, satyrique etc., 3rd ed. (Paris: Bibliothèque Derviche, 1871), 2:403.
20 Jean-Paul Bertaud, Choderlos de Laclos: L'auteur des Liaisons dangereuses (Paris: Fayard, 2003), 95; Delmas and Delmas, À la recherche, 32; Béatrice Didier, Choderlos de Laclos, les liaisons dangereuses: pastiches et ironie (Paris: Éditions du Temps, 1998), 143; Ron Rosbottom, Choderlos de Laclos (Boston: Twayne Publishers, 1978), 45; Seth, "La fortune," in Laclos, Les Liaisons dangereuses, 797; Versini, Laclos et la tradition, 150–1.
21 See Didier, Choderlos de Laclos, 143. See also Versini, Laclos et la tradition.
22 Versini's comparison between Saint-Aubin and Laclos, alongside the works of other novelists, in Laclos et la tradition is the most thorough of such analyses and establishes characters from various eighteenth-century novels as types. See also Stéphanie Genand, Le Libertinage et l'histoire: Politique de la séduction à la fin de l'Ancien Régime (Oxford: Voltaire Foundation, 2005), 49–50. Genand suggests that "dangerous liaisons" undergoes a transformation from theme to topos toward the end of the Ancien Régime, and she sees Laclos as a turning point with regard to both the moral tradition and the development of the topos. Genand also cites Laclos et la tradition to observe that Versini's study situates this shift from theme to commonplace (lieu commun) prior to the publication of Laclos's novel. Genand, 49.
23 Joan Hinde Stewart, Gynographs: French Novels by Women of the Late Eighteenth Century (Lincoln: University of Nebraska Press, 1993), 21–2. For further evidence of women's success in the literary marketplace in the eighteenth century, see Aurora Wolfgang, Gender and Voice in the French Novel, 1730–1782 (Aldershot: Ashgate, 2004), 5–10.
24 Stephanie M. Hilger, Women Write Back: Strategies of Response and the Dynamics of European Literary Culture, 1790–1805 (Amsterdam: Rodopi, 2009), 16.
25 Hilger, 21. "In one of the earliest attempts to define a canon of French eighteenth-century fiction, René Étiemble's 1966 Pléiade anthology Romanciers du XVIIIe siècle,

the absence of *romancières* is especially palpable." See also Martine Reid, introduction to *Femmes auteurs du dix-huitième siècle*, ed. Ángeles Sirvent Ramos, María Isabel Corbí Sáez, and María Ángeles Llorca Tonda (Paris: Honoré Champion, 2016), 20. In an assessment of the number of eighteenth-century women writers currently featured in the prestigious Pléiade editions, Reid observes the absence of female writers and notes that the genre-based anthologies only represent a handful of women.

26 Reid, 9–22.
27 See Hilger, *Women Write Back*, 28. Like Reid, Hilger interrogates the implications of "gendered categorization" and the ambiguous referent of "women's literature" that conflates and confuses writer, subject matter, and readership.
28 These include anthologies, such as Raymond Trousson, ed., *Romans de femmes du XVIIIe siècle* (Paris: Robert Laffont, 1996) and Aurore Évain, Perry Gethner and Henriette Goldwyn, ed., *Théâtre de femmes de l'Ancien Régime*, 4 vols. (Paris: Classiques Garnier, 2011–15), Reid's Femmes de Lettres series for Gallimard in its Folio 2€ collection, the Littérature et Genre collection under her direction at Honoré Champion, and the Modern Language Association's Texts and Translation series. For additional references, see Hilger, *Women Write Back*, 19–21. While recognizing the increased visibility granted to women writers through online editions, Hilger also warns against the "ghettoization of literature of women," claiming that their exclusion from print, which continues to be valued over digitized forms, "establishes a new bias based on old premises." Hilger, 26.
29 SIEFAR (website), accessed January 5, 2020, see http://siefar.org/; Sanam Nader-Esfahani, ed., "Works of Fiction and Non-Fiction in French by Women in the Eighteenth Century," Database on Harvard Dataverse, last modified December 16, 2019. See https://doi.org/10.7910/DVN/DXFSR6; Suzan van Dijk, ed., *Women Writers* (website), accessed January 5, 2020, neww.huygens.knaw.nl/.
30 Martine Reid, ed., *Femmes et littérature: Une histoire culturelle* (Paris: Gallimard, 2020).

Chapter 6

REJECTED ENCOUNTERS WITH WOMEN WRITERS:
THE CASE OF *LES PENSÉES ERRANTES*

Caleb Shelburne

Eighteenth-century French books are known for their substantial prefaces, but *Les Pensées errantes; avec quelques Lettres d'un Indien* (*Stray Thoughts; with Several Letters from an Indian Man*) takes this convention to the extreme. Published anonymously in 1758, this small book has an outsized preface: of the 334 pages in the text, 213—almost two thirds—are prefatory. The remainder is a distinct text, comprising an unfinished epistolary novel referenced by the subtitle. The majority of the text is a preface without a book—or as it is labeled, a "Preface that contains everything."[1] Faced with this apparent misunderstanding of the appropriate function of a preface, Friedrich Melchior Grimm—editor of the influential journal *Correspondance littéraire* (*Literary Correspondence*)—quipped, "I do not know the author of this work, of which the form is singular and the substance detestable."[2]

Setting aside the question of substance for now, Grimm's sensitivity to the identity of the author offers one lens through which to understand the text's unusual form. The form mediates the encounter between reader and author, manifested in Grimm's frustration at not knowing her. I say "her," because although no author or editor's name is given, the frontispiece proudly displays "Par Mme. ***," and there are references to the author's experiences as a woman throughout the text.[3] Although it is by no means representative, *Les Pensées errantes* evokes many of the challenges facing eighteenth-century French women writers. While the tone is often playful, the seemingly nonsensical structure functions to reject certain reading practices of the period—that is, the book carefully mediates the encounter between reader and author, permitting certain kinds of interactions while precluding others. Through reflecting on my own encounter with the text, I aim to draw attention to the structures of power that necessarily bear upon the moment of encounter. The study of literary form as a way of mediating, and in certain cases, rejecting, encounters between readers and writers shows the structural inequalities facing eighteenth-century French women writers—as well as these writers' creative countertactics.

Reading Les Pensées errantes

My journey to *Les Pensées errantes* was a series of coincidences. As a sophomore in college, a chance conversation led me to Christie McDonald's class on the French Enlightenment, and after a few weeks, I applied to work as her research assistant. Her current project was the eighteenth-century section of *Femmes et littérature* (*Women and Literature*), a two-volume collection that consolidates and thematizes existing research on women writers in French literature.[4] A month or two into this work, McDonald assigned me the task of determining how *Les Pensées errantes* might fit into her analysis.

I dwell on this haphazard path because chance is a central theme in *Les Pensées errantes* and a key aspect of encountering. But first, further information on the structure of the book is necessary.

As indicated by the title, the book is divided into two parts: a series of *pensées* (thoughts) on a variety of subjects, and an unfinished epistolary novel. The *pensées* are preceded and followed by short sections explaining the structure of the book—altogether, these three components comprise the "preface that contains everything." More than thoughts alone, *pensées* were an established genre, a form of philosophy written in disconnected fragments broaching numerous subjects without always stating a main argument. Famous examples from the French tradition include Blaise Pascal's *Pensées* (1670) and Denis Diderot's *Pensées philosophiques* (1746). While both of these cases may have been motivated by external circumstances—Pascal's *Pensées* was a posthumous collection of his unfinished writings, and Diderot was most likely avoiding censorship—the fragmented nature of *pensées* as a genre could also be a deliberate choice.[5] Its flexible argumentative structure supported wide-ranging reflection and facilitated unexpected connections between disparate topics. Like other philosophical genres, *pensées* were considered unsuitable for women writers. Besides *Les Pensées errantes*, only two other women writers published *pensées*, and neither was well received.[6]

Epistolary novels, by contrast, were deemed "light" and conventional modes of fiction—ostensibly more appropriate for a woman's romantic imagination. Of course, many epistolary novels, such as Charles-Louis Montesquieu's *Lettres persanes* (Persian Letters) and Françoise de Graffigny's *Lettres d'une Péruvienne* (Letters from a Peruvian Woman), can be read as philosophy in their own right. Indeed, the epistolary novel appended to *Pensées errantes* raises many of the ideas discussed in the more explicitly philosophical *pensées* genre.[7] As they were fictional and generally judged more on the basis of style and plot than philosophical substance, epistolary novels were one of the few genres open to women. Anything demonstrating more originality or reflection—philosophy, science, etc.—was considered unbefitting, and even unattainable, for a woman to publish.

By means of a ruse, *Les Pensées errantes* avoids the expectation that women writers could only succeed in fiction. At the beginning of the preface, the author expresses her frustration with novelists' tendency to provide pedantic and trite "portraits" of their characters, as well as "love letters and pretty verses," that fill space without advancing the plot.[8] After completing her own novel, she sought to remove all such digressions to streamline the narrative. However, she was unwilling to discard them altogether, and so decided to move all these digressions to the preface—this preface that the unsuspecting reader has picked up. From the introduction, it appears that the novel, stripped of its portraits, love letters, and verses, comes after the preface. Each prefatory *pensée* is therefore labeled with an alphanumeric *renvoi* (reference) to an associated point in the novel, and many of them include a brief quotation to provide context. For example, *pensée* O3 starts with a quote from the novel—"All things considered, I would have been a bad Turkish woman . . ."—and then continues with a comparison of the status of women in France and "Turkey."[9] Altogether, there are ninety-four *pensées*, ranging from A to P4.

The introduction frames each *pensée* as a rejected piece of the novel, like an endnote that instead appears in the preface. Already, the author is presenting a subtle critique: the *pensées*, a genre associated with such towering figures as Pascal and Diderot, are framed here as a collection of paragraphs removed from a woman's novel for the sake of clarity. The author thus insists that philosophy is inherent to novels as well, even as she self-consciously mocks novels' conventionality. But beyond this critique, the ploy of a novel allows her to address her audience in a traditionally masculine mode. Where *pensées* alone would have been deemed an unsuitable genre for a woman writer, the idea of a source novel encourages the reader to still consider it the work of a woman. As Antoinette Sol suggests, what at first appears to be a playful book quickly reveals itself to be defiant.[10]

After working through some two hundred pages of relatively dense *pensées* with no apparent through line and frequent shifts in scope, the reader arrives at a brief explanatory epilogue which concludes the preface. Here, the author reminds the reader of the novel she had promised at the beginning but confesses that it is not yet complete. The reason is characteristically mysterious: "Narsam is none other than myself, and my story is unfinished because I am not yet old."[11] "Narsam" is mentioned nowhere else, but as one contemporary reviewer noted, the context suggests it must be the name of the missing novel's heroine.[12] The "Several Letters from an Indian Man" are offered in lieu of the missing story of Narsam, admittedly meager consolation for the disappointed reader. The entire book—*pensées* and half-finished epistolary novel—is thus arranged around the novel promised at the beginning but later revealed to be missing, the history of Narsam who is apparently "none other than" the author.

Reading as Encountering

In Diderot's *Encyclopédie, ou dictionnaire raisonné des sciences, des arts et des métiers* (*Encyclopedia or Systematic Dictionary of Sciences, Arts, and Trades*, 1751–72), the act of reading is construed as an encounter between a reader and an author. In the article on literary and scientific works ("ouvrages"), Louis Jaucourt contends that studying a book is useful, but "nothing educates the mind like the act of writing and composing something oneself."[13] Jaucourt's point is that knowledge cannot be fully developed through reading because of the physical separation between reader and writer. Writing offers no guarantee of perfect knowledge but is more apt to hone one's ideas.

If reading is a useful but limited way of developing one's knowledge, what can be done to maximize its utility? An unsigned article on books ("livres") proposes a number of criteria for book selection, with the most important criterion being the author: "the life of the author, their profession, their rank; if something remarkable had characterized their education, studies, [and] way of life."[14] While other attributes like the quality of the publisher and the number of editions are relevant, knowledge of the author is considered paramount. The more one is confident in their expertise on the subject, the longer they took to write the book, and the more renowned the work, the more one can assume the book is worth reading—even if it is only an imperfect projection of the author's knowledge.

By evoking this understanding of reading, I do not intend to identify a specific "Enlightenment" theory of reading. Instead, I aim to show one common—though not universal—interpretation of reading that continues to this day: an encounter of two or more minds, that of the reader(s) and the author(s). Jaucourt, for instance, praises "those excellent authors whose works are like friends," treating the book as a virtual "friend" standing in for its author.[15] When Jaucourt selects a scientific work on the basis of its author's education or simply for their potential as a friend, he is using the text to simulate an encounter with its author. And when I read *Les Pensées errantes* as a way to understand one eighteenth-century French woman's perspective on the legal and social status of French women, I am likewise using the book to encounter this author.

The idea of authorship has received much critical attention, often challenging Jaucourt's conception of an encounter between two minds. In "The Death of the Author," Roland Barthes writes that a text is "a tissue of quotations drawn from the innumerable centers of culture."[16] For Barthes, a book is not the product of one mind, but rather a palimpsest of various cultural influences. Books can be collective endeavors, where one person's contributions are almost impossible to measure and where overall attribution of the volume to one editor is equally questionable. However, it is clear from the *Encyclopédie* articles that the commonplace understanding of authorship in eighteenth-century France defined texts as the products of individual minds.

In the introduction to this volume, Virginie Greene and Jérôme Brillaud discuss a wide range of interpretations of encountering, among which one common through line is the idea of chance. Louis Althusser is especially insistent on this point. Imagining a world of independent, parallel, falling raindrops (an image he takes from Epicurus),[17] he contends that the "aleatory" encounter of two drops begins a "chain reaction" of further encounters until we have what we have today.[18] While the Big Bang is one example, Althusser moves beyond science, shifting from politics to the economy, arguing that everything arises from one such random encounter, one such throw of the dice. The encounter is aleatory insofar as neither its causes nor its effects can be determined from how the dice fall.[19] Althusser's encounter is thus contingent and arbitrary rather than subject to fixed, universal laws. Encounters are coincidences, not convergences.

Reading—at least as I described it above—has a structure that precedes any individual encounter: the assumption that there is an author who wrote the text. As Jaucourt describes, the written word is an imperfect medium, allowing the reader to access the knowledge and experiences of the author, at least in part. Books enable encounters with individuals that might otherwise be inaccessible, liberating ideas from their human creators. But for Jaucourt, this human embodiment always comes *before* the encounter through the book. There is certainly something aleatory in reading, to think with Althusser, but it is always an encounter structured by one's knowledge of the author, one's familiarity with the publishing house, etc. And in eighteenth-century France, one significant feature of this pre-encounter structure was the consideration of gender.

Reading Women Writers

As the contributors to *Femmes et littérature* and many other scholars have documented, women's authorship was always subject to additional barriers. First to consider is material context. Because women's names were taken from their husband or father, they did not have a legal right to their own name, meaning they could not sign contracts with publishers without permission from their male guardian.[20] Women were already at a disadvantage with publishers, and men's control of money further restricted women's ability to self-publish.[21]

Second, women's reputations were more precarious than men's, increasing the associated social risks of publication. Louise d'Épinay, a close associate of Rousseau and Diderot, tells the story of Mademoiselle d'Albert, whose first book (published anonymously but soon found to be hers) caricatured some of her noble acquaintances in a manner considered disgraceful for a young, unmarried woman—or any woman, for that matter. Despite her family's efforts to buy back and destroy all of the copies, d'Albert was jailed in the Bastille for a few months and found her reputation ruined, forcing her to move to a convent.[22] Neither was this social risk limited to little-known or young authors. No less renowned a figure than the *salonnière* (salon hostess) Anne-Thérèse de Lambert believed that no woman of quality should publish. When some of her writing was printed without her consent, she had all of the copies bought back.[23]

Finally, as mentioned above, women were deemed only able to write in certain genres—and even in those genres, their capacity for "genius" was considered limited. It was widely assumed that women were guided by their emotions rather than their rationality and thus could not contribute to the sciences, philosophy, or theology.[24] If women chose to write, they were more suited for "less serious" genres, most of all novels. Whence the feint of the missing novel in *Les Pensées errantes*: a way to mollify, at least temporarily, those who might otherwise neglect a book written by a woman. The very fact that these "less serious" genres such as novels were associated with women often led the genres themselves to be treated as minor, creating a vicious circle connecting sexist ideas of women's capacities to genres deemed less significant or difficult to write. There was also the elusive concept of *génie*, roughly translatable as "genius," which was generally believed to be unique to men. Women were considered less imaginative, incapable of creative projects beyond their own experiences, and thus unable to produce truly original work.[25] Even if women could be authors in supposedly simple genres like novels, they still lacked the uniqueness of men's work.

Denigrating women's authorship in this way mirrored the real-life treatment of many intellectual women. The author of *Les Pensées errantes* complains that some of her male friends turn their conversation to *douceurs* (sweet talk) out of a commitment to *galanterie* (gallantry) in their relationships with women. If they could read in my interior, she writes in *pensée* S, they would understand her sincere preference for a more "natural tone, and that I want only to be a man for them."[26] She is thus one of the many women writers who hoped to be treated as men or—in the rather exceptional case of Olympe de Gouges—as androgynous, so that their intelligence would be taken seriously.[27]

One response to the biases against women writers was to conceal one's name. Anonymity was common among eighteenth-century writers for men and women alike, most often to deflect criticism until the book had proved successful, when their name might be willingly revealed. This tactic was further incentivized by the relatively small social circle of writers who were mostly members of the Parisian economic elite. Pseudonyms served a similar purpose, and in some cases included false gender identification: women identifying as men and vice versa.[28] Women writers may have been more likely to adopt these strategies because of the material and social barriers they faced. Joan DeJean argues that women often preferred to separate their "personal identity and authorial identity" for these reasons.[29] In this vein, Antoinette Sol's analysis of *Les Pensées errantes* interprets the construction of "margins" (the conceit of the *pensées* as endnotes to the missing novel) as a way of "[negotiating] between her position as a woman and as an author."[30] As Sol points out, this model of anonymity preserves the gendered voice without the threat of personal identification.

While anonymity allowed women to mitigate some of the risks of publishing, it hardly addressed the fundamental suspicion of their ability to write. Until the mid-twentieth century, the bibliographic standard was to attribute anonymous or pseudonymous works to men, and even in cases where a woman's name is identified, commentators often assumed she received help from her husband. One Enlightenment-era admirer of *Les Pensées errantes*, seeking to prove women's capacity in traditionally masculine fields through this example, worried that "it will only be through naming herself that she will be able to persuade us that this is the work of a woman."[31] Even this supportive reader is apparently unconvinced by the large "Par Mme. ***" on the frontispiece, but revealing her name would hardly preempt the usual criticisms of women writers: the work is unoriginal, presumptuous, or if otherwise unassailable, ghostwritten by some man in her life. Specifying a name would simply allow this criticism to concentrate on one individual. Gender thus determined how this reader, despite (or perhaps because of) their feminist pretentions, encountered *Les Pensées errantes*. Only a named encounter might convince the critics of a woman's abilities, but this too was unlikely: even encounters with *femmes de lettres* in real life, for instance in salons, seem to have done little to change understandings of women's intellectual capabilities.[32]

These dismissals of women's ability to write in certain genres hint at an implicit understanding of how women's writing should be read. A decade before *Les Pensées errantes* appeared, Diderot anonymously published his first novel, *Les Bijoux indiscrets* (*The Indiscreet Jewels*), the tale of a Congolese sultan who obtains and uses a magic ring that, when pointed at a woman, forces her "jewels" (i.e. genitalia) to tell her sexual history.[33] Diderot's satirical allegory has come to represent the desire for knowledge of women's sexuality and of women generally.[34] Although such readings tend to obscure some of the book's nuance, the allegory offers one way of interpreting the encounter between reader and female author, wherein reading functions like the magic ring, using the book to access her identity in ways that might be impossible in person.[35] Women's supposed lack of *génie* meant that it was neither possible nor desirable for a woman to write about anything other than herself—thence the recurring argument that a woman's book is only as good as the woman who wrote it. And the quality of a woman was usually structured around her sentimentality and sexuality, which were typically seen as being at odds with her rationality, among other things. A (male) reader might thus read women's work as an encounter with the woman as a sexualized body rather than a rational mind. As Linda Williams suggests, this makes reading more akin to pornographic voyeurism than *Encyclopédie*-style intellectual sharing.[36]

Take, for example, Charlotte-Élisabeth Aïssé, whose private letters were distributed in manuscript form. Aïssé, who had been purchased as a young girl from a slave market in Constantinople by a French ambassador, was an object of fascination during her life but even more so after her death, when her tragic story came to light. Her aristocratic lover proposed to her on multiple occasions, but she always refused, afraid that her lower social status might damage his reputation. An early death led to popular rumors that she had succumbed to heartbreak—a fitting end for a woman who came to epitomize feminine modesty. Yet the primary interest of her letters, then and perhaps still today, was the question of her sexual history, especially in her relationship with her adopted father.[37]

In the introduction to the first print edition of her letters, the editor explains that they have decided not to correct or update the manuscript text, since it is, with all its imperfections, the best representation of its author: "The heart guided the pen of Mademoiselle Aïssé; truth, sentiment, this happy simplicity, and naturalness are the characteristics of this short collection."[38] The appeal of the book, as described by this editor, was that it offered a chance for privileged access to this exotic woman's interiority, with a scarcely concealed focus on her sexuality. Aïssé's manuscript text could have served as a model for one of Diderot's stories of the magic ring, but where their *bijoux* lead to scandal, her letters confirm her legendary modesty for most readers.

The framing of Aïssé's work recalls Claude-Joseph Dorat's analysis of women writers' fiction, where "the attraction of their sex is communicated to their works."[39]

While Dorat was a prominent defender of women's authorship, his statement on their specific strengths demonstrates how gender set the expectations of the encounter even before it had taken place.

Rereading Les Pensées errantes

The epigraph of *Les Pensées errantes* should cue the reader to the strangeness of what is to follow: "*Non semper ea sunt, quae videntur*" (things are not always what they seem).[40] By only showing its author obliquely, the book's structure prevents the *bijoux indiscrets*-style of reading, where the book is used to access the woman's experiences, especially her sexual history. The *pensées* indeed present her private thoughts—recall her wish for her male friends to see her "interior" so they could appreciate her sincere wish to be treated as an equal—but there is no specific woman behind the text. Instead, we encounter a shifting, fragmentary voice that occasionally mentions romance but jumps to other topics too quickly for the reader to draw conclusions.

In *pensée* S, which begins with her frustration at her treatment by male friends, the author offers a more explicit statement on the intent behind this structure. Turning to "lovers" that court her too boldly, she explains, "If someone takes one step too many towards me, I take two steps back and thus, bit by bit, he will lose me entirely, all the while believing himself victorious."[41] A confrontation might damage a valuable relationship, so "this manner of fighting rather sweetly in retreat" offers the "surest" path to a satisfactory compromise.[42] Besides offering a fresh perspective on romantic entanglements, this passage offers a response to the "aleatory" interpretation of encountering. The author's tactical retreat is an alternative to "playing double or nothing" with one violent confrontation, ending either in an intimate relationship or a definitive break.[43] In the game of love, nothing can be left to chance: both results are too risky for this author. The analogy between romance and reading alluded to in the previous section looms behind this *pensée*. The author may not be able to control who encounters her, either in flirtatious conversation or in reading her words, but she intends to mediate how they do so. It is this act of mediation that explains the bizarre structure of the book.

Les Pensées errantes initially left reviewers perplexed, which I believe was precisely the intention, but curiosity in the author's identity soon won out. In 1806, Antoine-Alexandre Barbier credited a then-unknown woman named Bonne-Charlotte Bénouville with the book.[44] For the following two centuries, this attribution was left unquestioned. Then, just a decade ago, Mathilde Chollet demonstrated that the text was almost entirely copied from the personal diaries of another unknown woman, Henriette de Marans. The *pensées* were recorded day by day as her private reflections.[45] The book's central feint is therefore quite sincere: the notes from her diaries are framed as endnotes for a history of Narsam, and "Narsam is none other than myself." "Narsam" is also an anagram of Marans, a hidden jibe at how readers tended to conflate women writers with their protagonists in the *bijoux indiscrets*-manner.

While the revelation of the author's identity offers important insights for the historian, it is crucial that we remember how the book's structure sought to mediate our encounter with its author. My own notes on the text reflect this. I initially followed the Bénouville attribution, before learning of Chollet's research on Marans. Revising my notes was not simply a matter of using the "find and replace" function in my word processor to correct the name. I wrote up an abridged biography of Marans, compared it to Bénouville's, and then reassessed the main themes of the book through this new information.

It is only in the years since that I have tried to imagine the book as it was in 1758. Setting aside Chollet's valuable insights into Marans—as I have attempted to do for you by concealing her name until this final section—allowed me to attend more directly to her care in formulating the book. Her gender and voice are never concealed, but any attempt to access her identity is nevertheless deflected. For each step I take towards her, she takes two away from me. If we read the text's structure as rejecting a particular kind of encounter through reading, we learn something about the position of eighteenth-century French women writers that no biographical analysis alone could reveal. Marans' text shows us that she recognized how gender scripted encounters with women's writing. Rather than confronting this tendency in a risky battle, she loses the reader in tactical retreats, playing with the form to reject (as much as possible) this kind of encountering. In doing so, she asserts her right to be encountered on her own terms.

As a historian, I have been trained to read texts through what I can discover about their author and their context. This way of encountering historical figures is not reducible to seeking out a magic ring, nor does it entail denying women writers originality, as eighteenth-century understandings of *génie* might have it. Nevertheless, it scripts our encounters before they occur. With Althusser, we might note that the causes and the effects of such an encounter remain aleatory, but the range of possibilities is always already restricted. *Les Pensées errantes* offers an example of how one author sought to mediate encounters with herself, and in doing so, makes visible and implicitly critiques the assumptions behind these would-be encounters. As one reviewer wrote of her choice to call herself "Mme. ***," "it is, in some way, to resemble the Gods who, hidden from our eyes behind the stars [asterisks], are content with making themselves known through their marvels."[46] We may reach behind the stars, but we should never allow that knowledge to obscure their brilliance.

Notes

1 Henriette de Marans, *Les Pensées errantes; avec quelques Lettres d'un Indien* ([Paris]: Hardy, 1758), 1. All translations mine unless otherwise noted.
2 Friedrich Melchior Grimm, review of *Les Pensées errantes; avec quelques Lettres d'un Indien*, by [Henriette de Marans], ed. Henri Duranton, *Correspondance Littéraire* 5 (July 15, 1758): 115.

3 Marans, *Les Pensées errantes*, e.g. 53–5, 121–3, 168–73.
4 See Christie McDonald's chapter "Le dix-huitième siècle: 1715–1793," in *Femmes et littérature: Une histoire culturelle*, vol. 1, *Moyen Âge–XIII siècle*, ed. Martine Reid (Paris: Gallimard, 2020), 717–944.
5 Robert Niklaus, "Les 'Pensées Philosophiques' de Diderot et les 'Pensées' de Pascal," *Diderot Studies* 20 (1981): 201–17.
6 [Élisabeth] Guibert, *Pensées détachées de Mme Guibert* (Bruxelles: Couturier fils, 1771); Mme de Damas, *Pensées morales* ([Paris]: Desenne, 1799).
7 Antoinette Sol, "'Se repandre en paroles': Notions of Identity in Mme de Bénouville's *Pensées Errantes*," *Intertexts* 4, no. 2 (Fall 2000): 130.
8 Marans, *Les pensées errantes*, 8.
9 Marans, 164–7.
10 Sol, "'Se repandre en paroles,'" 136.
11 Marans, *Les pensées errantes*, 212.
12 Élie-Catherine Fréron, review of *Les Pensées errantes; avec quelques Lettres d'un Indien*, by [Henriette de Marans], *Année Littéraire*, July 15, 1758, 210.
13 Louis Jaucourt, "Ouvrage [Arts | Science]," in *Encyclopédie, ou dictionnaire raisonné des sciences, des arts et des métiers, etc.*, ed. Denis Diderot and Jean le Rond d'Alembert (University of Chicago: ARTFL Encyclopédie Project, December 1765), 11:722, see http://encyclopedie.uchicago.edu/. Translation mine.
14 Denis Diderot and Jean le Rond d'Alembert, eds., "Livre [Littérature]," in *Encyclopédie, ou dictionnaire raisonné des sciences, des arts et des métiers, etc.* (University of Chicago: ARTFL Encyclopédie Project, December 1765), 9:609–10, http://encyclopedie.uchicago.edu/. Translation mine.
15 Jaucourt, "Ouvrage," 722. Translation mine.
16 Roland Barthes, "The Death of the Author," in *Image, Music, Text*, trans. Stephen Heath (London: Fontana Press, 1977), 146.
17 Louis Althusser, "The Underground Current of the Materialism of the Encounter," in *Philosophy of the Encounter: Later Writings, 1978–87*, ed. Olivier Corpet and François Matheron, trans. G. M. Goshgarian (London: Verso, 2006), 168–9, cited in the Introduction to the present volume by Jérôme Brillaud and Virginie Greene, 6.
18 Althusser, 169.
19 Althusser, 193.
20 DeJean, *Tender Geographies: Women and the Origins of the Novel in France* (New York: Columbia University Press, 1991), 4.
21 Joan Hinde Stewart, *Gynographs: French Novels by Women of the Late Eighteenth Century* (Lincoln: University of Nebraska Press, 1993), 5–6.
22 Louise d'Épinay, review of *Les Confidences d'une jolie femme*, by Mademoiselle d'Albert, ed. Denis Diderot et al., *Correspondance littéraire, philosophique et critique* 8 (January 1775): 439–42. See also McDonald's "Le dix-huitième siècle" in *Femmes et littérature*, footnote on 781–2.
23 Isabelle Brouard-Arends, "Lambert, Anne-Thérèse Marguenat de Courcelles, marquise de (1647–1733)," in *Dictionnaire des femmes des Lumières*, ed. Huguette Krief and Valérie André (Paris: Honoré Champion éditeur, 2015), 673.
24 McDonald, "Le dix-huitième siècle," in *Femmes et littérature*, 727–33, 853–4.
25 McDonald, 727–33.
26 Marans, *Les pensées errantes*, 53.
27 Olympe de Gouges, "Pronostic sur Maximilien Robespierre, par un animal amphibie," 1792, 9.4.155, Les archives de la Révolution française, Bibliothèque nationale de France, https://catalogue.bnf.fr/ark:/12148/cb37236069q.

28 The case of Anne-Marguerite Du Noyer demonstrates both uses. During her first years writing and publishing the *Quintessence des Nouvelles* (1711–19), she pretended to be a man, only later revealing her name. Then, after her death in 1719, the male editors who succeeded her adopted the persona of a young female editor. See Suzanna van Dijk, *Traces de femmes: présences féminines dans le journalisme français du XVIIIe siècle* (Amsterdam: APA-Holland University Press, 1998), 81–131, esp. 120–7.
29 DeJean, *Tender Geographies*, 3.
30 Sol, "'Se repandre en paroles,'" 135.
31 [Jean-Charles de la Louptière], review of *Les Pensées errantes; avec quelques Lettres d'un Indien*, by [Henriette de Marans], *Journal des Dames* 1 (May 1761): 179.
32 McDonald, "Le dix-huitième siècle," in *Femmes et littérature*, 755–65.
33 Denis Diderot, *Les bijoux indiscrets*, 2 vols. ([Paris]: [Durand], 1748), http://gallica.bnf.fr/ark:/12148/btv1b8613354b.
34 Most famously, in Michel Foucault, *The History of Sexuality*, vol. 1, *The Will to Knowledge*, trans. Robert Hurley (New York: Vintage Books, 1988).
35 Nancy K. Miller, *French Dressing: Women, Men, and Ancien Régime Fiction* (New York: Routledge, 1995), 3–6.
36 Linda Williams, *Hard Core: Power, Pleasure, and the "Frenzy of the Visible"* (Berkeley: University of California Press, 1989), 1–3.
37 For more information on Aïssé, see Benedetta Craveri, "Preface," in *Lettres à Madame C*, by [Charlotte-Élisabeth] Aïssé (Paris: Payot & Rivages, 2009), 5–25. For other examples, see Charles-Augustin Sainte-Beuve, "Mademoiselle Aïssé," in *Lettres de Mademoiselle Aissé à Madame Calandrini*, by Charlotte-Élisabeth Aïssé, ed. Jules Ravenel, (Paris: Gerdès, 1846), 3–61; Henri Courteault, *Mademoiselle Aïssé, le chevalier d'Aydie et leur fille* (Paris: Société des bibliophiles françois, 1908).
38 Charlotte-Élisabeth Aïssé, *Lettres de Mademoiselle Aïssé à Madame C . . .* (Paris: La Grange, 1787), iii. This "Avis de l'éditeur" appears at the beginning or at the end of the book in different versions, but the pagination is the same.
39 Claude-Joseph Dorat, "Extrait des Mémoires du comte de Comminges," in *Lettres en vers et oeuvres mêlées* (Paris: S. Jorry, 1767), 38, https://gallica.bnf.fr/ark:/12148/btv1b8617174n. Translation mine.
40 Marans, *Les pensées errantes*, frontispiece. The quote is from Phaedrus' *Fables*, book IV.
41 Marans, 54.
42 Marans, 54.
43 Marans, 54.
44 Antoine-Alexandre Barbier, *Dictionnaire des ouvrages anonymes et pseudonymes composes, traduits ou publiés en français, avec les noms des auteurs, traducteurs et éditeurs; accompagné de notes historiques et critiques* (Paris: Imprimerie Bibliographique, 1806), 3:207, see http://books.google.com/books?id=peRRAAAAcAAJ.
45 Mathilde Chollet, "Une ambition féminine au siècle des Lumières: éducation et culture au château: les journaux de Mme de Marans (1719–1784)" (doctoral thesis, Université du Maine, 2014), 178–9, 187–90. Chollet and Krief argue that the work may have been a collaboration between Bénouville and Marans, with the former writing the final epistolary novel as a response to Marans' *pensées*, in Mathilde Chollet and Huguette Krief, eds., *Une femme d'encre et de papier à l'époque des Lumières: Henriette de Marans (1719–1784)* (Rennes: Presses universitaires de Rennes, 2017), 99–102.
46 [Louptière], "Les Pensées errantes; avec quelques Lettres d'un Indien," 178.

Chapter 7

ENCOUNTERING WOMEN WRITERS AND THEIR TEXTS:

LOUISE DE KERALIO'S PIONEERING ANTHOLOGY

Vicki Mistacco, Wellesley College

Louise de Keralio's *Collection des meilleurs ouvrages français composés par des femmes, dédiée aux femmes françaises* (Collection of the Best French Works Composed by Women, Dedicated to French Women, 1786–1789, twelve volumes)[1] marks a radical break with traditions then governing readers' encounters with women writers and their texts: namely, the exemplary women worthies tradition going back to the Middle Ages and Christine de Pizan[2] and the tradition of fragmented ahistorical galleries or alphabetical dictionaries illustrated in the eighteenth century by male compilers, such as La Porte, La Croix, and Billardon de Sauvigny.[3] Keralio brings together image and text, male and female writers, celebration and erudite history in an attempt to forge a new cultural narrative that would take account of women writers and bring about a more inclusive sense of national identity or, in her terms, "le génie national" (the genius of the nation).

In this assessment, I am in complete disagreement with Carla Hesse, who dismisses the *Collection* as "not especially innovative," as merely a continuation of the women worthies or *femmes fortes* tradition that she dates to the Renaissance, and as just another example of "separatist" as opposed to "integrationist" feminism. "Although the work is organized chronologically," she concludes, "it retains the structure of a series of timeless exemplary portraits, offered as models to the women writers of her own age."[4] In my view, this appraisal, which Hesse has repeated in a number of publications, is both unjustified and surprising.

Keralio's *Collection* is the first true anthology of French women's writing composed by a woman. An important distinction must be made between compilations, such as biographical dictionaries (La Croix, *Dictionnaire historique portatif des femmes célèbres* [Portable Historical Dictionary of Celebrated Women]; Briquet, *Dictionnaire historique, littéraire et bibliographique des Françaises* [Historical, Literary and Bibliographical Dictionary of French Women], 1804) or sketches of women writers (Ann Ford Thicknesse, *Sketches of the Lives and Writings of the Ladies of France*, 1780–1781), which may incorporate brief quotations from their works, and compilations which present whole works or substantial selections from them, sparing the reader the need to search for them elsewhere. When I use the term *anthology*, I am referring to the latter type of compilation, that is, to an anthology of women's *literature*. By this standard, earlier compilations by women, such as Marguerite Buffet's *Nouvelles observations sur la langue française, avec l'éloge des illustres savantes tant anciennes que modernes* (New Observations on the French Language with a Eulogy to Illustrious Learned Women, Both Ancient and Modern, 1668) and Jacquette Guillaume's *Les dames illustres* (Illustrious Ladies, 1665) do not qualify.

Unlike previous compilers, Keralio proposes a serious history of the development of French literature in which women's contributions would be foregrounded and contextualized:

> The intention to raise a monument to the glory of French women distinguished in literature, led me naturally to examine the state of letters in France, in each of the centuries where I noticed the name of one or several learned women; it would have meant raising them or lowering them all to the same level, if I had neglected to make important remarks on the times in which they lived, the impression their mind must have received from the genius of the nation (*le génie national*), from prejudices of the moment, from the progress around them of science and the arts. [...] It seemed to me that a general picture [...] would be clearer, more precise and more useful than disconnected observations [...].[5]

Women's literary history would be embedded in literary and cultural history *tout court*; it would be part of an emerging grand narrative of Frenchness and would avoid becoming, as in the women worthies and dictionary traditions, "remarks lacking in coherence and cohesion, unlikely to become engraved in the memory of readers, especially that of women and young ladies."[6] Keralio is not presenting timeless exemplars or sketchy alphabetical entries. She is experimenting with a new historiography designed to counter the fragmentation of knowledge still prevalent during the Enlightenment.[7]

Keralio's project was ambitious to say the least: in thirty-six volumes of four to five hundred pages each, issued to subscribers at the rate of two a month, she will bring together first, *selections* from distinguished works by the most celebrated women of the nation,[8] from Heloise to Madeleine de Scudéry. These will include writings, such as Christine de Pizan's *La Cité des Dames* (The City of Ladies), as yet found only in manuscripts. Keralio is in fact the first known woman critic of Christine and her first major anthologist, devoting nearly five hundred pages to her works.[9] After Scudéry will come an impressive, amazingly prescient, collection of often *complete* works by women working in all genres, including history and philosophy:

> one shall see published the *complete works* of Madame de Motteville, of Mademoiselle de Montpensier, of Madame de Villars, of Ninon de Lenclos, of

Madame de Sévigné, of Madame and Mademoiselle Deshoulières, of Madame de la Fayette, of Madame de Villedieu, a poem by Mademoiselle Cheron, a few pieces by Mademoiselle de la Vigne and Mademoiselle Descartes, by Madame Daulnoy, by Mademoiselle de la Force, by Madame de Saint-Onge, by Mademoiselle Bernard, by Mademoiselle de Lussan, by Madame de Murat, by Madame de Gomez, by Madame de Villeneuve, by Mademoiselle de Lubert, by Mademoiselle Fauques, &c. The best plays by Mademoiselle Barbier and by Madame de Graffigny; the poems of Madame de Montégut of Toulouse, the works of Madame Dacier, of Madame du Châtelet, &c.[10]

She never finished the project. Its sheer magnitude, financial difficulties and the onset of the Revolution brought it to a halt. At the brink of exhaustion, unable to keep up the rhythm of two volumes a month, she apologizes to subscribers: "Obliged to pursue two works at once, which each demand long and arduous research, I was unable to meet the precise commitments that I had made to the public regarding the timetable for delivering this Collection, whose first volumes require almost as much work as the *Histoire d'Élisabeth*" (History of Elizabeth); "The Author's health was gravely affected by the continuous labor required of her by two works, for the perfection of which she could not overdo her research. She was compelled to suspend it completely; this forced inactivity has delayed delivery of this collection [...]. Once rest has restored her strength, she expects to give herself over with new zeal to works that can please and be of use to her country."[11] The publication of the last known volumes, V and VI, was announced in the *Journal de la librairie* (Book Trade Newspaper) on 11 July 1789, just three days before the fall of the Bastille. The misogyny that would soon come to dominate revolutionary politics created an unpropitious climate for the continuation of a project such as Keralio's, intended to highlight women's achievements in the public sphere.[12]

Here is what we have. Following an abridged history of the state of letters in Gaul, volume I (1786) introduces the letters of Heloise. Christine de Pizan occupies three quarters of volume II and spills over into volume III (both 1787) which continues with the sixteenth century and the writings of Marguerite de Navarre. Volume IV (1787) is devoted to major sixteenth-century writers including Louise Labé, Hélisenne de Crenne, and Marguerite de Valois, and a cascade of lesser known figures. In the early prospectus at the Bibliothèque de l'Arsenal, she says she will include in her anthology "a few others whose remaining works were only printed once, scarcely read since, and perhaps unjustly forgotten."[13] Her collection implies a discriminating point of view and selection, but she occasionally gives in to the encyclopedic tendencies of her era (see, for example, IV:184).[14] From Volume IV, Keralio jumps to volumes IX through XIV (1787-1788) in which she reproduces, with only a brief introduction, the entire 1754 edition of the letters of Sévigné. She picks up in 1789 with volumes V and VI which take us through the rest of the Renaissance up through early seventeenth-century theater, via a long section on Scudéry. As Joan DeJean wrote two hundred years later, "had Keralio completed her anthology, she would have provided an alternative history of French literature until the Revolution, a narrative demonstrating the deficiency of any French literary history that omits the contributions of women to every period."[15]

We can already glean from the frontispiece to the first volume [figure 7.1], which she commissioned from a well-known artist and foremost book illustrator, Le Barbier the elder, how her approach differs from that of previous compilers of women writers and "women worthies," both male and female. At first glance, it looks as if this will indeed be another "women worthies" compilation, down to the evident intent to produce a beautiful book worthy of bibliophiles. We have the discrete elements characteristic of that format in the form of medallions on the column portraying individual women writers. The commemorative column stands as a visual analog of Keralio's *written* monument to the glory of distinguished French women writers. The laurel garland reinforces the idea of glory as does the quotation from Ariosto inscribed below. The winged figure with a quill writing on a great scroll appears to be a stand-in for the compiler herself. The Gothic architecture in the background may refer to the past she will exhume or perhaps the era that was the source of her inspiration. Inspiration is suggested by the billowing vapors. With her right hand, she points to the medallion portraying Christine de Pizan. Of all the books, folio volumes and scrolls in this image, only one, borne by a putto in the lower left, bears a title: *La Cité des dames*. Its author Christine de Pizan, then, figures as a precursor.[16] She too was a compiler of illustrious women and their deeds; she too sought to build a permanent monument to their glory, a citadel that would forever protect them from misogynist calumny.

However, if we take into account allegorical personifications first illustrated in Cesare Ripa's 1603 handbook, *Iconologia* (Iconology), and still prevalent in the late eighteenth century, a closer look at the winged figure discloses Keralio's difference from the tradition of women worthies epitomized by Christine. For the winged woman writing is not just a writer celebrating women but, for the eighteenth-century viewer, a familiar personification of History writing in the book of history [figure 7.2, Trajan's Column; figure 7.3, Ripa *Iconologia* 1709].[17] Thus, the frontispiece represents Keralio's *new* approach to women's literary history: the inscription of the memory of individual French women writers into a *continuous* historical narrative recounting the move toward Enlightenment and the progress of French culture toward the perfect realization of its *génie national*. Books coexist in the image with the visual arts as related signifiers of culture. Throughout the anthology, in text and illustrations, progress toward Enlightenment is traced by metaphors of light. Here the quotation from Ariosto's *Orlando furioso* (1532)– literally translated, "From their beautiful and glorious works a great light has spread throughout the world"–and the flames on the heads of the putti, symbolizing intellect,[18] reinforce the theme of women's contributions to Enlightenment by means of their written words. In Ripa's iconography, History looks backward to the past as she writes. Here she looks to the medieval figure of Christine de Pizan, who, in her own as yet imperfect way given the time in which she wrote, also tried to build her city, that is her book, on a bedrock of history. In the words of Keralio, "The only valid idea presented by the construction of the City of Ladies, is to lay its foundations on those of history."[19]

As in the Ripa prototype, History rests her foot on stone, "for history must always have a firm foundation, be based on facts, the truth, and be written with objectivity."[20] Keralio's role models for writing history are first and foremost the Benedictine monks of Saint-Maur who in their *Histoire littéraire de la France* (Literary History of France, 1733–1763) had implemented a new method for discovering historical truth grounded in archival research. It entailed the patient accumulation and scientific study of original manuscript documents and the critique of these authentic historical records based on reason. So detailed and exhaustive was their research that in the twelve volumes they completed, beginning in pre-Christian times, they only managed to reach the year 1167. Keralio acknowledges her debt to the work of "the learned and tireless authors of the *Histoire littéraire de la France*" in her abundant footnotes and in the preface, where they come first in a long list of erudite sources, mostly historical and, understandably, all male.[21] And she details her own forays into the archives to unearth original documents preserving artistic traces of the past "in the manuscripts in the king's library, in that of Saint-Germain-des-Prés"—this was the locus of the Benedictines of Saint-Maur—"of M. le Marquis de Paulmy, and in all those holding manuscripts of medieval centuries, and even of the sixteenth century."[22] If she places such emphasis on *inédits* (unpublished works) or original sources, if she gives such meticulous scholarly references,[23] and if, for example, she weighs at great length the documentary evidence for and against the existence of Clémence Isaure, the putative founder in the Middle Ages of the famous *Jeux floraux* (Floral Games) competition and thereby the supposed female patron of the entire French poetic tradition, it is precisely to legitimize her own literary history as conforming to the rigorous historical principles set forth by the Benedictines of Saint-Maur. In *De re diplomatica* (1681), considered the founding work of diplomatics and Latin paleography, Jean Mabillon, a Benedictine of the Congregation of Saint-Maur, had established the method for the scientific analysis of historical documents that would become the model for all types of historical inquiry.

> The existence of the foundation of these games no longer seems to be a problem, and we believe we must prefer to that of a single historian the authority of the learned authors of the general history of Languedoc, who gave this work the merit of *proof founded on the most authentic acts and titles*. It is difficult to believe after them authors who present themselves with no other authority than their opinion, and who, although not lacking in merit for their time, did not then recognize enough *the need for order and reason in establishing every type of historical fact.*[24]

In this, one of many scholarly controversies she addresses in the *Collection*, Keralio's reliable source is *Abrégé de l'histoire générale de Languedoc* (Abridged General History of Languedoc) by the Benedictine monks Joseph Vaissette and Claude Devic of the Congregation of Saint-Maur (1749). Like the *Histoire littéraire de la France*, it assembles an abundance of original documents which it subjects to an exacting critique. This lengthy development about Clémence Isaure and the

Jeux floraux in volume II is essential for understanding Keralio's historical reasoning and methodology: she looks for proof in "authentic" primary sources, archives, legal documents, etc., and then applies reason and logic to tease out the historical truth. She confronts a range of sources and opinions. In the end, regarding Clémence Isaure, she turns the documentary evidence adduced by one authority (Guillaume Catel, *Mémoires sur l'histoire du Languedoc* [Memoirs on the History of Languedoc], 1633) against him, using her own textual analysis and reason to refute his conclusion that Clémence Isaure was merely a fiction (II:91–100). Now she can claim with authority that a woman is at the origin of French poetry. While her erudition is astounding–she seems to have read every available source–she comes, alas, to the wrong conclusion. Clémence Isaure, it turns out, is a mythical figure whose origin rests on an *authentic* 1524 archival document *falsely* proclaiming she had made a legacy to the city of Toulouse that enabled it to restore and perpetuate the *Jeux floraux*. (One possible explanation for this fraud is that city magistrates wanted to avoid taxation on, or scrutiny of, the personal fortunes they used to finance the poetic contest.) From there the legend grew, giving rise to centuries of debates between believers and skeptics.[25] Like other intellectuals of her time, then, Keralio implements the Enlightenment tools of science and reason. Furthermore, like the medieval monks she discusses in this volume, Keralio plays the role of keeper of the archives. She contributes to historical memory by discerning, assembling and copying authentic original texts, preserving for posterity "the source of enlightenment."[26]

Her historical approach calls for a rejection of panegyrical writing. Far from parading before her readers a series of timeless, exemplary women worthies, as Christine de Pizan and other protofeminist precursors had done, Keralio offers impartial, carefully balanced, occasionally even harsh, judgments of women writers. Hers is a clear-eyed "well-considered esteem."[27] As Jean Sgard notes: "she wants to give, in an encyclopedic collection, a history of female genius, a body of knowledge concerning them. By focusing her efforts on women's creativity and their access to culture, she is probably the only one to have intuited the danger of a simple moral idealism."[28] She may be credited today with having recognized the importance of Christine de Pizan and brought her out of oblivion.[29] But, as much as she praises her for her intellect, for her political and moral vision and for her effort to write the history of a monarch when there were no models to follow, she is also quick to point out Christine's flaws as a writer—her "bad verses,"[30] for instance—and as a historian—factual errors and omissions and, precisely, showing only the good side of king Charles V.[31] In her view, not all of Christine's defects can be attributed to the still imperfect state of letters and the French language in the fifteenth century. "Christine was capable of doing better," she concludes at one point,[32] yet elsewhere she rates her *Chemin de longue étude* (The Path of Long Study) above Guillaume de Lorris and Jean de Meun's more celebrated *Roman de la Rose* (Romance of the Rose)[33] and claims that, had she lived during more enlightened times, she would have been "a prodigy among men."[34]

"A prodigy among men": this epithet highlights an important innovation in the *Collection*. Women's writing coexists with men's. Keralio initiates this method of placing women's texts in dialogue with men's with the first woman writer discussed at length, Heloise, whose literary legacy, a correspondence, is by nature dialogic. Keralio comes into her own with the figure of Heloise, breaking free from the rigid, repetitious century-by-century format (*State of Letters in Gaul in the Third Century, State of Letters in France in the Tenth Century ...*) borrowed from the *Histoire littéraire de la France*. With Clémence Isaure, origin and instigator of French poetry, and Christine de Pizan, public intellectual, first woman historian, modest and virtuous defender of women, and alter ego of Keralio,[35] Heloise, in dialogue with, and equal to, her male interlocutor, forms a trio of emblematic women writers whose treatment illustrates the anthologist's original approach to women's literary history. Keralio includes excerpts of Abelard's responses to Heloise's letters. She compares their writing and pronounces on them both: "There is more warmth, more eloquence, and perhaps more passion in Heloise's letter."[36] Throughout her anthology, she devotes extended passages to male authors and their works. To view women's writing in their cultural context, she obviously must also consider the writing of men. True to her historical principles, she judges them with impartiality and a certain revisionist originality: she praises Du Bellay while denigrating Ronsard, she recognizes Villon's genius but compares him unfavorably to Charles d'Orléans and questions his place in literary history.[37] She judges Christine against Charles d'Orléans and finds her diction wanting.[38] In Keralio's anthology, history results from the encounter between literature by women and literature by men and from the clash of multiple viewpoints. To these one should add encounters and clashes between French literature and the literatures of other European cultures. Keralio compares French and English theater and devotes a long note to Elizabeth Montagu's appreciation of Shakespeare.[39] She compares women novelists of France and England to those of other European nations[40] and she discusses the influence of Italian and Spanish theater on that of France.[41] Adopting a cosmopolitan perspective which takes into account different social institutions and other national differences, Keralio fosters a better understanding not only of women's place in the *French* literary tradition but of what constitutes Frenchness itself and the French patrimony.[42]

The benefits of this dialogic method are evident in her treatment of the history of the reign of Henri IV. (In the eighteenth century, history was considered a branch of literature.)[43] Keralio cites many male historians, but she also offers *in extenso* the memoirs of Marguerite de Valois[44] and the history of Henri's loves as told in the memoirs of Louise de Lorraine, Princess of Conti.[45] Ahead of her time, Keralio recognizes the historical value of women's "particular memoirs": "their observations, although devoid of that depth that only men can attain, have at times a finesse that men in turn do not always possess."[46] To create a complete cultural narrative, we need *both* perspectives. In her pioneering anthology, Keralio places women and men on the same footing in a shared cultural context and judges them by the same standards. This is still a radical idea. In the late eighteenth century, Keralio was attempting to write a dialogic history of French literature that has yet to be written in the twenty-first.

Keralio's feminist subtext calls for inclusion of women's literary achievements in the French patrimony. As much as it is a monument to the glory of French women

Figure 7.1 Frontispiece, Louise de Keralio, *Collection des meilleurs ouvrages français composés par des femmes*, vol. I, 1786. FC7.R5406.786c, Houghton Library, Harvard University.

Figure 7.2 Victory, Trajan's Column, Rome (Image © J.C.N. Coulston.) Reproduced with the permission of J.C.N. Coulston.

Figure 7.3 Cesare Ripa, *Iconologia*, ca.1709. Image by Vicki Mistacco. GEN (MS Eng 1188), Houghton Library, Harvard University.

writers, her *Collection des meilleurs ouvrages français composés par des femmes* adumbrates a new literary history and a new cultural narrative: she proposes an *experimental* literary history using the most modern historical methods and distilling from disparate sources a continuous and impartial narrative of women's share in the progress of French letters and in the expression of France's *génie national*. Ultimately, through illuminating encounters between image and text, male and female, French and foreign, she aims for no less than a revision of the French reader's sense of self.

Notes

1 The known volumes are numbered I to XIV, minus volumes VII and VIII which were never composed. I discovered in inventories in legal documents at the Archives nationales and the Archives départementales de Paris (AN MC/ET/X/781; AD de Paris, D4B6, carton 105, doss. 7454 and D4B6 carton 113 doss. 8071) that three more volumes (XV, XVI, XVII) once existed. They seem never to have been distributed and I have found no trace of them either in libraries or bookseller catalogs.
2 Lists or collections of "preuses" (lady worthies) such as we find in Jehan Le Fèvre's *Livre de Leesce* (Book of Gladness, 1380–1387) predate Christine de Pizan's milestone *Livre de la Cité des Dames* (Book of the City of Ladies, 1405). I am grateful to Christine Reno for pointing this out (email, 5 Sept. 2016).
3 In the form of discrete letters about French women writers addressed to an unnamed lady, Joseph de La Porte's *Histoire littéraire des femmes françaises, ou Lettres historiques et critiques* (Literary History of French Women, or Historical and Critical Letters, 1769) continues the gallery-of-famous-women tradition, even though he proceeds chronologically, quotes extensively from their works and claims to be offering women's literary history. The alphabetical entries in Jean-François de La Croix's *Dictionnaire historique portatif des femmes célèbres* (Portable Historical Dictionary of Celebrated Women, 1769) and Edme-Louis Billardon de Sauvigny's portrait gallery with selections, *Le Parnasse des dames* (The Parnassus of Ladies, 1773) are similarly discontinuous and ahistorical. Keralio scarcely acknowledges the existence of these compilations and rarely uses them as sources. By my unofficial count, there is only one reference in her anthology to La Croix, five to La Porte and three to Billardon de Sauvigny ("who had worked before me on a monument honoring women," III:277).
4 *The Other Enlightenment: How French Women Became Modern* (Princeton: Princeton University Press, 2001), 87. I develop my objections to Hesse's view in a forthcoming book on Louise de Keralio.
5 *Collection des meilleurs ouvrages français composés par des femmes, dédiée aux femmes françaises*, (Paris: l'Auteur; Lagrange [vols 5 and 6: l'Auteur; Maradan], 1786–89), I:ix–xi.
6 *Collection*, I:x.
7 Chantal Grell, *L'histoire entre érudition et philosophie: Étude sur la connaissance historique à l'âge des Lumières* (Paris: Presses universitaires de France, 1993), 279–84.
8 *Collection*, "Avis" I:vi.
9 Nadia Margolis, "Modern Editions: Makers of the Christinian Corpus," in *Christine de Pizan: A Casebook*, ed. Barbara K. Altmann and Deborah L. McGrady (New York: Routledge, 2003), 254
10 *Collection*, I:v–vi. Emphasis mine.
11 *Collection*, III:1; "Avis," XI:n.p. A letter reveals just how many demanding projects she was trying to juggle at once: "I had to do forced labor to finish my history of Elizabeth whose last two volumes are finally going to appear at the beginning of next month, to bring to six volumes at the same time my collection of the best works of French women, and to pursue different things unrelated to these occupations. My health has

suffered from it [...]" (letter to Dubois de Fosseux, 7 November 1787). The "different things" included extensive reviews of new books coming out of England for *Le Censeur universel anglais* and the editing and marketing of books by others that she published secretly with Lagrange. Women not being allowed to be publishers, the books only bore the Lagrange imprint.

12 For an overview of this ideological evolution, see Eliane Viennot, *Et la modernité fut masculine: La France, les femmes et le pouvoir 1789-1904* (Paris: Perrin, 2016).

13 Prospectus: *Collection des meilleurs ouvrages français composés par des femmes*, BR-23234, Bibliothèque de l'Arsenal, 2.

14 Although she claims to be collecting the *best* works by women, she nevertheless feels compelled to include in her presentation of seventeenth-century theater the tragedies of Mademoiselle Cosnard and Madame de Saint-Balmont, even though she judges them to be utterly lacking in "genius" for the genre and believes that their works are deservedly forgotten (*Collection*, VI:407, 427-28).

15 Joan DeJean, "Classical Reeducation: Decanonizing the Feminine," in *The Politics of Tradition: Placing Women in French Literature*, ed. Joan DeJean and Nancy K. Miller, spec. issue of *Yale French Studies* 75 (1988), 29.

16 For a discussion of this frontispiece and the central position it accords to Christine de Pizan in a feminocentric literary history and a historiographic tradition in defense of women, see Margarete Zimmermann, "Gedächtnis-Korrekturen: Das literaturgeschichtliche Archiv der Louise-Félicité Guinement de Kéralio" (Memory Corrections: The Literary-historical Archive of Louise-Félicité Guinement de Kéralio), in *Das Schöne im Wirklichen-Das Wirkliche im Schönen*, ed. Anne Amend Söchting, Kirsten Dickhaut, Walburga Hülk, Klaudia Knabel and Gabriele Vickermann (Heidelberg: Universitätsverlag C. Winter, 2002), 523. Although she draws attention to the importance of iconography in the *Collection*, Zimmermann does not further elaborate on the allegorical meaning of the winged woman or explore in any depth other images in the anthology.

17 Ripa's work enjoyed multiple editions and translations and was widely disseminated throughout Europe. "The *Iconologia* became the standard reference work for the representation of allegories, providing examples of how to represent abstract ideas in visual terms" (Edward A. Maser, *Cesare Ripa: Baroque and Rococo Pictorial Imagery. The 1758-60 Hertel Edition of Ripa's "Iconologia" with 200 Engraved Illustrations* [New York: Dover, 1971)], x). It continued to inspire eighteenth-century treatises, such as Jean-Baptiste Boudard's *Iconologie tirée de divers auteurs* (Iconology drawn from Various Authors, 1759) and Charles-Étienne Gaucher's undated *Iconologie, ou Traité de la science des allégories ... en 350 figures gravées d'après les dessins de MM. Gravelot et Cochin, avec les explications relatives à chaque sujet* [par Gaucher] (Iconology, or Treatise on the Science of Allegories ... in 350 Engraved Figures based on the Drawings of MM. Gravelot and Cochin, with Explanations of Each Subject). Ripa's iconography was largely culled from ancient sources such as the representation of Victory in a similar pose on Trajan's column in Rome. Reproductions in prints and books of Domenico Guidi's acclaimed marble group at Versailles, *The Genius of History Writing the Deeds of Louis XIV in the Book of Time* (1677-1686), kept the symbolism current into the eighteenth century (Kevin E. Kandt, *Schlüteriana III: Studies in the Art, Life and Milieu of Andreas Schlüter* [Berlin: Lukas Verlag, 2015], 164-65).

18 Cesare Ripa, in Maser, *Cesare Ripa: Baroque and Rococo Pictorial Imagery*, 154.

19 *Collection*, III:32.

20 Ripa, in Maser, 122.

21 *Collection*, I:xiii. For insights into Keralio's originality with respect to her male sources, see Marie-Ange Croft, "La réception des *Premières oeuvres poétiques* (1581) de Marie de Romieu sous l'Ancien Régime: de Guillaume Colletet à Louise de Kéralio," in *Sciences et littérature, suivi de Fortunes des oeuvres d'Ancien Régime*, ed. Solange Lemaitre-Provost, Esther Ouellet, Marilyne Audet and Lou-Ann Marquis (Paris: Hermann, 2013), 247–51. Croft points out that Keralio was the first to remark a similarity between Marie de Romieu's defense of women, "Brief Discours que l'excellence de la femme surpasse celle de l'homme" (Brief Discourse on the Superiority of Woman over Man), in response to a misogynist satire, and Christine de Pizan's. She notes further that Keralio was the first to stress the feminist aspect of Romieu's poem and the pantheon of Renaissance women that the poet inserts at the end: "which makes of the poem a kind of precursor very close in spirit to her own compilation" (ibid., 250).
22 *Collection*, I:xiv.
23 On the use of annotation in the second half of the eighteenth century by women historians emulating the erudite practice of the Benedictines of Saint-Maur, see Pellegrin, "L'histoire et son annotation. La mise en scène des sources par trois historiennes du XVIIIe siècle: Lussan, Thiroux et Kéralio," in *Les Femmes et l'écriture de l'histoire 1400–1800*, ed. Sylvie Steinberg and Jean-Claude Arnould (Mont Saint-Aignan: Publications des universités de Rouen et du Havre, 2008), 269–95.
24 *Collection*, II:84; emphasis mine.
25 Marie-Louise Couadau, "Clémence Isaure ou l'invention d'un mythe méridional," *Midi: revue de sciences humaines et de littérature de la France du Sud*, no. 2 (Mar. 1987), 48–51; Pierre-Louis Boyer, *Clémence Isaure: Vérités sur une chimère toulousaine* (Biarritz: Atlantica, 2010). Given Clémence Isaure's legendary significance for the French poetic tradition, it is not surprising that Louise d'Alq, the only other woman to compose an anthology of French women's writing prior to the twentieth century, also came down on the side of believers: "It's true they wanted to snatch Clémence Isaure away from us [...], but historians went back to the sources" (*Anthologie féminine* [Paris: Bureaux des Causeries familières, 1893], 25).
26 *Collection*, I:112.
27 Louise de Keralio, *Histoire d'Elisabeth, reine d'Angleterre* (Paris: L'Auteur; Lagrange, 1786–88), IV:347n.
28 "Collections pour dames," in *La Tradition des romans de femmes: XVIIIe–XIXe siècles*, ed. Catherine Mariette-Clot and Damien Zanone (Paris: Champion, 2012), 29.
29 Keralio was capitalizing on renewed interest in Christine thanks to the publications of philologists Boivin (1736) and Sallier (1751) which adopted the rational critical approach of the Maurists (Earl Jeffrey Richards, "The Medieval 'femme auteur' as a Provocation to Literary History: Eighteenth-Century Readers of Christine de Pizan," in *The Reception of Christine de Pizan from the Fifteenth through the Nineteenth Centuries: Visitors to the City*, ed. Glenda K. McLeod [Lewiston: Edwin Mellen Press, 1991], 118; Margolis, "Modern Editions," 255). By way of an introduction to the writer, she reprints the memoirs they had written under the auspices of the philologically-oriented Académie des Inscriptions et Belles-Lettres, of which her father, a historian to whom she attributes her education (*Collection*, I:vii) and passion for history, was also a member. He no doubt facilitated her access to their studies which may have sparked her interest in Christine.
30 *Collection*, II:343.
31 *Collection*, II:212–13. She makes a similar accusation that Christine only named women worthy of praise in *La Cité des Dames* ("One might object to her that she did

not show the opposite traits," III: 48), further proof of her rejection of the women worthies model.
32 *Collection*, II:295.
33 The passage is emblematic for the extremely subtle variations and the attention to cultural context in Keralio's judgment of Christine: "This fiction is rather ingenious for the time in which allegory reigned above all. But one may especially note regarding poetic conceptions, images and choice of subjects, that Christine de Pizan was infinitely superior to Jean de Meun and Lorris. One may compare what one has seen of the romance of the Rose with the selections from *path of long study*, and certainly the advantage will not go to the famous and much celebrated romance" (II:325–26). Objectivity results from this interplay between judgment and context: "It is through the examination of the circumstances and the times that, according to what it was possible for men to do, one may reach a fair assessment of what they did" (I:189).
34 *Collection*, II:128.
35 On Christine de Pizan as a model for Keralio, see Karen Green, *A History of Women's Political Thought in Europe, 1700–1800* (Cambridge: Cambridge UP, 2014), 209.
36 *Collection*, I:395–96.
37 *Collection*, III:173.
38 *Collection*, III:169.
39 *Collection*, III:28–29.
40 *Collection*, V:16–19.
41 *Collection*, VI:345–47.
42 In so doing, she also anticipates the discipline of comparative literature, of which Germaine de Staël's *De la littérature* (On Literature, 1800) would become the first great example.
43 See *Collection* V:456.
44 *Collection*, IV:309–497.
45 *Collection*, V:104–314.
46 *Collection*, V:444.

Chapter 8

CHÂTELET, LAVOISIER, CHARRIÈRE: NEGOTIATING THE BORDERLANDS OF THE REPUBLIC OF LETTERS

Ian Van Wye

Some encounters are personal; others are socially mediated. In this sense, a writer is a representative of something more than a single mind or an individual oeuvre. There is another dimension to consider—that of being a representative of an intellectual tradition, a culture, a language, or a nation. This idea quickly came to the fore in the research I conducted in concert with Christie McDonald. Together, we became interested in how eighteenth-century francophone women writers served as intermediaries in transnational philosophical and scientific debates, especially by way of translation—and in doing so not only represented their own voices, but also cast light on the mores and traditions of other societies, thereby offering an implicit exposé of those of their own.

This hypothesis emerged through a close examination of translations of plays, novels, and scientific and historical texts, as well as of what might be called "reworkings"—loose adaptations, in French, in which ideas, themes, and even plotlines from works in other languages were recast in new molds that were seen as more suitable for women writers. It also emerged through consideration of a larger question: at a time when women played no small role in intellectual culture, could it really be true that they left little in the way of written records of their accomplishments, as one common story goes?

To a large degree, the fact that this question has to be posed at all is the result of a historical sleight of hand. Women writers disappeared from the mainstream historical record in the decades following the French Revolution, as a study of revised editions of the bibliographies compiled by Jean-François de la Harpe (1736–1803) and Charles Palissot de Montenoy (1730–1814) reveals. Though still synonymous with an imprecise notion of "progressivism" for many—perhaps because of the titillating tenor of its rhetoric, its impiety, or its radicalism—the Revolution in fact represented a significant setback for women and for women writers in particular. The National Assembly articulated a distinction between active and passive citizenship, the latter being reserved for women and others who were deemed unfit to fully participate in civic life[1]—a distinction redolent of Kant's views on women and servants. As a result, women were even denied intellectual property rights under the revolutionary regime, further signaling their exclusion from the intellectual sphere.[2] In the years following the Terror, Henri Grégoire and other surviving politicians attempted to refashion a semblance of order in the French literary world by establishing a patronage system for writers—one from which women would be excluded.[3]

Palissot himself, in the introduction to the 1803 edition of his bibliography, confessed that he had succumbed to the "seductions of society" when writing the 1770 edition, and that he presently intended to point out which of the writers he had included previously were "Tartuffes"—a name which, in spite of its male connotation, he applied to women as well as men.[4] His targets included Madame de Genlis, guilty of "la manie de juger tout le monde (the bad habit of judging everyone)"; Madame de Graffigny, guilty of being a poor imitation of Fontenelle; and Madame Deshoulières, about whom he wrote, "elle a été soupçonnée, comme la plupart des femmes beaux-esprits de nos jours, d'avoir eu peu de part aux ouvrages qui portent son nom (she was suspected, like many of the *bel-esprit* women of our time, of having little to do with the works that bear her name)."[5] The names of these writers were effaced by way of demotion, singled out as evidence that French literary culture had become decadent, even frivolous.

And yet the work of a different category of women writers has survived: that of women translators, in many cases because their translations and reworkings provided fuel for ongoing intellectual debates. Of particular note, too, was the way in which so many of these women's translations, if not rising to the level of complete reworkings, could be described as low fidelity—that is to say, they were expanded, edited, and redacted, and sometimes even prepared in bad faith, with the aim of drawing attention to the erroneous or absurd nature of the original. In many cases, these women translators' loyalties lay with intellectual movements in France, often led by men with whom they collaborated. Under the aegis of a foreign author's name or ideas, they demonstrated their faithfulness to and enthusiasm for national culture, as well as their faith (however subtly it was conveyed) in their own ideas. More importantly, Christie McDonald and I hypothesized that this tactic served as a means by which women could voice their opinions in philosophical, literary, and scientific debates without facing the censure of male writers, who often disparaged their intellectual abilities even as women hosted so many of the *salons* at which they mingled.

We identified two distinct mechanisms. First, women could choose to translate or adapt one text and not another, giving primacy to perhaps one of several competing voices, thereby conveying an original opinion. Second, women could alter works for a francophone audience, adding explanatory notes and even illustrations, cutting and revising the original text as they saw fit, and in so doing demonstrate their own creativity and erudition—qualities that often found expression in oral culture but which were overlooked on the page. Both mechanisms are particularly salient in the cases of the natural sciences and philosophy—and both fields benefited from the largely overlooked contributions of women in the eighteenth century. Three especially notable writers in this vein are Émilie du Châtelet, Marie-Anne Lavoisier, and Isabelle de Charrière, all of whom translated or reworked significant scientific and philosophical texts with the aim of introducing their ideas to a broader audience. In doing so, they helped to establish the Enlightenment as the age of the encounter.

Émilie du Châtelet

Émilie du Châtelet (1706–49) never lived to see the French Revolution, but she participated in its equally momentous scientific counterpart in the first half of the eighteenth century, all by way of translation. She was in the vanguard of Newtonian physicists in France at a time when most other scientists, virtually all of them men, still gave primacy to the ideas of Descartes. Today, du Châtelet is perhaps most famously associated with Voltaire, with whom she lived and worked as an intellectual collaborator at Cirey.

Before turning to physics she began with economics, translating Mandeville's *Fable of the Bees* around 1735, though this work is infused with a significant amount of her own thinking. Her choice of Mandeville was important in and of itself, too: this translation bolstered Voltaire's own critique of thinkers like Pascal, who denounced luxury, by setting it on firmer social-scientific ground.[6]

Du Châtelet understood herself to be an active participant in such debates; in the introduction to her translation of the *Fable of the Bees,* she refers to translators as "les négocians de la république des lettres (mediators of the republic of letters)."[7] The term "négocians" means something like "merchants" or "intermediaries" in the commercial sense, and carries a further connotation of cleverness. This was the role to which Émilie du Châtelet and many other women writers dedicated their lives: they were the ones who introduced new ideas from abroad to France, who made them accessible in the French intellectual marketplace, and who argued that people needed these ideas—that they had value and that they were an improvement upon the status quo.

In the late 1730s, she also set out to improve upon the work of Voltaire in physics and metaphysics alike. Voltaire had recently published his *Éléments de la philosophie de Newton* (*Elements of the Philosophy of Newton*, 1738), with significant assistance, he conceded, from the more scientifically minded du Châtelet.[8] She, for her part, published an article in the *Journal des savants* in which she noted an error that Voltaire had made in his discussion of mirrors and optics, and in which she posited a clearer distinction between gravitation and attraction.[9] Du Châtelet did, however, praise Voltaire for the care he took in refuting the ideas of Descartes, describing his work as "peut-être le plus grand service que l'on pût rendre à notre nation en fait de Philosophie (perhaps the greatest service that one could render the nation in the field of philosophy)"[10]—a description that du Châtelet may have intended to apply to her own work as well, given that she was engaging with and critiquing Voltaire as an intellectual equal. Indeed, by 1740 she had produced an original treatise of her own, the *Institutions de physique* (*Foundations of Physics*), which was a synthesis of the ideas of Newton and Leibniz.[11] It was in this work that du Châtelet attempted to elucidate the metaphysical implications of this new understanding of the physical sciences, something Voltaire was unable to do in his *Éléments*.[12]

Du Châtelet's crowning accomplishment was her translation of Newton's *Principia*, a project that would consume the last decade of her life. To this day, it remains the only version in French, and a new edition of the translation was issued as recently as 2015. While Newton's ideas had entered circulation in France, they were far from being accepted as common currency—and it was in the midst of this debate that du Châtelet made her most significant contributions to the study of physics, heavily annotating Newton's work and again offering a synthesis of Newtonian and Leibnizian principles.[13] Here, her conception of herself as a "négociant" finds its fullest expression in the crossing of national and disciplinary boundaries in the quest for an improved science of the physical universe.

Du Châtelet gave her manuscript of the *Principia* to the Bibliothèque du Roi (the King's Library) days before her death in 1749, though the first edition was not published until a decade later. The reluctance of even her close collaborators to accept Newtonian principles is at least partly to blame—Alexis Clairaut, who was charged with publishing the translation after du Châtelet's death, refused for some time to embrace Newton's law of universal gravitation.[14] It was not until the arrival of Halley's comet in 1759, predicted in accordance with Newtonian principles by another woman, Nicole-Reine Lepaute, that there was definitive proof that Newton, and by extension du Châtelet, had been right all along.[15]

Voltaire contributed an introduction and an ode dedicated to both Newton and du Châtelet to the translation, which constitutes a remarkable statement on the role of language in science. He deems the author and translator to be "deux prodiges (two prodigies)," but he also notes that du Châtelet's version of the *Principia* is in some ways superior to Newton's: while Voltaire saw Latin as a dead, inflexible language, in vernacular French there existed the possibility of a translator creating a new scientific lexicon for the modern age, one with terminology better suited to the ideas it described.[16] The use of a living language also widened the circulation of the *Principia*, transforming it from a recondite work reserved for scholars into a text that could be encountered by men and women without knowledge of classical languages. In this sense, transnational sources—Newton, Leibniz—became, in the hands of a translator such as du Châtelet, the bedrock of an explicitly Francophone conception of the natural sciences and its role in the French public sphere.

Lavoisier

Du Châtelet is not the only scientist to have furthered a hypothesis by way of translation. Marie-Anne Lavoisier (1758–1836) is not as well-known as her husband Antoine, though their early marriage—Marie-Anne was only thirteen at the time—would paradoxically prove to be a boon to her own scientific knowledge. She was tutored by Antoine Lavoisier's colleague Jean-Baptiste Bucquet, who maintained his own laboratory and taught classes in chemistry.[17] She became an important chronicler of her husband's work, and her writings and drawings were included in the official record of his laboratory.[18] Later, she would discuss advances in chemistry at a scientific salon she held twice a week,[19] and would continue to promote Antoine Lavoisier's work even after he was sentenced to death, most notably by writing the preface to his *Mémoires de physique et de chimie* (*Memoirs of Physics and Chemistry*), which remained unpublished until 1805.[20]

In spite of her prominent social role, she situated her own work very much within the private sphere. Her English-language skills were far superior to those of her husband, and she viewed herself as his personal translator.[21] This was perhaps most true in the case of her 1788 translation of the work of Irish scientist Richard Kirwan, whom Antoine Lavoisier had criticized for his promotion of the theory of phlogiston. This translation, titled *Essai sur le phlogistique, et sur la constitution des acides* (*An Essay on Phlogiston, and on the Constitution of Acids*, 1787), was published unsigned but was nonetheless praised by the Academy of Sciences in Paris.[22] In this case, translation was used as a means of making ideas accessible to critique—Antoine Lavoisier's own work could only be properly understood if the ideas of which he was critical were also made available to the French public. In this case, Marie-Anne Lavoisier played the role of a *négociante* in bad faith, transmitting erroneous ideas across borders with the aim of furthering advances in French chemistry—a philosophy of translation that would later be echoed in John Stuart Mill's defense of free speech in *On Liberty* (1859).

Marie-Anne Lavoisier played the opposite role as well, keeping her husband apprised of less conjectural developments in England, where research into the chemistry of the respiratory gases was being conducted by scientists including Joseph Black and Henry Cavendish. At a time when chemistry experiments increasingly required complex laboratory apparatuses, Marie-Anne's skills as an engraver—she is believed to have studied under Jacques-Louis David—allowed for the transmission not just of ideas but of research practices as well. She made detailed drawings of her husband's ice calorimeter, which allowed for accurate measurements of heat energy, as well as of his efforts to capture and analyze the exhalations of his research subjects.[23]

Later, Marie-Anne Lavoisier would produce signed translations, most notably of Kirwan's *On the Strength of Acids*, and was named as the illustrator of Antoine Lavoisier's *Traité élémentaire de chimie*[24] (*Elements of Chemistry*, 1789). Her translations won her the acclaim of scientists including Marsilio Landriani and Horace Bénédict de Saussure, though she tended to adopt a self-deprecating posture that downplayed her abilities as an original thinker.[25] This was a common theme that emerged in the cases of so many of the women translators encountered during research towards this essay: a tendency to view translation as something less than an act of creation, something more like the work of a disciple. It is difficult to know how to interpret these protestations of unoriginality in the case of translation in particular, though it is likely that they were conditioned by very specific cultural tropes—perhaps written in obeisance to the view, promoted by Rousseau, A. L. Thomas, and Palissot himself, that women were capable of emotional insight but not original intellectual labor. Palissot would note apropos Madame de Sévigné, one of the few women writers of whom he approved, that she wrote with great "sentiment" and "imagination" without "laboring over books."[26] The fact that a translation could successfully be produced by a woman meant that it was, *ipso facto*, a "lower" form of intellectual expression in the eyes of such men—hence Lavoisier's tendency to downplay the importance of her work. It is also possible, of course, to read some amount of irony into such disclaimers.

Charrière

Strict translations were not the only "Trojan horse" used by women writers to convey original arguments. Take, for example, the technique of transcription—whether real or, as in many cases, fictive. It was possible, for instance, to play with the idea of happenstance—what if an epistolary novel were to be stitched together from letters supposedly found in a dusty drawer?

Isabelle de Charrière, née Belle van Zuylen (1740–1805), was born in the Netherlands, wrote in French, and spent much of her life in Switzerland—circumstances that must have at least partly inspired the subject of a 1793 novel she titled *Lettres trouvées dans des portes-feuilles d'émigrés* (*Letters Found in the Portfolios of Émigrés*). Much like translation, the "found letters" genre allows for a distancing of the work from the author, even as the final product is very much an act of original creation—a novel. In some ways, this anonymizing tactic only served to make the reading experience more intimate for those who saw past the formal conceit of the title; the letter, so vital to both intellectual and affective exchange in the eighteenth century, here becomes the author's mode of address to the reader. Charrière herself claimed that there was little difference between her letters and her novels—she highlighted the commonalities of style and noted that she only wrote about topics of interest to her in both cases.[27]

Charrière was far from unique as a practitioner of the epistolary novel, but she would come to experiment with even more radical forms of transcription: original reworkings of philosophical texts, couching their ideas in the more feminine mode of the novel. She was a close friend of Benjamin Constant, and spent the final decade of her life responding to the philosophical writings of Immanuel Kant, which had become increasingly popular in Revolutionary France. Many scholars now recognize that Charrière's 1795 novel *Trois femmes* (*Three Women*) is in fact a response to Kant's 1793 essay, "On the common saying: That may be correct in theory, but it is of no use in practice." Here, Kant set out to defend deontological ethics against its consequentialist detractors, who would later count among their ranks none other than Charrière herself. It was in this essay that Kant actually argued against the autonomy of women,[28] a situation Charrière sought to remedy in *Trois femmes* by offering readers three unmarried female characters, all capable of acting as free moral agents despite the absence of paternal authority.[29]

Furthermore, these protagonists face some of the same dilemmas that Kant posed in his essay—most notably the moral quandary referred to as the *depositum*, in which someone is entrusted with something of value and must decide what to do with it after the original owner has gone missing.³⁰ In contrast to Kant, the moral decisions of these three characters are guided by consequentialist ethics, and Charrière's novel is able to capture what she perceived as the myopic shortcomings of strict Kantianism. In this sense, *Trois femmes* can be seen as a revival of the pre-Revolutionary genre known as the *conte philosophique,* or philosophical tale, exemplified by Voltaire's *Candide.*³¹ It is also an example of a woman writer using the novel—a form uniquely suited to showing rather than telling—to covertly advance an argument by way of literary example. If *Trois femmes* succeeds as a novel qua novel—which it does, as testified to by its availability in English translation and its publication as a mass-market paperback in France— then the very fact of its plausibility necessarily casts doubt on Kant's ideas. It also stands as an example of what it means to encounter Kant in a transnational context, and to situate his ideas in a milieu defined by the particulars of French history—in this case the Revolution, which drove Charrière's characters to Germany (an inverse echo of her reworking of Kant in French), and about which Kant himself hedged (claiming that the king had in fact "abdicated" by summoning a consultative body, the Estates General).³²

Both Charrière's brand of ethics and her novelistic style of writing had fallen out of favor by the time of the Revolution, however. Influenced by Henri Grégoire, the Revolutionary government had settled on Kantianism as a national moral doctrine,³³ and Carla Hesse argues that Charrière's novel is "at every level a searing *cri de coeur* against the emerging cultural vision of the Committee of Public Instruction in Paris."³⁴ For Hesse, Charrière's critique is not purely academic; it is a retelling of Kant's moral fable from the perspective of "outlaws" who have been denied full moral worth, and for this reason she deems Charrière to be one of the early antecedents of Michel Foucault, who would also set out to rewrite Kant in his own essay titled "What is Enlightenment?"³⁵

*

One of the most striking aspects of translation is its explicitly internationalist purview. Each of the texts discussed here represents a transnational encounter by nature of its origins—and such encounters should not be taken for granted, as Antoine Lavoisier's own struggle to gain access to English-language scientific texts reveals. In this sense, Charrière, Lavoisier, and du Châtelet all embody the latter's conception of the "négocian," someone who not only transmits ideas across borders but also tailors them to the audience waiting on the other side. Translation is in this way a comparative act as well, allowing the nation-states of the eighteenth century to take stock of their standing in the global realm of ideas.

Examples of translation and rewriting abound in fields beyond science and philosophy, too: Octavie Guichard translated many of the classics of English literature, including Samuel Johnson's *Rasselas* and David Hume's *History of England.* Madame Riccoboni did the same for English theater, publishing an anthology for French readers in which she revised many of the plays as a means of making them more comprehensible to her audience. As she wrote in the preface to

Le Nouveau Théâtre Anglais (*New English Theatre*): "On ne doit pas s'attendre à une servile exactitude dans cette traduction; en rendant les mots d'un auteur, on ne rend pas toujours sa pensée: souvent même on la change à son désavantage (One should not expect servile exactitude in this translation; in translating the words of an author verbatim, one doesn't always capture his or her meaning—often, one even changes it to the disadvantage [of the original idea])."[36] This statement is in no small part an assertion that women are capable of engaging with the ideas of male authors, and that they can rephrase and thus strengthen their arguments for new audiences.

The research into women writers from which the examples in this essay have been drawn constitutes one of the capstones of Christie McDonald's scholarship, and not by accident. An encounter, at least a fruitful one, requires varying degrees of flexibility, humility, and, above all, ingenuity. The paradigmatic feature of an encounter is perhaps circumlocution (in the positive sense, as the term is used by modern language instructors). The strategies employed by the women writers discussed in this essay are all variants of circumlocution—encounters with foreign texts provided a window of opportunity rather than an impediment to self-expression. The encounter—whether in the *salon* or on the page—was an essential part of intellectual culture as experienced and promoted by women in the eighteenth century.

Above all, the stories of these three women writers should serve as encouragement to scrutinize the ways in which we construct the past. To simply lump these writers into the category of "overlooked luminaries" is to do them and the historical record a disservice. Thinkers on the order of Émilie du Châtelet, Marie-Anne Lavoisier, and Isabelle de Charrière were anything but ignored or overshadowed in their own time. As women, they faced unique challenges, as their biographies reveal. And yet they also managed to make names for themselves, in spite of the hostility that sometimes greeted them in their respective fields. They belong in a category of study that transcends the dichotomy of famous and obscure, one that seeks to understand why certain writers were actively suppressed through an examination of politics, gender, and canon formation. Appreciating these individuals is not so much a matter of rediscovering them as it is one of removing the clouded spectacles that prevented us from seeing them all along. In doing so, we can come to better understand how the intellectual encounters that these women writers enabled live on in a larger history of ideas extending unto the present.

Notes

1 Joan Scott, *Only Paradoxes to Offer: French Feminists and the Rights of Man* (Cambridge: Harvard UP, 1996), 34–35
2 Scott, 37.
3 Jean-Luc Chappey, "Canonisation littéraire et remise en ordre politique et sociale entre révolution et empire," *Revue d'histoire littéraire de la France* 114, no. 1 (2014): 18–19.
4 Charles Palissot de Montenoy, *Mémoires pour servir à l'histoire de notre littérature* (Paris: L'Imprimerie de Crapelet, 1803), iii–vii. All translations mine unless otherwise noted.

5   Palissot, *Mémoires*, 355, 371, 247–8.
6   Felicia Gottman, "Du Châtelet, Voltaire, and the Transformation of Mandeville's Fable," *History of European Ideas* 38, no. 2 (2012): 219–20.
7   Gottman, 220.
8   Linda Gardiner Janik, "Searching for the Metaphysics of Science: the Structure and Composition of Madame Du Châtelet's *Institutions de physique*, 1737–1740," *Studies on Voltaire and the Eighteenth Century* 201 (1982): 87–8.
9   Émilie du Châtelet, "Lettre sur les elemens de la philosophie de Newton," *Journal des sçavans* (September 1738): 537–40.
10 Du Châtelet, 535.
11 Keiko Kawashima, *Émilie du Châtelet et Marie-Anne Lavoisier : Science et genre au XVIII Siècle*, trans. Ayako Lécaille-Okamura (Paris: Honoré Champion, 2013), 140–3.
12 Gardiner Janik, 88.
13 Isaac Newton, *Principes mathématiques de la philosophie naturelle, tome I*, trans. Émilie du Châtelet, ed. Michel Toulmonde (Paris: Amalivre, 2015), 20–3.
14 Newton, 40.
15 Newton, 40.
16 Newton, 57–9.
17 John B. West, "The Collaboration of Antoine and Marie-Anne Lavoisier and the First Measurements of Human Oxygen Consumption," *The American Journal of Physiology, Lung Cellular and Molecular Physiology* 305, no. 11 (2013): L778.
18 Jacques G. Ruelland, "Marie-Anne Pierrette Paulze-Lavoisier, Comtesse de Rumford (1758–1836): Lumière surgie de l'ombre," *Dix-Huitième Siècle* 36 (2004): 103.
19 Ruelland, 103.
20 Ruelland, 108.
21 Keiko Kawashima, "Women's Translations of Scientific Texts in the 18th Century: A Case Study of Marie-Anne Lavoisier," *Historia Scientiarum* 21, no. 2 (2011): 128.
22 Kawashima, 131.
23 West, "The Collaboration of Antoine and Marie-Anne Lavoisier," L777–81.
24 Kawashima, "Women's Translations of Scientific Texts," 132.
25 Kawashima, 132–3.
26 Palissot, *Mémoires*, 360.
27 Susan Van Dijk, "Les topoï 'féminins' dans des fictions épistolaires et des correspondances véritables: Mesdames de Graffigny, Riccoboni et Charrière," in *L'épistolaire au féminin: Correspondances de femmes (XIIIe–XXe siècles)*, ed. Brigitte Diaz and Jürgen Siess (Caen: Presses Universitaires de Caen, 2006), 40.
28 Carla Hesse, "Kant, Foucault, and *Three Women*," in *Foucault and the Writing of History*, ed. Jan Goldstein (Cambridge, MA: Blackwell, 1994), 91–2.
29 Judith Still, "Isabelle de Charrière's *Three Women*—Adopting and Adapting Hospitality After Kant," *German Life and Letters* 64, no. 1 (2011): 28–9.
30 Still, 24–8.
31 Hesse, "Kant, Foucault, and *Three Women*," in Goldstein, *Foucault and the Writing of History*, 90.
32 Reidar Maliks, "Was the French Revolution Really a Revolution?," *Oxford University Press Blog*, July 14, 2015, see https://blog.oup.com/2015/07/french-revolution-bastille/.
33 Hesse, "Kant, Foucault, and *Three Women*," in Goldstein, *Foucault and the Writing of History*, 88–9.
34 Hesse, 90.
35 Hesse, 85.

36 Madame Riccoboni, *Le Nouveau Théâtre Anglois* (Paris: Humblot, (1769)), vol. 1, x–xi, cited in Marianne Charrier-Vozel, "Mme. Riccoboni, traductrice de Hugh Kelly," in *La traduction des genres non romanesques au XVIIIe siècle: actes du colloque international tenu à Metz les 14–15 mars 2003*, eds. Annie Cointre and Annie Rivara (Metz: Centre d'études de la traduction, 2003), 187. Translation mine.

Chapter 9

WOMEN'S FICTIONS AND TRANSLATIONS IN SUPPORT OF ENLIGHTENMENT VALUES

Monique Moser-Verrey

During the eighteenth century both in France and in Europe, the values brought forth by the Enlightenment were embraced by a much larger part of the reading public than is traditionally acknowledged by historians of philosophy and literature. The political battles between the *philosophes* and the so-called *antiphilosophes* are a distraction hiding the general progress of science and rationality. Looking back on half a century of scholarship in French and comparative literature, I will show how women researchers progressively uncovered forgotten and even hidden contributions of emancipated women writers whose works were published in the years preceding the French Revolution. This research interest, which intersects with Women's Studies, is of course much broader than the case study offered here. I intend to highlight the itinerary that led Christie McDonald and I from close readings of dialogue in French philosophical novels, tales, and drama to broader scopes—including global studies as well as the impact of book trade and translation on the progress of Enlightenment values across Europe.

Although the dominant approach to literary texts in general and to dialogue in particular was inspired by structuralism in linguistics and in the social sciences, the work Christie McDonald and I did on Denis Diderot (1713–84) in the 1970s transcended pure formalist and ideological studies; it uncovered philosophical lessons on the conditions of possibility of communication or readability, as it were.[1] As my work was inspired by Paul de Man's teaching at the University of Zurich,[2] I proposed to understand the very ambiguous relationship between Jacques (or "James") and his Master in Diderot's novel *Jacques le fataliste et son maître* (*James the Fatalist and his Master*, 1796)[3] as an allegorical representation of the difficulties that constantly defeat successful communication while maintaining the interdependence of another conversing couple—namely, that of the narrator and his reader. As Diderot's explicit narrator puts it: "James and his Master ... are good for nothing when separated, like Don Quixote and Sancho, and Richardet and Ferragus."[4] This allusion to Cervantes's novel and Ariosto's epic poem links the present story to the chivalric romance and its parodies where no encounter is more important than that of a desirable woman. The sexual aspect, rather than the ideal, of this encounter is precisely what intrigues James' Master. By holding off on retelling the story of his first experiences, James manages to lead his Master wherever he wants during their ongoing journey. In this novel, no power struggle fully establishes a reversal of the social hierarchy between master and slave (as in Hegel's dialectic), but the give-and-take of dialogue prevails.

Inspired by Derrida's reading of Rousseau,[5] Christie McDonald chooses to juxtapose the study of dialogue and the study of utopia because both seem to raise the question of intersubjectivity. McDonald sees intersubjectivity as a movement between the same and the other which defeats the presuppositions of logocentrism by questioning the pursuit of a unifying origin. James' fatalism provides such an origin by pointing to a first inscription of everything on the famous big scroll in which he believes. However, the encounter of Europeans with eloquent Tahitians in Diderot's *Supplement to Bougainville's Voyage* (1771 or 1772)[6] opens up the discourse to very different horizons. McDonald's analysis of the various dialogues offered by Diderot in his *Supplement* proves how productive the interdisciplinary encounter by which she begins this essay can become in literary criticism. But the English version of her insightful study does not include the references to Derrida we find in her original French article.[7] Indeed, the book version of her work on dialogue and writing presents the discussion of *De la grammatologie* (*Of Grammatology*, 1967) in a separate chapter that includes Paul de Man's dialogue with Jacques Derrida concerning Rousseau's texts.[8]

The word *supplément* is intriguing both in Diderot's and in Derrida's texts. The full subtitle of Diderot's work provides the following clarification: "or dialogue between A and B on the drawback to binding moral ideas to certain physical actions which bear none." In the text, A and B agree that the moral rules of the civilized world are contrary to the rule of nature and welcome the examples of free love in the Tahitian society they read about in the *Supplement to Bougainville's voyage*. McDonald suggests that their conversation corresponds to Derrida's understanding of supplementarity. But this is not the end of the story, for the next conversation between A and B seems to depend on what the women—who were left behind as A and B went for a stroll together—will want to do. B is rather annoyed: "The women again! You can't take a step in any direction without running straight into them."[9] A suggests nevertheless that they should read to them the dialogue between Orou, the Tahitian Father, and the Almoner, his French guest, in which the utopian sexual habits of the Tahitians overwhelm the honest clergyman from France. Unfortunately, the reading does not take place, so the women's point of view on this matter remains unknown. The two men conclude that the women would not have offered their views on the topic of sexuality anyway.

Diderot is well known for having lifted religious taboos and given ample space to women's unruly thoughts and words about sexuality in his libertine novels. In his plays, which were meant to educate the public and replace the teachings of the Church, female characters are paragons of virtue. This is true of the character Constance in his play, *The Natural Son* (1757). It is also true of Voltaire's comedy *Nanine* (1749), and Madame de Graffigny's play, *Cénie* (1750). Such young and attractive female characters are eloquent defenders of Enlightenment values. In his famous *Letter to M. D'Alembert on Spectacles* (1758) Jean-Jacques Rousseau, Diderot's philosophical foe, vigorously attacks women on stage, observing that in modern plays "it is always a woman who knows everything, who teaches everything to men."[10] He categorically denies them the wisdom, knowledge and philosophy to which modern authors like Diderot, Voltaire, and Madame de Graffigny entrust young heroines like Constance, Nanine and Cénie. Rousseau argues that nothing on stage compares to what we see in real life, because pretty young women truly don't know much. Yet he sees the benefits of using their voices to proclaim the truth and teach virtue on stage: "I do not deny... that such preceptors can give weight and value to their lessons."[11] The debate on the social impact of theater that divided the once amicable *philosophes* is closely linked to cultural politics in Rousseau's hometown of Geneva.

In the mid-1750s, when Voltaire moved to Geneva, theaters were closed by religious decree. Like many of the Genevan elite, he worked to have them reopened and to have plays performed again in the Calvinist Republic. Since the seventh volume of Diderot and d'Alembert's *Encyclopédie* was close to completion and was to include an article on Geneva, the *philosophes* seized the opportunity to promote the idea of establishing a decent theater in Geneva, where comedians would be regarded as honest people—in short, an institution whose example would spur the reform of theaters throughout Europe.[12] By opposing his fellow *philosophes*' innovating projects, Rousseau identified a specific problem of the French Enlightenment. In his footnotes, he laments the fact that priests follow their interest by tormenting the *philosophes*, while the latter take pride in imposing their opinions. If everyone spoke in good faith, he argues, persecutions and disputes would end.[13] He claims that in his Protestant hometown of Geneva, theologians and ministers are themselves *philosophes*, referring more precisely to "M. le professeur Vernet."[14] In more recent studies concerning the history of religion, we find that in eighteenth-century Europe, an important religious Enlightenment took place among Jews, Catholics, and Protestants. It is not surprising that, in order to illustrate the Protestant side of this movement, David Sorkin dedicates an entire chapter to Jacob Vernet (1698–1789) focusing on his theology, his teaching, and his pastoral leadership in Geneva.[15]

A distinguished man of letters himself, Vernet had served as a tutor in a wealthy French family and traveled around Europe before being named professor of *belles lettres* and later of theology in Geneva. Since French was considered at the time the universal language of culture, many Protestant families from the European aristocracy chose to entrust the schooling of their children to well-educated young men and women from the Protestant French part of Switzerland and foremost from Geneva. This was the case for Belle de Zuylen, who would later publish under the name of Isabelle de Charrière (1740–1806). The eldest daughter of Diederik Jacob, Baron van Tuyll van Serooskerken from Utrecht, Belle was raised by Miss Jeanne-Louise Prevost from Geneva and spent some time with her in this town when she was ten years old in order to become fluent in the French language. When Miss Prevost left the van Tuyll family to settle in Geneva, she continued to correspond with her pupil, keeping her informed about social, literary, cultural, and religious events. Around Christmas 1753, she reports how the ministers of her church preach against the "strong minds" who want to replace the Christian religion by a natural religion—that is to say, by no religion at all. She seems surprised to hear that this could be an issue in her town since, after reading Mr. Vernet's book,[16] she cannot doubt the truths of the holy Gospels and recommends the beauties of religion to the thirteen-year-old Belle.[17] Vernet was a prolific translator, editor, and writer; he even edited some of Voltaire's publications in Geneva. As a pastor, he also honored Rousseau's request to return to the Protestant faith after having chosen Catholicism for some time.

The reading public in Geneva was aware of the ongoing dialogue between Protestant theologians and the *philosophes*, and so were educated women. Belle de Zuylen was introduced to these debates at a very young age and avidly read modern plays, tales and novels by Voltaire and Rousseau. At her family's chateau in the Netherlands, she even acted in plays including Voltaire's *Nanine,* wrote poetry, and also published a tale. She was a brilliant young lady very critical of the old nobility around her and eager to converse and correspond with intellectuals. She finally married Charles-Emmanuel de Charrière, the Swiss tutor of her brothers, returned with him to Switzerland, and spent her adult life at his manor in Colombier near Neuchâtel. The novels, tales, and plays of Isabelle de Charrière are a lively contribution to the spirit of the Enlightenment, including the emancipation of women. They were first aimed at her immediate surroundings: Neuchâtel, Lausanne, and Geneva but after the Revolution, they reached France, England, Germany and even America. Women of letters like her were not easily noticed within the Republic of Letters, but Charrière worked very hard to have a presence in the public sphere. In 1784, for instance, she published in Geneva a short epistolary novel[18] which was a feminist response to *Le mari sentimental* (*The Sentimental Husband*, a recent Swiss novel depicting a reasonable gentleman driven to suicide by his selfish wife). Charrière's shrewd reversal of the perspective caused quite a controversy in Geneva. *Letters from Neuchâtel* (1784) and *Letters from Lausanne* (1785) were printed locally, but *Caliste* (1787)—her most sentimental novel—was immediately distributed in Paris by Prault, imprimeur du Roi (the Royal Printer).[19] Later on in her career, she became fascinated with book illustrations and managed to include lovely prints illustrating important encounters[20] in her philosophical tale *Three Women: A Novel by the Abbé de la Tour*, which was published in 1798 by Pierre Philippe Wolf in Leipzig but printed by Orell-Füssli in Zurich, and finally released in 1799.[21] She did not doubt that her tales were worthy of engravings produced by renowned artists following her specific directions. As in other illustrated sentimental novels and moral tales of the last third of the eighteenth century, the gorgeous line-engravings of that time usually illustrate elaborate textual *tableaux* found in the novel itself. If Diderot's domestic comedy introduced on the stage the aesthetic of the *tableau*—or the self-explanatory, moving encounter of the protagonists—this new dramatic style was actually even more effective in the narration of sentimental and moral tales. It thus became fashionable to produce expensive editions of both plays and novels, inserting prints to illustrate sentimental and virtuous *tableaux* illustrating the moral values of Enlightenment.[22]

We have seen how Charrière developed an autonomous literary career in an environment and time that supported Enlightenment values and—although she was not religious herself—was joined in her lively salon[23] at Colombier by foreign guests and local intellectuals, including Protestant ministers who were Enlighteners and writers themselves. But during the same period, the French Catholic Enlightenment was caught in political battles that very sadly led some of its prominent leaders, like Adrien Lamourette (1742-94), to the guillotine.[24] As a theologian of Reform Catholicism, Lamourette had an impact on Madame de Genlis (1746-1830) when she was the governess of the children of the Duc d'Orléans (1747-93).[25] Both Lamourette and Genlis were inspired by Rousseau's philosophy. In her novel of education *Adelaide and Theodore* (1782), that both followed and criticized Rousseau's *Emile* (1762), Madame de Genlis combined a Christian education with access to learning both for young ladies and princes. She also designed the moral and intellectual preparation needed for a future Enlightened monarch. Her pupil, Louis-Philippe, was to be the last king to reign in France during the Restoration from 1830 to 1848. The fact that he was educated by a woman is exceptional. French aristocrats were traditionally educated by clergymen who also produced educational and recreational books for their pupils. Historical anecdotes offered multiple themes linked to the Church or the nation that could both instruct and please young people. The Catholic Enlightenment produced new educational books as well as new collections of anecdotes, tales, and plays, which were not financially supported by any institution but were attractive enough to sell on the free market. The illustrated tale collections sold by Baculard d'Arnaud and Louis d'Ussieux in the early 1770s seem to have inaugurated in France the industrialization of novelistic literature.[26]

I will now focus on the publications of the virtually unknown French author Louis d'Ussieux (1744-1805) to find out how he contributed to the emancipation of women and how much he relied on women's fiction to please a growing feminine readership. D'Ussieux was born to André Dussieux and Marie de Borie in Angoulême, France. He was educated by the Jesuits in his hometown, was tonsured in 1764, and was sent to seminary in Strasburg for further studies. But since the Jesuits were banned from France in the late 1760s, he eventually left the Company of Jesus, got married, and settled in Paris, where he spent most of his life. While Isabelle de Charrière was publishing her first novels in Switzerland, he started editing, in collaboration with the father of his second wife, A.-C. Bellier-Duchesnoy (1739-1810), the *Bibliothèque universelle des dames* (1785), a huge collection of 18mo booklets offering the essentials of literature, philosophy, science, and the arts in a well-designed, handy and open-ended succession of lessons written by a group of men of letters and at first intended to educate young ladies throughout Europe.[27] Following the biblical model, this collection begins with a discourse on the globe, its formation, and its geography, quoting contemporary naturalists like Buffon and explorers like Cook and Forster, but also alluding where possible with deference to the Scriptures and the Ancients. Vivienne Mylne's study of all sections of the *Bibliothèque* shows that while it widely follows Rousseau's ideas on women's education, it also includes contradictory material and does not present a coherent educational project. It rather "stands as a valid testimony to the variety of ideas, in the late eighteenth century"[28] and resembles other collections produced by financially successful writers who were educated by the Jesuits in the south of France. At that time, d'Ussieux had also become a respected French *littérateur*,[29] much like his friend Jean-Antoine Roucher (1745–94), the moving spirit of the *Bibliothèque universelle des dames*.

It would be fascinating and not totally implausible to imagine an encounter between Isabelle de Charrière and Louis d'Ussieux in Paris just before the outbreak of the Revolution. They could indeed have been introduced to each other by Jean-Baptiste Antoine Suard and his wife Amélie Panckoucke Suard, who was a writer and a *salonnière* (salon hostess) herself. When Charrière lived in Paris from January 1786 to August 1787, she was a guest at Madame Suard's salon. Being one of the founders and collaborators of the *Journal de Paris* (1777–92), the first daily paper in France, d'Ussieux of course had professional ties with Monsieur Suard. While d'Ussieux was in charge of announcing and discussing plays in the literary section of the paper, Suard was the royal censor of theatrical materials and performances. From 1785 on, he also became the censor of the *Journal de Paris* and, as a prolific literary journalist, contributed several articles to this daily paper.

Although Charrière and d'Ussieux both embraced Enlightenment values, they did not share the same political ideas and religious creeds. Raised in the Protestant faith, Charrière belonged to an aristocratic family and was born at Slot Zuylen near Utrecht,[30] in the United Provinces, Europe's oldest Republic. Raised as a Catholic, d'Ussieux actually aspired to be granted a title of nobility in the French monarchy. Ironically this was to happen in 1789.[31] During the Revolution he narrowly escaped the guillotine, most likely thanks to his masonic friends. So did Suard, who traveled to Switzerland and Germany during the Reign of Terror. However, d'Ussieux's friend Roucher was beheaded in 1794. Despite the important differences separating Charrière and d'Ussieux, they could have agreed on the necessity of giving women an excellent education. Charrière tutored several young women from high-standing families in Neuchâtel while d'Ussieux edited the *Bibliothèque universelle des dames* and also produced elegant collections of moral tales suited for young ladies around Europe.

Women's contributions to French literature have certainly been neglected ever since literary history became a well-established discipline in the nineteenth century. In previous centuries, women writers' names also sometimes remained hidden behind those of their editors, whose authority served to widely circulate women's translations and women's fictions. We will see that d'Ussieux also used his authority as a *littérateur* to circulate women's texts without naming the true authors. Today we find this shocking, but in fact it was not unusual during the Ancien Régime to be considered the author of a text for having presented it in print to the public, regardless of who actually wrote it.

D'Ussieux was an assiduous student of literature and of history who wanted to serve the Republic of Letters with various partners. When the Jesuits were finally expelled from Strasburg in 1767, he moved to Mannheim and tried to convince Charles-Théodore, the elector of the Palatinate, to support *L'Europe littéraire*, a journal he planned to sell to subscribers along with a new version of Diderot and d'Alembert's *Encyclopédie*. But his project was short-lived. Did he also visit other courts in Württemberg and Bavaria looking for support? When did he fall in love? When did he renounce his religious vows? When did he get married? Who was his first wife? We know that in 1768, he published an essay in Paris on the state of French literature in which he took the *philosophes*' side, defined the proper "architecture"[32] of books, and affirmed his patriotism and love of the French monarchy. He then promptly turned his theory into practice and started making a living by producing various kinds of publications in collaboration with colleagues, printers, engravers, and foremost, his first wife.

We know very little about Madame d'Ussieux—not even her full identity.[33] As a former lady-in-waiting at the court of Württemberg,[34] she must have been fluent in German. In 1770, her elegant French imitation of the first modern novel in German literature, Wieland's *Don Sylvio von Rosalva*, appeared with a better selling title: *Le Nouveau Don Quichotte*.[35] By definition, the imitation of a poem or a novel takes liberties with the original to adjust it to the taste of the potential clients. This was unacceptable to German intellectuals living in Paris, such as Georg Adam Junker—a respected professor of German at the *École militaire* (Military School)—who championed faithful translations that allowed the reader to appreciate the differences between French and German culture. In response to his criticism, Madame d'Ussieux wrote a preface to justify her work and concluded saying: "In one word, I tried to turn a German production into a French book."[36] Sixteen years later, Charles Joseph de Mayer, the editor of *Le cabinet des fées*, preferred her translation to a more literal one and published it to conclude his vast collection of fairy tales.[37] This is the only publication of a contemporary author that directly gives credit to Madame d'Ussieux for her writing. An extra bio-bibliographical entry was added at the end of the section identifying the authors of the collection's tales.

> DUSSIEUX (Madame), we have already spoken about this lady in the *Notices*, it is known that she translated the novel *Don Silvio of Rosalva* by Wieland. She gave to the public two volumes of *Sentimental tales*. Her style is always lively and her tone sentimental or passionate, we found the tale *The Armenian Princes* extremely touching.[38]

Here we learn that Madame d'Ussieux not only translated from German to French; she also wrote short works of fiction. *Les princes d'Arménie*, which opens the second volume of d'Ussieux's *Décaméron françois* in 1774, was translated into German and published in Vienna four years later.[39]

Two collections of beautifully illustrated short works of fiction identified as *nouvelle* or *anecdote* were published in Paris and widely distributed in Europe by Louis d'Ussieux. The titles of the collections alluded to well-known models from the sixteenth and the seventeenth centuries. The first collection was called *Le Décaméron françois* (1772–5) and the second *Les nouvelles françoises* (1775–81). Each tale was published separately, but they were eventually combined into five-story volumes sold by subscription. The first series contained two volumes and the second one had three. As a historian of literature, Monsieur d'Ussieux commented on the evolution of tales in his preface to the *Décaméron françois*, concluding that he was presenting sentimental moral tales to the public. The main theme of those tales is love and fortune, as in earlier models—including Charles Sorel's five-story volume, *Les nouvelles françaises où se trouvent divers effets de l'amour et de la fortune* (1623). D'Ussieux's sixteen tales (one issue features two stories) dwell on love and fortune in a variety of historical circumstances chosen around the globe. I am convinced that this editorial project was a joint venture by Monsieur and Madame d'Ussieux. But Madame d'Ussieux's early death left her husband at a loss as to how to finish a work that had already been advertised and paid for by subscribers. Comparing closely the *fleurons* that adorn the title pages of the first volume and the second volume of the *Décaméron françois*, we discover a telling difference. In 1772 (see Figure 9.1), the rococo scene—an allegory of the authors—

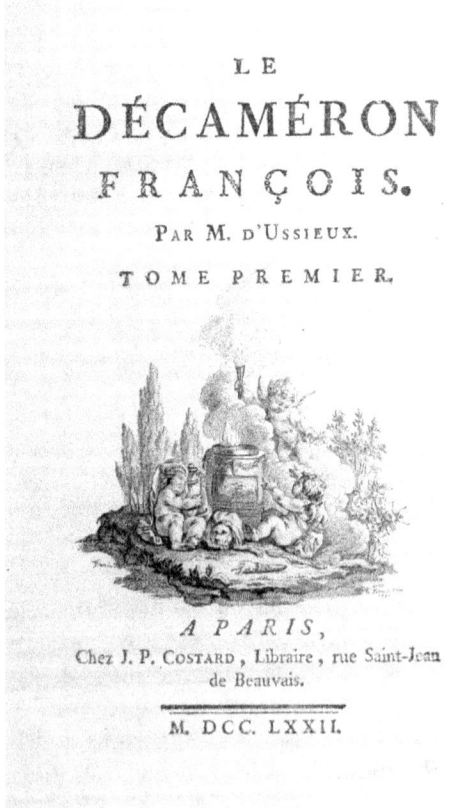

Figure 9.1 D'Ussieux's Fleuron. Designed by F. Clerc and etched by E. Fessard, 1772. Title page to Louis d'Ussieux, *Le Décaméron françois*, vol. 1 (Paris: Costard, 1772). Image courtesy of the *Bibliothèque des livres rares et collections spéciales*. Direction des bibliothèques, Université de Montréal.

is full of harmony and joy, but in 1774 (see Figure 9.2), the same scene looks very sad. The female putto that was sitting on the left side now turns away, is bending over, and has been covered up by a sheet. The flame of its lamp has been blown out and the dog resting nearby stirred up.

According to these *fleurons*, Madame d'Ussieux probably passed away sometime between 1772 and 1774, but her writings continued to be published by her widowed husband. Thus we find in 1781 the addition of a translation from a German author, Hans Ernst von Teubern, in the third volume of the *Nouvelles françoises*.[40] Originally published in 1767 in Leipzig, Teubern's anecdote illustrates the contemporary French invasion of Corsica. It was timely subject matter that needed some rewriting for a French audience when Madame d'Ussieux was busy translating Wieland. It is likely that she also worked on the translation of this historical tale in order to give it a more sentimental turn. In the German original, the soldier Dubois falls in love with Gioconda, a Corsican girl. His acquaintance

Figure 9.2 D'Ussieux's Fleuron. Anonymous. Title page to Louis d'Ussieux, *Le Décaméron françois*, vol. 2 (Paris: Dufour, 1774). Image courtesy of the *Bibliothèque des livres rares et collections spéciales*. Direction des bibliothèques, Université de Montréal.

with the enemy is, of course, unacceptable, and he is eventually judged and executed. In the French version, Gioconda saves her lover and reconciles the French with the Corsican democrats—lead by Pasquale Paoli (1725–1807)—through her eloquent and philosophical speech in the final scene.

If we remember now how the *philosophes* used attractive young women on the stage to proclaim Enlightenment values—a dramatic device sharply denounced by Rousseau in his *Lettre à D'Alembert*—it is striking to find the same strategy used here to confront an inhumane application of martial law. Gioconda's plea for peace and goodness is not an isolated instance in d'Ussieux's collection of tales and anecdotes where women resist tyrannical power plays and violence. The frontispiece of *Dubois et Gioconda* (see Figure 9.3) shows the heroine acting in the same way that she speaks. We see her separating her lover and her brother, who are about to kill each other.

I would argue that in the *Décameron françois* and the *Nouvelles françoises*, the anecdotes with footnotes and references to various historians are Louis d'Ussieux's own compositions, because they could easily be turned into plays. He also published a well-researched historical drama[41] and certainly hoped for a career as a dramatist. But most of the tales in his collections are less academic and more sentimental. Are they Madame d'Ussieux's fictions or translations, like *The Armenian Princes* and *Gioconda*? Certainly not all of them, for after she died, the advertised collection was completed with slightly rewritten stories from the seventeenth century, the majority of which were originally produced by women writers like Catherine Bernard or Charlotte-Rose de Caumont de la Force, as Henri Coulet has shown.[42] The recycling[43] of moral tales and other texts already published in France during the seventeenth and the early eighteenth century was, in fact, not new in d'Ussieux's career as an author, translator, and editor. The same year that d'Ussieux's wife published her *Nouveau Don Quichotte*, he also published with the same printer a short version of the discovery and conquest of the Indies by the Portuguese,[44] which is essentially drawn from the Abbé Prévost's *Histoire générale des voyages* (1746–59, 15 volumes). It could be that d'Ussieux's interest for the discovery of new worlds was triggered by family ties with André Thévet, the Franciscan explorer, cosmographer and writer, born in Angoulême in 1516. We know that d'Ussieux's baptism certificate is signed by Marie Thévet, his godmother and grandmother.

Then, d'Ussieux seems to have translated a two-volume collection of Spanish tales, first published in 1772.[45] But in reality, he modernized and edited existing French translations of Spanish novellas published during the seventeenth century as well as French tales exploiting Spanish anecdotes. The two volumes contain more texts by women authors whose identity I was able to confirm.[46] Out of twelve tales I could trace back to their sources, seven were written by women, two of whom were French, Catherine Bernard (1663–1712) and Anne de La Roche-Guilhen (1644–1710). Both contributed to the genre of the *nouvelle espagnole*, which was quite popular in the 1690s. The second volume of d'Ussieux's collection is filled with stories by María de Zayas y Sotomayor whose *Novelas amorosas y ejemplares* (1637) and *Desengaños amorosos* (1647) had already been translated and adapted to the expectations of the Parisian market in 1680.[47] During the reign

Figure 9.3 Frontispiece to *Dubois et Gioconda: Nouvelle corse* (Paris: Brunet, 1781). Designed by Desmaisons and etched by Madame Ponce. In Louis d'Ussieux, *Nouvelles françaises*, vol. 3 (Paris: Nyon l'aîné, Belin, 1784), 5–61. Image courtesy of the *Bibliothèque des livres rares et collections spéciales*. Direction des bibliothèques, Université de Montréal.

Figure 9.4 Vignette to *Dubois et Gioconda: Nouvelle corse* (Paris: Brunet, 1781). Designed by Desmaisons and etched by Madame Ponce. In Louis d'Ussieux, *Nouvelles françaises*, vol. 3 (Paris: Nyon l'aîné, Belin, 1783), 5–61. Image courtesy of the *Bibliothèque des livres rares et collections spéciales*. Direction des bibliothèques, Université de Montréal.

of Louis XIV, the adaptation of foreign literatures to French standards was promoted by the Académie Française. The translators thus took great liberties with the foreign originals. D'Ussieux obviously worked with the existing translations and adapted them once again to the contemporary expectations of the Parisian market, which was indeed now embracing Enlightenment values. But his endeavors were not revolutionary; they were still meant to serve the French monarchy by lifting the tradition to meet modern expectations.

It is interesting to note that women's fictions, which had long been criticizing the abuse of power, were obviously welcome to support the effort of promoting Enlightenment values and of giving a sentimental turn to historical tales. D'Ussieux of course emulated his model Baculard d'Arnaud (1718–1805), whom he called "the writer of the heart."[48] Both were educated by the Jesuits and so was Jean

Regnault de Segrais (1624–1701), who was also a model for d'Ussieux because he favored women in his *French Tales* (1656–7) and promoted Madame de La Fayette's novels under his own name. Of course, Segrais was Madame de La Fayette's secretary at the time and did not have to live off his publications' revenue. But the world was changing fast in the 1770s and 1780s. Since he did not receive a pension from an aristocratic family, d'Ussieux had to seek business opportunities with his elegant book productions. A hard-working *littérateur*, he was successful with many of his book projects and managed to sell them all over Europe. Today, national libraries—from Lisbon to Saint-Petersburg—hold his illustrated tale collections. Several tales were also popular enough to be immediately translated into other European languages. This interest also reminds us that beautiful products coming from Paris were highly regarded all around Europe during the eighteenth century. Even Isabelle de Charrière always awaited books and prints she ordered in Paris with great anticipation.

It remains to be seen what networks, specifically, helped d'Ussieux reach wealthy subscribers among princes, aristocrats, and patricians, as well as their wives and daughters. This is, of course, a question to be determined by historians of the book trade. But I suppose d'Ussieux, as a former Jesuit, kept enough friends within the Society of Jesus to be able to benefit from its long-established networks. The Freemasons also effectively supported the Enlightenment and its progress. Louis d'Ussieux, like many cultural agents engaged in the book trade, was a Freemason. In January 1782, he extended an invitation to Benjamin Franklin on behalf of the Neuf-Sœurs Parisian Lodge, of which he was a member.[49] D'Ussieux is remembered as a *littérateur* along with his Freemason collaborators Barthélémy Imbert and Antoine Roucher.[50] The variety and number of his publications is praised and listed with special attention given to his illustrated translation of Ariosto's *Orlando furioso* (1775–83) in four volumes[51] because five of the artists and engravers also belonged to the Neuf-Sœurs Lodge.[52] But this precious translation has also been criticized for being a cultural appropriation that was untrue to the original Italian poem. Monsieur d'Ussieux had turned an Italian production into a French book, just as Madame d'Ussieux had turned a German production into a French book. Both books were meant to magnify the good taste and elegance of the French monarchy and were applauded by an impressive crowd of cultural agents who adhered to Freemasonry and were also mostly Catholic Enlighteners. D'Ussieux was not alone. He belonged to a majority that was abruptly unsettled by the Revolution. The Grand Orient of Paris, to which the Neuf-Sœurs Lodge reported, was placed under the auspices of the Grand Master Louis-Philippe-Joseph duke of Chartres,[53] the future Duc d'Orléans, who was executed in 1793. Many other members of the Lodge lost their lives; since d'Ussieux was lucky enough to survive, he found a new way to uphold the moral principles of the Lodge,[54] focusing on basic needs of humanity like salt and wine.[55]

Let me conclude this essay on the support Enlightenment values received from women writers by reflecting on the appropriation of their original tales in expensive, beautifully illustrated books meant to entertain and uplift the elite of the Ancien Régime. We saw how the *philosophes* entrusted their precepts to attractive female characters in their plays, but in Diderot's *Supplement to Bougainville's Voyage*, the dialogue between A and B also introduces a fictitious female voice. The anecdote about Miss Polly Baker's plea against unjust laws in New England—those which punish single mothers while ignoring the responsibility of fathers—eloquently supports Diderot's point about Nature's blessing of bearing healthy children. It is clear in the dialogue between A and B that this anecdote is not B's invention, but the original author is not named.[56] This was the norm in conversation, for anecdotes were designed to call in question the ruler's authority. At a time in which it was considered indecent for women to publish their fiction, the name of an editor could also protect them. But why would women writers from the seventeenth century have needed anyone's protection in the 1770s? Although d'Ussieux adapted the language of their sentimental tales to more effectively support Enlightenment values, we can appreciate that the moral lessons to be drawn from these love stories were designed by real women like María de Zayas y Sotomayor, Mademoiselle de La Force, Catherine Bernard, Anne de La Roche Guilhen, and Madame d'Ussieux. The striking examples provided by their characters reached a large European audience and supported love, peace, truth, and virtue in countless private homes. As historians and translators, these women also facilitated encounters with other cultures and other times. A study of the reception of their tales in the countries that provided new translations during the nineteenth century could help us understand what "urgent questions"[57] the hidden women writers' moral imagination was able to raise for the centuries to come. In the same manner, the ethnographic imagination of the *philosophes*, studied by Christie McDonald, is of great interest to our globalized world today.

Unexpected encounters are a rich source of discoveries. By applying this method to marginal figures of the literary Enlightenment we were able to discern varying effects of the religious Enlightenment. In the north of Europe, the ideas propagated by the Protestant Enlightenment led Isabelle de Charrière to an autonomous creativity that was not perceived at the time by a very large audience but which has become very popular today—not only among feminist students of eighteenth century French literature, but also with the general reading public. At the same time, women authors from the seventeenth century helped a professional editor from the south of France, who was a Catholic Enlightener, to propagate Enlightenment values all over Europe without revealing to this vast readership which tales were originally written by women. Today d'Ussieux is hardly known as an author and the women writers associated with his publications remain absolutely invisible.

Notes

1   See *The Canadian Review of Comparative Literature* 3, no. 1 (1976), a special issue on dialogue edited by Christie V. McDonald. Our contributions address Diderot's unsettling narrative strategies as well as intertextuality and intersubjectivity in his complex text, which challenges the reader at every turn.

2. It was during this time that Paul de Man was working on *Allegories of Reading: Figural Language in Rousseau, Nietzsche, Rilke and Proust* (New Haven and London: Yale University Press, 1979).
3. This novel was posthumously published in French in 1796, but it was circulated through Melchior Grimm's *Literary Correspondence* at the end of the 1770s and probably written in the early 1770s. Diderot never published his philosophical fantasies, reflections, or tales during his lifetime, but did share them with friends.
4. Denis Diderot, *James the Fatalist and his Master: Translated from the French of Diderot* (London: printed for G. G. and J. Robinson, 1797), I:201, *Eighteenth Century Collections Online,* Gale, accessed March 23, 2020.
5. Jacques Derrida, *De la Grammatologie* (Paris: Minuit, 1967).
6. In the same way as with *James the Fatalist and his Master*, this text was circulated but not published in Paris before 1796.
7. Essay originally published in French by Christie V. McDonald, "Le dialogue, l'utopie: *Le Supplément au voyage de Bougainville* par Denis Diderot," *Revue canadienne de littérature comparée* 3, no. 1 (1976): 63–74. For an example of the productive critical interface made possible by McDonald's approach, see also my "Jacques le fataliste et son maître: interdépendances," directly preceding McDonald's essay in the same special edition of the *Revue canadienne de littérature comparée* 3, no. 1 (1976): 51–62. McDonald later included an English version of her article in a book-length study on dialogue, separating the theory (Derrida and de Man) from the analysis of Diderot's tale. See Christie V. McDonald, *The Dialogue of Writing: Essays in Eighteenth-Century French Literature* (Waterloo: Wilfrid Laurier University Press, 1984), 63–72.
8. McDonald, *The Dialogue of Writing,* 18–29.
9. Denis Diderot, *Rameau's Nephew and other Works*, trans. Jacques Barzun and Ralph H. Bowen (Indianapolis: Hackett Publishing Company, Inc. 2001), 228.
10. Jean-Jacques Rousseau, *Letter to d'Alembert*, in *The Collected Writings of Rousseau*, ed. and trans. Allan Bloom, Charles Butterworth, and Christopher Kelly (Hanover: University Press of New England, 2004), 10:287.
11. Rousseau, 287.
12. Friedrich Schiller is best known for having elaborated on this matter in his essay, "Theatre Considered as a Moral Institution." See John Sigerson and John Chambless, trans., The Schiller Institute, see https://archive.schillerinstitute.com/transl/schil_theatremoral.html.
13. Rousseau, *Letter to d'Alembert*, 258–9.
14. Rousseau, 260.
15. David Sorkin, *The Religious Enlightenment: Protestants, Jews and Catholics from London to Vienna* (Princeton: Princeton University Press, 2008), 67–111.
16. Jacob Vernet. *Traité de la vérité de la religion chrétienne, tiré principalement du Latin de feu Mr. J. Alphonse Turrettin* (Geneva: Henri-Albert Gosse & Comp., 1740).
17. Isabelle de Charrière/Belle de Zuylen. *Œuvres complètes* (Amsterdam: G. A. Van Oorschot, 1979), 1:36.
18. For more details see Isabelle de Charrière, *Letters of Mistress Henley Published by her Friend*, trans. Philip Stewart and Jean Vaché (New York: The Modern Language Association of America, 1993).
19. We owe the material bibliography to Cecil P. Courtney. Details are indicated in Isabelle de Charrière/Belle de Zuylen, *Œuvres complètes*, VIII:610–15 and also in C. P. Courtney, *Isabelle de Charrière (Belle de Zuylen): A Biography* (Oxford, Voltaire Foundation, Taylor Institution, 1993), 741–66.

20 For more detail on these encounters, see my "*Rencontres gravées pour Hermann und Dorothea de Goethe et Trois femmes d'Isabelle de Charrière*," in *Topographie de la rencontre dans le roman européen*, ed. Jean-Pierre Dubost (Clermont-Ferrand: Presses Universitaires Blaise Pascal, 2008), 363–87.
21 Isabelle de Charrière/Belle de Zuylen, *Œuvres complètes*, IX:762–63.
22 See much more on this topic in *Gestes admirable ou la culture visuelle de l'imprimé / The Visual Culture of Print. Eighteenth-Century Fiction* 23, no. 4 (2011), guest editor Monique Moser-Verrey, Université de Montréal.
23 This salon was also the center of an impressive "virtual salon" based on an extensive correspondence. See my *Isabelle de Charrière: salonnière virtuelle. Un itinéraire d'écriture au XVIIIe siècle* (Paris: Hermann, 2013).
24 Sorkin, *The religious Enlightenment*, 261–309.
25 Sorkin, 269.
26 Angus Martin, "Baculard d'Arnaud et la vogue des séries de nouvelles en France au XVIIIe siècle," *Revue d'Histoire littéraire de la France* 73, no. 6 (November–December 1973): 982–3.
27 A.-C. Bellier-Duchesnoy, *Bibliothèque universelle des dames. Première classe: Voyages* (Paris: Bibliothèque de S. A. S. Madame la princesse Des Deux-Ponts, 1785), I:1–2.
28 Vivienne Mylne, "The Bibliothèque *Universelle des Dames* (1785–97)," in *Women and Society in Eighteenth-Century France*, ed. Eva Jacobs (London: The Athlone Press, 1979), 136.
29 According to Voltaire, *les gens de lettres* (well-read persons) possess a philosophical spirit and if they also show good taste, they are perfect *littérateurs*. See "Gens de lettres," in *Encyclopédie, ou dictionnaire raisonné des sciences, des arts et des métiers, etc.*, ed. Denis Diderot and Jean le Rond d'Alembert (University of Chicago: ARTFL Encyclopédie Project, December 1765), 7:599b.
30 Her father Diederik Jacob, Baron van Tuyll van Serooskerken presided at times the provincial Ridderschap and supported the House of Orange against the French invasion in 1747.
31 See Nicole Brondel, "Ussieux, Louis d'," in *Dictionnaire des journalistes, 1600–1789*, ed. Jean Sgard (Oxford: Voltaire Foundation, 1999), II:976.
32 Louis d'Ussieux, *Essay sur l'état actuel de la littérature française* (Paris, 1768), 78.
33 D'Ussieux's marriage certificate, in the archives of the Parisian notary Pierre Paulmier (March 1784) indicates that he was the widower of Jeanne Herrfort, obviously a German name.
34 Jean-Chrétien-Ferdinand Hoefer, ed., *Nouvelle biographie générale depuis les temps les plus reculés jusqu'à nos jours, avec les renseignements bibliographiques et l'indication des sources à consulter* (Paris: Firmin Didot frères, 1854–77), 45:820.
35 Madame d'Ussieux, *Le Nouveau Don Quichotte, imité de l'allemand de M. Wieland*, 4 vol. (Bouillon: De l'Imprimerie de la Société Typographique, 1770).
36 Madame d'Ussieux, "Lettre du traducteur à Monsieur***," in *Französische Übersetzervorreden des 18. Jahrhunderts*, ed. Wilhelm Graeber (Frankfurt am Main: Peter Lang, 1990), 185. Translation mine. For more details, see my "Wieland imité par les d'Ussieux ou l'adaptation de productions étrangères à Paris autour de 1770," in *Traduire et illustrer le roman au XVIIIe siècle*, ed. by Nathalie Ferrand, *SVEC* no. 5 (2011): 93–114.
37 C. M. Wieland, *Les Aventures merveilleuses de Don Silvio de Rosalva, traduites de l'allemand de M. Wieland, par Madame d'Ussieux*, in *Le Cabinet des fées* 36 (Geneva and Paris: Barde, Manget & Compagnie and Cuchet, 1786).

38 *Le Cabinet des fées*, 37:361. Translation mine.
39 Louis d'Ussieux, "Les princes d'Arménie, nouvelle," in *Le Décaméron françois* 2 (Paris, Dufour, 1774), no. 6, 1–66. Published in German as *Die Armenischen Prinzen. Eine Erzählung aus dem Französischen des Herrn d'Ussieux von I. A. E. V. G.* (Wien: In der Ghelenschen Buchhandlung, 1778).
40 Originally written by H. E. Von Teubern, *Dubois und Gioconda, eine korsische Erzählung* (Leipzig und Züllichau: bey der Waysenhaus- und Frommannischen Handlung, 1767). Louis d'Ussieux, "Dubois et Gioconda. Nouvelle corse," in *Nouvelles françaises* 3 (Paris: Brunet, 1781), no. 11, 5–61.
41 Louis d'Ussieux, *Les Héros français, ou le Siège de Saint-Jean-de-Lone, drame héroïque en 3 actes et en prose, suivi d'un Précis historique de cet événement* (Amsterdam et Paris: Lajai, 1774).
42 Henri Coulet, ed., *Nouvelles du XVIIIe siècle* (Paris, Éditions Gallimard, Bibliothèque de la Pléiade, 2002), 1468–9.
43 Memory, imitation, and cultural appropriation contribute to the evolution and expansion of art and literature. "Cultural recycling" is a useful metaphor to assess this historical as well as intercultural process. See Walter Moser, "Le recyclage culturel," in *Recyclages: Économie de l'appropriation culturelle*, ed. Claude Dionne, Silvestra Mariniello and Walter Moser (Montréal: Les Éditions Balzac, 1996), 48.
44 Louis d'Ussieux, *Histoire abrégée de la découverte et de la conquête des Indes par les Portugais* (Bouillon: De l'imprimerie de la Société Typographique, 1770).
45 Louis d'Ussieux, *Nouvelles espagnoles, traduites de différents auteurs par M. D'Ussieux*, 2 vol. (Madrid: Ruault, 1772).
46 See my "*Nouvelles espagnoles* (1772) traduites par Louis d'Ussieux," in *Ainsi passe le texte: Mélanges en hommage à Madeleine Jeay*, ed. Véronique Duché, Yen-Maï Tran-Gervat and Daniel Maher (Paris: Classique Garnier, 2018), 113–30.
47 María de Zayas y Sotomayor, *Nouvelles de Dona Maria de Zayas, traduites de l'Espagnol*, 5 vol. (Paris: G. Quinet, 1680).
48 Louis d'Ussieux, "Préface," in *Le Décaméron françois*, (Paris: Costard, 1772), I:x. Translation mine. Baculard d'Arnaud was also educated by the Jesuits who are known to have encouraged an apostolate of the pen since the 16th century and favored the production of books.
49 See the letter from Louis D'Ussieux to Benjamin Franklin, [dated before] 22 January, 1782, the National Archives, Founders Online, see https://founders.archives.gov/documents/Franklin/01-36-02-0318.
50 Louis Amable, *Une Loge maçonnique d'avant 1789. La R. . L. . Les Neuf Sœurs* (Paris: Félix Alcan, Éditeur, 1897), 313.
51 Louis d'Ussieux, *Roland furieux, poème héroïque de l'Arioste. Traduction nouvelle par M. d'Ussieux*, 4 vol. (Paris: Brunet, 1775–83).
52 Louis Amable, *Une Loge maçonnique*, 313–14.
53 Louis Amable, 389.
54 "The goal of F. . M. . is to improve the fate of men." Louis Amable, 399. Translation mine.
55 Louis d'Ussieux, *Corps législatif. Conseil des Anciens. Opinion de Dussieux, d'Eure-et-Loir, sur la resolution du 24 pluviôse, relative à l'impôt du sel, séance du 9 ventôse* (Paris, Imprimerie nationale, an VII, 1799). As collaborator of François Rozier's *Cours complet d'Agriculture* (1801–05), d'Ussieux contributed the article "Traité théorique et pratique sur la culture de la vigne, avec l'art de faire le vin . . ." This *Traité de la vigne* was also published separately (Paris: Delalain, 1801).

56 Christie McDonald has conducted extensive research on the various versions of this anecdote originally invented by Benjamin Franklin. See Christie McDonald, "Anxiety of Change: Reconfiguring Family Relations in Beaumarchais's Trilogy," in *Eighteenth-century Literary History, an MLQ Reader*, ed. Marshall Brown (Durham: Duke University Press, 1999), 190.
57 Christie McDonald, "On the Ethnographic Imagination in the Eighteenth Century" in *French Global: A New Approach to Literary History*, ed. Christie McDonald and Susan Rubin Suleiman (New York: Colombia University Press, 2010), 238.

Chapter 10

STOWE MEETS THOMAS: WHAT IS LITERARY PROPERTY?[*]

Gary Wihl

Before intellectual property became an established term in law in the 1870s, there was a rather more vague precursor called "intangible property"—in effect a contradiction in terms, a property in name only, which could be owned and valued but without an actual material existence. Full of paradoxes and peculiarities, intangible property nonetheless took on central importance as part of the historical development of Anglo-American copyright law. To quote Oren Bracha, a scholar of copyright law:

> Copyright was ... reimagined as ownership ... over an intangible object of property ... During the second half of the nineteenth century, this aspect of copyright underwent a fundamental doctrinal and conceptual change ... a novel concept of copyright as ownership of intellectual works appeared.[1]

This essay examines the pivotal transformation of intangible property into modern intellectual property by looking closely at the well-known case of *Stowe v. Thomas* (1853). The case involved a battle over copyright infringement when a German publisher produced an unauthorized translation of Harriet Beecher Stowe's immensely successful novel, *Uncle Tom's Cabin*.[2] Stowe sued the publisher but lost the case. At the time, copyright law was much narrower in scope and did not confer rights to the author over adaptations or translations of her work. This case has been the subject of extensive legal commentary, standing at that critical juncture in the development of copyright law discussed by Bracha. But the most "novel"[3] (in the words of her attorneys) principle at stake concerned conflicting interpretations of what constitutes the property of the author. Although the rights of the author have since been settled in expansions of the US Copyright Act and in international copyright treaties, the effort to attach features of a literary text to stronger definitions of property has led to heightened protectionism that is in conflict with the original, constitutional goal of copyright, the advancement of the arts and letters for the public good. *Stowe v. Thomas* remains a valuable source for understanding the unintended consequences of a particular reduction of textuality into a legal definition of property, with particular relevance to a literary work that serves the public good.

The mid-nineteenth century in the US marked a turning point in the market for literature and other types of printed material. The volume of publication increased, as did the demand for literary works, domestic and imported. Prior to the growth of the market and the publishing industry, authors could rarely, if ever, make a living through the sale of literary works (excluding maps, dictionaries, medical reference works, etc.—all good sources of income for printers); the stake in protecting creative work through copyright was low. There was no significant pressure to exercise the author's rights over publication when the readership and ownership of books was small. As serial publication grew, as schools and literacy grew, as certain authors like Charles Dickens or Mark Twain could actually become celebrities, the effort to protect the author's rights and rewards spurred the development of copyright law as we basically know it today. Contemporary debates in copyright no longer question the author's ownership of a creative work; rather, in a crowded and lucrative marketplace, primarily driven by the cultural industries, the issue is primarily piracy versus originality, not the question of authorship as such as the fundamental source of originality and creativity. From the inconspicuous germ of "intangible property" we have now reached the point where copyright has been reduced to the expression of any idea in a "tangible" form. To quote the Visual Artists Rights Act of 1990, encoded in 17 U.S.C., § 102(a), "Copyright … subsists … in original works of authorship fixed in any tangible medium of expression."[4] From the dubious claim in favor of "intangible property" we have moved to full property rights of any original content on the level of its mere material appearance—from a sketch for a painting drawn on a napkin to an unpublished novel--as long as that content is fixed in a tangible medium of expression. How did we move swiftly from intangible property to legal ownership of original content in a tangible medium and what exactly is owned by the author? A medium links ownership to something tangible but we continue to struggle over questions of ownership. How can the author own a particular fragment of a commonly shared medium of expression? Have we solved the problem of literary property or become bogged down in a muddle?

From its foundation in American constitutional and common law, copyright has been framed by philosophical goals: specifically, the advancement of knowledge for the public good and the diffusion of knowledge to promote the arts and sciences.[5] But over time, the exfoliation of the law, in revisions to the Copyright Act and in decisive cases, has served less and less as a vehicle for the advancement of knowledge as articulated by the Framers. By the time we arrive at recent revisions to the Copyright Act, the advancement of arts and letters appears to be specifically excluded as a test for copyright protection. I refer again to the 17 U.S.C. § 102, "Subject matter of copyright: In general": "The term 'literary works' does not connote any criterion of literary merit or qualitative value: it includes catalogs, directories, and similar factual, reference, or instructional works and compilations of data … the definition of 'pictorial, graphic, and sculptural works' carries with it no implied criterion of artistic taste, aesthetic value, or intrinsic quality."[6]

The modern standard of "advancement" is sheer abundance of material, with no clear measure of quality or value. Of course, literature and the arts may progress for all sorts of reasons, unrelated to copyright, including better education and the attractions of the marketplace—that is a question for literary scholars and critics, not lawyers. But can we trace any actual advancements in the arts and letters back to copyright protection? That question frames the foundational principles of copyright in the US Constitution. But the law has become less interested in that issue; actually, that understates the situation. If anything, the complaint today is that we are surrounded by too much knowledge, too many books and sources of entertainment, the unprecedented dissemination of texts, artworks, scholarship in multiple media. Where the issue of protection arises, it is less frequently a matter of whether or not protection should be granted in the first place (as it was in *Stowe v. Thomas*) but rather whether or not there is harm to the owner's right to reap reward for the use and/or circulation of copyrighted material.

I do not mean to suggest that courts and the government, as the grantor/adjudicator of copyright, should play the role of arbiter of literary value. Rather, I want to open up a line of inquiry that suggests a closer tie between the development of literary property, out of intangible property, and the courts' characterization of the literary text. In fact, the so-called materiality of the text, where property and creativity meet, is rather more of an encounter in an unpredictable way, where an author becomes dispossessed of the whole idea of controlling one's language in the name of a singular self. To quote the editors' application of Althusser to the theme of this volume, "The materialism of the encounter combats the principles of reason, necessity and eschatology as well as the quests for origins and ends. It posits that there is no eternity in any laws of my world, that any accomplished fact will be revoked by an unpredictable and undecipherable fact yet to be accomplished."[7]

Stowe v. Thomas stands at the center of an extraordinary, possibly unique, combination of public good (the cause for abolition) and the creation of a best seller. But the importance of this case for the development of copyright law is obscured by the conflict over "intangible property" that was at the center of the legal arguments. To sum up the case: F. W. Thomas, the publisher of a German newspaper, *Die Freie Presse*, in Philadelphia, commissioned and published in serial form a German translation of Harriet Beecher's Stowe's novel, *Uncle Tom's Cabin*, starting on January 1, 1853. The novel is said to have sold 300,000 copies in its first year, was adapted on stage, parodied by some, and translated into German by another translator Stowe commissioned.[8] The immense, unexpected success of the novel raised new questions about the application of copyright law. At the time the novel was received as a strong call for abolition, but in retrospect its impact on copyright legislation perhaps is its real legacy. In a Bill of Complaint, Stowe sued Thomas to block the publication of his competing translation in the Federal Circuit Court of the Eastern District of Pennsylvania. The court found in favor of Thomas, however, under a strict interpretation of federal copyright law, which at the time did not extend the author's rights of publication to editions, translations, adaptations—in short, works that could be classified as derivative. That legal understanding was to come almost twenty years later, when the US Copyright Act was amended by Congress to include specifically those property rights.

The complaint filed by Stowe's attorneys, Samuel H. and Samuel C. Perkins, suggests that the underlying issue was financial, the harm to Stowe's expected income from the competing translation she had already commissioned. But if her motivation had been primarily increasing her income, she would have been better off suing her publisher, Jewett, who made most of the money off the enormous sales of the novel. Furthermore, Thomas offered to settle with Stowe and pay her a share of the proceeds, but she rejected the offer. The question before the court quickly turned into what was truly novel about the case. Before an infringement could be argued, the court needed to define what in fact Stowe owned. What was literary property? And even if that could be determined in law, would that apply to translations of creative work? From the outset, her attorneys in the case would have to deploy some ingenuity at a time when translation was not protected in law. The crux of this case was about property as an intangible owned by the author. How could legal categories apply to the product of the literary imagination as expressed through characters, plot, or style? Do we have a robust definition of what these literary terms actually represent from the "intangible" partly public/partly private world of source texts, themes, allusions, to say nothing of deliberate parodies and adaptations—areas that remain thorny to this day?

The definition of "intangible" is further complicated by the fact that it emerges as an issue of property in a case involving translation. Is a translation a literal duplication of a pre-existing work––merely a copy? In that sense, perhaps it is covered by the terminology of protecting copies in the law at the time. Or it is just another, independent manifestation of the *urtext* based on the same content as the original, already in the public domain. But in that case, is there further latent absurdity in that the *urtext* itself could be re-translated back in the first language, producing a competing parallel "original" language version? Part of these confusing struggles have to do with the application of pre-existing terms like "copy," in the law, to very broad features of the literary text.

At first glance, one would think that, leaving aside the merits of Stowe's writings, her pro-abolitionist stance as a writer would be immediately recognized in law as serving the public good—and indeed, part of Justice Grier's decision in the case rests on his belief that if even Stowe cannot own all derivations of her work, it needs to get out there, to the broadest possible public, even beyond its 300,000 copies in circulation. A passionate abolitionist, Stowe provides a highly sentimental description of the cruelty and sorrow of the life of the American slave, whipped, sold, and traded, dispossessed of family and friends, subjected to fear and danger. The literary quality of the novel is debatable: the plot is melodramatic, with deaths, reconciliations, escapes or tortures, inserted with arbitrary timing by the author to pull at the reader's heartstrings every fifteen pages or so. The style is condescending by modern standards, putting into the voices of the slaves heavily colloquial speech, and the story is made up of contrasting human portraits in the extreme, from the evil Simon Legree to the high-minded, yet indolent, St. Clare. But pure and simple, it was a success and it has become part of the American vocabulary of abolition and of efforts, pro and con, to establish an image of dignity for African Americans.

The issue of property arose before any other questions about the political message of the novel. From the outset, the arguments in the case took on a weirdly metaphysical vocabulary, which one could imagine sounded like a debate over philosophical principles but in retrospect looks more like arguments from a seminar in literary theory. Legally, literary property—what Stowe actually owned as an author and could claim to protect—would have to be based in common law rather than federal statutes, since the statute was silent on the topic of property. What exactly did she own? The words on the page? That would seem to diminish entirely the labor and originality of the author, reducing it to nothing but "signs" that could be substituted by any linguistic convention, a *reductio ad absurdum* in the view of her attorneys. But on the other hand, was it not equally absurd for her to claim as property, broadly depicted, sentimental characters who of course resembled all sorts of stereotypical characters in works of fiction, and which she freely admitted derived from her reading of published slave narratives? A robust definition of literary property would appear to give her a "monopoly" over fiction that was contrary to the whole philosophical principle of the public's interest in the circulation of ideas and the promotion of learning. It would be absurd to claim ownership of expressions of abolition or of slavery; it would be equally absurd to define literary property as mere words on a page devoid of their intended meaning, the strictest possible application of the word "copy" from the federal statute. The issue of translation exposed the vagueness of the entire concept of literary property within the legal framework of copyright, but also the need for the court to come to a legal decision that settled as best as it could the vexing issue of property. There was no legal basis for protecting ownership of an idea, then or now. The court could never commit so gross an error. Translation raised the persistent issue of public good, the free circulation of ideas and images, versus the rights of the author to print, reproduce, and disseminate the products of her intellectual labor.

At this critical legal/literary/philosophical juncture, there are many traps and pitfalls, and on the whole, I would have to say that Stowe's attorneys unfortunately fall into more of them than Thomas's attorneys, who focused correctly on the limits of what Grier could decide as a matter of law. Because the federal statutes concerning copyright refer to printing and selling copies of a work, Stowe's attorneys were faced with the immediate task of expanding the definition of copy in an effort to protect Stowe's interests. Nothing in the language of the statutes provided a robust meaning for the word "copy," so they resorted to arguments from common law, including reaching over to cases and laws from England. Again, they could not make a substantive intellectual argument, claiming that Stowe owned the topic of abolition, or the concept of slaves as property that could be bought or sold, or broad plot elements like whipping or charity, escape or rescue. Instead, they used common law to propose rather metaphysical arguments about a literary work as the product of an author's mind, as intellectual labor that cannot be reduced to mere "signs" on a page:

An author is the "creator," the "efficient cause" of a thing ... he is the creator of the ideas—the thought—the plan—the arrangement—the figures—the illustrations—the argument—the style of expression. The exclusive right to sell these is what is secured by copyright. The right is original, inherent; a right founded on nature, acknowledged, we think, at common law ... a right ... more deeply rooted than the right to any other property ... Particular language—words of one tongue as distinguished from words of another—are but the signs of his ideas. A perfect translation will present the identical creation and mental production, in a way that the sign is never thought of.[9]

If translations—mere signs of an author's original ideas—are permissible, then ideas become *publici juris* public property and may be retranslated back into English by a third party. And so it goes; the author's copyright is voided by translation. Note that labor, originality, the mind of the author are all being argued as protected property in the abstract. There is not a single reference to any passage, character, theme, description, or quotation from *Uncle Tom's Cabin*.

The relationship of common law on property, as applied to literary works, and federal statues, is another long and twisted story. The separate states offered copyright protection as a matter of common law property, but it was the federal government that defined copyright as a matter of statutory law. The connection was confusing, and in fact became the crux of an earlier, pivotal copyright case before the Supreme Court, the first of its kind, *Wheaton v. Peters* (1834).[10] I only wish to point out that Stowe's attorneys were testing a weakness in the copyright law having to do with common law notions of property, as the natural right to own the product of one's labor, as opposed to the federal law, that conferred a limited monopoly on the actual printing and selling of copies of books, charts, maps. But even in the earlier Wheaton case, which concerned Peters' publication of an abridgement of Wheaton's comprehensive record of Supreme Court decisions, the justices struggled mightily with the definition of "property,"[11] in particular its intangible nature, and narrowly ruled that the interests of the public good outweighed the protection of Wheaton's labor. The court was divided, however; the case served to highlight inherent problems in copyright law, legally and philosophically, but failed to settle the matter. Legal scholarship gives the *Wheaton* case greater significance than the *Stowe* case because Wheaton seemed to set up a contest between the most basic philosophical principles: all the natural rights of authors drawing on the greatest historical era of natural rights legislation versus the growing effort to downplay common law at the state level in favor of asserting federal law, the philosophy of the public good. However, the *Stowe* case is one of the few that specifically concerns literary property, as opposed to the publicly held, judicial opinions of the court, as in the *Wheaton v. Peters* case.

Thomas's lawyers shot back by immediately exposing the vagueness of property as an issue of intangibles—in this case, thoughts:

Writing and thinking are separate things, and the results of distinct gifts and separate labours. Thought is the gift of heaven; style or ease of writing, comes from art. The thought may be more meritorious than the style; but the thought, independent of its language, cannot be protected; and therefore literary property attaches not to the thoughts as expressed, but to the expressions of the thoughts.[12]

Furthermore, "every author appropriates thoughts from others."[13] Translations, in fact, enhance the value of original works, by increasing the circulation of ideas. Far from being injured, or "pirated," Stowe's work is increased in value. Once a book is published, the intangible property of "ideas," if indeed it can even be called a definite form of property, joins with the ideas of the public. Only the singular expression, in the material form of words on a page, can be "copied" and therefore protected by law.

This all begins to sound more and more like debates in literary theory between intentionalists—the work as the product of the human mind—and formalists—the work as an autonomous literary object, with a specificity of language that cannot even be paraphrased. And this literary debate remains as unresolved today as the legal debate over the concept of literary "property"—except that in the legal situation, a decision must be made. Both sides cannot co-exist indefinitely. The case is either in favor of Stowe or in favor of Thomas.

I have tried to make clear up to this point that the apparent philosophical conflicts in this case—What is an individual thought versus what is a public thought? Can a thought be owned? Do thoughts exist apart from words?—are pseudo-metaphysical arguments that draw on intellectual traditions (natural rights, the progress of the arts) which are weirdly transformed when they enter into the legal terminology for property. Justice Grier, as I said earlier, is now seen as having erred in ruling in favor of Thomas, because over time the author's rights have been extended to include translations, abridgments, and adaptations. But I would suggest that Grier's primary concern was to avoid legitimizing a monopoly over ideas, which could have far worse consequences. It was only the ingenuity of later justices who were able to exploit a distinction between ideas and expressions that allowed authors greater rights over their works—but at the expense of inadvertently downplaying the importance of ideas in the public sphere. Grier may have had in mind Jefferson's remarks on copyright: "If nature has made any one thing less susceptible than all others of exclusive property, it is the action of the thinking power called an idea, which an individual may exclusively possess as long as he keeps it to himself; but the moment it is divulged, it forces itself into the possession of every one . . . Its peculiar character, too, is that no one possesses the less, because every other possesses the whole of it."[14] Grier seems to echo these very words in his opinion in favor of Thomas.

Grier's decision correctly focuses on the legal ambiguity at the center of the *Stowe v. Thomas* case, for which there is no clear answer in common law: "In order to decide what is an infringement of an author's rights, we must inquire what constitutes literary property." Interestingly, Grier does not talk like an intentionalist or a formalist, attaching property or possession to the author's words or to thoughts. Instead, he asks, what happens when any idea is published; it is the act of publication, not composition, that concerns him. And here he tests an extension of the term "copy," not in the sense of mere words but rather in the sense of what is publicly shared via the act of publication: "[W]hen [an author] has published his book, and given his thoughts, sentiments, knowledge or discoveries to the world, he can have no longer an exclusive possession of them ... The author's conceptions have become the common property of his readers."[15] There is almost a modern notion of a creative commons at work here, since common property suggests a resource that cannot be diminished by further use, in lectures, parodies, criticisms, abridgements. And in fact, by the time this case was tried, the reality was that the characters in Stowe's novel were on the stage, in burlesques, comedies, parodies, and dramas, none of which Stowe controlled or attempted to control.[16] Although Grier sounds like he is speaking the same language as Thomas's lawyers, his opinion is actually broader in scope in attempting to recapture some of the original intent of copyright law, to further the progress of the public sphere, to zealously guard against the possibility of using the law to monopolize the circulation of ideas.

In retrospect, Grier is mocked for mistaking the eventual thrust of the law in favor of Stowe, when he concludes, "Uncle Tom and Topsy are as much *publici juris* as Don Quixote and Sancho Panza. All [Stowe's] conceptions may be used and abused by imitators, play-rights, and poetasters."[17] But in fact, far from a casual reference to a literary classic, Grier is making reference to the actual situation that Cervantes faced, when the popularity of book one of *Don Quixote* led to many successful sequels. So frustrating was this to Cervantes that he went to the trouble of killing off his knight in his own sequel.[18] But the point Grier makes is very concrete: What is the afterlife of a literary creation once it leaves the hands of the author and catches the popular imagination? In its concreteness, Grier sidesteps the irresolvable abstractions of property in the legal arguments for and against. Legal definitions of property did not offer any clear guidance in the *Stowe v. Thomas* case. The real issue at stake was the extent to which the law might permit an author to control sentiments, criticisms, adaptations of her work, a risk that in Grier's eyes set a far more dangerous precedent than any measurable harm to the author's income from the sale of her original work.

The case remains instructive for modern discussions of copyright because it reminds us of the law's original intent, to promote the public good. As definitions of protection and property have gained strength in copyright law, ideas have been pushed into the background to take care of themselves, as neutral meanings in public space, not owned by anyone but without any measure of service to the public good. Stowe was actually in the ideal situation: a powerful voice for abolition *and* a commercial success. Her efforts to fix a premature concept of literary property disrupted the balance she actually achieved and have left us with a profusion of literary works—all very well protected, but with a radical separation of ideas and expressions, in a state of imbalance no clearer than the metaphysics of the translation debate. Ideas cannot be owned; expressions are with difficulty recycled back into the literary commons out of which they come and to which, from a literary point of view, they should return.

I conclude with a few speculations. Where parties in a copyright dispute would really suffer no harm, in terms of being able to share substantial revenue, the court should set some sort of threshold for admission. There are now false incentives in place, to protect fragments of songs or pieces of music, or elementary designs, which, by their very popularity only invite overprotection for the sake of exaggerated harms. More speculatively, could there be a closer relationship between the legal process and the actual literary process? I have tried to suggest that the development of intangible property left an unfortunate split in law between ideas as free but neutral in meaning and expressions that really only capture the surface features of text. It is interesting to recall that at the time natural rights arguments about property were taking hold in the law, as Lyman Patterson has argued,[19] philological science was developing at a rapid rate in the reconstruction of ancient languages and grammars, in comparative linguistics, in the establishment of hermeneutics, in the creation of historical dictionaries, in higher standards of scholarly editing—all pointing to a much greater awareness of the components of literary expression. A rather more nuanced definition of intellectual property might see utility and originality going hand in hand, as they do in literary studies, where poets and novelists actually try to imitate each other for the sake of progress, a genuine commons of tropes, genres, plot structures, allusions. Copyright, now squarely in the hands of the author, appears to have succeeded in promoting the flourishing of the arts. We live in a time of unprecedented artistic, literary, scholarly productivity. But we could limit the law's tendency to focus on the margins of this productivity by asking for interventions where substantial infringement occurs, based on principles of textual coherence. I do not imagine any retraction of author's rights over derivative works. Where there is reasonable reward, rather than imaginary harm, let derivative works advance the progress of the arts and knowledge.

Translation, ironically, is the very model for literary production, neither a literal copy nor a new representation of the *urtext* but in fact an imitation that combines similarity with difference. In an exchange with Jacques Derrida on theories of translation, Christie McDonald neatly captures this point when she writes, "If meaning remains intact from one language to another [and] is transmissible and susceptible to the legitimate operation of readability ... it is because it first of all conforms to the rule according to which a good translation follows the internal logic of what is called the 'original.'"[20] Her emphasis on the terms "original" and "logic" derives from her reference to Walter Benjamin on translation, whom she quotes in her remarks: "'Fragments of an amphora which are to be glued together must match each other in the smallest details, although they need not be like one another. In the same way a translation, instead of resembling the meaning of the original, must lovingly and in detail incorporate the original's mode of signification.'"[21] How different the arguments in *Stowe v. Thomas* could have been, had the legal terms of debate, limited to copy and idea, benefited from theoretical advances in our understanding of literary production, of which translation, according to McDonald, serves as model for a general understanding of the relationship of reading to writing.

Notes

*   Earlier, preliminary versions of this chapter were presented at a conference on Copyright and Culture, Jagellonian University, Krakow 2015 and at a faculty seminar, Osgoode Law School, York University, Toronto, 2016. I thank the members of the faculty seminar for valuable comments and questions which led to many clarifications in my argument. For editorial assistance in the preparation of this chapter, I thank Catherine Mros, a Ph.D. student in the English Department, Washington University in St. Louis. For assistance with the legal documentation of the case examined in this chapter, I thank Rachel Cheng, a law student at the University of Chicago.

1. Oren Bracha, "The Ideology of Authorship Revisited: Authors, Markets, and Liberal Values in Early American Copyright," *Yale Law Journal* 118, no. 2 (2008–2009): 224. Bracha's essay offers an in-depth historical analysis of the major components of copyright law, of which property is only one. His larger argument questions the emphasis placed on romantic concepts of originality as the prime driver of developments in copyright law. He argues for much greater influence of market forces and the commercial interests of publishers for the increasing protections of authors' rights. On copyright and literary history, see Martha Woodmansee and Peter Jaszi's "The Law of Texts: Copyright in the Academy," *College English* 57, no. 7 (1995): 769–87, which focuses on the romantic sources of our concepts of authorship and questions whether these sources are overprotecting creative or scholarly works, limiting the possibilities for collaborative work and the application of the "fair use" principle. Meredith L. McGill's "The Matter of the Text: Commerce, Print Culture, and the Authority of the State in American Copyright Law," *American Literary History* 9, no. 1 (1997): 21–59, and "Copyright and Intellectual Property: The State of the Discipline," *Book History* 16, no. 1 (2013): 387–427, trace the competing influences of natural rights theory (going back to Locke) as the grounds of authors' ownership of their labor.
2. *Stowe v. Thomas* 1 Pitts, 82 (E.D. Penn, 1853), see https://law.resource.org/pub/us/case/reporter/F.Cas/0023.f.cas/0023.f.cas.0201.2.pdf, decided by Justice Robert Grier in favor of Thomas. Focusing on the conflicting interpretations of property in this case, Melissa Homestead writes, "The case proved to be a legal dead-end ... but Stowe's failure is nevertheless revealing and instructive. By filing suit, Stowe attempted to enlarge dramatically the legal domain of the author in American copyright law, giving authors more powerful proprietary rights and the possibility of greater profits at the expense of readers." Melissa Homestead, "'When I Can Read My Title Clear': Harriet Beecher Stowe and the *Stowe v. Thomas* Copyright Infringement Case," *Prospects: An Annual of American Cultural Studies* 27 (2002): 202.
3. *Stowe v. Thomas*, "S.H. and S.C Perkins, for Mrs. Stowe", 201.
4. 17 U.S.C. § 102(a).
5. See US Constitution, art. I, § 8, cl. 8: "To promote the Progress of Science and useful Arts, by securing for limited Times to Authors and Inventors the exclusive Right to their respective Writings and Discoveries" and the Copyright Act of 1790: "An Act for the encouragement of learning, by securing the copies of maps, charts and books to authors ... during the times therein mentioned."
6. 17 U.S.C. § 102.
7. Introduction in Encounters: Choice and Chance, p. 7 and note 33.
8. On the publishing success of Stowe's novel in the larger context of the struggle of nineteenth-century female authors' efforts to achieve financial independence, see Susan

Coultrap-McQuin, *Doing Literary Business: American Women Writers in the Nineteenth Century* (Chapel Hill and London: University of North Carolina Press, 1990), 86. For a specific discussion of the financial terms of Stowe's contract with her publisher, Jewett, and for the deterioration of their relationship over income from *Uncle Tom's Cabin*, see Susan Geary's "Harriet Beecher Stowe, John P. Jewett, and Author-Publisher Relations in 1853," *Studies in the American Renaissance* (1977): 345–67.
9 *Stowe v. Thomas,* "S.H. and S.C. Perkins, for Mrs. Stowe", 202.
10 *Wheaton v. Peters,* 33 US (8 Pet.) 591 (1834). See https://supreme.justia.com/cases/federal/us/33/591/. The Wheaton case is not cited in the Stowe case. For detailed discussion of this case see Lyman Rae Patterson, who uses this case to trace the confluence of multiple legal and philosophical sources in copyright law. Lyman Rae Patterson, *Copyright in Historical Perspective* (Nashville: Vanderbilt University Press, 1968), 203–21.
11 *Wheaton v. Peters.*
12 *Stowe v. Thomas,* "Mr. Goêpp and B. H. Brewster, contra", 205.
13 *Stowe v. Thomas,* 205.
14 Thomas Jefferson to Isaac McPherson, August 13, 1813, in *The Founder's Constitution* 3, eds. Philip B. Kurland and Ralph Lerner (Chicago: The University of Chicago Press, 1986), see http://press-pubs.uchicago.edu/founders/documents/a1_8_8s12.html.
15 *Stowe vs. Thomas,* "Grier, Circuit Justice", 206.
16 See Stephen Best on the "ubiquity" of *Uncle Tom*'s characters on the stage: hysterical Topsies, fugitive Elizas, calculating Legrees, and indolent St. Clares. Best cites a "sea of parodies, revisions, and thefts, achieving immense fame and influence within months of the appearance of Stowe's sentimental novel in serial form." Stephen Best, *The Fugitive's Properties: Law and the Poetics of Possession* (Chicago and London: The University of Chicago Press, 2004), 138.
17 *Stowe vs. Thomas,* "Grier, Circuit Justice", 208.
18 As Stanley Rothenberg notes, "Notwithstanding the [Spanish] Royal Privilege of exclusivity to print and sell the book, it did not mention derivative works or otherwise extend to a sequel, i.e. the use of the characters in new and different adventures. In fact, unauthorized sequels were a common practice at the time. Thus Don Quixote, one of the most enduring and best-loved characters in world literature, and his sidekick Sancho Panza, were free for the taking by any free-loading novelist. And so, along came Alonso Fernandez de Avellaneda (pseud.) in 1614 with publication of his unauthorized sequel." Stanley Rothenberg, "What if *Don Quixote* Had Been Copyrighted?," *Journal, the Copyright Society of the USA* 50 (2002–2003): 534.
19 Patterson, *Copyright,* 214–15.
20 See Jacques Derrida, *The Ear of the Other: Otobiography, Transference, Translation: Texts and Discussions with Jacques Derrida,* ed. Christie McDonald, trans. Peggy Kamuf (Lincoln and London: University of Nebraska Press, 1988), 117.
21 Walter Benjamin, "The Task of the Translator", trans. Harry Zohn, in *Illuminations,* ed. and intro. Hannah Arendt (NY: Harcourt Brace Jovanovich, 1968), cited by McDonald in Derrida, *The Ear of the Other,* 119.

Chapter 11

FORM ENCOUNTERS SENSE: THE SEMIOLOGICAL DIMENSIONS OF WAGNERIAN ANTI-SEMITISM

Jean-Jacques Nattiez

The following article falls within the context of the research that I have conducted in recent years about Richard Wagner's anti-Semitism, which led me to publish a book on the subject.[1] My intention here is to attempt to show how studying this aspect of the composer's thought and body of work raises questions that might interest colleagues and students preoccupied by the encounters between music and literature, and more specifically, encounters between music, opera, ideology and politics. Unsurprisingly, the theme of encounter was at the heart of the music/literature seminar that Christie McDonald invited me to co-lead with her in 1981 and 1983 in the Department of French Studies and at the Faculty of Music of the Université de Montréal. For my part, an essay emerged from this encounter, "Proust as Musician," which I had the pleasure of dedicating to her in thanks for the many suggestions that I received from her.[2]

Defining the nature of such an encounter first implies that we agree on the nature of this anti-Semitic content by specifying in which symbolic forms it is manifested in Wagner. We must also define the meaning of these words. Here, the word "symbol" is not a particular type of sign that, in contrast to Saussure's arbitrary sign, designates an analogical relationship between the signifier and the signified—like, for example, the blindfolded woman and the scale used as symbols of justice (Lady Justice)—but instead a form whose property is that of *reference*: referring back to abstract relationships like in symbolic logic, just as much as to relationships of image, affect and narrative, as in stories, myths, films, visuals arts, dreams, games, etc. By "symbolic form", I mean—following Ernest Cassirer and Jean Piaget[3]—that essential concept for enterprises of comparative semiology which attempts to describe the particular operating methods of each system of signs: a musical work does not function semiologically like verbal language; an opera libretto does not work in the same way as theoretical writing about opera, etc. These distinctions are crucial for my proposition. Is Wagner's anti-Semitism only present in his theoretical writings where it is denotatively evident? Where is it in the text of his opera librettos or in the action represented on stage? Furthermore, where is it in the music, which is often considered in the formalist traditions forged in the nineteenth century as referring back only to itself?

Wagner wrote six anti-Semitic texts. Here I'll focus principally on the very first, *Das Judenthum in der Musik* (*Judaism in Music*), written and published in 1850.[4] In this text, there are citations that expose the anti-Semitic dimension of Wagner's thought, I believe, beyond the shadow of a doubt. It manifests itself on the level of his physical description of the Jew, but also in his description of language, song, and financial dominance in economic life.

First of all, the physical appearance of the Jew: "We shall attempt to understand the involuntary repulsion aroused in us by the personality and customs of the Jews, in order to justify this instinctive feeling which is obviously stronger and more overpowering than our desire to be free of it. We are deliberately distorting our own nature if we feel ashamed to proclaim the natural revulsion aroused in us by Jewishness."[5] And: "In ordinary life the Jew … strikes us first by his outward appearance which, whatever European nationality we belong to, has something unpleasantly foreign to that nationality. We instinctively feel we have nothing in common with a man who looks like that … this unpleasant freak of nature."[6]

For Wagner, the Jew doesn't have a language that belongs to him, and Hebrew will remain a dead language. "The shrill, sibilant buzzing of his voice falls strangely and unpleasantly on our ears. His misuse of words whose exact shade of meaning escapes him, and his mistakenly placed phrases combine to turn his utterance into an unbearably muddled nonsense. Consequently, when we listen to Jewish speech we are involuntarily struck by its offensive manner and so diverted from understanding of its matter. This is of exceptional importance in explaining the effect of modern Jewish music on us."[7]

As for the song of the synagogue, Wagner continues, "we cannot fail to notice that it has not come down to us in its purity … Who has not been convinced that the musical divine service in a popular synagogue is a mere caricature? Who has not had feelings of repulsion, horror and amusement on hearing that nonsensical gurgling, yodelling and cackling which no attempt at caricature can render more absurd than it is?"[8]

The Jew, therefore, as much by his language as by his songs, is situated outside of each of the national communities of Europe. His dominance in economic life is all the more most disturbing and reprehensible: "As the world is constituted today, the Jew is more than emancipated, he is the ruler. And he will continue to rule as long as money remains the power to which all our activities are subjugated … [T]he artistic taste of our times [has been given] into the custody of busy Jewish hands."[9] And Wagner goes after Mendelssohn and Meyerbeer: "To become human with us signifies, first of all, for the Jew: to cease to be a Jew."[10] Addressing himself to the two composers, he writes: "Without a backward glance, take part in this work of redemption through self-denial [*selbstvernichtend*], for then we are one and indivisible. But remember that your redemption from the curse laid on you can be achieved by only one thing, that that is the redemption of Ahasuerus— decline and fall [*der Untergang*]!"[11]

There is no doubt of Wagner's anti-Semitism in his theoretical writing, but looking at the librettos is another question entirely. This is where it seems necessary to take into consideration their specificity as symbolic form, in order to fully recognize the specificity of the encounter between anti-Semitic thought and the world of opera.

Adorno already affirmed, in 1962, that the characters of Alberich and Mime in the Tetralogy, and Beckmesser in *The Master-Singers of Nuremberg* were caricatures of Jews. In the space that I have been allotted, I will only use the example of Beckmesser, the ridiculous character who sets out to win the contest for Eva's hand in marriage by serenading her at dawn. Yet a segment of Wagnerian musicological literature has refused, in the strongest terms, this interpretation, based on the fact that Beckmesser is the image of a good German bourgeois from the Christian community of Nuremberg. My position is that Beckmesser is not a Jew, but an *allegory* of the Jew.

Wagner republished his anti-Semitic essay, under his real name, a few months after the premiere of *The Master-Singers*, on June 21, 1869, because he wanted to clarify its meaning, as he says explicitly in the letter that he addressed to Madame Mouchanoff, the person to whom he dedicated the essay.[12] Wagner's anti-Semitism is fueled here by personal rancor directed towards Eduard Hanslick. This is the product of an encounter between a composer and musical critic who had been hostile towards him. Wagner had, quite evidently, taken offense to Eduard Hanslick's anti-Wagnerian attacks in his famous essay *The Beautiful in Music* (*Vom Musikalisch-Schönen*) in 1854.[13] However, Beckmesser is none other than a caricature of Hanslick. One can first refer to the second and third drafts of the libretto of *The Master-Singers* (written between November 14 and 18, 1861): Beckmesser wasn't yet named Beckmesser, but Veit Hanslich. Was Hanslick Jewish? This is far from certain, and, need I add, it has no importance. What matters is what Wagner thought. In the 1869 republication of *Judaism in Music*, he adds a section in which he tries to make Hanslick Jewish by discovering an alleged Jewish origin, "carefully camouflaged," he writes.[14]

We can see, therefore, that we can be certain of the Jewish nature of Beckmesser by transitively linking two types of information: Hanslick is defined as a Jew in the theoretical work and Hanslich was the initial name of Beckmesser in the drafts. To these textual and philological pieces of information, we can also add a third element of proof, a third encounter, which may be surprising: the music itself.

Due to the traditional semiological conception of music as pure form, therein lies a dimension of the problem that has been particularly contested.

I will only cite a declaration from Pierre Boulez, among many others: "The real anti-Semitism of the Wagner who wrote *Judaism in Music*, and that you find in his correspondence, has nothing to do with the content of his music."[15] If Boulez recognizes music as having a political connotation, it is not at the level of semantic content whose existence he generally denies, but from the point of view of the connotations of its form: "Wagner's music refuses by its very existence to carry the ideological content that it is accused of transmitting."[16]

Despite my great admiration for Boulez, I disagree. For Boulez, music cannot be the vehicle of meaning. Yet the case of *The Master-Singers* brings forth a refutation. In the second act, to woo Eva, Beckmesser sings a serenade whose music is particularly ridiculous. And Wagner wrote in *Judaism in Music*: "If we were repelled by his appearance and his speech, his song will engage our attention only to the extent that we exclaim at so absurd a phenomenon."[17]

As the British musicologist Barry Millington has demonstrated, the melismas of Beckmesser's serenade in *The Master-Singers* are a musical caricature of the music of the synagogue. To demonstrate this, Millington compared this passage to the transcription of the declamation of a Jewish cantor, Gershon Sirota, recorded at the very beginning of the twentieth century, of the prayer "Retzai" for which the appoggiaturas and melismas are analogous to those of Beckmesser's serenade, with the characteristic jumps by sixths, alternations between fourths and fifths, and melismatic flourishes within a single syllable.[18]

One might think that a recording from the beginning of the twentieth century is not proof, as *The Master-Singers* was created in 1869. But we have access to an extraordinary piece of information reported by Cosima Wagner, Richard's wife, in her diary on March 14, 1870,[19] that evokes the encounter of Wagner's work with the Jewish community. After a performance of the opera in Vienna, on February 27, 1870, a daily newspaper reports that, in Cosima's words, "Among other things the J[ews] are spreading a story around that 'Beckmesser's song' is an old Jewish song which R. was trying to ridicule" and that the performance was followed by whistling and yelling, by unarticulated shouting and hullabaloo. And there were other protests of the same genre in Mannheim (March 5, 1869) and in Berlin (April 1, 1870). This proves that the music of the Serenade was recognized in Germany and in Austria by the members of the Jewish community as a caricature of the music of the synagogue.

To characterize Wagner's anti-Semitism, we must therefore recognize the specificity of each of the symbolic forms involved. In his theoretical writings, his anti-Semitism is denotatively evident. In the librettos, Wagner never explicitly characterizes his characters as Jewish, but their Semitic dimension can be demonstrated by calling on resources of philology and by projecting on the text of the libretto information from a theoretical text that illuminates its content. As for his music, contrary to a widely accepted formalist notion, it may convey meaning thanks to the stylistic processes used and by the citation of a well-defined musical corpus. Not infrequently, musicologists are obliged to admit that Wagner's theoretical writings have an anti-Semitic content, even if one of them, Dieter Borchmeyer, practiced an odious form of musicological negationism by deleting the anti-Semitic texts from his edition of Wagner's complete works, under the pretense that "they would diminish/pull down the intellectual level of his edition"![20] Musicologists are more reluctant to admit the Semitic dimension of Wagner's characters: Alberich, Mime, Hagen, Beckmesser, Kundry. You can count on one hand—I cite among them the remarkable book by Marc Weiner, *Music and the Anti-Semitic Imagination*[21]—those who admit that a work of music can be qualified as anti-Semitic. This is nevertheless the case, but for this, the semiological function of both libretto and music must be better illuminated. In particular, we must recognize that music is not only a game of "forms in movement" that refers only back to itself, as Eduard Hanslick argued in 1850, but is also a semiological system in which one can recognize meaningful dimensions by bringing to light its encounters with the theoretical context that commented on it, the dramatic context that accompanied it, and its function as citation: music acquired religious significance outside of the context of a lyrical work, but, if its origin is recognized, it is preserved thanks to the encounter between synagogue music and an opera scene.

Translated by Anne Ratnoff

Notes

1 Jean-Jacques Nattiez, *Wagner antisémite: Un problème historique, sémiologique et esthétique*, followed by Wagner's texts, trans. Marie-Hélène Benoit-Otis (Paris: Christian Bourgois éditeur, 2015).
2 Jean-Jacques Nattiez, *Proust musicien* (Paris: Christian Bourgois éditeur, 1984); 2nd ed., 1999. For the English translation of the first edition, see Nattiez, *Proust as Musician*, trans. Derrick Puffett (Cambridge: Cambridge University Press, 1989).
3 See Ernst Cassirer, *Philosophie der symbolischen Formen* (New Haven: Yale University Press, 1953); in English as *The Philosophy of Symbolic Forms*, trans. Ralph Manheim (New Haven: Yale University Press, 1953). See also Jean Piaget, *La formation du symbole chez l'enfant*, 6th ed. (Neuchâtel-Paris: Delachaux et Niestlé, 1976), 194.
4 Richard Wagner [R. Freigedank, pseud.], "Das Judenthum in der Musik," *Neue Zeitschrift für Musik* 33, no. 19 (September 3, 1850): 101–7, and no. 20 (September 6, 1850): 109–12. See critical edition in Jens Malte Fischer, ed., *Richard Wagners "Das Judenthum in der Musik: Eine kritische Dokumentation als Beitrag zur Geschichte des Antisemitismus"* (Frankfurt: Insel Verlag, 2000), 139–96. (The difference between Judenthum—with an H—and Judentum—without an H—follows the spellings used by these two publications.)
5 Wagner, Richard, "Judaism in Music," in *Richard Wagner—Stories and Essays*, trans. Charles Osborne (London: Owen, 1973), 24–5. The citations of Wagner are taken from this English translation unless otherwise noted.
6 Wagner, "Judaism in Music," 26.
7 Wagner, 28.
8 Wagner, 33.
9 Wagner, 25.
10 Nattiez, *Wagner antisémite*, 50. Translation mine—Trans.
11 Wagner, "Judaism in Music," 39. We surmise that this final sentence of Wagner's anti-Semitic essay drove certain commentators to see Wagner as a predecessor of the Holocaust. In the book cited, I attempted to demonstrate that, at the time of its writing (1850), this note alluded instead to "the idea of decline and disappearance" and "cultural self-destruction."
12 Richard Wagner, *Das Judenthum in der Musik* (Leipzig: J.J. Weber, 1869).
13 Eduard Hanslick, *The Beautiful in Music*. ed. Morris Weitz, trans. Gustav Cohen (New York: The Liberal Arts Press, 1957). See also the critical edition in German: Eduard Hanslick, *Vom Musikalisch-Schönen. Ein Beitrag zur Revision der Aesthetik der Tonkunst* [1855], ed. Dietmar Strauss (Mayence: Schott, 1990).

14 Nattiez, *Wagner antisémite*, 614. Translation mine—Trans.
15 Pierre Boulez, *Points de repère: Regards sur autrui,* ed. Jean-Jacques Nattiez and Sophie Galaise (Paris: Christian Bourgois éditeur, 2005), 2:163. Translation mine—Trans.
16 Boulez, 163.
17 Wagner, "Judaism in Music," 29.
18 Barry Millington, "Nuremberg Trial. Is There Anti-Semitism in *Der Meistersinger?*", *Cambridge Opera Journal* 3, no. 3 (November 1991): 247–60. For a comparison of the traditional prayer and Beckmesser's serenade, see the musical examples in Nattiez, *Wagner antisémite,* 385–9.
19 Entry from March 14, 1870 in *Cosima Wagner's Diaries,* ed. Martin Gregor-Dellin and Dietrich Mack, trans. Geoffrey Skelton (New York: Harcourt Brace Jovanovich, 1978), 1:199.
20 Richard Wagner, *Dichtungen und Schriften,* ed. Dieter Borchmeyer (Frankfurt: Insel Verlag, 1983), 10:187. Translation mine—Trans.
21 Marc Weiner, *Wagner and the Anti-Semitic Imagination,* 2nd ed. (Lincoln, NE: University of Nebraska Press, 1997).

Chapter 12

"UN AUTRE MOI-MêME": BETWEEN THE SELF AND THE OTHER IN PROUST'S CORRESPONDENCE[1]

François Proulx

Studies of Marcel Proust's correspondence have noted its mirror-like aspect.[2] In a recent edition of newly discovered letters to Pierre de Polignac, Jean-Marc Quaranta comments that Proust appears to be writing about himself, and in a sense to himself, when he offers literary advice to his correspondent.[3] Martin Robitaille observes a principle of mimicry at work in Proust's most formative epistolary relationships, with his mother, and later with Robert de Montesquiou,[4] as missives to each end up reflecting their recipient's respective style, parroting their phrases and redeploying their epistolary tactics, in a writing practice akin to Proust's celebrated pastiches. According to such readings of his correspondence, Proust either negates the other by projecting his self (as with Polignac) or negates his self by incorporating the other (as with his mother or Montesquiou). The result is a portrait of Proust the letter-writer as highly solipsistic, in line with some of his pronouncements, for instance in his novel where the narrator describes friendship as a "fatal ... abdication of the self,"[5] that he does not believe in the possibility of any meaningful engagement between self and other.

Rather than argue directly against such characterizations, I want to ask whether some of Proust's letters might suggest a different mode of encounter with the other, one where, rather than seeing only himself in the other, or seeking to mimic and therefore incorporate him or her, Proust comes to imagine his addressee as a kind of other self, connected yet distinct, figuratively present despite being absent. In Proust's letters to the composer Reynaldo Hahn (1874–1947), his onetime lover and lifelong most intimate friend, I propose to see a rehearsal of the complex play of pronominal and subjective positions—the writer who writes "I" but is not the person saying "I," the reader who somehow recognizes and better understands herself through the prism of that "I"—that underpin Proust's novel *À la recherche du temps perdu* (*In Search of Lost Time*).

Another Myself

In a 1921 letter to the scandalous aristocrat Élisabeth de Gramont (in a lesbian relationship with Natalie Clifford Barney since 1910, and divorced from the Duc de Clermont-Tonnerre as of 1920),[6] Proust writes: "... since you tell me that you will see Reynaldo Hahn on Wednesday, he is another myself [c'est un autre moi-même] to whom you could say whatever you like to my intention." The letter is known only through a sales catalog, which cites just this sentence fragment and the sentence immediately after.[7] According to a paraphrase provided in the catalog, the statement concerns a favor that Proust's correspondent wants to ask him, something she perhaps hesitates to write in a letter. The nature of this favor remains a mystery, as Élisabeth de Gramont's letters to Proust preceding and answering this one have not reached us.

The phrase "another myself" sounds clumsy in English, but it is not at all unusual in French. As a locution it is attested in two major nineteenth-century reference works of the French language, the Bescherelle brothers' *National Grammar* (1834)[8] and Émile Littré's *Dictionary of the French Language* (1863–73). In the *Littré*, the sub-entry under "même" describing the pronominal construction "moi-même," "toi-même" and so on (myself, yourself ...) is immediately followed by an explanation of this locution: "Another myself, a person whom I love as much as myself, who is like myself, who may represent me in all matters ..."[9] The sub-entry then provides nine citations of canonical writers using the phrase, for instance Corneille in *Attila* (1667): "J'ai lieu de vous aimer comme un autre moi-même" (I have reason to love you as another myself). This list includes four citations of Racine, whose plays are among the major intertexts of Proust's novel.[10] A link between Racine and Reynaldo Hahn exists in Proust's manuscript notebooks: Hahn had composed choruses for a staged performance of Racine's play *Esther* starring Sarah Bernhardt in 1905. In a scene from the manuscript, these choruses are not only mentioned by the narrator but performed by Hahn himself (sitting at a piano), singing with the adult narrator's mother, as the narrator and his father listen intently, in a moment of familial and domestic bliss.[11] Intended for a sequence known as "Conversation with *Maman*" at a time when Proust envisioned his project as a hybrid essay to be titled "Against Sainte-Beuve" (in late 1908 or early 1909),[12] the scene was not retained by Proust for the more developed published version of the *Recherche*. We do not know if Proust directly associated the locution "un autre moi-même" with Racine, who uses it in three plays (*The Thebaid*, *Mithridate*, *Bérénice*). Nevertheless, the locution belongs to a classical, Racinian French heritage which under Proust's pen is tied to queerness[13] and to Reynaldo Hahn.[14]

According to French classical philology, the concept of the friend as "another self" can be traced back to Pythagoras. In *The Life of Pythagoras* (1706), André Dacier explains: "No one understood the essence of friendship better than Pythagoras. He was the first to say that 'all is shared between two friends' and that 'a friend is another self' [un autre nous-mesme]; this observation provided Aristotle with the basis for his fine definition of friendship as 'one soul that lives in two bodies.'"¹⁵ In Descartes's treatise *The Passions of the Soul* (1649), the locution appears in a slightly different context, as part of a reflection on the nature of (heterosexual) love:

> But the principal attraction comes from the perfections that one imagines in a person who one thinks could become a second oneself [un autre soi-même]. Along with establishing a difference of sex in human beings … nature has implanted certain impressions in the brain that bring it about that at a certain age and season one regards oneself as defective—as forming only one half of a whole whose other half must be a person of the opposite sex—so that the acquisition of this other half is represented by nature, in a confused way, as the greatest of all imaginable goods.¹⁶

The shift to love, and to sexual difference, introduces the notion of error. In the opposite sex, according to Descartes, perfect identity and reciprocity are not found but "imagined": they are an impression, a confusion, a lure.

Proust had studied Descartes extensively (mostly the *Discourse on Method* of 1637) as part of the philosophy *baccalauréat* examination he passed in 1889.¹⁷ In the *Recherche*, the narrator's reflections on the self and the other, as he grieves the dead Albertine, take on a Cartesian quality, decrying the conflation of the self and the other as an "illusion":

> The bonds between ourselves and another person exist only in our minds. Memory as it grows fainter loosens them, and notwithstanding the illusion by which we want to be duped and which, out of love, friendship, politeness, deference, duty, we dupe other people, we exist alone. Man is the creature who cannot escape from himself, who knows other people only in himself, and when he asserts the contrary, he is lying.¹⁸

This is not quite the narrator's final say on the question, as the revelations of the final volume about the power of art to bridge the self and the other are yet to come. Still, one can wonder: when Proust describes his lifelong intimate friend as "another self," is he simply employing a locutionary shortcut? In doing so, is he "lying" (to use his own term) to Élisabeth de Gramont, as well as, in a sense, to Reynaldo Hahn, and to himself? Or might he be alluding to another kind of experience, to a different form of relation between the self and the other that, while it in no way corresponds to the abyss of unknowability between the narrator and Albertine, might nevertheless underlie the structure of his novel?

Particularity, Reciprocity, Possibility

Proust's first encounter with Reynaldo Hahn took place in 1894, when he was twenty-two years old and Hahn was nineteen: they likely met in Madeleine Lemaire's salon on May 22.¹⁹ In Proust's earliest surviving letter to Hahn, from [July 18?], he asks for a "rendezvous," "at my place or yours"—a chaste proposition, since they both lived with their parents at the time—"or at the terrace next to the water basin at the Tuileries"—on the surface, an equally respectable location, given the specified time, "one of these coming afternoons."[20] Yet the latter option also carries a less than chaste connotation, given that the Tuileries garden were a notorious queer cruising spot, as attested by an 1893 letter from Reynaldo Hahn himself.[21] From that first exchange, the pair would go on to develop and maintain a sustained epistolary practice characterized by particularity, reciprocity and possibility.

Starting in the amorous phase of their relationship in 1894–6, but also beyond it, throughout the intimate friendship that lasted to the end of Proust's life, letters from each bestow upon the other an exceptional status, using superlative terms. "You [are] truly the person whom, along with *Maman*, I love the most in the world," Proust declares in July 1896[22]; "o my little Reynaldo, o my great affection in life," he writes on a dedicated copy of his translation of John Ruskin's *Bible of Amiens* in 1904.[23] During Proust's last illness in the fall of 1922, Hahn, having recently spoken with Proust's brother Robert (a renowned surgeon), pleads with Marcel to accept treatment in a wrenching final letter: "I need not tell you how much I regret not having [the] slightest influence on you. I know that no one can sway your decisions and that I am powerless to bring about what I consider reasonable and desirable for my dearest friend, for one of the people I will have loved the most in my life."[24]

The pair's closeness is emphasized by a remarkable complicity and reversibility, as evidenced by their sometimes-interchangeable nicknames ("Buncht" and "Bunibuls," with numerous declensions and variants).[25] Not limited to naming, but always tied to writing, Proust and Hahn's reciprocity also extends to perspective and presence. In a letter from 1896, Proust tells Hahn: "You write to me, with that rapid elegance I so admire in your letters, equal to the most remarkable quips of the 17th century: 'Tell me what I think about it.'"[26] The query concerns a quatrain by Mallarmé,[27] on which Hahn seeks Proust's explanation and opinion. Proust's judgement, Hahn writes, will become his own; in his concise formula, collapsing "you" into "I" and using only the present tense, Proust's opinion, which he does not yet know, nevertheless already *is* his opinion. Echoing Hahn in turn, Proust responds to his correspondent by quoting his admirable quip, judging it to be "well above Mallarmé's verses"[28] and equal to the *Grand Siècle* writers he himself so admires. This principle of reciprocity is also repeatedly evoked at times of grief. After the death of Hahn's father, in June 1897, Proust writes to him: "I love you with all my heart … Distance is nothing, my little Reynaldo. I am always by your side." When years later Hahn loses his mother in March 1912, Proust is unable to attend the funeral ceremonies but again writes: "I am closer to you than to me."[29]

Interchangeability gives rise to varied potentialities, some of which are fantasy scenarios, tied to illicit imaginings. Proust writes to Louis d'Albufera in May 1908, possibly displacing his own complex sentiments of desire and clandestineness toward his correspondent onto the figure he describes as a "brother":

> As for what you tell me regarding my friends, if you mean Reynaldo, you are right to think that he is a friend to me: the dearest, the best, a brother. If I were to

learn that he had murdered someone, I would hide the body in my bedroom, so that I could be held as the guilty one."[30]

Other possibilities are more concrete and positive, as Hahn, for over two decades, served as Proust's emissary for a wide range of missions around Paris: everything from contacting publishers, to soliciting reviews or influencing votes for the Goncourt Prize or the Legion of Honor, to finding jewelers for custom-designed gifts. Proust writes to Marie Nordlinger in February 1904: "Thanks to Reynaldo (everything I have ever done has always been 'thanks to Reynaldo') I was able to see Wisthler [sic] one evening."[31] Even more significantly, in a September 1907 letter to Hahn himself, Proust describes his correspondent as a generative horizon of possibility, present day and night: "But how often each day, each night, my heart melds into the thought of Buninuls, how often I curl up inside him, and in fact, whatever else may occupy my thoughts, his dear little mininulsity [mininulserie] and his face remain at my horizon and compose it."[32] The thought of Hahn, in other words, is the background against which Proust's other thoughts can form—including thoughts of his future novel, which are not far off in the fall of 1907.

"Writing to myself"

In his authoritative biography of Proust, Jean-Yves Tadié imagines Reynaldo Hahn's "disappointment" in seeing neither his name nor those of his works mentioned in *À la recherche du temps perdu*.[33] Setting aside the question of Hahn's perceived absence in the published text of Proust's novel,[34] I want to reflect on two aspects of Hahn's presence during its first phase of composition, the years 1908–13.[35] Proust's correspondence describes Hahn's presence in two ways: the first is literal and physical, as Hahn made Proust "thousands of visits"[36] at his apartment on boulevard Haussmann between his installation in December 1906 (following the death of his mother) and the declaration of war in August 1914, always at night-time and despite unfavorable odds that Proust would actually be able to receive him. As Proust explains to another correspondent in January 1910:

> The only being I see from time to time is Reynaldo, since he visits frequently at unreasonable hours, and one time out of every six, I am done with my fumigation and that time I allow him to enter, since he is so used to my illness, and does not mind receiving my answers on little pieces of paper if I am unable to speak...[37]

There is "something almost conjugal about these near-daily visits, like the relations between the married Swann and Odette," muses Tadié.[38] Céleste Albaret, Proust's housekeeper from 1914 until his death in 1922, remarks that Hahn enjoyed an exceptional status: he was the only person allowed to enter Proust's apartment unannounced, and walk straight into the bedroom if Proust was awake and not in the middle of a "fumigation." Hahn also left without being accompanied by her, a privilege she appeared to resent.[39] It was during some of these frequent visits (before Albaret took over from previous domestics) that Hahn was given another unique privilege: he was perhaps the first person to read an early version of what became *Du côté de chez Swann* (*Swann's Way*), or rather, to have it read to him by the author.[40]

Since these night-time conversations took place in person, there are no surviving traces of them save for brief mentions in Proust's letters to other correspondents. Yet Hahn's "presence" during the first years of composition of Proust's novel is also frequently described, in a second, more figurative manner, in Proust's letters to Hahn when one of them is away from Paris. If for instance Hahn travels abroad to conduct a musical work or give a conference, or when Proust spends the summer at the seaside resort of Cabourg, Proust explains that, as part of his creative process, he discusses his work-in-progress with Hahn out loud, even as Hahn is physically absent. Early on, descriptions of these scenes place the pair's relationship under signs of literary exemplarity, through comparisons to famous writers' friendships; later, they come to blur the divide between Proust and Hahn's real lives and the parallel world of Proust's fiction. In October 1908, Proust writes from Versailles, where he has retreated to a hotel in order to work:

> Bunibuls I cannot schwrite you tonight since I must schwork.[41] And yet how many topics of conversation would there be with Bunibuls, since I may say of the two of us, as Ruskin said of Carlyle, 'that he was now in all of England the only person with whom he could agree on matters of praise and blame.'[42]

John Ruskin was an important influence for Proust who translated two of his works. Thomas Carlyle also carries a biographical significance for Proust and Hahn, since a French translation of Carlyle's *On Heroes, Hero-Worship, and The Heroic in History* (1841) figures among their readings during their shared sojourn in Brittany, away from their parents, in the fall of 1895.[43]

Similarly, in August 1910, Proust writes from Cabourg:

> Flaubert's entreaties in his solitary retreat, asking Bouilhet 'Are you pleased with me?,' or those of a little girl to her doll are nothing compared to the words I say out loud out all night long: 'O my bunibuls, don't you think this is just schweet etc.' Perhaps the name of Reynaldo, as Virgil would say (and quite rightly so), travels all the way to my neighbors' ears . . .[44]

Flaubert's longtime friend Louis Bouilhet (1821–69) played an essential role in the genesis of many of the novelist's works. Flaubert would submit pages of his manuscript to Bouilhet's critique during the latter's often weekly visits to his retreat in Normandy, and the two men shared an extensive correspondence.[45] Here Proust appears to paraphrase a letter from May 10, 1855, when Flaubert was working on *Madame Bovary*: "Are you pleased? Am I lovely?"[46] In the next sentence he references Virgil's *Eclogues*, where Book VI opens with an address of dedication to a man named Varus: "'tis of you, Varus, our tamarisks shall sing, of you all our groves. To Phoebus no page is more welcome than that which bears on its front the name of Varus."[47] Both citations are revealing in what they convey about Proust's ambition and self-image: a long friendship between a pair of nineteenth-century male writers, tied to a revolution in the genre of the novel; a classical text, not without a homoerotic component (it is from Book II of the *Eclogues*, about a shepherd's love for a boy, that André Gide will borrow the name *Corydon*). Yet we also get a sense of Proust's vulnerability, and perhaps even of his gender-bending sensitivity, in the no less remarkable middle comparison, as the adult writer likens himself to a young girl talking to her doll.

In his letters to Hahn during the first phase of composition of the *Recherche* (1908–13), Proust repeatedly gives accounts of these conversations in absentia. In November 1911, he pleads to Hahn: "You would listen with as much indulgence as Zadig[48] if whenever I am alone (which is always) you heard me say repeatedly: 'My poor schweet' or 'How do you like that my schweet.'"[49] In January 1912, he opens a letter by stating: "My dear little Bi-ni-mels, I have just spent the night chatting with you, asking: 'Is pretty? You like?'"[50] A short letter from an undetermined date, possibly early 1912, goes further in conflating both presence and absence, and the fictional world of Proust's work-in-progress to the real world inhabited by Hahn:

> My dear little Gunimels
> It is I who shed tears when I read your little telegram,[51] but they were schweet tears. My schweet but I love only you. If I don't constantly remind you it's to avoid tyranny etc. . . . But I could not have gone to sleep without a good-night kiss, without having given you the kiss of Combray, I kiss your hand my Gunibuls.
> Buncht
>
> [p.s.: . . .] My schweet your little note from this morning will remain among the memories of our friendship and of my life (pleonasm) as one of the two or three things that have the most touched and delighted me[.][52]

The mention of the "kiss of Combray" is the only clue that allows Philip Kolb to date this letter, somewhat loosely, to the "[first months of 1912?]," since another letter, as we have seen, attests that Proust had read Hahn the "first 200 pages" of his manuscript in late November 1909.[53] Proust's letter not only merges reality with fiction but changes the cast and reverses the roles of what would become an emblematic scene of his novel. The pair who take center stage in the "drama" of bedtime[54] are no longer the young hero and his mother, but Proust and Hahn.[55] What's more, whereas in the novel it is the mother who bestows the good-night kiss,[56] in the letter it is Proust who gives it to Hahn. In the novel, the mother's kiss is compared to a "host for an act of peace-giving communion," a token of love and "real presence" that confers "the power to sleep."[57] In the letter, the kiss's power is no less miraculous, as it collapses the past into the present (in the same sentence, the verb tenses slip from the French past infinitive, "having given you the kiss," to the infinitive present, "I kiss your hand") and absence into presence (the letter is written after Hahn has left boulevard Haussmann, but Proust nevertheless "kisses his hand").

The postscript to this same letter playfully states that, for Proust, the words "of our friendship and of my life" constitute a "pleonasm," that is, a semantically unnecessary redundancy. In this logic, "my life" and "our friendship" are equivalents, as the self does not exist apart from the other. Another letter from December 1912, written when Hahn was traveling in Romania, further develops this reasoning:

> My good Schweet
> I send you a little schwello. You are by now so mingled to my thoughts, my sleep, my readings, that writing to you seems to me almost as schwocking as writing to myself.[58]

"Writing to myself": pleonastic, unnecessary, shocking. The epistolary relation, by definition a circuit, an exchange based on absence, finds itself short-circuited if the participants turn out to be always present to each other, to not be two but instead somehow one. In such conditions, why write at all? Perhaps for the same reasons that one would write a work that is neither an autobiography nor a conventional novel.

Self-Readers

For Emmanuel Levinas, the doubling and othering of the self into the "I" of writing is precisely what opens the possibility of interior exploration in the *Recherche*:

> Proustian reflection, structured by a separation between the *I* and its state, imparts its own accent to the inner life by a kind of refraction. It is as if *I* were constantly accompanied by another myself [un autre moi-même], in unparalleled friendship, but also in a cold strangeness that life attempts to overcome. The mystery in Proust is the mystery of the other.[59]

A friendship without equal, another self: Proust's correspondence and sustained dialogue with Reynaldo Hahn, both in his presence and in his absence, that "horizon"[60] against which the novel was conceived and nourished in its early years, appears as a laboratory, a space of experimentation and reflection (understood as both mirroring and contemplation) in which Proust worked out the play of distance from the self (as strangely other) and proximity to the other (as a potential other self) that would come to characterize his narration.

Levinas's use of an optical metaphor to describe the novel's operation on the self as "a kind of refraction" derives from a much-cited statement by Proust's narrator in *Time Regained*. This volume, which we now know as the final tome of the *Recherche*, is a posthumous assemblage by Proust's brother Robert and the editors of the NRF publishing house, based on six fair-copy notebooks ("cahiers de la mise au net") largely written in Proust's own hand and numbered XV to XX.[61] The famous passage comparing the novel to an "optical instrument" and stating that "every reader is ... the reader of his own self" can be found in Cahier XIX, in a long paperole (a series of sheets glued to a notebook page): "In reality every reader is, while he is reading, the reader of his own self. The writer's work is merely a kind of optical instrument which he offers to the reader to enable him to discern what, without this book, he would perhaps never have perceived in himself."[62] These sentences are immediately preceded by an odd double reflection, on "the invert who reads" a book written by an unspecified author and "gives to his heroines a masculine countenance," and about Racine who "himself was obliged, as a first step towards giving her a universal validity, for a moment to turn the antique figure of Phèdre into a Jansenist."[63] In its juxtaposition of Racine and "inversion" in the middle of a pronouncement about the relation of the reading self to the novelistic other, the sequence condenses and erases—but also makes visible, if we know how to read it—the earlier, discarded scene of the "conversation with *Maman*," where Reynaldo Hahn was not only named but made to be present in the narrative. In that scene, the mother singing the chorus along with Hahn is compared to "one of the young girls at Saint-Cyr rehearsing in front of Racine," collapsing the present with the distant past; her description further states that "the lovely lines of her Jewish face, filled with Christian gentleness and Jansenist courage, turned her into Esther herself,"[64] thereby telescoping[65] "antique" alterity into present identity, the mother's Jewish difference into "universal" sameness, and the mother's own voice into Hahn's—"you truly the person whom, along with *Maman*, I love the most in the world."[66] Such is, according to the revelations of *Time Regained*, the power of the instrument that is the book offered to the reader, through which she can encounter another self.

Notes

1 These reflections on the self and the other in Proust's correspondence are indebted to Christie McDonald, who invites us to ponder, in the context of a roundtable with Jacques Derrida, "... the pronoun 'I,' which is not only the addresser but the addressee, the one for whom one always writes, and only in his/her absence." Christie McDonald, "From one Genre to the Other," in Jacques Derrida, *The Ear of the Other: Otobiography, Transference, Translation* (1982), ed. Christie McDonald, trans. Peggy Kamuf (Lincoln: University of Nebraska Press, 1985), 48.
2 A book-length study of the topic is even titled "Proust as mirrored in his correspondence." Luc Fraisse, *Proust au miroir de sa correspondance* (Liège: SEDES, 1996).
3 Jean-Marc Quaranta, postface to Marcel Proust, *Lettres au duc de Valentinois*, ed. J.-M. Quaranta (Paris: Gallimard, 2016), 71–3.
4 Martin Robitaille, *Proust épistolier* (Montréal: Les Presses de l'Université de Montréal, 2003).
5 "Friendship [is] an abdication of the self ... Friendship is not merely devoid of virtue, like conversation, it is fatal to us as well." Marcel Proust, *Within a Budding Grove*, trans. C. K. Scott Moncrieff and T. Kilmartin, rev. D. J. Enright (New York: Modern Library, 2003), 664.
6 See the biography by Francesco Rapazzini, *Élisabeth de Gramont: Avant-gardiste* (Paris: Fayard, 2004).

7 Marcel Proust, *Correspondance*, ed. Philip Kolb, 21 vols. (Paris: Plon, 1970–93), XX, 334. Hereafter cited as *Corr*. Unless otherwise indicated, all translations are mine. The catalog cited by Kolb is *Catalogue Maison Charavay*, n° 713 (October 1963), lot n° 29585.
8 Bescherelle aîné, Bescherelle jeune and Litais de Gaux, *Grammaire nationale, ou grammaire de Voltaire, de Racine, de Fénelon . . . et de tous les écrivains les plus distingués de France*, 2nd ed. (Paris: L. Bourgeois-Maze, 1835–6), 157.
9 Émile Littré, *Dictionnaire de la langue française*, 4 vols. (Paris: Hachette, 1863–73). See littre.org/definition/même.
10 See for instance Antoine Compagnon, "Racine est plus immoral," in *Proust entre deux siècles* (Paris: Seuil, 1989), 65–107.
11 Marcel Proust, Cahier 2, f° 6 recto. NAF 16642, Bibliothèque nationale de France. See gallica.bnf.fr/ark:/12148/btv1b60004692/f8. This passage is transcribed, without the variants found on the manuscript, in *Contre Sainte-Beuve*, ed. Bernard de Fallois (1954) (Paris: Gallimard (folio), 1987), 118.
12 See Nathalie Mauriac Dyer, "Composition and publication of *À la recherche du temps perdu*," in *Marcel Proust in Context*, ed. Adam Watt (Cambridge: Cambridge University Press, 2013), 34–40.
13 In the novel, Racine's play *Esther* (1689), about the Persian queen who hides and later reveals her Jewish identity, is cited by the narrator during the revelations of *Sodom and Gomorrah*: trans. C. K. Scott Moncrieff and T. Kilmartin, rev. D. J. Enright (New York: Modern Library, 2003), 87–8.
14 One of Proust's private drawings for Hahn is a portrait of the composer draped in the titles of his works, including "choeurs d'*Esther*" ("choruses for *Esther*"). *Marcel Proust: Collection Marie-Claude Mante*, Paris, Sotheby's, May 24, 2018, lot 156, see sothebys.com/en/auctions/ecatalogue/2018/livres-et-manuscrits-pf1803/lot.156.html.
15 André Dacier, *La Vie de Pythagore, ses symboles, ses vers dorez et la vie d'Hiéroclès* (Paris: Rigaud, 1706), 100.
16 René Descartes, *The Passions of the Soul* (1649), § 90, trans. Jonathan Bennett, 2017, see earlymoderntexts.com/assets/pdfs/descartes1649.pdf.
17 See Luc Fraisse, *L'Éclectisme philosophique de Marcel Proust* (Paris: Presses de l'université Paris-Sorbonne, 2013), 699–710.
18 *The Fugitive*, trans C. K. Scott Moncrieff and T. Kilmartin, rev. D. J. Enright (New York: Modern Library, 2003), 607.
19 Philip Kolb, "Chronologie," in *Corr.*, I, 76.
20 *Corr.*, I., 308–9.
21 "[The Tuileries gardens] are always full of pederasts." Letter to Édouard Risler, paraphrased in Bernard Gavoty, *Reynaldo Hahn: Le musicien de la Belle Époque* (Paris: Buchet-Castel, 1976), 93.
22 [July 3?, 1896], *Corr.*, II, 88.
23 [Around February 24, 1904], *Corr.*, IV, 66.
24 [Shortly after October 21, 1922], *Corr.*, XXI, 515. The letter is typed; in the passage cited, Hahn crossed out "j'ai" and corrected it with "j'aurai" in pen, thereby replacing the past construction "person I have loved" with the future perfect "person I will have loved," and inferring that his love for Proust, rather than existing in the past, will continue into the future. *Collection Patricia Mante-Proust*, Sotheby's, Paris, May 31, 2016, lot 229, 88–9, see sothebys.com/en/auctions/ecatalogue/2016/livres-manuscrits-pf1603/lot.229.html.
25 For an insightful analysis of the Proust-Hahn correspondence including these playful nicknames, see Simone Delesalle-Rowlson, "'Le Bunibuls de Monsieur Proust' et la

philologie," in *Proust et les «Moyen Âge»*, ed. Sophie Duval and Miren Lacassagne (Paris: Hermann, 2015), 315–32.
26 [August 28 or 29, 1896], *Corr.*, II, 111.
27 See Philip Kolb, notes 6 and 7, in *Corr.*, II, 113–14.
28 *Corr.*, II, 111.
29 [March 25, 1912], in Françoise Leriche, "Lettres inédites du Kolb-Proust Archive," *Bulletin d'informations proustiennes* 26 (1995), 17.
30 [May 5 or 6, 1908], *Corr.*, VIII, 111; *Manuscrits et autographes*, Ader Nordmann, Paris, June 27, 2013, lot 112, see ader-paris.fr/lot/15316/3105662.
31 [Early February 1904], *Corr.*, IV, 54. On Proust and Whistler, see Kazuyoshi Yoshikawa, *Proust et l'art pictural* (Paris: Honoré Champion, 2010), 319–20, and "The Models for Miss Sacripant," in *Proust in Perspectives: Visions and Revisions*, ed. Armine Kotin Mortimer and Katherine Kolb (Urbana: University of Illinois Press, 2002), 248–51.
32 [September 1 or 2, 1907], *Corr.*, VII, 266.
33 *Marcel Proust* (Paris: Gallimard, 1996), 741. In 2018, J.-Y. Tadié reiterated this point in his lecture preceding a sale that included a few unpublished letters from Hahn to Proust ("Proust entre la littérature, l'amitié et l'édition," May 17, 2018, unpublished lecture for *Marcel Proust: Collection Marie-Claude Mante*, Sotheby's, Paris, May 24, 2018).
34 I consider that question in "Proust's Drawings and the Secret of the 'Solitary House,'" *Modern Language Notes* 133:4 (2018), 865–90.
35 During the war years, Hahn voluntarily enrolled in the French army, much to Proust's chagrin. From 1919, after Proust left boulevard Haussmann, Hahn found it more difficult to visit (*Corr.*, XVIII, 497, and XIX, 624). Starting in 1920, Hahn also spent multiple months of the year in Cannes and Deauville. See: Philippe Blay, "Chronologie," in *Reynaldo Hahn: Un éclectique en musique*, ed. P. Blay (Arles: Acte Sud/Palazzetto Bru Zane, 2015), 44–5.
36 Letter to Lucien Daudet, January 25, 1914, *Corr.*, XIII, 73.
37 Letter to Madame Gaston Arman de Caillavet (née Jeanne Pouquet) [shortly after mid-January 1910], *Corr.*, X, 31. "Fumigation" refers to an asthma treatment that involved burning a medicated powder.
38 Tadié, *Marcel Proust*, 295.
39 Céleste Albaret with Georges Belmont, *Monsieur Proust* (Paris: Robert Laffont, 1973), 275.
40 "I read the whole beginning (200 pages!) to Reynaldo and his response greatly encouraged me ... I now feel it is my duty above all else to work toward finishing this." Letter to Georges de Lauris, [shortly before November 27, 1909], *Corr.*, IX, 218.
41 To translate Proust and Hahn's epistolary "lansgage," which is formed by adding superfluous consonants (particularly "h" and "s") and modifying vowels in certain words, I make similar modifications to these words' English equivalents (often adding "schw"). Here for instance, I render "hescrire" [écrire] as "schwrite" and "trabouler" [travailler] as "schwork." Virginie Greene describes "lansgage" as "a mix of childish expressions, medieval spellings and phonetic notations of the manner of speaking of a foreigner of imprecise origin, a bit sibilant and speaking with a bad cold." Marcel Proust, *Lettres*, ed. Françoise Leriche with Caroline Szylowicz (Paris: Plon, 2004), 1240.
42 [October 24, 1908], *Corr.*, VIII, 253. As noted by Kolb, Proust paraphrases Ruskin's *Fors clavigera*, vol. IV, letter 37 (January 1874), in *The Works of John Ruskin* (London: Library Edition, 1907), XXVIII, 22.
43 Letter to Robert de Billy, [September 1895], *Corr.*, I, 426.

44 [August 4, 1910], *Corr.*, X, 157–8.
45 Antoine Albalat, *Gustave Flaubert et ses amis : avec des lettres inédites de Gustave Flaubert* (Paris: Plon, 1927), 7. See also Louis Bouilhet, *Lettres à Gustave Flaubert*, ed. Maria Luisa Cappello (Paris: CNRS éditions, 1996).
46 Kolb, note 10, *Corr.*, X, 158.
47 Virgil, *Eclogues, Georgics, Aeneid I–VI*, trans. H. R. Fairclough, rev. G. P. Goold (Cambridge, MA: Harvard University Press, H. R. Loeb Classical Library, 1999), 61–3. A tamarisk is a flowering shrub.
48 Zadig is Reynaldo Hahn's dog in this period: Proust famously addressed a letter to him, explaining his literary aesthetics in dog-accessible terms. [Shortly after November 3, 1911], *Corr.*, X, 372–4.
49 [Early November 1911], *Corr.*, X, 367.
50 [Shortly before mid-January 1912], *Corr.*, XI, 29.
51 Hahn's telegram has not reached us.
52 [early 1912?], *Corr.* XI, 39–40.
53 See above, n. 40.
54 *Swann's Way*, trans. C. K. Scott Moncrieff and T. Kilmartin, rev. D. J. Enright (New York: Modern Library, 2003), 58.
55 As we recall, an 1896 letter declared that "You [are] truly the person whom, along with *Maman*, I love the most in the world." See above, n. 22.
56 "My sole consolation when I went upstairs for the night was that Mamma would come in and kiss me after I was in bed." In later sentences the kiss is described more precisely as the young hero kissing his mother on the cheek. Proust, *Swann's Way*, 15.
57 Ibid.
58 [December 3, 1912], *Corr.*, XI, 309.
59 Emmanuel Levinas, *Proper Names*, trans. Michael B. Smith (Stanford: Stanford University Press, 1996), 102. Translation modified.
60 See above, n. 32.
61 See Robert Proust's correspondence with the NRF, *Les Années perdues de la Recherche, 1922-1931*, ed. Nathalie Mauriac Dyer with Alain Rivière and Pierre-Edmond Robert (Paris: Gallimard, 1999).
62 Marcel Proust, Cahier XIX, f° 29 recto, paperole. NAF 16726, Bibliothèque nationale de France. See gallica.bnf.fr/ark:/12148/btv1b6000680s/f83. *Time Regained*, trans. A. Mayor and T. Kilmartin, rev. D. J. Enright (New York: Modern Library, 2003), 322.
63 *Time Regained*, 321.
64 See above, n. 11.
65 In a different passage from *Time Regained*, the narrator observes that "it was a telescope that I had used to observe things which were indeed very small to the naked eye, but only because they were situated at a great distance, and which were each one of them in itself a world." *Time Regained*, 520.
66 See above, n. 22.

Chapter 13

EKPHRASING AS ENCOUNTER: "TRY SAY" WITH GEORGES DIDI-HUBERMAN AND HÉLÈNE CIXOUS

Ginette Michaud

> ...une rencontre qui ne serait pas une incroyable, improbable et miraculeuse imprévisibilité ne serait pas une rencontre. Une rencontre doit rester de rencontre, improbable, aléatoire, chanceuse, indémontrable et à jamais étrangère au savoir. On ne saura jamais, ce qui s'appelle savoir, si on a pu rencontrer quelqu'un—ce qui s'appelle rencontrer.
>
> Jacques Derrida, *H. C. pour la vie, c'est à dire...*,
> Paris, Galilée, 2002, p. 59.[1]

Deconstruction and the "arts of the visible"

As early as *Speech and Phenomena* (1967) and *Of Grammatology* (1967), Jacques Derrida examined the *mise en scène* of "appearances, phenomena, ideas, even visibility as such, in the history of philosophy."[2] This "old concern" of his "was brought up to date,"[3] as he put it, by *Memoirs of the Blind*, the art exhibition that he curated in 1989. Indeed, from the very beginning(s), his comprehensive critique of metaphysics was inextricably tied to the deconstruction of phenomenology, of the visible-invisible. In the philosophical tradition, this entails a calling into question of the theoretical authority exerted by the sense of sight, "understood from the time of the Greeks," as Éliane Escoubas reminds us, "as philosophy of presence, full presence, presence of the presenting presence."[4] Insofar as "from the time of the Greeks until the advent of phenomenology...everything starts with 'seeing,'" it comes as no surprise that blindness should be that which is "going to emerge and lead us in our critique of the philosophy of presence or phenomenology."[5] The lucidity of Derrida's gesture is thus readily apparent: by losing sight of...sight, he focuses his attention on the distinction between sight and vision—more broadly, on the question of "viewpoints" (in its equivocal sense in English), which structures the experience of seeing for the draftsman, who is a "blind seer" of sorts.

This *abocular* point of view aims to rethink the optical apparatus's very configuration, which in-forms, even pre-forms and de-forms every experience or perception in advance. By delving into the eye's configuration, Derrida tells another "story of the eye,"[6] through a kind of thinking that is "out of sight"—one whereby things are no longer anticipated, predicted, or foreseeable. In other words, he tries to go beyond immediate perception, appearance, apprehension, and prehension so as to make room for a-perception or for a "phenomenology of the inapparent."[7]

This other way of framing "the question of seeing and saying, of the invisibility at the heart of the visible"[8] is also a manner of seeing without fore-sight: "What does not to fore-see mean? ... For instance ... can one paint without fore-seeing, without design [*dessein*]? Can one draw [*dessiner*] without a design? That is to say, without seeing something coming?"[9] Indeed, the critique of *eidos*—which, as Derrida reminds us, means "determination of being ... in Plato," the "idea" but also the "contour of a visible form,"[10] i.e. the "image"—hinges on the corollary problem of the event, much like the *abocular* point of view that he contrasts with pure phenomenality. As such, art plays a central role here, particularly when it comes to the experience of the line [*trait*], which does "not merely designate some visible or some space," but rather, far more radically, comes about and *makes its way* as "stroke or *spacing*,"[11] as "the free opening of spacing";[12] it is, in short, "another experience of difference."[13]

Several questions arise here: what part does deconstruction play in the problem of the work of art? How does this point of view alter our gaze, even our approach to the optical apparatus that organizes sight? How does it compel us to rethink our relationship with the work of art, particularly in regard to the question of ekphrasis, which exceeds its strictly descriptive formal function? Indeed, when we think sight through a blind spot or a shadow, "out of sight"; when we heed Joyce's injunction, "[s]hut your eyes and see,"[14] we begin to *look* differently by "owning up to an experience where *nothing* is stable *anymore*,"[15] to quote the art historian Georges Didi-Huberman's *Essayer voir* (*Try See*). "When faced with the image," we must "willingly ... lose track of our own words" because "that is precisely where a new opportunity lies in wait for speech, writing, knowledge and even thought as such."[16] Indeed, the act of *looking* "transforms everything"; it even "rends language itself."[17]

Didi-Huberman: Try Say See

Whenever we transcribe sight, we invent another kind of phrasing—an *ekphrasing*. But how can writing account for the gaze's muteness, for the mute work of art? One of the most interesting aspects of Didi-Huberman's work is his willingness to take the "gaze's looming blurriness"[18] into account, to go beyond perception so as to rethink the latter from a nocturnal, even blind perspective (Derrida's "Thinking Out of Sight" isn't too far off). Using phenomenology as his starting point, Didi-Huberman unceasingly questions the very notions of "being" and "subject." As early as *L'homme qui marchait dans la couleur* (*The Man Who Walked in Color*, 2001), he critiques "the eye of perception," resolutely distancing himself from

Gestalt psychology in order to hazard another kind of liminal experiment, one that plays "on borders and through passages, ushering us toward uncanny, troubling states," leaving "visible space" behind for the uneasy experience of a "visual place": "We must conceive of visual place beyond the visible forms that circumscribe its spatiality; we must conceive of the gaze beyond our eyes. After all, we dream with our eyes closed."[19]

For Didi-Huberman, it is not so much a question of how to "try to say" as how to "try say":[20] it is a gesture that, through "'half-heard words,'"[21] poetically matches the image by conveying how sight discloses language. What matters here is the sensation of reaching the ends of language, of digging ever deeper until you lose yourself in the feeling of indescribability that lies at the heart of description. Yet it works out perfectly because both sides of the seeing/saying divide involve the same silence, the very same night wherein writing is tasked with becoming "clairvoyant"[22] by imagining an *interpretive* phrasing, "in the hazy or musical sense of the term, of course, without reference to any sort of iconographic deciphering."[23] Such is "the muteness of the gaze":[24] it is a "*summoning of language* in the very locus where it is still lacking."[25]

It thus comes as no surprise that, more so than phenomenological descriptions of visual artworks, Didi-Huberman favors literary descriptions that attempt such anamneses so as to "try say." Beckett, especially, is singled out as the quintessential spectator who is deprived of the use of language when faced with a painting. Quoting the *Three Dialogues*, Didi-Huberman holds Beckett up as "the paradigmatic writer ... of this kind of dialectic or "double distance": remembrance of the oldest forms ... *and* invention of the most radical forms of writing; a feel for the indescribable *and* linguistic experimentation within the bounds of this very powerlessness."[26]

Didi-Huberman revealingly grounds his reflection in that which rends sight, preventing it from straightforwardly deciphering what we think lies before our eyes. He dwells on that which quivers at the edge of perception, those instances when the visible (or *visuality*) emerges as distinct from seeing. Indeed, he accounts with unswerving analytic rigor for all of these wavering, fuzzy states in which we're fascinated by a fleeting form as language falls short. What does it mean, then, to look when we do not see anything—or so little or so poorly? With reference to James Coleman's work, Didi-Huberman writes in *Essayer voir*:

> It was as if I had grown weary of the language that had been available to me up to that point. I felt as though "undefined"—and not just indecisive, incapable of judgment—when faced with this image. Was I not myself the likeness of this undefinable form that stood before me, this form that had perhaps been devised by the artist so as to *undefine my language*?[27]

This lack is not a defect. Rather, it is the very condition of desire, of a still unexpected virtuality, of a new possibility: that language itself might open up. Didi-Huberman stresses the price we pay whenever we look: when faced with the image, we must (yet the same could be said of memory) own up to the "tedious sensation that arises whenever we delve into"²⁸ language, into the "[y]ou must go on"²⁹ of desire that reemerges "from the very bottom of the swell where language loses itself."³⁰ This "[y]ou must go on," writes the author of *Images malgré tout* (*Images in Spite of All*), is "the ethical formula that grounds the just relationship between desire and lack."³¹ And it is to this spacing, to this fluttering, that the essays of *Essayer voir* undoubtedly draw our attention, assaying "an experience that cannot be separated from its risk and its application."³²

Cixous: "Seeing with the Tongue"

If, as Derrida suggests in the aforementioned epigraph, every encounter must remain "alien to knowledge" and unpredictable, literally un-foreseeable; if, as Didi-Huberman invites us to think, it is necessary to rethink the relation between knowledge and sight so as to open up an unknown bypath between the French homonyms "*savoir*" and "*ça voir*," I would now like to further discuss the question of ekphrasis in light of Hélène Cixous's recent writings, as it is the site of an "encounter" between philosophy, art, and literature that allows us to reflect on what happens and comes to pass as an event between the visual and the sayable, between seeing and saying. The problem of transfer and translation from one art to the other is doubly relevant here considering its importance for Christie McDonald, whether it concerns music—so vital in her writings on Rousseau and Proust—or painting (I'm thinking here of *The Proustian Fabric*,³³ as well as of her beautiful volume, *Images of Congo*,³⁴ dedicated to her aunt Anne Eisner, a painter and ethnographer, not to mention *Painting My World*,³⁵ about her mother, Dorothy Eisner, who was also a painter).

Hélène Cixous's writings on art embody this new adventurous account of the encounter between drawing and writing. They chart a new path, both intimate and poetic, by intertwining seeing (be it a quasi-blindness) and reading, so as to listen and respond to the cry she hears in the "*pain*ting." As Hervé Sanson observes with reference to *Insurrection de la poussière* (*Insurrection of Dust*),³⁶ a work that subtly blends photographs and drawings by Adel Abdessemed with his handwritten exchanges with Cixous,

> languages are different; how to understand each other? Does something occur through misunderstanding itself—insuperable, irreducible? How to communicate when one wields words and the other images, solid bodies? How do we think through images, graphic lines? How does writing see and allow us to see?³⁷

As we know, Hélène Cixous has written extensively on the arts, as evidenced not only by *Poetry in Painting*,³⁸ but by her oeuvre as a whole. From *Portrait du soleil* (*Portrait of the Sun*, 1974) and *Portrait de Dora* (*Portrait of Dora*, 1976) to *Portrait of Jacques Derrida as a Young Jewish Saint* (2001) and "Portraits of Portraits: The Very Day/Light of Roni Horn" (2008), the portrait (among other matters) is steadily deployed in her thinking on aesthetics. An oft-quoted and discussed passage from "The Last Painting or the Portrait of God" has in fact become emblematic of her relationship with art as a whole: "I would like to write like a painter. I would like to write like painting,"[39] she states, a sentence whose ambiguous syntax hints at several possibilities: would she like to write as a painter paints . . . or writes? Is she talking about "painting writing" or "writing painting"?[40] The "two practices, foreign to each other yet bound to meet . . . not on one or the other side" but on the same "other stage," are summoned here "in the manner of a *shared enigma.*"[41] On the one hand, works of fine art are for Cixous "one with instances of language."[42] On the other hand, while it is true that writers have "an unusually harmonious way with words and the ability to make them new," this is merely the first step, as "one must then consider where one is going, what will come about, with the aid of a *given* writing, as one goes ever further, deeper into thought by way of painting, into painting by way of thought."[43] After all, painting already *thinks*; it already is a *cosa mentale*, to quote Leonardo da Vinci: "In search of his/her own idiom, the poet learns to write through painting as the painter makes his way through language, via its wealth of sentences and silences."[44]

This "unconditional admiration for the fine arts" has occasionally been made explicit by Cixous in terms of a "regrettably impossible equivalency,"[45] since painting possesses certain features that writing lacks, such as speed of execution; the right to repeat and to "repent"; the ability to *make* us see (*fairevoir*) time; and especially the ability "not to create hierarchies"[46] out of the subjects that painting chooses to depict. This is true, for instance, of the "root" that Cixous singles out in Alechinsky's work as the "being of beings," a "marvelous mixture of kinds of beings that rolls space into vegetal as well as human species," the "umbilical cord of the born artist": "The root is everything, Nature, sculpture, painting, drawing, fossil and embryo, baboon and god."[47] Thus, "[e]very painted subject is equal to every other":[48] a statement that echoes Derrida's statement *tout autre est tout autre* (every other is entirely other),[49] emphasizing the ethical equivalency of species and genders. And while Cixous is sensitive to the difference between these "poetic lookalikes"[50]—*Mais le Poème est fait en temps. Et le tableau sur espace.* (But the Poem is made of time. And the painting on space.)[51]—she is also attentive to the similarities that reveal "writing-or-drawing" to be "twin adventures."[52] Indeed, she acknowledges the utter equality of painting and writing in that both call for language that oversteps its own boundaries, whether visual or verbal, coining the beautiful word *co-vivance* (co-vival)[53] to describe how the writer and the artist are bound in the same creative gesture.

This sustained attentiveness to art has become more important still over the past decade, as Cixous has dedicated several substantial essays to artists such as Roni Horn, Simon Hantaï, Nancy Spero, Pierre Alechinsky, Luc Tuymans, and Adel Abdessemed. I would now like to highlight, without purporting to be exhaustive, some of the more striking traits of her poetics by reflecting on the simultaneously aesthetic, ethical, psychic and political scope of art and by drawing on the ancient trope of ekphrasis, that twin sister of literature.

In her contribution to an issue of *Études françaises* dedicated to this question, Hélène Cixous begins by "*excusing*" herself. Indeed, she claims to be unable to define her conception of ekphrasis as asked:

It won't make an EKphrase out of their EKphrases.

I looklisten and am compelled to face up to their appearance: these defiant people are none other than the EKphrases themselves, running along, passing me by, accompanying me, my choir, a choir for my cores [*cœurs*].

You have already guessed, before I even began *drawing* this address ... as you behold my face *painted* with worry, that I won't overeKphrase my tribe of EKphrases.

And for good reason. I ... have only ever EKphrased.[54]

Much could be said about the italicized verb that opens Cixous's non-answer. Indeed, this "excuse" is her idiosyncratic way of not evading the question "what is an EKphrase?," subverting it, or perhaps running along with it. Although Cixous "*excuses herself*" for being unable to write on this topic, it is obviously not for lack of things to say but rather because she believes the question escapes any predefined boundary due to its singular impetus: "I eKphrase as I breathe,"[55] she adds, a quote simultaneously inspired by Montaigne's *Essays* and Derrida's "Circumfession" ("I posthume as I breathe").[56] Furthermore, in the passage quoted above, we can see that Cixous's sentence rephrases the mode of encountering itself, as the beings she calls her "EKphrases" never manifest themselves directly, but only in an oblique, fleeting way (I will return to this quality later), as they appear and disappear at a pace similar to that of writing itself. The new trope of "ekphrasis" cannot thus merely settle for a pedestrian translation, even less for an already given knowledge. It must accompany, move alongside (a gesture that bespeaks some measure of longing) the work of art, in tune with its most tumultuous, dynamic, intense desire, yet without ever taking hold of it.

Moreover, by turning the Greek noun into a verb, Cixous kindles, with renewed energy, a trope that is all too often stabilized into a well-behaved reproduction of the painting or the image. The act of "eKphrasing" is thus given over to an unprecedented expansion, pushing back the limits of description or commentary, becoming breath, gesture, action, performative event. Here, the line or stroke of writing—which is also a drawing—delves into "what 'to see' may mean. And what 'to say' gives us to see,"[57] as Derrida puts it. Indeed, Cixous's "EKphrases" further underscore this chiasmus, which operates at the intersection of image and writing, where they poetically exchange their respective "insight" (*savoir*, to be understood here as "insight" into the "it" or "id" of *ça* in *ça voir*). For Cixous, painting and writing, even as they remain specific and different in their means, both "[n]eed to be translated into its other language."[58]

But what does it mean to see for Cixous? What does she see when she looks, from her nearly blind point of view, at a painting? "*My eyes constantly betray me. Near-sightedness and double vision accompany me, I write from up close, very close, one detail at a time.*"[59] Insofar as she argues, in *Relevé de la Mort* (*Keeping Track of Death*), that "we don't know what seeing means. When it comes to seeing, we know almost nothing,"[60] it is obvious that her approach to painting differs from that of Balzacian[61] realist-naturalist description, to say nothing of formal-semiological aesthetic erudition or art history, which she candidly admits to ignore. Instead, her approach to the work of art depends on another experience of seeing: that of language as such. "I love paintings the way the blind must love the sun: feeling it, breathing it in, hearing it pass through the trees, adoring it with regret and pain, knowing it through the skin, seeing it with the heart,"[62] she writes in "The Last Painting or the Portrait of God," where her "aisthesics" draw on all the senses (sound, touch, smell) that withdraw from vision.

As in her own writing, what Cixous favors in the work of art is "passion and passage,"[63] or what she calls, with reference to Clarice Lispector, "[t]he style of genesis. The style of *being in the course of* [en train de]."[64] She argues that this gerund is "the very first message"[65] of creation:

> Into which forms will the world which is (in the course of) being created be able to pour its tumultuous advent? How to write what is going to come what is coming what has just come what hardly is what has never been yet? How to write the thing about to be known, the first times, how to write for the first time? The unheard-of, the unseen, the mobile, the fragrance, the never looked at, the inside of a wardrobe, the gropings of thought.[66]

Going to see a painting, as she says of Hantaï's *Peinture* (*Écriture rose*),[67] implies first and foremost yielding to an enigma, to the unknown—and not just any unknown, but that which "everybody for all times immemorial has seen and recognized that it was: our unknown. The proper image of what is properly foreign to us inwardly."[68] That is what we must approach, meet and even come to know here, yet it is a knowledge that will forever border on non-knowledge: "To know? It is *to go towards*, by skipping from non-knowledge to non-knowledge. To not-know is an acknowledgment of the other. What gathers these unstable elements is the embrace of a look."[69]

The problem of art—its very being (provided we may still speak of essence)—is thus a stop-off point for unstable, turbulent and barely graspable phenomena (assuming this term maintains any relevance here): "They go past, they elude our grasp, they leave us trembling with searing memories."[70] Such is the surge of unstable messages that gets painted and of which the work keeps track, a vibration that the writer records and translates in turn via an "imagical"[71] sentence that doesn't seek to name but to *call* "it"—a thing, a being, i.e. these "physical *and* spiritual phenomena [that] present themselves and in that very second assert themselves and are gone."[72] Cixous focuses on writing, in all of its "fluttering fidelity,"[73] the exact moment when this metamorphosis springs forth and overtakes vision—the moment when these epiphanic phenomena of another kind take shape. Cixous is driven by these "amphibological refinements"[74] that solely an inventive instance of phrasing, in its meandering folds, can reveal. With marvelous precision, she then describes the moment when "the quaintness of the ambiguity"[75] is suddenly seen.

For Cixous, the moment when the limit fades is also when ekphrasis intimately touches on the question of sexual difference, on its advent beyond any border within a given language; when writing-painting compels us "to think the point of contact right to the communion between subject object active passive."⁷⁶ Significantly, this moment also entwines the poetical and the political in her eyes, as evidenced by this exemplary ekphrasis that could perhaps stand for all the others, regarding *In Search of Lost Time* (of course, I thought of Christie McDonald's meditations on Proust while reading it):

> The young girl he [the narrator] desires is not one, she is one of the components of the *little band* of young girls, she is *one or another of the "beings" or "creatures" or "types"* taken straight out of the sculpture studio of the French bourgeoisie, and yet she is forever unique but which is she? Who is she? Or rather which what is she? Because the narrator immediately declares that he is mad not about a certain young person but about *this* profound and multiple *this* that is collected under the proper name of this particular young girl. This *this* named Albertine, and sometimes one sometimes another of these totally surprising and unexpected types, isolated from their place and social class of origin, unclassifiable, equivocal, part vegetable, part animal, part honeysuckle, part pussy willow, part aeroplane ... This sharing-out of the visible universe where order, property or propriety reigns, along with the law of the separation of genres, genders, classes, species, kingdom.⁷⁷

Here, Cixous gives us an excellent description of this vibratory oscillation between *who* and *what*, exemplarily embodied by Albertine, who is a "fleeing being, being in flight."⁷⁸ Perhaps every instance of writing, every artistic process—as long as it accepts to think through the question "who am I?"—seeks, like Proust's novel, the moment that makes every signature literally, literarily impossible, when both generic and sexual gender dissolve into multiplicity or overpopulation: an intensification that secretes an unqualifiable "pinch of difference, a sexual sprinkling, a slight exaltation"⁷⁹ among these uncharacterizable "beings of unclear gender, human or musical or amorous, who recognize one another and deliver resounding messages in an ecstatic exchange of correspondences, identities, othernesses and enchanting supersubjectivities." Art—writing or painting—goes toward "that which meanders and flows ... by spilling over"⁸⁰ into the book or the painting, that which

> meandrogynes, that invents and saves the fragile, sumptuous mysteries of differences: sexual differences, and also "properly individual difference," the one which prevents an individual still alive, still formless, from being instituted and cadaverised in the state of a sexual, social identity, or of an identity of age and species: ... living being, ... according to circumstances, varies the context, the encounter, the season, going through diverse possibilities of incarnation in one day, changing epochs as well as species.⁸¹

The work's moment is the "mystery of the Advent," "[g]ermination in painting," "[w]hat happens *before* the work," preparing "[t]he wedding of the outside with the inside."⁸² This incessant beginning has always "already begun": "[i]t looks like the nave of a theatre before the birth of the play, that is, of the world. A luminous matrix whose very presence has evocative force: there's going to be some being. What? Who?"[83]

Standing before the work, Cixous is in the position of the dreamer, waiting for "the voice of the painting which floats hidden in the far end of the canvas, which attracts, which waits to be followed, to be sought, to be dreamt, to be hoisted up from the depths where it is being prepared."[84] A striking aspect of her approach to the work of art is that she conceives of it as neither subjective nor objective: indeed, the work of art is no object, but a thing, the "support for a main subjectile."[85] And in "First to Be Astounded," an essay on Pierre Alechinsky—her alter ego, a "paintwriter"[86] with whom she has repeatedly collaborated—she writes: "Now the canvas is set. It is all stretched out. It shivers. It is not fixed at all. A breath of air causes it to stir softly. With a sigh. Held lightly by drawing pins only, it could go away."[87]

This attention to stirring, to breath, to the source is constant in Cixous's writings on art. It is in this sense that writing and painting are bound by a common cause or thing: both engage with instantaneity,[88] *live*liness of execution, the fragmentary and the passage; both "invoke the invisible alongside the visible,"[89] pursuing the enigmas and mysteries of vision; lastly, both call on the imagination of the viewer/reader, challenging him/her in the process: "[W]hat matters to me most, in art, are works of being: works which no longer need to proclaim their glory, or their magisterial origin, to be signed, to return, to make a return to celebrate the author."[90] And in *Lemonade Everything Was So Infinite*, she adds: "Was not an 'art'-'work,' was not an object, was not the beautiful result of an ambition, hadn't been reached, aimed at, desired as a goal, hadn't been made for another to admire it."[91]

Cixous's ekphrastic writing thus gives rise to the "[s]cene of a passage between the image and the text."[92] Her essays—an open form of thought that is "simultaneously theoretical and poetical"[93]—are "transitional writings, just passing through, offbeat texts that lay bare a fleeting aspect of their own birth."[94] Likewise, as Cixous writes with reference to Clarice Lispector, we may say of Cixousian ekphrasis that "[w]ith writing she sees. She writes in order to see, she writes without having seen what is going to be written, then what she writes enables seeing."[95] In Cixous's work, then, the painting's reading-writing is indeed an *encounter*, in the strongest sense of the term, between the language of the painter and her own. But a true "encounter" runs counter to one and the other, since we don't know *who* signs that which takes shape between them.

One last (double) image in closing. We have seen that for Didi-Huberman as well as for Cixous the expression "touching with the eyes" gives rise to a poetics of the image that is not only new but unheard of, hitherto unseen, not yet *perceived* in a phenomenological sense. We find another eloquent example of this intensified exphrasing/ekphrasing in *Bark*, a retelling of Didi-Huberman's visit to the extermination camp at Auschwitz, where he comments on "three small strips of bark" he gathered while there, depicting them "as the three letters of a script preceding all alphabets":[96] "I looked, with the idea that looking would perhaps help me to read something that had never been written."[97] He then describes these few "pieces of bark"⁹⁸ as "pieces of skin, already flesh,"⁹⁹ images of a scratched, torn, ripped skin, but also "a surface of apparition endowed with life,"¹⁰⁰ a subjectile for "this unwritten thing he attempt[s] to read"¹⁰¹ which "[a]ppears through apparition, and not just through its appearances."¹⁰² Didi-Huberman recalls at the end of his essay that the word "bark" (*écorce*, *scortea*, "mantle of skin") has a double meaning: that of *cortex*, which ties it to the epidermis, and that of *liber*, the "part of the bark that serves even more easily than the *cortex* itself as a writing material."¹⁰³ Again, he speaks of this liminal, bordering space "where words and images meet," where "[t]hose things that fall from our skinnings (*écorchements*), those barks of images and texts [are] arranged and phrased together."¹⁰⁴

A similar image, bound to the skin, to the intimate, hypersensitive body, emerges in Cixous's essay on Adel Abdessemed's drawings. Glossing this work, which was inspired by the famous kiss the two lovers exchange on the beach in *From Here to Eternity* (1953), Cixous hyperbolizes this image as the Image of all Ekphrasis and says of this "moving epiphany" that it is not only "[t]he Image of the Kiss" but "the Kiss-image"¹⁰⁵ itself, thus suggesting that it is more than a mere analogy and that every image "tremble[s] from the Kiss of eternity":¹⁰⁶

> The image of the Kiss. The Kiss-image. The Image escapes us, but not before having struck us. For a second we have touched immortality. The Kiss immortalizes us, the whole it remains . . .
>
> The Kiss cannot be seen. It pounces on us and knocks us into the abyss of the sky. It does not rest until it has left us wounded burned marked by its visit. It is a spirit, a fateful trembling of the being, the violent encounter of two bodies that want to form a single god. The Kiss is neither masculine nor feminine, it is warlike, vanquished and victorious, it is the sea having been with the sun, fire mixed with water . . .

This Kiss-image could very well be the most unbelievable encounter Derrida ever dreamt up, the most erotic form of Ekphrase ever imagined. It is an encounter of another kind where the work of art "bumps into us, knocks us over, rolls us frantic to the edge of the universe, to the beginnings, where you I the sea thrash about in the ecstasy of genesis."¹⁰⁷

*Translated by Cosmin Toma**

Notes

* A different version of this text was published in French under the title "'J'eKphrase comme je respire . . .': poétique de l'*ekphrasis* dans quelques textes récents d'Hélène Cixous," in *Ententes—À partir d'Hélène Cixous*, ed. Stéphanie Boulard and Catherine Witt (Paris: Presses Sorbonne Nouvelle, 2018), 33–43.

1 ". . . an encounter that would not be unbelievably, improbably, and miraculously unpredictable would not be an encounter. An encounter has to remain casual [*de rencontre*], improbable, risky, fortuitous, unprovable, and forever alien to knowledge. One will never know—what is called knowing—if one was able to meet somebody—

what is called meeting." Jacques Derrida, *H. C. for Life, That Is to Say . . .* , trans. Laurent Milesi and Stefan Herbrechter (Stanford, CA: Stanford University Press, 2006), 64.
2. Michael Naas, "La nuit du dessin: Foi et savoir dans *Mémoires d'aveugle* de Jacques Derrida," *Cahiers de l'association internationale des études françaises* (AIEF) 62 (May 2010): 254. Translation mine—Trans.
3. Jacques Derrida, "Drawing by Design," trans. Laurent Milesi, in *Thinking Out of Sight: Writings on the Arts of the Visible*, ed. Ginette Michaud, Joana Masó, and Javier Bassas, with new translations by Laurent Milesi. (Chicago: The University of Chicago Press, forthcoming 2021), 104.
4. Éliane Escoubas, "Derrida and the Truth of Drawing: Another Copernican Revolution?," trans. Paul Milan, *Research in Phenomenology* 36 (2006): 202.
5. Escoubas, 202–3.
6. See Georges Bataille, *Story of the Eye*, trans. Joachim Neugroschel (London: Penguin Books, 2001). Translation mine—Trans.
7. Jacques Derrida, "Lignées," in Micaëla Heinich, *Mille e tre, cinq* (Bordeaux: William Blake & Co., 1996) (no. 981, n.p.). Translation mine—Trans.
8. Jacques Derrida, "The Philosopher's Design," trans. Laurent Milesi, in *Thinking Out of Sight*, 97.
9. Jacques Derrida, "Thinking Out of Sight," trans. Laurent Milesi, in *Thinking Out of Sight*, 33.
10. Derrida, 42.
11. Derrida, 47.
12. Derrida, 38.
13. Derrida, 47.
14. James Joyce, *Ulysses* (1922; repr., London: Penguin Books, 2000), 45. In *Worstward Ho* (London: John Calder, New York: Grove Press, 1983), 11, Samuel Beckett rewords it as "[c]lenched staring eyes." In *Abstracts et Brèves Chroniques du temps. I Chapitre Los* (Paris: Galilée, 2013), 63, Hélène Cixous strikingly renders this lesson in turn: "[k]illing images. Saving visions. Close your eyes lest I pierce them." Translation mine—Trans.
15. Georges Didi-Huberman, *Essayer voir* (Paris: Minuit, 2014), 52. Translation mine—Trans.
16. Didi-Huberman, 52.
17. Didi-Huberman, 49.
18. Georges Didi-Huberman, *L'homme qui marchait dans la couleur* (Paris: Minuit, 2001), 58. Translation mine—Trans.
19. Didi-Huberman, 58–9.
20. Beckett, *Worstward Ho,* 17, cited in Didi-Huberman, *Essayer voir*.
21. Samuel Beckett, *A Piece of Monologue*, in *The Collected Shorter Plays* (New York: Grove Press, 2010), 269, cited by Didi-Huberman in *Essayer voir*, 97.
22. Didi-Huberman, 85.
23. Didi-Huberman, 85.
24. Didi-Huberman, 49.
25. Didi-Huberman, 50.
26. Didi-Huberman, 82.
27. Didi-Huberman, 52.
28. Didi-Huberman, 54.
29. Samuel Beckett, *The Unnamable*, in *Three Novels: Molloy, Malone Dies, The Unnamable* (New York: Grove Press, 2009), 407, cited by Didi-Huberman in *Essayer voir*, 54.
30. Didi-Huberman, 53.

31 Didi-Huberman, 54.
32 Didi-Huberman, 55.
33 Christie McDonald, *The Proustian Fabric: Associations of Memory* (Lincoln: University of Nebraska Press, 1991). See also Christie McDonald and François Proulx, ed., *Proust and the Arts* (Cambridge: Cambridge University Press, 2015).
34 Christie McDonald, ed., *Images of Congo: Anne Eisner's Art and Ethnography, 1946–58* (Milan: 5 Continents Editions, 2005).
35 Christie McDonald, ed., *Painting My World: The Art of Dorothy Eisner* (Suffolk: ACC Editions, 2009).
36 Hélène Cixous, *Insurrection de la poussière. Adel Abdessemed*, followed by A. A. and H. C., *Correspondance* (Paris: Galilée, 2014). Adel Abdessemed's drawings also accompany *Ayaï! Le cri de la littérature* (Paris: Galilée, 2013) and Cixous has written on his work elsewhere: "Lettre à Adel" [2015] (*Études françaises*, 37–45); "The Secret in the Tarp," in *Adel Abdessemed: From Here to Eternity* (Manhattan and Los Angeles: Venus, 2015), n.p.; and *Les Sans Arche d'Adel Abdessemed et autres coups de balai* (Paris: Gallimard, 2018).
37 Hervé Sanson, "D'apesanteur liés," review of *Insurrection de la poussière: Adel Abdessemed*, suivi de *A. A. H. C.: Correspondance*, by Hélène Cixous, *Continents manuscrits*, 2015, see http://coma.revues.org/610. Translation mine—Trans.
38 Hélène Cixous, *Poetry in Painting: Writings on Contemporary Arts and Aesthetics*, ed. Joana Masó and Marta Segarra (Edinburgh: Edinburgh University Press, 2012).
39 Hélène Cixous, "The Last Painting or the Portrait of God," trans. Sarah Cornell, in *"Coming to Writing" and Other Essays*, ed. Deborah Jenson (London and Cambridge, MA: Harvard University Press, 1991), 104.
40 Frédéric Regard, "Un effet de Manche: lecture de 'K. A Notebook' de Maria Chevska et Hélène Cixous," in *Cixous sous X, d'un coup le nom*, ed. Marie-Dominique Garnier and Joana Masó (Paris: Presses Universitaires de Vincennes, 2010), 99. Translation mine—Trans.
41 Regard, 99.
42 Hélène Cixous, *Le Voyage de la racine alechinsky* (Paris: Galilée, 2012), 30.
43 Hélène Cixous, *Luc Tuymans: Relevé de la mort*, vol. 1 (Paris: La Différence, 2012), 31.
44 Cixous, 32.
45 Sanson, see http://coma.revues.org/610. Translation mine—Trans.
46 Sanson, 125.
47 Cixous, *Le Voyage de la racine alechinsky*, 11, 14, 18, and 12. Translation mine—Trans.
48 Cixous, *Luc Tuymans*, 88.
49 Jacques Derrida, *The Gift of Death*, trans. David Wills (Chicago: The University of Chicago Press, 2008), 82.
50 Hélène Cixous, "Spero's Dissidances," trans. Laurent Milesi, in Cixous, *Poetry in Painting*, 22.
51 Hélène Cixous, *Le Tablier de Simon Hantaï: Annagrammes*, followed by H. C. and S. H., *Lettres* (Paris: Galilée, 2005), 41. Translation mine—Trans.
52 Hélène Cixous, "Without End, No, State of Drawingness, No, Rather: The Executioner's Taking Off," trans. Catherine A. F. MacGillivray, in *Stigmata: Escaping Texts* (London & New York: Routledge Classics, 2005), 17.
53 Cixous, *Insurrection de la poussière*, 21.
54 Hélène Cixous, "Quand H. C. essaie de s'*excuser*," *Études françaises* (2015) 51(2): 207. Emphasis mine ("*drawing*" and "*painted*"). Translation mine—Trans.
55 Cixous, "Quand H. C. essaie de s'*excuser*," 208.

56 Jacques Derrida, "Circumfession," in Jacques Derrida and Geoffrey Bennington, *Jacques Derrida*, trans. Geoffrey Bennington (Chicago and London: The University of Chicago Press, 1993), 26.
57 Derrida, "The Philosopher's Design," 97.
58 Cixous, "Quand H. C. essaie de s'*excuser*," 210.
59 Cixous, *Luc Tuymans*, 45.
60 Cixous, 25.
61 Olivier Ammour-Mayeur, "Hokusai: source d'un imaginaire de la littérature au xxe siècle (Hélène Cixous/Henry Bachau)," *Lettres romanes* 56:1–2 (2002): 143; www.brepolsonline.net/doi/abs/10.1484/J.LLR.3.49. Translation mine—Trans.
62 Cixous, "The Last Painting or the Portrait of God," 106.
63 Hélène Cixous, "Seeing with the Tongue: The Lispector Apocalypse," trans. Laurent Milesi, *Matador* (No. 0, 2012): 24–5.
64 Cixous, 24–5.
65 Cixous, 24–5.
66 Cixous, 24–5.
67 This movement, this urge *toward*, is essential for Cixous: "I didn't want to talk about painting or about Hantaï, she says. Rather I wanted to talk about my adventure, the painting's adventure, my going-to-encounter a thing said to be a painting . . ." Cixous, *Le Tablier de Simon Hantaï*, 11.
68 Cixous, "Seeing with the Tongue," 24–5.
69 Cixous, 24–5. As Cixous writes elsewhere: "All I know is that I feel things, I proceed via mysteries, I feel enigmas, and these enigmas are like flashing lights which make me advance. There are sparks in the night and I advance towards them. If I saw everything in advance, I wouldn't say anything anymore, or else I'd be a philosopher. I think that poetical work is a nocturnal work. It's a semi-oneiric work made up largely of divination and not of knowledge." In "Interview with Hélène Cixous," with Catherine Anne Franke and Roger Chazal, *Qui Parle* 3:1 (Spring 1989): 174.
70 Cixous, "Seeing with the Tongue," 24–5.
71 After the title of Hélène Cixous's text for Ernest Pignon-Ernest, "L'imagie d'Ernest," in *Face aux murs. Ernest Pignon-Ernest* (Paris: Delpire, 2010), 121–9.
72 Cixous, "Seeing with the Tongue," 24–5.
73 Cixous, 24–5.
74 Cixous, 24–5.
75 Cixous, 24–5.
76 Cixous, 24–5.
77 Hélène Cixous, "How Not to Speak of Algeria," trans. Eric Prenowitz, in *Volleys of Humanity: Essays 1972–2009*, ed. E. Prenowitz, (Edinburgh: Edinburgh University Press, 2011), 171–2.
78 Cixous, 171 and 173. It is this lifting of limits that is political for Cixous: "[i]t is not confusion we witness, but a deconstruction, an extension of the zones of exchange, a lifting of demarcations, the development of what in politics would be an accomplishment of the dream of the liberation of national flows, of a transnational intermingling." Cixous, 172.
79 Hélène Cixous, "Volées d'humanité," in *Rêver croire penser. Autour d'Hélène Cixous*, ed. Bruno Clément and Marta Segarra (Paris: CampagnePremière, 2010), 15. Translation mine—Trans.
80 Cixous, "Seeing with the Tongue," 24–5.
81 Cixous, 24–5.

82 Hélène Cixous, "First to be Astounded," trans. Laurent Milesi, in *Alechinsky. À contre-vent* (Paris et New York: Galerie Lelong & Co., 2012), 3.
83 Cixous, 4.
84 Cixous, 5.
85 Cixous, 7.
86 Cixous, *Le Voyage de la racine alechinsky*, 39.
87 Cixous, "First to Be Astounded," 5.
88 This privileged access to the present itself is what both writing and painting seek according to Cixous: "For me, that is what painting is, the chance to take hold of the third person of the present, the present itself." Cixous, "The Last Painting or the Portrait of God," 105.
89 Mary Bryden, "Hélène Cixous and Maria Chevska," in *Women and Representation*, ed. Diana Knight and Judith Still (University of Nottingham: WLF Publications, 1995), 106.
90 Cixous, "The Last Painting or the Portrait of God," 116.
91 Hélène Cixous, *Limonade tout était si infini* (Paris: Des femmes, 1982), 189, cited by Bryden in "Hélène Cixous and Maria Chevska," 107.
92 Regard, "Un effet de Manche," in Garnier, *Cixous sous X*, 114.
93 Didi-Huberman, *Essayer voir*, 83.
94 Regard, "Un effet de Manche," in Garnier, *Cixous sous X*, 116.
95 Cixous, "Seeing with the Tongue," 24–5.
96 Georges Didi-Huberman, *Bark*, trans. Samuel E. Martin (Cambridge, MA, and London: The MIT Press, 2017), 5.
97 Didi-Huberman, 5.
98 Didi-Huberman, 5.
99 Didi-Huberman, 120.
100 Didi-Huberman, 120.
101 Didi-Huberman, 5.
102 Didi-Huberman, 118.
103 Didi-Huberman, 120.
104 Didi-Huberman, 120–1.
105 Cixous, "The Secret in the Tarp," n.p.
106 Cixous, n.p.
107 Cixous, n.p.

Chapter 14

CARING FOR ENCOUNTERS

Verena Andermatt Conley

In the wake of the great voyages and discoveries, encounters are often thought of as meetings on distant lands between European conquerors and the native Other. First in a pen and ink, and later in copperplate in his *Nova reperta*, Jan Van der Straet—called Stradanus—famously depicts Amerigo Vespucci's discovery of the New World.[1] He shows the Tuscan traveler, dressed in layers of cloth and armor, arriving on *terra firma,* staring at a nude female who rises from her hammock to greet him while other natives are roasting what looks like human limbs in the background (Figure 14.1).

In the spirit of Michel de Certeau's well-known analysis of the engraving in the *Nova Reperta*, Vespucci, staring intently, his left hand firmly gripping his staff and gonfalon while letting his astrolabe hang from his right, projects upon the woman the feminine component of his own forename: *America*.[2] This scene, a subject of Vespucci's letters describing his discovery of the Americas, has become the bedrock of myriad (and often heroic) myths of encounter of the Other in the New World. They call forth images of white men disembarking from frigates and galleons, seeking gold and bringing civilization to scantily clothed natives. Exotic encounters and glorious conquests become the stuff and substance of a good deal of literature and painting. Yet already less than a century following the Columbian discoveries, Montaigne surmised in his *Essays* that the colonial enterprise (attributed to Spain under Charles V and Philip II) had managed to wreck half of the planet:

> The universe will fall into paralysis; one member will be crippled, the other in full vigor. I am much afraid that we shall have very greatly hastened the decline and ruin of this new world by our contagion, and that we will have sold it our opinions and our arts very dear.[3]

The voices decrying the violence that Montaigne observed in his time grew louder in the eighteenth century when philosophers (many in admiration of Montaigne) began to take colonial humanism to task. Theirs was a relentless and often devastating critique of what they felt to be appropriative encounters. Such nuanced and better-informed reports are part and parcel of literatures dear to Christie

Figure 14.1 Jan Van der Straet, "Amerigo Vespucci Discovers America" (circa 1587–9). Reproduced in accordance with the Metropolitan Museum of Art's Creative Commons Zero (CC0) policy.

McDonald: Montesquieu in his *Lettres persanes* (*Persian letters*, 1721), Voltaire and the native in "L'Ingénu" ("The Huron," 1767), Diderot and the Tahitian islanders in his *Supplément au voyage de Bougainville* (*The Supplement to Bougainville's Voyage*, 1771), La Condamine's tales of his travels up the Amazon, or even Rousseau who described alterity remarkably in his letters, discourses, reveries and diatribes.

With Christie McDonald as our guide, we delight in following what the above writers and philosophers had begun when taking stock of the sorry history of discoveries. Yet, today, at a time when communication and exchange move in every direction, all over the globe and at the speed of light, encounters are everywhere and nowhere. They occur fleetingly, in the physical world, but even more, often unbeknownst to us, in new media. In the stream and flow of moving texts and flashing images, they become the matter of sensors and tracking devices. Databases and algorithms now seem prerequisite to the idea of encounter and discovery. Vespucci's astrolabes, compasses, and sextants have given way to mobile devices that communicate with countless satellites, orbiting all over our earthly planet like electrons buzzing about an atom. Conceived in think tanks and laboratories, making use of new modes of exchange, contemporary strategies of marketing are priming "subjects of interest" for the countless humans they seek to charm and also control. It now appears that cultural differences that had made possible encounters with others—even that of Stradanus' figure of "Vespucci discovering America"—have become quaint, faint, and remote.

Yet, we do not have to follow such an extreme. In the humanities, encounters today take place with other types of knowledge, primarily from the sciences. The classical division between subject and object, hence between a self and an "other," tends to erode and disappear. Attention to new materialisms appeals to open systems and, more recently, to quantum fields and to discoveries in microbiology that call in question all binaries, to begin with, the division of self and (its often subservient) other, but also the lines of divide separating human and animal, things animate and inanimate or—as Claude Lévi-Strauss showed with obstinate passion—the demarcation of nature and culture.

Since 1979 at least, there has been a call for a "new alliance" between the humanities and the sciences. Isabelle Stengers argued for an enchanted nature to replace the inert counterpart found in older museums of natural history. Born in Belgium in 1949, Stengers studied chemistry before turning to philosophy to help her rethink official science. An avid reader and interlocutor of Alfred North Whitehead, Gilles Deleuze, Félix Guattari, Bruno Latour, and others, Stengers rejects the idea that life seeks a condition of homeostasis—in other words, a dynamically balanced continuity. As a student, she joined chemist and future Nobel Laureate Ilya Prigogine to study what they called "far from equilibrium conditions" and "dissipative structures," or the frequently unforeseen shifts that upset the idea of homeostasis of a system.[4] Seeking to ally the humanities with the applied and social sciences, Gilles Deleuze and Félix Guattari engage Prigogine and Stengers' creative reflections on the delicate and often tenuous character of living and inorganic orders. Their work on chaos theory—on what they call *chaosmos*—and on deterritorialization and rhizomatic thinking runs contrary to closed orders (such as the second law of thermodynamics) that predestine the end of things and of time.[5] The world as we see it now—such as in the throes of the present COVID-19 pandemic—is subject to sudden and even unpredictable connections and becomings.

In their reflections on "becoming microscopic," "becoming animal," "becoming other," even "becoming tick," Deleuze and Guattari assumed that order is ephemeral and all phenomena continually come out of and revert to a dark and unfathomable world of shadows, a *"fuscum subnigrum"*—in other words, a universal chaos.[6] "How" the universe works has to be continually reimagined in its ongoing formation and reformation, in its emergence both *from* and *within* chaos, in beginnings that begin over and again.[7] It could be said that Deleuze and Stengers think "processually," favoring areas where the give-and-take of force and circumstance induce change and where environmental shifts alter the face of things. In that sense they return to the art of analogy that, until the advent of the "new scientific spirit," had been at the core of all inquiry into what then were called the secrets of nature.[8] Tending to locate its beginnings in Descartes, for whom reason was a "matter of mind" and not of bodily, organic life, historians of modern philosophy can be apt to overlook Whitehead's legacy of process that Deleuze, Guattari, Stengers, and others have resurrected and redesigned in their work on sensory activity and ecology.⁹ It is this strange but enthusing push-and-pull of regression (to a quasi-medieval sensorium) and progression (toward a science of affect), I argue, where encounters become nexuses of relations and thus, in a strong philosophical sense, *events*. They lose their hostile animus of the kind felt in Stradanus's iconic image of Vespucci's encounter with the Other. They take place *between* "subjects," *among* humans as well as *across* species and things. The world, Stengers argues, no longer emerges from the subject as it had in Kant. In building on the work of Whitehead, she studies how the subject emerges from the world.[10] The subject is a "feeling" of and for its world. As Stengers puts it: "I produce myself qua feeling that which is not me."[11] To feel is to be affected. Sensation and affect, that is, a certain materiality, move (through) a "subject" that enters in relation with humans and things both animate and inanimate. The Cartesian idea that conceives reality as constructed of bits of matter that exist independently of one another is superseded by an event-based or process-oriented ontology. Stengers adds that events are primary and depend on each other (2011: 201). A (single) person is a continuation of overlapping events of relational encounters, with the consequence that "identity" remains forever an abstraction. Valuation and reaction become functions of creativity that construct the world. Reality is conceived as composed of processes of dynamic "becoming" rather than static conditions of "being." All physical things change and evolve continually. All organisms shape the world and are shaped by it. The universe is not finite but instead, evolves. "Essences" such as matter are mere abstractions. Perception is not limited to living, self-conscious beings. The term, "prehension" (from the Latin *prehendere*, to seize), indicates a kind of perception that can be conscious or unconscious. It can apply to people as well as to electrons. Stengers comments on how Whitehead rejects the theory of representative perception, in which the mind has only private ideas about other entities. Prehension indicates that the perceiver actually incorporates aspects of the perceived thing into itself.[12] Rather than being independent, entities are constituted by their perceptions and relations, though there are always some obligations and constraints. Stengers explains relational encounters as perceptions that occur in two modes: causal efficacy (or physical prehension) and presentational immediacy (or conceptual prehension).

A relational encounter, she clarifies, is an event, that is, in Whiteheadian terms, a prehension and a concrescence. If a prehension is something that is grasped, for Whitehead it is also likened to a "folding over." A concrescence holds together different, even contradictory terms in a tension that cannot be resolved. Concrescences open onto fabulations—that is, onto inventions, onto new ways of thinking and of assembling. In the words of Brian Massumi, because it is relational by its very nature, an event needs care and attention to a "dividual-transindividual complexity."[13] Of its own duration, an event does not happen in chronological time.[14] When cared for, an event can be made to last so as to precipitate other events and new encounters that, in turn, will engender other sensations and perceptions of space-times in locations that do not have to be contiguous. The subject is no longer the conscious master of itself, no longer, either, an entity that goes out to encounter the Other and take control of what it finds. The "subject" is traversed, even riddled, by affects and emotions that continually change it. If a trace of animus—fear of attraction, recoil before what seems unsettling—is felt in the English usage of "encounter" (as in Stephen Spielberg's *Close Encounters of the Third Kind* [1971], a wildly successful science fiction nail-biter), its experiential inflection is surely felt in the French *rencontre*, where a meeting of the known and unknown have heuristic potential. When discussing paternal relations in "Of the Affection of Fathers for their Children," in the second volume of the *Essays*, Montaigne ties this heuristic potential to the pleasure of inquiry into the world at large.[15]

In the pages he devotes to how he lives with his ill health, his travel to Italy, and his own relation with his immediate kin, Montaigne suggests that encounters have to be tended to with care. When we reinvent them as *rencontres* at the level of sensation, affect and intensity, we find ourselves practicing what, in a different yet correlative context, Brian Massumi calls a "situational openness."[16] In such cases, "subjects" are conditioned by others and by a collective and very plural texture of the encounter. They no longer have autonomy in respect to what they meet; rather, they (or we) experience encounters as collaborations and negotiations. Encounters fold into an aesthetics and an ethics—that is, a political art through which subjects can also invent and reinvent a world in common. Negotiations take place between subjects coming from different practices, rather than between those belonging to the same disciplines. To enable such encounters, boundaries have to be porous. The tensions and intensions of concrescences aspire to collective fabulations, speculations, to experiment with experience and hence, to open ourselves up to new possibilities.

Care for the event of encounter is also a *care of the possible*, which for Stengers can be understood as a kind of pragmatic practice.[17] Caring necessitates the thinking of possible openings on the one hand and, on the other, of predicting their consequences. Care of the possible entails speculating on how Earth is becoming inhabitable and, in practical measure, on how to inhabit it. For starters, it is incumbent upon all subjects to be critical of the concepts undergirding the past ravages of humanistic binary thinking. Subjects have to change their habits and their *habitus*. They have to live as collaborators—not as dominator or dominated. Oriented toward a relational future, subjects who inhabit the world today must think and act in "sympathy"[18] or "sympoietically"[19] with their environment, but in any case, with *care* understood as an ethical, aesthetic, and ecological commitment.[20]

To practice care is not just to care *for*, as in the humanistic paradigm that usually puts women in the role of caregivers expected to work selflessly (and in conditions of drudgery) and that the Pope invoked not long ago in his encyclical, *On Care for Our Common Home* (2015). Rather, the "subject" would live the encounter as event, with care and joy. In such an *ethos*, the "subject" folds and unfolds. As Deleuze, Guattari, and Stengers would say, it draws new diagrams and creates new assemblages. It becomes part of an ecology of practices; it collaborates with attentive sympathy. Even in the blitz of new media, it is not assimilated into priming and marketing but, rather, lives the intensity of events as relational encounters while projecting, imagining, and fabulating future modes and practices of care. Such a new "subject" is very different from the humanistic one that pitted the West against the rest of the world. "Westerners," as Bruno Latour calls them, may still wonder what will happen when the former "other" will sit at the table and share negotiations for the construction of a common world.[21] Such a commonality is, of course, what we would wish to happen—to see clichés of a subservient other begin to dissipate.

As we have seen, many representations of encounters deal with what in the age of humanism had been called the New World. Representations of "savages" such as those in the copperplate engravings in Stradanus's *Nova reperta*, but also in French accounts of travel, from André Thevet to Joseph-François Lafitau and others, are now remainders of a humanistic tradition under siege. To further honor Christie McDonald's attention to the visual medium, a 1914 painting by Jeannie Augusta Brownscomb, "The First Thanksgiving at Plymouth," illustrates the point.[22] At a long table, lightly positioned on a diagonal angle, are gathered nineteen men, women, and children. Lifting his folded hands toward heaven, a priestly, wizened man stands, his eyes closed, giving thanks to the Lord. A few native chiefs with colorful headdress (generally worn by Plains Indians!) sit at the very end of the table while in the background and at a distance from them, several other natives and one white man—for whom space is unavailable at the crowded table—huddle together, looking on with perplexity.

Even the chiefs sitting at the end of the table gaze at the scene innocuously, without participating in the ceremony that seems to be far from their ken. The rendering of this first Thanksgiving at Plymouth, a depiction of a foundational narrative of the United States, riddled with clichés, nonetheless moves away from the earlier confrontational representations or from those descriptions of the encounter on American shores where gentlemen happen upon naked indigenous women, wild men, and beasts. If the narrative in the picture does not completely *exclude* what is strange or foreign, as Charles Blow argued in an editorial published on Thanksgiving Day 2019, it also fails to *include* or call attention to the natives.[23]

Brownscomb's painting stands in strong contrast to what we know of Thanksgiving in the twenty-first century and of encounters. The latter are now rethought, rewritten, and re-presented as events taking place between co-equals, drawing on different areas of expertise, who enter into collaboration and negotiation, none of which presupposes the supremacy of Western knowledge, be it that of science, nature, technology, forms of government, or religion. There are now multiple natures[24] and sciences.[25] The former "others" are sitting at the table, eating and speaking in a new sharing of voices, be it in Jean-Luc Nancy's *Le partage des voix* (*Sharing Voices*, 1982) as both a sharing and a dividing of voices or, as Guattari would have it, with their mouths full—that is, by descending into matter, affect, and sensation.[26]

We can see the shift in sensibility, in ethics, and in aesthetics when we look at a recent depiction of encounters in the work of the Canadian Cree artist and member of the Fisher River Band, Kent Monkman, specifically in two of his monumental paintings under the title *mistikôsiwak* (*Wooden Boat People*) on exhibit in the Great Hall at the New York Metropolitan Museum of Art (December 27 to April 9, 2020). In the words of the artist, the paintings rewrite the history of exclusion that began with the first encounters. They fabulate other ways of inhabiting and being in common. The two murals, "Welcoming the Newcomers" (2019) and "Resurgence of the People" (2019), are produced in a multimedia style. Working from photographs of live models, Monkman employs a team of assistants, much as in the workshops of the great Baroque painters, by way of a collaboration before the artist brings the final touches to the painting.[27] Blending a series of well-known history paintings by Delacroix, Leutze, and others with the academic style of Bouguereau and Tissot, Monkman reimagines the encounter between Europeans and indigenous people.

"Welcoming the Newcomers" stages the event of encounter as something relational, in no way built on surprise, opposition or exclusion. The natives welcome the new arrivals, and, for the most part, lend the travelers a helping hand. The new arrivals do not descend from majestic galleons but fight for their lives after their vessel, a minuscule form in the upper right corner, appears to have been shattered and wrecked. Hailing from different ethnicities, social classes, those who arrive are not all white, nor do they bear the trappings of conquerors, Puritans or Pilgrims. As in the older copperplates, the painting is populated by humans *and* animals. We catch sight of the fin of a whale that might have caused the craft carrying the "wooden boat people" to capsize. A blond white man, perhaps a reimagining of Vespucci, is seen reaching for the breast of an indigenous woman (America?) while a beaver, standing erect on his palmate paws, appears both to salute him and to defend her. From a certain point of view the event can be seen depicting a care of a "relational encounter" in which the natives indiscriminately welcome and reach out to people from different backgrounds: white sailors, African slaves, and people from a gamut of ethnicities, possibly hired deck hands, and indentured servants. Seen thus, the mural would visibly undo existing binaries and clichés. It makes ethnic and gender boundaries porous by depicting on its surface other ways of migrating and inhabiting. Though dealing with history, the mural shifts its content from the usual catalogue of heroic scenes to more quotidian operations, notably in "Welcoming the Newcomers" where the crouching nude extends helping hands to save from drowning a black and a Caucasian, and behind them an olive-skinned victim, who all reach for dear life. Women who converse while tending to and nursing children belong to the new assemblage. The mural stages a quasi-utopian *rencontre* in which heteroclite humans and animals come together to build a world in common.

A companion mural, "Resurgence of the People" (2019), imagines the aftermath of the disastrous colonial invasion. In the upper left corner, a handful of survivors, four armed white men brandishing AK-47s and a pistol, are shown gesticulating wildly and triumphantly, unaware of the fact that the island on which they stand is rapidly disappearing with rising seas of climate change. The "people" seen in larger format in the bottom half of the painting are not sitting around a table. They are gathered in a moving boat or hanging on its sides waiting to be rescued, collectively imagining new "possibles" that will require their care. They are not mourning a vanishing culture as in Delacroix's *Natchez* (1835, also at the Metropolitan Museum of Art), but row toward the spectator and, out of frame, away from the impending disaster that is the consequence of Western *incurie* (lack of care).[28] This relational encounter is made possible through the collaboration of a collectivity that includes again different ethnicities, sexualities and a panoply of animals. The totemic Canadian beaver (whose population was almost eradicated after the encounter with the *voyageurs*) is seen sitting next to a child, grouped with the "people" composed of Native Americans, Asians, Africans, as well as Caucasians. A white man is being rescued by a black man while—standing much like George Washington crossing the Potomac—a gender-fluid figure, a nude in high heels, is putatively a self-portrait of Monkman in guise. Everyone is engaged in collective thought and action; the people exude a sense of collaboration and creative assembly. The water surges, but so do the people. Their resurgence—from the Latin *surgere*, to rise, also related to sap—their force, and their capacitation activate new possibles. In Monkman's paintings, a care of the event of encounter is felt through what Massumi calls trans-individual complexities.[29] In an accessible style of the academic tradition, the painting seems to be in concert with the moment that is 2019, a time of often-tragic migrations owing to climate change and to political upheaval to which the painter would wish to sensitize his spectators. "Resurgence of the People," a remake of sorts of Emmanuel Leutze's famous painting, "Washington crossing the Delaware" (1851) during the American Revolutionary War of 1776—also on display at the Metropolitan Museum—lacks the traditional depth of field of history paintings.[30] Elements of "décor"—that is, the expanse of the agitated sea and the low-flying and ominously dark clouds—are not simply background, but function as actors themselves. Such actors function elsewhere in a vastly different but possibly complementary context—what Bruno Latour and Frédérique Aït-Touati call the "new climate regime," to which a new aesthetics and new ethics have the task of sensitizing humans.[31] Sitting at the negotiating table or, as here gathered in a boat, human subjects attempt to evade what Stengers calls "the coming barbarism,"[32] the result of binary thinking of the self as opposed to the other and, in turn, the consequent desire to colonize and control. In the fabulations of Stengers and here of Monkman, negotiations and the sharing of voices reach across divides. This reaching across involves not only animals such as the beaver, but also "things" which are part of the scene of negotiation that stages new and different events. Human actors do not move about against an immobile décor.[33] There is no more foreground and background, but only, in the lexicon of Deleuze and Guattari, a *plane of immanence* and smooth consistency.

Taking leave of the two monumental paintings, we can say that on these planes of immanence, events of encounter happen at once between humans, between humans and other species, and between humans and things. In this way, as Stengers and others would have it, the world is a vibratory continuum in which humans and all other organisms feel with and for ambient milieus. They collectively shape and are shaped by them. The shift from a hostile encounter between a conscious subject and a presumably inert object, a conqueror and something to be conquered, moves in the direction of a care of the encounter and, as said, even more, a *rencontre,* that opens on to new *assemblages* (a translation of Guattari's concept of "agencements"). As new materialisms have reshaped the humanities and undone the essentializing character of humanism, the making and reshaping of these assemblages or *agencements* can only be ongoing. As Deleuze and Guattari and now Stengers, Latour, Haraway, Barad, Tsing, and others remind us,[34] the world is always in becoming, in a continuous vibration where bundles of matter constantly shift and where humans and things of any kind—organic and inorganic alike—enter in ephemeral and precarious relations or assemblages with other species and things.

By way of abrupt conclusion, a care of the *encounter*, or else, a *rencontre,* begs us to consider how to assemble, how to gather, how to collaborate, and how to create. Building on Christie McDonald's studies of ethics, we can say that when taking leave of a conquest or appropriation, we shift toward a care of encounter—a collective *rencontre*. We enter into negotiations with multiple others, humans, animals, and things both animate and inanimate in a world that, however precarious, is always in process. Such is Christie McDonald's world, and such is the world we wish to bring before us.

Notes

1 Dated *c.* 1587–9, penned in brown ink with brown wash, the image in its first state (19 x 16.9cm) is held in the Metropolitan Museum of Art. See www.metmuseum.org/art/collection/search/343845. Philip Galle executed a copperplate version in Stradanus' *Nova Reperta* (1580). For different readings of the *Nova Reperta* see Lia Markey, ed., *Renaissance Invention: Stradanus'* Nova Reperta (Evanston: Northwestern University Press, 2020); Lia Markey, "Stradanus *Nova Reperta* in Renaissance Florence," *Renaissance Quarterly* 65, no. 2 (Summer 2012): 385–422.
2 Michel de Certeau, *L'Écriture de l'histoire* (Paris: Éditions Gallimard, Bibliothèque de l'histoire, 1975), ii; *The Writing of History*, trans. Tom Conley (New York: Columbia University Press, 1992), ii.
3 Michel de Montaigne, "Of coaches," *Essays* III, 6, in *Essays* and *Travel Journal* in *The Complete Works of Montaigne*, trans. Donald Frame (Stanford: Stanford University Press,1957), 693.
4 Ilya Prigogine (1917–2001) was a Belgian physicist and chemist born in Russia. He received the Nobel Prize in 1977 for his contributions to irreversible thermodynamic processes and especially to the theory of dissipative structures. Working with him, Stengers discovers that science can be treated not only objectively but with passion. When co-writing with him *La Nouvelle alliance: Métamorphose de la science* (Paris: Gallimard, 1979), translated as *Order Out of Chaos* (New York: Bantam Books, 1984), Stengers claims to have understood that "another science" is possible. See Isabelle Stengers in dialogue with Frédérique Dolphijn, *Activer les possibles* (Bruxelles: Esperluète, 2018).
5 E.g., today's reader of *A Thousand Plateaus: Capitalism and Schizophrenia* (Minneapolis: University of Minnesota Press, 1987) discovers threads of Stengers' way of thinking about habitat and environment woven through their many remarks concerning territorialization. Ongoing deterritorialization (and reterritorialization) disrupts homeostasis. It would be tantamount to an encounter.

6 Gilles Deleuze, *The Fold*, trans. Tom Conley (Minneapolis: University of Minnesota Press, 1993), 76-7.
7 In one of his first texts originally published in French in 1953, Deleuze's "Causes et raisons de l'île déserte," (*Desert Island and Other Texts, 1953-74*, ed. David Lapoujade, trans. Michael Taormina [Cambridge: Semiotexte/MIT Press, 2004], 9-14) contrasts Daniel Defoe's *Robinson Crusoe* (1719) and Jean Giraudoux's *Suzanne et le Pacifique* (1921) to inventively show how beginnings are re-beginnings.
8 Gaston Bachelard—in his *Nouvel esprit scientifique* (1934, published in English as *The New Scientific Spirit* [Boston: Beacon Press, 1984])—and Georges Canguilhem—in his *Idéologie et rationalité dans l'histoire des sciences de la vie* (1977, published in English as *Ideology and Rationality in the History of the Life Sciences* [Cambridge: MIT Press, 1988]) and *La Connaissance de la vie* (1952, published in English as *Knowledge of Life* [New York: Fordham University Press, 2008]), a work summing up his reflections—informed Michel Foucault in his studies of epistemological ruptures. One of these ruptures, the shift from analogy to representation at the outset of the seventeenth century, signaled the beginning of what Foucault called the "scientific gaze." See the third chapter of *Les Mots et les choses: une archéologie des sciences humaines* (Paris: Gallimard, 1966); in English, *The Order of Things: An Archeology of the Human Sciences* (New York: Pantheon, 1971).
9 In arguing for the supremacy of man as a thinking machine, Descartes—almost slyly it seems—divorces the human subject from sentient beings and things in nature at large. On the subtlety of Cartesian thinking, see Christopher Braider, *The Matter of Mind: Reason and Experience in the Age of Descartes* (Toronto: University of Toronto Press, 2012).
10 Trained in mathematics, professor of science and philosophy at Cambridge before migrating to Harvard in 1924, Alfred North Whitehead (1861-1947) wrote copiously about how thinking, born of sensation, becomes a force of logic and ecology such as in *Adventures of Ideas* (Cambridge: Cambridge University Press, 1933), *The Concept of Nature* (Cambridge: Cambridge University Press, 1971, reed.), *Essays in Science and Philosophy* (New York: Philosophical Library, 1947), *Nature and Life* (Cambridge: Cambridge University Press, 1934), *Process and Reality: An Essay in Cosmology* (Cambridge: Cambridge University Press, 1929), and *Science and the Modern World* (Cambridge: Cambridge University Press, 1926).
11 Isabelle Stengers, *Thinking with Whitehead: A Free and Wild Creation of Concepts*, trans. Michael Chase (Cambridge: Harvard University Press, 2011), 295.
12 Stengers, 295.
13 Brian Massumi, *The Power at the End of the Economy* (Durham: Duke University Press, 2015), 36.
14 See Gilles Deleuze, *The Fold*, trans. Tom Conley (Minneapolis: University of Minnesota Press, 1993), 101.
15 Montaigne, *Essays* II, 8, 278-93. Reflecting on how analogy and process bear on this essay—in *La logique du vivant* (Paris: Gallimard, 1970); published in English as *The Logic of Life: A History of Heredity*, trans. Betty E. Spillmann (New York: Pantheon, 1973)—François Jacob stresses the importance of encounter as process in the history of genetics and of science in general.
16 Massumi, 65.
17 Isabelle Stengers and Eric Bordeleau in "The Care of the Possible: Isabelle Stengers Interviewed by Eric Bordeleau," trans. Kelly Ladd, in *Scapegoat: Architecture, Landscape, Political Economy*, no. 01 "Service" (Summer 2011): 12-13, 16-17, 27.

18 Massumi, 54.
19 Donna Haraway and Martha Kenney, "Anthropocene, Capitalocene, Chthulhocene," in *Art in the Anthropocene*, eds. Heather Davis and Étienne Turpin (London: Open Humanities Press, 2015), 260.
20 Erin Manning and Brian Massumi, *Thought in the Act* (Minneapolis: University of Minnesota Press, 2014), 108.
21 Bruno Latour, *We Have Never Been Modern*, trans. Catherine Porter (Cambridge: Harvard University Press, 1993), 47.
22 The 1914 painting hangs in Pilgrim Hall, Plymouth, Massachusetts. See https://en.wikipedia.org/wiki/Jennie_Augusta_Brownscombe#/media/File:Thanksgiving-Brownscombe.jpg. Brownscombe remade another in 1925 with the Pilgrims seen as if in reverse shot. In this painting, there remains only one Indian chief seated at the table, see https://nmwa.org/works/thanksgiving-plymouth.
23 Blow argues that, contrary to the "Pilgrim-centric view so often presented," Native Americans provided most of the food. Brownsombe's painting (and so also another by Jean Leon Gerome Ferris) "feature[s] the native in a subervient position, outnumbered and crouching on the ground at the edge of the frame." Charles Blow, "The Horrible History of Thanksgiving," *New York Times,* November 27, 2019, see www.nytimes.com/2019/11/27/opinion/thanksgiving-history.html. While a few Native Americans actually do sit at the table, they are marginalized.
24 Eduardo Viveiras de Castro, *The Inconsistency of the Indian Soul: Encounters of Catholics and Cannibals in Sixteenth-Century Brazil* (Chicago: Prickly Paradigm Press, 2011).
25 Bruno Latour, *War of the Worlds: What about Peace?*, trans. Charlotte Bigg, ed. John Tresch (Chicago: Prickly Paradigm Press, 2002); see also Stengers, *Thinking with Whitehead*.
26 Félix Guattari, *Chaosmosis: An Ethico-Aesthetic Paradigm*, trans. Paul Bains and Julian Pefanis (Bloomington: Indiana University Press, 1995), 124.
27 See www.metmuseum.org/press/exhibitions/2019/the-great-hall-commission-kent-monkman. Because of the spread of the COVID-19 virus, the gallery is now closed.
28 See www.metmuseum.org/art/collection/search/436180.
29 Massumi, *Power*, 36.
30 See www.metmuseum.org/en/art/collection/search/11417.
31 Bruno Latour and Frédérique Aït-Touati, "Décor as Protagonist: Bruno Latour and Frédérique Aït-Touati on Theatre and the New Climate Regime," interview by Sébastien Hendrickx and Kristof van Baarle, *Etcetera*, January 7, 2019, see https://e-tcetera.be/decor-is-not-decor-anymore/.
32 Isabelle Stengers, *In Catastrophic Times: Resisting the Coming Barbarism*, trans. Andrew Goffey (London: Open Humanities Press, 2015).
33 Bruno Latour and Frédérique Aït-Touati, "Décor as Protagonist."
34 See in particular Karen Barad, "No Small Matter: Mushroom Clouds, Ecologies of Nothingness, and Strange Topologies of Spacetimemattering," in *Arts of Living on a Damaged Planet: Ghosts and Monsters of the Anthropocene*, eds. Anna Tsing et al. (Minneapolis: University of Minnesota Press, 2017); Donna Haraway, *Staying with the Trouble: Making Kin in the Chthulucene* (Durham: Duke University Press, 2017); Anna Tsing, *The Mushroom to the end of the World: On the Possibility of Life in Capitalist Ruins* (Princeton: Princeton University Press, 2017).

Chapter 15

PRIVATE LIVES, PUBLIC HISTORY: ENCOUNTERING THE FILMMAKER ISTVÁN SZABÓ

Susan Rubin Suleiman

István Szabó is one of the few Hungarian filmmakers to have earned a major international reputation over the past half century. His 1981 film, *Mephisto*, was the first by a Hungarian director to be awarded the Academy Award for Best Foreign Film, and he has received many other prizes and awards over his long career.[1]

Szabó, born in Budapest in 1938, belongs to what I have called the "1.5 generation"—that is, people who were children in Europe during World War II.[2] My definition of this term refers specifically to Jewish child survivors of the Holocaust and to their memory of persecution and trauma; but it can apply to anyone who experienced World War II as a child in countries where the war was fought, not only to Jews. Szabó's family were assimilated Jews who had converted to Catholicism before he was born, but he remembers his grandparents as still observing some Jewish rituals. He himself had to be hidden during the Nazi occupation of Hungary (1944–5), since the Nazis' racial theories made conversion irrelevant.

The major fact about experiencing trauma as a child is that one is not able to fully understand what is happening. Of course most adults do not "fully understand" either, but at least they have a vocabulary and certain concepts that allow them to try and make sense of their experience; young children lack not only these tools for understanding the events around them, they often don't even remember those events later on, except in the most fragmentary and incomplete way. Yet, despite—or perhaps because of—their lack of understanding and coherent memories, children who experience trauma are affected by it very deeply. Childhood trauma has crucial consequences for an individual's personality precisely because the child has no way of explaining the experience to him or herself; and children have even less control over what happens to them than the most helpless adult. Jewish children in Europe during the war often survived in hiding with false names, separated from their parents, having to pretend to be someone else at a time when they barely knew who they were to begin with. Non-Jewish children also suffered;

they often experienced bombardment, displacement, and separation from parents, especially from their fathers who were in the Army.

Szabó himself is very conscious of the importance that his experience during the war had for him, and for all those of his generation. In one of the first interviews he gave, when he was twenty-five years old, right after the success of his first short films that had been presented at an international film festival, he told his interviewer how he came to make his ten-minute-long film "Variations on a theme," which is about the war: "It was born of the understanding that my generation too, even though we were barely eight years old when the war ended, is a generation wounded by war. Half of my friends lost their fathers in the war. I did too. No more war!"[3] More than fifty years later, in a conversation I had with him in Budapest in October 2017, he mentioned that he had recently been invited to a film festival in France whose theme was "Film and War," and added with a laugh: "It looks like just about all of my films fit the rubric!" That's because of his childhood during World War II, he said. "That marks you, you don't just move on from it."[4]

Before I ever met István Szabó in person, I had encountered some of his films. I must have seen *Mephisto* in the 1980s, though I have no memory of doing so. I vividly recall seeing his next film, however: *Colonel Redl*, released in 1985. Starring the marvelous Austrian actor Klaus Maria Brandauer—who had also been the star of *Mephisto*—*Colonel Redl* takes place in the waning years of the Habsburg Empire: it ends with archival footage of the assassination of Crown Prince Franz Ferdinand and of the first battles of World War I. The story focuses on the life of an army officer, Alfred Redl, who rises from an impoverished peasant childhood in the far eastern region of the empire, Galizia, to the highest post in the Habsburg intelligence service, only to die an ignominious death by his own hand when it turns out that he has sold military secrets to the Habsburgs' historic enemy, the Russian Czar. Colonel Alfred Redl was a real person, an out and out traitor and double agent who used his highly privileged position to collect large sums for the secrets he sold over a period of more than five years.[5] In Szabó's film, however, he appears as a complex character—a closet homosexual and a parvenu never comfortable in his own skin—who gives away secret information only once, in a fit of self-hatred. The figure that Szabó draws of him could have stepped out of the pages of Joseph Roth's celebrated novel *The Radetzky March* (1932), or of Sándor Márai's posthumous bestseller *Embers* (1942), which also feature Habsburg army officers in the waning years of the Empire.

Colonel Redl made a profound impression on me. When I thought about it afterward, I realized it was not only because of the psychological complexity of the main character but also because several scenes take place in Budapest, which was second only to Vienna as a capital of the Austro-Hungarian Monarchy (as the Habsburg Empire was also known after the "compromise" of 1867, which accorded a degree of autonomy to Hungary). Budapest is my native city; I was born there just a year and a half after Szabó himself. Like him, I was a young Jewish child in hiding in 1944–5; unlike him, I left the country with my parents a few years after the war, and for more than three decades I never looked back. Once we arrived in the USA, I was bent on becoming an American girl, with no complications.

Throughout middle school, high school, college, graduate school, then marriage, motherhood, and the first years of a teaching career, I almost never thought about Budapest and talked about it only rarely with my two sons, despite the fact that my mother—whom my sons knew and loved—never lost her thick Hungarian accent. But she too avoided reminiscing about Budapest. She was resolutely focused on the present, and her memories of Hungary—the anti-Jewish laws of the 1930s, the war, then Communism—were mostly not the kind to wax nostalgic about.

Then, things shifted. In 1984, after my mother had fallen ill (it was the beginning of her dying, which occurred four years later), I returned to Hungary for two weeks with my sons and became temporarily what I called "a tour guide of my own life." That return trip jogged my earliest childhood memories: the war, but also the time after it, when life in Budapest seemed quite wonderful for a while. The outings to the Buda hills with my mother, the walks along leafy Andrássy Avenue right near our apartment building in Pest, the summers spent in a resort town nearby where I learned to dance and swim, all that came back to me with a power that surprised me. Compelled, I started to write about my childhood. My scholarly and teaching interests also took a sharp turn, as I embarked on new courses about literature and films of the Holocaust and about memory of World War II and the Occupation in France. Until then, I had specialized in literary theory, avant-garde movements, feminist criticism; those interests did not disappear, but they were upstaged by my new ones. It was as if the return to Budapest had opened a door I had kept resolutely shut for many years; once I opened it, I discovered a new terrain that stretched all the way from Budapest to Paris.

True, the "memory boom" in literary and cultural studies was also taking off around that time, so my personal (re)turn corresponded to a wider intellectual turn in academic scholarship. Pierre Nora's immensely influential volumes on *Les Lieux de mémoire* appeared between 1984 and 1992, and Claude Lanzmann's epochal film *Shoah*—which insisted not so much on the events of the Holocaust as on survivors' memories of them—appeared in 1985. But looking back on it, what strikes me as significant is the way the collective phenomenon intersected with my personal history. The by-now almost hackneyed dictum that "all scholarship is autobiographical" found here a solid confirmation.

Still, my involvement with Hungary, and with the films of István Szabó, might not have continued without the intervention of History with a capital H. The fall of the Berlin Wall in 1989 opened up Hungary, like the rest of Eastern Europe, to the world. In 1991, I saw Szabó's first English-language film, *Meeting Venus*, featuring an international cast headed by Glenn Close and the French actor Niels Arestrup. The film recounts the rocky but ultimately successful road taken by a production of Wagner's *Tannhäuser* at the Paris Opera in 1990. The production was slated to celebrate post-Wall Europe, where international cooperation would be the norm. But the Hungarian maestro Zoltán Szántó[6] (played by Arestrup) has to struggle against multiple obstacles in getting to opening night. These include in-fighting among the singers, due to national as well as personal rivalries— already, the demons of nationalism were rearing their heads, as Szabó realized. Frustrating demands from the French labor unions, Szántó's deteriorating marriage back in Budapest, and his stormy love affair with the diva Karin Anderson (played by Close) add further complications. At one point, Szántó returns to Budapest for a few days with Anderson, who is giving a recital there; this causes a serious break in his marriage (the ending of the film leaves that question unresolved), but also gives Szabó a chance to take his hero back to his native city. Budapest plays a major role in many of Szabó's films—it's a city he clearly loves and has filmed beautifully. But in *Meeting Venus*, all the scenes in Budapest take place indoors—the concert hall, the conductor's apartment, the hotel where the diva is staying.

It's all the more curious that the memory I carried with me for many years was of the conductor proudly showing off the city to his new love. It was only upon seeing the film again in preparation for writing this essay that I realized my error and began to ponder its significance. In my memory, Szántó took Andersen up to the "Fisherman's Bastion," a neo-Gothic structure on Castle Hill from where one has a panoramic view of the city. Nowadays it's always full of tourists, and it's not a spot that Szabó particularly likes—it does not appear in any of his films, while the Danube and its bridges, and some streets near the river on the Pest side, with turn-of-the-century apartment buildings, recur almost like a leitmotif in his work. Was my false memory linked to the fact that my mother had once written to me, around the time I was getting ready for my first return to Budapest in 1984, that the Fisherman's Bastion was among the few things she still remembered of the city of her youth? In a conversation I had with Szabó in Budapest in December 2017, I mentioned that I loved his films because they raised questions that made the audience think. But he pointed to his head and said, "Not here." Then he pointed to his heart: "Here." What he seeks in his films, he said, is first of all to touch a viewer's emotions, not her reason. My own experience of *Meeting Venus* seems to bear that out. Of course, he wants the viewer to think as well, and indeed my false memory spurred a lot of thinking—but feeling comes first.[7]

Less than a year after seeing *Meeting Venus*, in the spring of 1992, I received a letter sent to my Harvard address: a new Institute for Advanced Study had just been founded in Budapest, and I was invited to join the first cohort of Fellows, starting in September. The writer of the letter clearly had no knowledge of my Hungarian background; the invitation was addressed to the Harvard professor, not to the fledgling autobiographer seeking traces. Of course, I jumped at the opportunity. In the beginning of February 1993, I moved to Budapest for six months. The Collegium Budapest, located in a historic eighteenth-century building on Castle Hill, a stone's throw from the Fisherman's Bastion, provided a roomy office and a community of scholars, as well as a comfortable apartment in a nice part of town. The time I spent there was like a dream—a dream recorded, for every night I would sit at my laptop and write in detail about the day's activities: my meetings with Hungarian colleagues, lectures I heard (and also gave) at the Collegium and elsewhere, exhibits I attended, films I saw (only Hungarian ones—I wanted to educate myself), and perhaps most importantly, the walks I took around the city, often circling back to the neighborhood where I had grown up. And then there were the endless conversations with friends and strangers about the meaning and the consequences of "the Change," as the end of the communist regime was called in Hungary. At the end of those six months, I had a huge manuscript that, with cutting and pruning, would eventually be published as a memoir, *Budapest Diary: In Search of the Motherbook*. My love affair with the city and the talks with Hungarians about how their lives had been transformed by the larger history after 1989 constituted, along with my almost-obsessive search for traces of my childhood and family, the heart of the book.

Among the films I wrote about in detail in *Budapest Diary* was István Szabó's *Sweet Emma, dear Böbe (Édes Emma, Drága Böbe)*, which I saw in Budapest in July 1993, a few months after its release. Once again, I found that Szabó's preoccupations and my own had intersected. *Sweet Emma, dear Böbe* is a film about "the Change"— about what happens when two young women schoolteachers from the provinces— who had been trained to teach Russian in high school and who live in quasi-impoverished circumstances in a teachers' dormitory in Budapest—are suddenly told that they will have to teach English from now on, and learn it quickly. Russian would no longer be offered as part of the curriculum. As I wrote in my diary that evening, "Szabó is merciless in showing the effects of 'the Change' even on the smallest institutions: petty bickering among the teachers, desperate attempts by former Communists to divorce themselves from their Party past, and everywhere a generalized anxiety about the future."[8] The story of Emma and Böbe does not end well. Like many others, the two young women are caught by a huge historical wave that threatens to drown them. The "new Europe," Szabó seemed to be saying, brings with it new freedoms, but also new hardships and even death to people with minimal resources. Naturally, I loved the film!

Although I met many intellectuals and even one or two filmmakers while I was in Budapest, it never occurred to me to try and meet István Szabó. I hadn't seen enough of his films, hadn't written about them, and he was famous. What reason could I possibly give for wanting to meet him? The fact that I admired his films and felt a kinship with his preoccupations was not enough.

Now fast forward to 2000. *Budapest Diary* had been published in 1996 and I was at work on a book that would take several more years to complete, focusing on public and private memories of World War II and the Holocaust. I was also working with my dear friend Christie McDonald on another project, our jointly edited volume about "French global"—which caused us to spend a lot of time together, delighting us both. In my original plan, the "memory book," as I called it, would be focused exclusively on France, even though the broader issues it raised—about trauma, memory, national identity, Jewishness—were relevant to other times and places.

But that summer, in Paris, I saw István Szabó's film *Sunshine* (1999), and realized that I must write about it for the memory book. It's hard to describe the deep emotion and deep personal involvement I felt while watching that film. It was in English (starring Ralph Fiennes, Jennifer Ehle, Rosemary Harris), but it was about Hungary—and not only Hungary but Jews in Hungary. Almost double the length of Szabó's other films (it's three hours long), *Sunshine* tells the story of a Jewish family in Hungary over four generations, from the "Golden Age" of Hungarian and Hungarian-Jewish history in the late nineteenth century to the end of communist rule. The story is of Jewish assimilation, followed by the upheaval of World War I, then a growing climate of anti-Semitism culminating in the anti-Jewish laws of the late 1930s, then war again, deaths in the Holocaust, a diminished life under communism, and finally a kind of liberation after 1989.

The three main protagonists, father, son and grandson, are all played by Fiennes, in a tour de force performance. The first assimilated generation of the Sonnenschein family "Magyarizes" its name around 1900 in a patriotic gesture, changing it to Sors (which means fate in Hungarian). The next generation converts to Catholicism in order to allow the champion fencer Adam Sors to become a member of the army's fencing team, which does not admit Jews. Adam then leads the Hungarian team to victory at the 1936 Olympics—but after that high point, it's all downhill. Adam is murdered in an atrocious way in a forced labor camp for Jews during the war, while his teenage son watches in horror. (Szabó based this episode on the real-life murder of the Hungarian Jewish fencing champion Attila Petschauer, who was beaten to death in a camp by Hungarian gendarmes in 1943.) After the war, Adam's son Ivan—whose voice we have occasionally heard as the film's narrator—enters the communist secret police, presumably in response to the helplessness he felt as a teenager witnessing his father's murder. Fiennes plays him with a stiffness of affect that suggests post-traumatic stress disorder. But Ivan soon becomes disillusioned with the hard-line communist regime and in 1956 he joins the crowds demanding reform. After the failure of the 1956 uprising, he spends time in jail as a "counterrevolutionary." Not long after his release and the death of his beloved grandmother, the narrative takes a huge leap forward in time to 1989, beyond communism. Ivan now decides to take back his family's Jewish-sounding name and announces that he "breathes freely for the first time."

Dubbed into Hungarian, *Sunshine* (*A napfény ize* [a taste of sunshine]) received enormous attention in Hungary and stirred up some heated debates. While many viewers, especially among Jews, loved the film, others criticized it. It shouldn't have been made in English, some said; it made Hungary look bad in the eyes of Western viewers, said others; still others said that Szabó's handling of the postwar period was not true to the way things really were. And what did Szabó think he was accomplishing by having Ivan take his name back? Was he suggesting that all those whose names had been "Magyarized" generations earlier should revert to their Germanic (or Serbian or Czech or Romanian) names? Only anti-Semites made suggestions like that! And so on.[9]

In the USA, passions were not aroused; the film received mixed reviews in the press. Some critics objected to having a single actor play all three major roles; others found the characters not complex enough, especially when compared to Szabó's earlier films with their rich attention to individual psychology. Jewish audiences by and large loved the film, and it also had many screenings among Hungarian-Americans. As for me, I wrote a long essay about the film that was published in a journal in 2001 and eventually found its way into my memory book.[10] And this time, I did seek out an opportunity to speak with István Szabó. Just around the time I was finishing my article, in the fall of 2000, Columbia University organized a symposium around the film, with Szabó in attendance. I flew down to New York for the event. After the screening, a historian and a literary scholar specializing in Hungary discussed the film with him, and then the audience had a chance to ask questions. I raised my hand and asked a question, which I hoped would show that I had really studied the film. He answered appreciatively, and I felt authorized to go up to him afterward. I was too shy to speak Hungarian with him, especially since his English is excellent. But I was thrilled to have met the man, after having been acquainted with some of his films over many years.

Thus began a personal acquaintance that has meant a great deal to me. In 2006, while I was in Budapest to attend a conference, Szabó agreed to meet me for a formal interview to talk about his work. As part of my preparation, I watched his first three feature films, in Hungarian, which had established his international reputation as a young filmmaker in the 1960s: *The Age of Daydreaming* (*Az álmodozások kora*, 1965), *Father* (*Apa*, 1966), and *Love Film* (*Szerelmesfilm*, 1970). All of these films featured young men and women of Szabó's generation, who came of age after the war, under communism. Since that was also my generation, these films gave me a glimpse of what I might have become, had my family not left Hungary in 1949. The question of emigration is raised in each film, and in *Lovefilm* it is central: the film tells the story of a young couple who have loved each other since childhood, but who are separated in 1956 when she decides to leave the country after the uprising and he decides to stay. Among Szabó's early films, it is the one that struck me most deeply—for obvious reasons, given my own displacements, but it is also formally among Szabó's most complex works, a memory film that skips around among different moments in the lives of its protagonists, from the time of the Nazi occupation in 1944 to the "Young Pioneer" years of the early 1950s, then the 1956 uprising and the "softer" years of the late 1960s. Running through it like a guiding thread is an existential question that I found fascinating: how do individuals make choices at historically critical moments—that is, moments such as war and revolution, when public history interferes blatantly with private life? Szabó has asked this question, in one form or another, in most of his films. In *Love Film*, the lives of the two protagonists are permanently inflected by the choices they make in 1956, one choosing to leave Hungary, the other to stay. My family left before 1956, but I imagine that my parents must also have struggled with the question—and their decision to leave obviously determined the rest of my own life.

On a sunny day in September 2006, I met Szabó in a café on Castle Hill, not far from the Collegium Budapest. He arrived punctually, and we got down to our interview with no preliminary chitchat. We spoke in English to make it easier to transcribe (I had brought along a voice recorder), and also I thought that the distance provided by another language might allow him to talk more freely. Our conversation lasted more than two hours; we talked about his childhood, the war, the question of emigration (why did he and his mother stay in Hungary after the war, when they could have emigrated to New York where an uncle lived?), and the complications of Jewish identity in Central Europe.[11] Although he was brought up as a Catholic, he said, people still thought of him as Jewish. "In this part of the world, that's how it goes," he said. "The exclusion of those who don't belong?"

I asked. "Yes, exclusion is the most important element of the tribe mentality. Those who aren't Hungarian..." Rereading the transcript of that interview today, when Hungary's prime minister Viktor Orbán rests his power and his popularity on the hatred he foments of "migrants," I realize how prescient Szabó was—more exactly, how correctly he diagnosed the "tribe mentality" that seems to be gaining ground all over Europe at present.

One thing that was very much on Szabó's mind during our conversation was the painful subject of a recent "scandal" around his name, which had occupied the Hungarian press for several months and had also been reported in the *New York Times* and other newspapers abroad. The previous January, a journalist had published a long article exposing his discovery that for several years when Szabó had been a student at film school, he had written reports for the secret service about his classmates and others linked to the institution.[12] Given Szabó's longstanding reputation in Hungary as a filmmaker of integrity, whose concerns encompassed ethical questions as well as the ways that individual lives are inflected by History, this revelation devastated many people. But didn't they realize, Szabó told me, that he had been an eighteen-year old boy forced into cooperating with the secret service along with many others, including two of his classmates? And that the whole episode lasted only a few years, that it was over before he had even made his first film? He felt angry and frustrated, convinced that he had been targeted precisely because of his international reputation: "They needed someone they could attack, and since I'm the best known..." He didn't explain who "they" were, but it hardly mattered: "they" were whoever stood to gain (or thought they did) from exposing compromising facts about the communist years. After the opening of secret service archives all over eastern Europe in the 1990s, it became clear that in Hungary, as in other communist countries, half the country had been writing reports about the other half! While some who did that undoubtedly acted out of ideological conviction, many others had been forcibly enrolled, by means of threats and blackmail, into acting as "agents" during the harsh years immediately following the 1956 uprising.

In January 2000, just after he had finished a long novel in which he expressed his lifelong admiration for his father, the celebrated writer Peter Esterházy discovered, to his horror, that the same father had written reports for the secret service for more than two decades, from 1957 to 1979. Esterházy wrote a book about his discovery, and his description makes it clear that the system itself—which went to absurd lengths in enrolling and overseeing its so-called agents—was the main culprit, not those it forced into its clutches.[13] Nevertheless, and even for those who were able to escape from those clutches relatively quickly, like Szabó and his classmates (that too was part of the system's absurdity: people could be "disenrolled" just as they had been enrolled, for no obvious reason), the whole experience must have been fraught with feelings of guilt as well as helplessness. They could, after all, have refused to cooperate and faced the consequences. Easier said than done.

These days, as I get ready to write a book on Szabó's work, I have been struggling with the question of how much importance to ascribe to that painful episode from his youth. It is clear that I cannot simply ignore it, even if the book is not a biography but a study of his films. But I cannot make it a centerpiece either. Szabó himself has said that everything one needs to know about it is in his films. Following that lead, one could argue that his emphasis on existential and ethical choices in individual lives, as well as his oft-repeated statement that private lives can be destroyed by History, have their source in that youthful experience. Such an insight does not get us very far, however, in understanding his films; it reduces their general import, and the importance of Szabó's concerns, to mere personal history. But the theme that underlies all of Szabó's oeuvre is precisely that personal history is indissociable from public history (History with a capital H), which is always ready to interfere with, and often to destroy, individual lives.

The challenge, here as in many other instances, is to acknowledge a traumatic personal past—whether your own or someone else's—without letting it overwhelm you. One thing one can learn from encountering István Szabó (the man and his films) is that complexity is all.

Notes

1 Most of Szabó's films are in Hungarian, but *Mephisto* and several others are in German and he has also worked in English. All of his films have been shot principally in Budapest.
2 Susan Rubin Suleiman, "The 1.5 Generation: Thinking About Child Survivors and the Holocaust," *American Imago* 59, no. 3 (Fall 2002): 277–95.
3 István Szabó, "Három kisfilm sikeréröl a rendezővel, Szabó Istvánnal" ("About the Success of Three Short Films, with the director István Szabó"), interview by Eva Lelkes, *Film, Szinház, Muzsika,* February 15, 1963. Clipping, István Szabó, "Personal Folder, 1963–1982," Hungarian National Film Archive, Budapest.
4 István Szabó, in discussion with the author, Budapest, October 20, 2017.
5 John R. Schindler, "Redl—Spy of the Century?", *International Journal of Intelligence and Counterintelligence* 18, no. 3 (2005): 483–507.
6 The similarity in names, Szabó-Szántó, is intentional—Szabó himself directed a production of Tannhäuser in Paris around 1990, and based the film partly on his own experience. In a playful gesture, he gave several male characters in the film names that translate into "szabó," which means "tailor" in Hungarian": Schneider, Tailleur, Sarto.
7 István Szabó, in discussion with the author, December 14, 2017. The idea that he wants his films to affect viewers' emotions, and by extension to "help them live," is a longstanding one with Szabó and recurs in many of his published interviews. See, for example, the long interview with András Szegő from 1987, "Ingerelnek a felfuvalkodott, gőgös emberek" ("I can't stand swellheaded, arrogant people"), reprinted in *Beszélgetések Szabó István Filmrendezővel [Conversations with Filmmaker István Szabó]*, ed. Zsuzsa Radnóti (Budapest: Ferenczy Kiadó, 1995).
8 Susan Rubin Suleiman, *Budapest Diary* (Lincoln: University of Nebraska Press, 1996), 172.
9 I discuss the Hungarian debates in detail in my book *Crises of Memory and the Second World War* (Cambridge: Harvard University Press, 2006), 128–31.
10 Susan Rubin Suleiman, "Jewish Assimilation in Hungary, the Holocaust, and Epic Film: Reflections on István Szabó's Sunshine," *Yale Journal of Criticism* 14, no. 1 (Spring

2001): 233–52. Revised version in Suleiman, *Crises of Memory and the Second World War*, chapter 5.
11 An edited version of the interview appeared in the online film journal *Kinokultura* in 2007. Susan Rubin Suleiman, "On Exile, Jewish Identity, and Filmmaking in Hungary: A Conversation with István Szabó," in *Kinokultura* special issue 7 "Hungarian Cinema" (February 2008), see www.kinokultura.com/specials/7/hungarian.shtml.
12 András Gervai, "Egy ügynök azonosítása" ("The identification of an agent"), *Élet és Irodalom*, January 27, 2006.
13 Péter Esterházy, *Javított Kiadás: Melléklet a Harmonia Caelestishez* (Budapest: Magvető, 2001). The book has been translated into many languages, but not into English. I first read it in French: *Revu et corrigé* (Paris: Gallimard, 2005). An English rendering of the title would be "Revised Edition: Appendix to *Harmonia Caelestis*"—*Harmonia Caelestis* being the title of the novel Esterházy had just finished, a paean to his father, when he discovered the latter's hidden past.

Chapter 16

CREATION AND RE-CREATION ACROSS CULTURES
AND DISCIPLINES:
TAHITIAN ENCOUNTERS FROM BOUGAINVILLE
TO GAUGUIN AND BEYOND

Christie McDonald

Charles Darwin described the experience of encountering something for the first time: "First impressions at all times very much depend on one's previously acquired ideas."[1] Writers, philosophers, travelers, and artists have met and engaged with "what they did not know"—what was lost or was without precedent—as a propelling force to understand and create. With some hindsight, they give us an idea of how the exhaustion of certain ideas creates an opening for the emergence of others: thinking across boundaries from a given time and place to the beliefs of later generations. Understanding and interpretation often depend on that which from the past can be brought to bear on the experience of unprecedented encounters. Although this question has no geographical limit, Tahiti and its history offer spectacular examples of how encounters become flashpoints for understanding cultural, philosophical, political, as well as aesthetic change. My purpose here is to look briefly at how the encounters Louis de Bougainville describes upon arriving in Tahiti in the eighteenth century and those of Paul Gauguin in the nineteenth generated debate and modernist myths of the primitive that have reached into the twentieth and twenty-first centuries.

While the word "encounter" comes from the old French *encontre* (opposite or contrary) and *encontrer* (to go against), originally meaning meeting in battle, it has taken on more diffuse meanings of engagement through face-to-face experience—in difficulty or opposition, accidentally or not, as well as amorous meetings. I am going to use the word "encounter" largely in the sense of discovery and self-discovery through what is received from the outside and by accident.

Roland Barthes wrote about the necessity of bringing diverse disciplines together to enable new configurations of thought:

> The idea of the work comes not necessarily from the internal recasting of each of these disciplines, but rather from their encounter in relation to an object which

traditionally is the province of none of them. It is indeed as though … *interdisciplinarity* … cannot be accomplished by the simple confrontation of specialist branches of knowledge … It begins *effectively* when the solidarity of the old disciplines breaks down—perhaps even violently, via the jolts of fashion—in the interests of a new object and a new language neither of which has a place in the field of the sciences that were to be brought peacefully together.[2]

Barthes situated a new object and its "methodological field" between what he called the work (closed and unified in meaning) and the text (open-ended in interpretation between writer, language, and reader, extended later to other media). That was in 1971. Much has happened since then in a world where change is accelerating (for better and worse): from economic and climate change, political realignment, to the continuing information revolution with the advent of social media. These changes make an interdisciplinary approach all the more necessary today and allow us to return to the Enlightenment in which broad questioning across what we now call disciplines (prior to their separation in the nineteenth century) brought about extraordinary social and political transformation.

I recently visited Tahiti, where a temporal gap of about a thousand years existed between the settlement of the islands—now believed to have come down from Taiwan through the linguistic study of the Austronesian languages[3]—and their later so-called "discoveries" by Europeans. These "discoveries" took place in a remarkable ten-year period: from 1767 with the voyage of the first British sailor Samuel Wallis, to that of France's Bougainville, through to James Cook's third voyage in 1777. Their stays on the island and the narratives that they wrote about their experiences fascinated the Europeans who read them, providing a vision of Tahiti for Westerners as a utopian paradise.

This European myth did not simply emerge, however, from these travel accounts alone. Almost twenty years before Wallis, Bougainville, and Cook set out on their voyages, Jean-Jacques Rousseau wrote his breakout work, the *Discourse on the Origins of Inequality* (1754-5); itself a rewriting of the book of Genesis, this discourse traced the hypothetical stages of society from life in nature through to civilization—a story of how moral regress and decay accompanied technological "progress." Rousseau viewed contemporary European society as corrupted by inequality, inauthenticity, and a degenerate socio-political system. He did not believe reform possible without recreating the foundations of society. In his account of the fall from nature—and this is critically important—there is no original sin, but rather a secular account of how humankind entered into society through physical necessity, passing through a transitory golden age between nature and culture. Meanwhile, Rousseau's friend with whom he was later disaffected, Denis Diderot, was leading the great collective Enlightenment project of the vast *Encyclopédie* to showcase the advances of learning, culture, science, and technology, in order to—its stated goal—change humankind's way of thinking. To his contemporaries, for whom the advancement of culture and technology were celebrated as progress and the way forward, Rousseau represented a kind of genius pariah in his condemnation of culture.

Rousseau doubted the ability of contemporary travelers to comprehend what they saw and reliably narrate their observations. He credits the writers of antiquity (especially Homer and Herodotus) as better able to observe culture[4] and invokes the need for philosophers to understand cultures other than one's own. For his capacious view of the relationship between humans in general and the specifics of particular societies, the great twentieth-century structural anthropologist Claude Lévi-Strauss deemed Rousseau the first ethnographer. Indeed, Rousseau's important social and theoretical construct for society in the *Social Contract* presupposed his first hypothetical history of inequality moving from nature to culture in the *Discourse on the Origins of Inequality*.

Bougainville Encounters Tahiti

Louis de Bougainville set out in 1766 on the frigate *Boudeuse* and the storeship *Étoile* with several scientists.[5] In a daily log, he records nautical information (coordinates, wind, sea) as well as commentary. What most strikes Bougainville and his crew upon their arrival in Tahiti is the welcome of the people:

> A crowd of Indians [sic] welcomed us on the shore with the most emphatic demonstrations of happiness. Not one carried any arms, not even sticks. The chief of this settlement led us to his home where we all sat down on the ground, they brought fruit, water and dried fish and we had a golden age meal with people who are living in that happy time.[6]

How were they to interpret what they were witnessing since they did not know what had happened with Wallis (who had precipitated violent engagements), had no previous knowledge of the place or culture, and did not speak the language? Unaware that the Tahitians may have sought to make peace following their experience with Wallis, Bougainville searches in the first moments for a way "to describe correctly what we have witnessed," writing in his journal that Tahiti is a scene "worthy of Boucher's brush"[7] and that "one would need Fénelon's pen, to depict it, Albani's or Boucher's brush."[8] The hospitality of the people recalls Virgil for Bougainville: "O Venus, for they say it is you who grant rights to those who seek hospitality, may it be your pleasure to make this a happy day [for those who set out from Troy and one of our descendants will remember]."[9] Note that in the *Aeneid* reference material, it is Jupiter, the god of sky and thunder—not Venus the goddess of love—who is interpellated.[10] Then, when not far from reefs with the wind falling calm and a "violent current" driving them towards breakers, Bougainville again turns to Virgil[11]: "into shallow water and swirling sandbanks he [god of the winds] drives us, a pitiable sight to see."[12] Bougainville's points of reference for comprehending this unprecedented encounter with Tahiti and Tahitians are thus, by his own admission, from the long tradition of Western art and literature.[13] Finally, trying to understand Tahitian religion and death rituals, of which he saw no trace, he cites Cicero to caution about what constitutes knowledge, or the lack thereof: "Let us not treat as knowledge things about which we are ignorant and lend our assent to them."[14] Bougainville's familiarity with these classical texts is impressive; as an educated man, he had also read contemporaries such as Rousseau, Buffon, and most likely the earlier travel literature.[15] The recourse to Virgil and Cicero demonstrates Bougainville's reliance on his learned cultural toolkit to understand a situation entirely new to him.

Bougainville's observations about Tahitian society include a view of women and the ease of sexual mores: "We are offered all the young girls ... These people breathe only rest and sensual pleasures. Venus is the goddess they worship. The mildness of the climate, the beauty of the scenery, the fertility of the soil everywhere watered by rivers and cascades, everything inspires sensual pleasure."[16] It is easy to see why, when he decides to name this place, he again turns to a tradition he knows: "And so I have named it New Cythera (the island of Aphrodite)."[17] His contemporaries would have in mind Watteau's early eighteenth-century painting, "Pilgrimage to Cythera," as a reference (even though that is a departure rather than arrival). In sum, Bougainville sees himself "transported into the Garden of Eden" on the interior of the island—a scene reminiscent of Virgil's *Eclogues*.[18] The naturalist Philibert Commerson had a similar reaction in a letter to the astronomer Le Français de la Lande, although his reference differs: "I gave it the name Utopia or fortunate, that Thomas Moore had given to his ideal republic: I did not yet know that M. de Bougainville had named it the New Cythera."[19] Only later did Commerson learn that "the inhabitants had named the island Tahiti," which signifies rushing toward the water.[20] He concludes: "The name I had thought to give it was appropriate for a country, the only one on the planet perhaps, where men are without vices, prejudice, without needs or dissension."[21] Yet like Wallis, who staked a claim for King George before him, Bougainville took "possession" of the island without informing the indigenous people, planting a flag to mark an act of domination. In 1909, the French Geographical society of Paris erected a memorial statue to honor Bougainville by artist Antide-Marie Péchiné, which in 1968 was moved from the quay in Papeete to its current location in Bougainville Park, Papeete.

Bougainville published a revised narrative from his journal, *Voyage autour du monde* in 1771, leaving out nautical details of the journal, updated and informed by the Tahitian named Autouru who came to France with him and from whom he learned about the culture: including the mores of marriage, the making of bark cloth for clothing and canoes with outriggers, and more. In this work, he rails against armchair thinkers like Rousseau—to whom his own models of thought about Tahiti were ironically indebted:

> I neither quote nor contradict anybody, and *much less do I pretend to establish or to overthrow any hypothesis* ... I am a voyager and a seaman; that is, a liar and a stupid fellow, in the eyes of that class of indolent haughty writers, who in their closets [*cabinets*] reason *in infinitum* on the world and its inhabitants, and with an air of superiority, confine nature within the limits of their own invention.[22]

In his diatribe advocating for experiential knowledge, Bougainville intended to validate such travelogues and those who wrote them. Although he and his crew only stayed for nine days in Tahiti, his descriptions of the island and its people—his view of Tahiti as a paradise—nevertheless launched a myth which would carry through to the beginning of the twentieth century.

After writing a review of the published *Voyage Round the World* for his friend Grimm's cultural newsletter, *Literary Correspondence*, which was not published at the time, Diderot set about writing a radical little work of his own, *The Supplement to Bougainville's Voyage*, published posthumously some twenty years later, in 1796. Whether Rousseau believed in his hypothetical history going back to an origin in nature, or Bougainville thought he had truly discovered a "natural" society in Tahiti, Diderot's title involving a fictive "supplement" offers a deconstructive strategy *avant la lettre* in which encounters need not only be first encounters. In it, as I have argued earlier,[23] Diderot's works suggests that comprehension between cultures requires a complex set of dialogues. Two readers, A and B (schematized characters right out of the dictionary order of the *Encyclopédie*), together read and comment upon Bougainville's descriptions of Tahiti's presumed sexually free yet somewhat regulated society—a community based on an alternative family structure with all property in common. Diderot may have been responding to Rousseau's *Discourse on the Origins of Inequality* or to Bougainville's attack on thinkers like himself and Rousseau who had never travelled. In any case, what is at issue is the role of fiction as a supplementary strategy to what one does not know or understand (materially, culturally and ethically) of other societies, and as a way toward critique of one's own. The elders dictate the fate of the young women, who are assumed to desire most of all bearing children, in a society where fertility constitutes the highest value. Yet, in Diderot's text one almost never hears from the women, with the exception of a female outcry against the injustice of laws not in Tahiti, but in New England; in a seemingly unrelated anecdote within the dialogue, a Miss Polly Baker defends herself in court against the injustice of the laws penalizing her for having five children born out of wedlock. Diderot effectively targets both French society and colonial America,[24] indirectly pointing out discrepancies between the assertion of moral principles (in sexuality, marriage, and religion) and interpretations of a culture newly encountered and quickly assimilated into socio-political debate.

In the *Supplément*, Diderot gives voice to Tahitians, creating an encounter between a Tahitian husband, father, and elder who reveals the joys and perils of hospitality (in a society close to nature) and a French chaplain (the Almoner) who defends arbitrary (and hypocritical) customs of European society and religion. In a lengthy speech, the old man speaks to his people: "Weep, unhappy Tahitians! Weep—not for the going but for the coming of those wicked and ambitious men."[25] He rails against the intrusion of Bougainville and other Europeans whose appropriation of the island people of Tahiti transgressed their freedom and innocence, brought disease and the potential for their future enslavement, while sowing the seeds of a civilizing mission on the part of Europeans—an argument later used to legitimate colonialism in the nineteenth century.

Were Bougainville, Diderot and Rousseau asking relevant questions for their time? I believe that in their different ways they were, despite leaving largely unexamined the relationship of their dominance over indigenous peoples as well as the autonomy and equality of women within European and Tahitian society. In turn, both Bougainville and Diderot mention a surprising revelation concerning the naturalist Philibert Commerson: that his valet turned out to be a woman disguised as a man. Jeanne Baret, a botanist who accompanied Commerson as lover and caretaker, turned out in fact to be the first woman to circumnavigate the world. Whether her sex was discovered by Tahitian men on a beach (wanting to give her "Cytheran hospitality," as Bougainville alleges), or she was gang raped by French crew members later in New Ireland Province seems to be in question.[26]

What each side (Tahitian and European) projected in these first encounters has been the subject of much discussion. Miscommunication first began when Wallis and his crew interpreted what they perceived to be lascivious behavior of the women as sexual invitation, which in reality was a display of female power intended to humiliate those, particularly men, toward whom it was directed; "the noa (unrestricted) power of women [associated with fertility] was inimical to the ra'a (restricted, sacred) power of men, destroying their mana or ancestral power."[27] Historians, anthropologists, and art historians have been untangling the parallel versions of the meetings between people in the Pacific and Europe. Both sides drew on myths: Western versions assume European agency and passivity of the islanders. The islanders, on the other hand, assumed their own agency and believed that they had conjured the event of European arrival.[28] A volunteer crew member, Charles-Félix-Pierre Fesche, wrote, when a murder occurred of an islander by one of the crew, that the Europeans—not the islanders (following Montaigne's lead)—were the barbarians.[29]

By the mid 1800s, the society that had existed before the contact with Europeans had come close to extinction because of diseases such as syphilis and tuberculosis, with estimates ranging from a maximum of 35,000 people to as few as 8,000. William Bligh arrived on the *Bounty* in 1788 in order to gather breadfruit to transport to the Caribbean as food for slaves. By the 1790s, George Vancouver noted that the Tahitians had already become dependent on European exchange; whaling ships (from the 1790s on) brought alcoholism, disease, and slavery. Missionaries (including a permanent Anglican settlement from 1797) suppressed local customs. In a sense, the creation of a European idea of this land of plenty and pleasure, as a utopian idea, was accompanied by its destruction at the hand of modern invaders: a "dangerous supplement." If it is clear that Western versions presumed that history began with the arrival and agency of the Europeans, it also becomes clear that Enlightenment encounters of discovery began the intertwining of cultures from then on.

Loving Tahiti

Accounts of sexually welcoming Tahitian women would have seemed likely for libertine novels in the tradition of Laclos and—more radically—Sade. Yet it was the tradition of the sentimental novel—from the translations of Richardson's work through Rousseau's *New Heloise,* to Bernardin de Saint Pierre's *Paul and Virginia,* and a series of novels by women writers only now coming into full view[30]—that provided a literary tradition as backdrop to colonization in the nineteenth century. Historian Matt Matsuda argues that the French reconfigured "possession into passion," with the "legacies of sentimentalism into the age of the nation: imperialism ... registered in languages of love."[31] Whether through a sense of exotic sensualism or political relationship, love became key to governing structures—to the resistance to colonialism and to the alliances that were formed in French Polynesia. The imposition of European boundaries interrupted networks and connections from centuries of migration and navigation in the Pacific, creating "points of crossing."[32] Matsuda points out that "the Pacific [was] ... less a site of colonial history or expansionist territorial mastery than of highly unstable and charged encounters ["among European, Oceanic, American, and Asian temporalities and geographies"], especially for the French."[33] What differed in the earlier explorations from the sixteenth-century European Renaissance (Spanish, Portuguese, Dutch, French), or the French Enlightenment— eighteenth-century explorations and expansions looking for new trade routes, cultures, and scientific observations—was that by the end of the nineteenth century, imperialism turned into appropriations of territory and people. The change from voyages of discovery to identification with nation states and global domination married "a 'civilizing mission' to the romantic legacies of discovery voyages."[34]

The quintessential novel that influenced a generation of readers—from Paul Gauguin to Marcel Proust—about life in the colonies was Pierre Loti's wildly successful 1880 autobiographical fiction, *The Marriage of Loti.* Loti—who had dreamed of the colonies from childhood—became a naval officer, following in the footsteps of his late brother Julien who had lived for two years in Tahiti. But the island turned out not to be the paradise described by Bougainville a century before. Congregational missionaries sent from London[35] had suppressed much of traditional Tahitian life: from the annual festivals, to the dancing of the *upa-upa* (considered indecent because very sexualized), to traditional songs and the imposition of what are called grandmother or Mother Hubbard dress ("civilized" modest shift dresses that covered the entire body of the so-called "naked natives").[36] Loti stayed long enough to take a child lover (whom he abandoned) and create a story that took for granted the inequalities of colonial life; the novel inspired Delibes to write an opera, *Lakmé* (1883) Lakme, and Reynaldo Hahn a comic opera, *The Dream Isle* (1898). Loti promoted the cliché of a dying Polynesian culture in the wake of colonization and Christianization, making lost love and melancholic tragedy dominant themes rather than conquest and domination.

Gauguin Encounters Tahiti

The dominating narrative from Bougainville to Loti, Gauguin, and beyond, is that French Polynesia left behind the sense of freedom in a golden age paradise with the incursion of colonialism. How then to view the cross-current of encounters in Tahiti which unleashed Gauguin's remarkable creativity? Victor Segalen, in his introduction to Gauguin's fictive autobiography, *Noa Noa*, wrote that "Gauguin was a monster, an imperious monster,"[37] for his excessive talent, the range of his life (from sailor, to stock broker, to painter and exiled artist in Tahiti), and his transgression of norms. In a late text, "Before and After," Gauguin refers to the gravity of confession in the wake of Rousseau's *Confessions* and traces his mother's powerful family to a Borgia d'Aragon, viceroy in Peru, where he spent the early years of his life.[38]

When Gauguin decided to leave Europe and his family—abandoning five children (ironically, like Rousseau) along with his wife Mette—he chose Tahiti as a place that would allow him to create a new and unique kind of art, independent of his contemporaries and European traditions. It was then that his life began to intersect with the complex history in Tahiti. Gauguin had visited the World's Fair in 1889, where he saw international representations, including Tahiti among the French colonies, and the photographs of Charles Georges Spitz; these inspired hope that there he would find freedom where he could "love, ... sing, and die," as he wrote rather cruelly to his wife Mette in 1890.[39] The rest is "history": he stays for two years (1891–3), returns to Paris, goes back to Tahiti (1895), and finally lives out his life in the nearby Marquesa Islands (where he died in 1903). His life and art are probably the most celebrated and mythologized of modern Primitivism.

The hypothesis here involves the importance of precedents for understanding new experiences: I will focus now on how for Gauguin, expectations about the Tahitian past affect his cultural encounters. Because he both wrote and painted (along with creating ceramics and works on wood), Gauguin traced or partially invented the transformation of lived experience and perceptions into art. Looking for an idealized past, expecting to find "true" Tahitian culture, and the rejuvenation it would bring to his life and art, Gauguin—like Loti—was disappointed when he arrived: the overlay of culture, governance, and morality had erased much of what he had hoped to find. So, he goes in search of what remains of Tahitian culture in the people; with no extant art available in the Society Islands, Gauguin seeks to recreate it in his own work, equivalent in some ways to Diderot's fictional supplement, creating "a surrogate world of 'authentic' visual experience."[40]

How does Gauguin put together the precedents for what he was seeing and creating? Arriving in Tahiti, he brings along a collection of photographs and postcards which he uses to decorate his first hut outside Papeete. Among the photographs are: Manet's *Olympia*, Botticelli's *Venus*, Fra Angelico's *Annunciation*. He may well also have brought with him some transcriptions from *Promenades in London*,[41] a book written by his maternal grandmother, Flora Tristan, in which she deplored prostitution and the kind of unequal society in which women are victimized.

Gauguin then draws upon his multi-cultured interests in the painting *Ta matete* (*The Market*, 1892), for example, which depicts several women sitting in the place where prostitutes gathered in Papeete, flattening their bodies and gestures in stylized Mother Hubbard dresses. In *Noa Noa* (which meant fragrant scent), he wrote what could have been a label for this painting, echoing both his own life up to that point and his sense of Tahitian culture: "There is, in all of them, a love so innate that, whether mercenary or not mercenary, it is still Love."[42] No follower here of his activist feminist grandmother as he mixes prostitution and love, as well as his new life and European aesthetic, Gauguin nevertheless presents himself as a maverick—caught up in the conflict between considering himself as outsider and anti-colonialist at the same time that his very presence in Tahiti depended, in fact, on colonialism.

First conceived as a travelogue for Gauguin's 1893 Durand-Ruel exhibition, though not completed in time, *Noa Noa* evolved into a collaboration with the Symbolist poet Charles Morice.[43] The work is a fictive autobiography about Gauguin's early days in Tahiti, in which he fashions an image of himself for Europeans in general and in particular for French friends and colleagues. In describing his contact with Tahitian culture, he echoes the Rousseau playbook of nature before the onset of society:

> Civilization is leaving me little by little. I begin to think simply, to harbor no ill feelings or hate for my fellow being—indeed I love him. I have all the pleasures of a free life, both animal and human. I escape from inauthenticity, I enter into nature: with the certainty of a tomorrow just like today, as free, as beautiful, peace descends upon me.[44]

Gauguin progressively adds in sketches, woodcuts, and watercolors—not as illustrations of the narrative, but in parallel with the text. To explain his understanding of cultural and religious beliefs, he draws on the work of ethnologist Jacques-Antoine Moerenhout (a Belgian merchant and diplomat-turned-ethnographer who lived in Tahiti),[45] but he does not seek to be accurate or representative in creating his own works.

Gauguin describes a trip during which he acquires his first child bride—Tehura or Tehamana, aged thirteen—whom he brought, with the permission of her family, down from the countryside, comparing her innocence with the decrepitude of French colonial women. Gauguin seems to have found an ideal life with her: "Every day at the first ray of sun the light was radiant in my room. The gold of Tehamana's face flooded all about it, and the two of us would go naturally, simply, as in Paradise, to refresh ourselves in a near-by stream."[46] Gauguin thus makes his life an incontrovertible part of the story of his painting. Whether or not Tehamana existed as one person, or was rather a composite,[47] Gauguin begins to detach from portrait painting and to create meaning out of the innocence and beauty of a very young woman whose mystery he felt held some of the past he was seeking to retrieve. This is particularly relevant with respect to a series of works from the sketch in *Noa Noa* of *Manao tupapau* (*The Spirit of the Dead Watching*) to the painting *Manao tupapau*. Mario Vargas Llosa, in his novel about Gauguin and his grandmother Flora Tristan, *The Way to Paradise*, stays very close to Gauguin's own descriptions of how this painting of Tehamana came about: he comes home to find her in the dark alone and frightened; it is a supremely erotic scene in which sexual excitement (male sexuality, let's be clear) enables creativity—a theme throughout the parts of the novel about Gauguin. Yet without the attending figure (who is the spirit of death) behind the female figure on the couch, the painting can be interpreted as verging on child pornography, as biographer David Sweetman states. It is the first in a series of works that begin to rival Manet's *Olympia*:[48] the girl is looking back at the painter—not with defiance, but rather as a child who is both frightened and available. Perhaps Gauguin's intention was to out-shock Manet and Loti, adding an almost androgynous ambiguity to the body: the Mahu—which Gauguin brings into a number of paintings—indicated a third sex in Maori culture (both man and woman), similar perhaps to what we might call non-binary today.

A late painting defies the clear opposition between passivity and activity, *Te arii vahine, The Noble Woman*, 1896, for which the model is presumably his second young "wife," Pau'ura, with whom he lost one child and then had another. In it, she is depicted as Eve in a Tahitian Eden, with mangoes on the ground as the displaced forbidden fruit. Yet this Eve seems to be liberated from the Fall—unashamed or unaware of it. As with Rousseau's quest for an origin outside of or alongside the Judeo-Christian scheme of original sin that enables new ideas, associations, and histories, Gauguin's reconfigured Tahitian Eve seems to be even more liberated than Olympia on her couch.[49]

As his work became canonical, Gauguin's own view of women went largely unchallenged until the 1960s—that is, until post-independence critics of colonialism and feminists began to challenge the masculinist tradition.[50] Art historian Griselda Pollock asked provocative questions about the intertwining of gender and "the color of art history" in relation to the painting of Tehamana: how does Gauguin's male gaze impose meaning on a Tahitian woman, to which she seemingly could have no response? And how should a woman and a feminist art critic respond to such a painting?[51] The importance of gender in fields from art history to literature and philosophy raises questions more broadly from the eighteenth and twenty-first centuries—not only with regard to blindness to gender and inequality, but to the openings that reinterpretations provide.

What emerges from Gauguin's writing and his influence on artists and critics is the sense that continuous exploration and crossing boundaries constitute integral parts of Gauguin's monstrous genius. The 2017 exhibition *Gauguin Alchemist* demonstrated the way in which different media allowed Gauguin to make his own supplementary moves across high art (painting) and craft (wood carving and ceramics) to achieve new levels in his art-making, as he left representation behind for synthetic or conceptual art.[52] It is, as Gloria Groom puts it, precisely this capacity for "openness to fresh, unrehearsed discoveries that made him so influential for artists such as Vassily Kandinsky, Ernst Ludwig Kirchner, Henri Matisse, [and] Pablo Picasso and, [in Groom's and many peoples' eyes] that renders him so fascinating today."[53] Gauguin's artistic innovations were to become an inspiration and model for painters interested in Primitivism, particularly Pablo Picasso to whom he served as a kind of mentor. Gauguin's friend and editor, Morice, gave Picasso a copy—now unfortunately lost—of Gauguin's *Noa Noa* with which he identified and to which he added his own drawings. Picasso drew from

Gauguin's paintings, woodcuts, ceramics and drawings, even signing one work "Paul Picasso."[54] Matisse was also inspired by Gauguin, in among others, *The Joy of Living* (1905–16), later integrating his own memories of a visit to Tahiti in 1930 in wall coverings and tapestries *Oceania, the Sky* and *Oceania, the Sea* (1946), and the paper cut-out collage *Lagoon* in the book *Jazz* (1947).

Toward the end of his life, Gauguin insisted: "'I am a savage [primitive]. And civilized people have a presentiment of this; for there is nothing surprising, disconcerting in my works if not this "savage-in-spite-of-myself" aspect.'"[55] The sense of Gauguin's Primitivist project preceded Picasso's, particularly those works that explored origins. Gauguin told an interviewer in 1895 that "to produce something new you have to go back to the original source, to the childhood of mankind."[56] Picasso's *The Life* (1903)[57] recalls Gauguin's cosmological summum which Picasso saw in 1901, *Where Do We Come From? What are we? Where are we going?*

Does this painting answer the questions of Gauguin's title? Reading the painting from right to left, from birth to death, Gauguin suggests that what happened in Eden/Paradise was neither the fault of man nor woman, but somehow of both, as suggested by the androgynous figure in the center. Between the ideal of an innocent Tahiti and its loss in the present, between the ravages of a life (bringing disease to himself and likely all his lovers) and art, Gauguin associated himself as a civilized primitive: both in essays[58] and the great ceramic statue, *Oviri* (1894) depicting the Tahitian goddess of life and death that he wished to be his tombstone.

My visit to Tahiti in early spring of 2018 further stimulated questions about the way in which the encounters of travelers such as Bougainville would find interpretations as in Diderot's *Supplement* and create long-lasting myths that defied or redefined reality. One looks in vain for any work by Gauguin on the island, but still wonders at how his imperfect life and the lost histories he sought to re-imagine could enable such art. What was exhausted or ignored at a given moment can reemerge in new questions and forms: from the stories of Jeanne Baret whose own Mahu kind of existence has only recently been told,[59] to art historian Elizabeth Childs' "taking back Teha'amana"[60] with twentieth- and twenty-first-century artists from the Society Islands to Samoa and Auckland, to the exhibition "Paintings From Afar" at the Musée du Quai Branly—Jacques Chirac (2018). This exhibition revealed remarkable painting from the French colonial past including not only celebrated painters like Gauguin, but also a work by Marie-Antoinette Bouillard Devé (1920) of a sitting woman titled "Red Earth Woman from Cochinchina (Vietnam)," in dialogue with Gauguin's Polynesian work. An example closer to me is that of my aunt, Anne Eisner, who painted a series of women and children upon her return to New York during the 1950s from the ex-Belgian Congo (Democratic Republic of Congo). She created these works not simply in relation to a tradition inherited from Gauguin and Matisse, among others. More importantly, she focused on extensive encounters with Bantu and Mbuti Pygmy women with whom she lived in close proximity—foregrounding empathy and community rather than sexuality and dominance.[61] We continue to learn, I believe, from the way in which encounters are first apprehended and re-experienced as encounters anew as they are continually revised.

Notes

1. Charles Darwin, *Voyage of the Beagle* (Mineola: Dover, 2002), 437.
2. Roland Barthes, "From Work to Text," in *Image, Music, Text* (New York: Hill and Wang, 1977), 155–6.
3. Jared M. Diamond, "Linguistics: Taiwan's Gift to the World," *Nature* 403, no. 6771 (February 2000): 709–10.
4. See my "On the Ethnographic Imagination in the Eighteenth Century," in *French Global: A New Approach to Literary History*, eds. Christie McDonald and Susan Suleiman (New York: Columbia University Press, 2011), 223–40.
5. Among them the naturalist and follower of Rousseau, Philibert Commerson, who studied medicine, zoology and botany; the engineer-cartographer Charles Routier de Romainville; and the astronomer and mathematician Pierre-Antoine Véron, whose patron was the Royal Astronomer Lalande and who was later charged with observing Venus's transit in 1769.
6. Louis Antoine de Bougainville, *The Pacific Journal of Louis-Antoine de Bougainville, 1767–1768*, trans. John Dunmore (London: The Hakluyt Society, 2002), 61. Emphasis added.
7. Bougainville, 62.
8. François Fénelon (1651–1715) wrote *Les Aventures de Télémaque* (1693–4), which indirectly inspired Mozart's *Magic Flute* and, more directly, his *Idomeneo*; Francesco Albani (1578–1660) was an Italian Baroque painter of frescoes on mythological subjects; François Boucher (1703–70) was the French court painter since 1765. Bougainville, *The Pacific Journal*, 73.
9. Bougainville, 63.
10. The *Aeneid* I:731–3, trans. P. Vergili Maronis: Opera, ed. R. A. B. Mynors (Oxford University Press, Oxford, 1969). Michael Putnam, email message to author, December 19, 2019.
11. The *Aeneid* I:111, trans. Putnam.
12. Bougainville, *The Pacific Journal*, 71.
13. I thank my friend and colleague, the great classicist Michael Putnam for his assessment of Bougainville's knowledge of the *Aeneid*.
14. Cicero, *De Officiis*, I.6.18. This text was widely read in the eighteenth century. M. Tulli Ciceronis: De Officiis, ed. M. Winterbottom (Oxford University Press, Oxford, 2016).
15. From John Chardin (1643–1714)—a Protestant jeweler who published an immensely popular three-volume account of his trip to Persia, *Voyages De Monsieur Le Chevalier Chardin En Perse Et Autres Lieux De l'Orient (Travels in Persia* [1686, 1711]*)*—and Jean de Léry (1536–1613)—who two centuries earlier celebrated *Histoire d'un voyage fait en la terre du Brésil* (1578); to Maupertius (1698–1759)—who traveled to Lapland to make longitudinal measurements—and La Condamine (1701–74)—who went to South America for measurements at the Equator. Moreover, the Abbé Prévost (1697–1763) published a compilation of travel narratives, *Histoire Générale des Voyages* [1746–59, 15 vols.].
16. Bougainville, *The Pacific Journal*, 63.
17. Bougainville, 63. Cythera, an island off the south coast of Greece, was thought to be the birthplace of Aphrodite.
18. Bougainville, *Voyage autour du monde* (Paris: Presses de l'Université de Paris-Sorbonne, 2001), 213. My translation.
19. "Lettre de M. Commerson, docteur en médecine, et médecin botaniste du Roy . . ., 25 Feb. 1769. Sur la découverte de la Nouvelle Ile de Cythère ou Taïti", in Bougainville, *Voyage*, 402. My translation.

20 Bougainville, 402. Translation mine.
21 Bougainville, 402. Translation mine.
22 *A Voyage Round the World by Lewis de Bougainville*, trans. John Reinhold Forster (London: F.A.S. J. Nourse, bookseller to his Majesty and the Royal Academy, 1772), 26. Emphasis added. He continues on the same page: "This way of proceeding appears very singular and inconceivable, on the part of persons who *have observed nothing themselves*, and only write and reason upon the observations which they have borrowed from those same travelers in whom they deny the faculty of feeling and thinking." Emphasis added.
23 See Jacque Derrida's extensive analyses of the supplement in Rousseau's work, *De la grammatologie* (Paris: Minuit, 1967). Also my "The Reading and Writing of Utopia in 'Le Supplément au voyage de Bougainville,'" *The Dialogue of Writing: Essays in Eighteenth-Century French Literature* (Waterloo: Wilfrid Laurier University Press, 1984), 63–73.
24 Denis Diderot, "Supplement to Bougainville's Voyage," in *This is Not a Story and Other Stories* (Oxford: Oxford University Press, 1993), 88–91.
25 Diderot, 67.
26 See Bougainville, *The Pacific Journal*, entries from May 28–29, 96-7, and Glynis Ridley, *The Discovery of Jeanne Baret: A Story of Science, the High Seas, and the First Woman to Circumnavigate the Globe* (New York: Crown Publishers, 2010). As recent scholarship suggests, accounts differ, and Bougainville's after-the-fact entry may have invented the discovery of Baret as a woman in Tahiti in order to protect revelation about his crew's crime—punishable by death—from entry into history.
27 Anne Salmond, *Aphrodite's Island: The European Discovery of Tahiti* (Berkeley: University of California Press, 2009), 51.
28 Salmond, 459
29 Bougainville, *The Pacific Journal*, 265.
30 See my "Le dix-huitième siècle: 1715–1793," in *Femmes et littérature: Une histoire culturelle*, vol. 1, *Moyen Âge–XIII siècle*, ed. Martine Reid (Paris: Gallimard, 2020), 717–944.
31 Matt K. Matsuda, *Empire of Love: Histories of France and the Pacific* (Oxford: Oxford University Press, 2005).
32 Matsuda, 5.
33 Matsuda, 7.
34 Matsuda, 15.
35 The Protestant Congregationalists, who arrived from England in Tahiti at the end of the eighteenth century were very repressive; it was at their behest that a young Queen Pomare IV—who ruled from age fourteen between 1827 and 1877—famously expelled two French Roman Catholic priests from the islands in 1837, ultimately resulting in the queen being forced to accept the establishment of a French protectorate over Tahiti in 1842. By 1872, Tahiti was a colony of France in all but name, Pomare IV was a queen in name only, and France annexed Tahiti in 1880.
36 See Pierre Loti, *The Marriage of Loti (Rarahu)*, trans. Clara Bell [1930], 1st French ed. (London: T. Wener Laurie Ltd, 1880).
37 Victor Segalen, "Préface," in Paul Gauguin, *Noa-Noa: Séjour à Tahiti* (Paris: Éditions Complexe, 1989), 9. Translation mine.
38 *Paul Gauguin's Intimate Journals*, trans. Van Wyck Brooks (Bloomington: Indiana University Press, 1958). Born in Paris, Paul Gauguin (1848–1903) grew up in his very early years in Arequipa, Peru, after which he and his mother moved back to France. He went into the merchant marine (where he was coincidentally aboard the same ship as Loti), became a stockbroker, and had five children with the Norwegian Mette in an unhappy marriage before deciding to change radically and become an artist.

39 Letter to Mette, February 1890, cited in Elizabeth C. Childs, *Vanishing Paradise: Art and Exoticism in Colonial Tahiti* (Berkeley: University of California Press, 2013), 83.
40 Childs, 94.
41 Flora Tristan (1803–44) was a maverick feminist, socialist activist and author of *Peregrinations of a Pariah* (1838), *Promenades in London* (1840), and *The Workers' Union* (1843). See, among others, Norma Broude, "Flora Tristan's Grandson: Reconsidering the Feminist Critique of Paul Gauguin," in *Gauguin's Challenge New Perspectives After Postmodernism,* ed. Norma Broude (New York: Bloomsbury, 2018).
42 Nicholas Wadley, ed., *Noa Noa: Gauguin's Tahiti,* trans Jonathan Griffin (Oxford: Phaidon Oxford, 1985), 30.
43 See Wadley, 30.
44 Gauguin, cited in Wadley, 48. My translation.
45 Jacques-Antoine Moerenhout, *Voyages aux îles du Grand océan* (Paris: A. Maisonneuve, 1959); *Travels to the Islands of the Pacific Ocean* (Lanham: University Press of America, 1993).
46 Gauguin, cited in Wadely, *Noa Noa*, 37.
47 See David Sweetman, *Paul Gauguin: A Life* (New York: Simon and Shuster, 1995).
48 Sweetman, 325.
49 See Sweetman, 28–9.
50 See Abigail Solomon-Godeau, "Going Native: Paul Gauguin and the Invention of the Primitivist Modernism," in *The Expanding Discourse: Feminism and Art History,* eds. Norma Broude and Mary D. Garrad (New York: Harper Collins, 1992), 312–9.
51 Griselda Pollock, *Avant-gard gambits, 1888–1893: Gender and the colour of Art History* (London: Thames and Hudson, 1992).
52 See Gloria Groom, "Introduction," in *Gauguin: Artist as Alchemist,* ed. Gloria Groom (New Haven and London: Yale University Press, 2017), 20.
53 Groom, 20.
54 John Richardson, *A Life of Picasso* (New York: Random House, 1991), 263–4.
55 Paul Gauguin, *The Writings of a Savage*, ed. Daniel Guérin, trans. Eleanor Levieux (New York: Viking, 1978), xxxvi, cited in Ophélie Ferlier-Bouat, "The Alchemist and the Savage: Truth and Self-Reflection in Gauguin's Three-Dimensional Work," in Groom, 50–1, note 45.
56 Suzanne Blier, *Picasso's Demoiselles: The Untold Origins of a Modern Masterpiece* (Durham: Duke University Press, 2019), 39.
57 Exhibited in *Picasso: Blue and Rose*, Musée du Quai d'Orsay, Paris, September 2018–January 2019.
58 Paul Gauguin, *Oviri: Écrits d'un sauvage* (Paris: Gallimard, Folio, 1974); Gauguin, *The Writings of a Savage.*
59 See Michèle Kahn, *La clandestine du voyage de Bougainville* (Paris: Le Passage, 2014) and Ridley, *The Discovery of Jeanne Baret.*
60 Elizabeth C. Childs, "Taking Back Teha'amana: Feminist Interventions in Gauguin's Legacy," in Broude, 229–49.
61 See *Images of Congo: Anne Eisner's Art and Ethnography, 1946–1958,* ed. Christie McDonald (Milan: 5 Continents Editions, 2005); Christie McDonald, *The Life and Art of Anne Eisner (1911-1967): An American Artist between Cultures.* (Milan: Oficina libraria, 2020).

BIBLIOGRAPHY

Visual Artists Rights Act of 1990. In 17 U.S.C. § 102. 1990.
A.-C. Bellier-Duchesnoy, ed. *Bibliothèque universelle des dames. Première classe: Voyages,* Bibliothèque de S. A. S. Madame la princesse Des Deux-Ponts. Voyages, t. 1. Paris: 1785.
Abelard, Peter. *Letters.* Translated by Betty Radices. London: Penguin, 2003.
Ahmed, Sara. *Strange Encounters: Embodied Others in Post-Coloniality.* London and New York: Routledge, 2000.
Aïssé, Charlotte-Élisabeth. *Lettres de Mademoiselle Aïssé à Madame C . . .* Paris: La Grange, 1787.
Albalat, Antoine. *Gustave Flaubert et ses amis: avec des lettres inédites de Gustave Flaubert* Paris: Plon, 1927.
Albaret, Céleste, with Georges Belmont. *Monsieur Proust.* Paris: Robert Laffont, 1973.
Alq, Louise d'. *Anthologie féminine.* Paris: Bureaux des Causeries familières, 1893.
Althusser, Louis. *Philosophy of the Encounter, Later Writings, 1978–1987.* London: Verso, 2006.
Althusser, Louis. "The Underground Current of the Materialism of the Encounter." In *Philosophy of the Encounter: Later Writings, 1978–87,* edited by Olivier Corpet and François Matheron, 163–207. Translated by G. M. Goshgarian. London: Verso, 2006.
Amable, Louis. *Une Loge maçonnique d'avant 1789. La R. L. Les Neuf Sœurs.* Paris: Félix Alcan, Éditeur, 1897.
Ammour-Mayeur, Olivier. "Hokusai: source d'un imaginaire de la littérature au XXe siècle (Hélène Cixous/Henry Bachau)." *Lettres romanes* 56, nos. 1–2 (2002): 143–9, www.brepolsonline.net/doi/abs/10.1484/J.LLR.3.49.
Ariosto, Ludovico. *Roland furieux, poème héroïque de l'Arioste. Traduction nouvelle par M. d'Ussieux.* 4 volumes, in-4°. Paris: Brunet, 1775–83.
Arrangement between Mlle de Keralio and M. La Grange and their creditors. April 3, 1789. AN MC/ET/X/781. Archives nationales. Paris. September 17, 2015.
Augustine. *Confessions.* Edited by Michael P. Foley. Translated by F. J. Sheed. 2nd ed. Indianapolis: Hackett, 2006.
Bachelard, Gaston. *The New Scientific Spirit.* Boston: Beacon Press, 1984.
Backus, Irena. "John of Damascus, De Fide Orthodoxa: Translations by Burgundio (1153/54), Grosseteste (1235/40) and Lefèvre d'Étaples (1507)." *Journal of the Warburg and Courtauld Institutes* 49 (1986): 211–17.
Backus, Irena. *The Reception of the Church Fathers in the West.* 2 volumes. Leiden: Brill, 1997.
Backus, Irena. "Renaissance Attitudes to New Testament Apocryphal Writings: Jacques Lefèvre d'Étaples and His Epigones." *Renaissance Quarterly* 51, no. 4 (1998): 1169–98.
Badiou, Alain. *L'être et l'événement.* Paris: Éditions du Seuil, 1988.
Bankruptcy inventory. Fonds faillites. Archives départementales de Paris. Paris.
Barad, Karen. "No Small Matter: Mushroom Clouds, Ecologies of Nothingness, and Strange Topologies of Spacetimemattering." In *Arts of Living on a Damaged Planet: Ghosts and Monsters of the Anthropocene,* edited by Anna Tsing et al., 103–20. Minneapolis: University of Minnesota Press, 2017.

Barbier, Antoine-Alexandre. *Dictionnaire des ouvrages anonymes et pseudonymes composés, traduits ou publiés en français, avec les noms des auteurs, traducteurs et éditeurs; accompagné de notes historiques et critiques*. 4 volumes. Paris: Imprimerie Bibliographique, 1806. See http://books.google.com/books?id=peRRAAAAcAAJ.

Barchilon, Jacques. "Beauty and the Beast: From Myth to Fairy Tale." *Psychoanalysis and the Psychoanalytic Review* 46, no. 4 (1959): 19–29.

Barthes, Roland. "The Death of the Author." In *Image, Music, Text*, 142–8. Translated by Stephen Heath. London: Fontana Press, 1977.

Barthes, Roland. "From Work to Text." In *Image, Music, Text,* 155–65. New York: Hill and Wang, 1977.

Bataille, Georges. *Story of the Eye*. Translated by Joachim Neugroschel. London: Penguin Books, 2001.

Beaulieu, Alain. "La politique de Gilles Deleuze et le matérialisme aléatoire du dernier Althusser." *Actuel Marx* 34, no.2 (2003): 161–74.

Beckett, Samuel. *A Piece of Monologue*. 1979. In *The Collected Shorter Plays*. Reprinted. New York: Grove Press, 2010.

Beckett, Samuel. *The Unnamable*. 1953. In *Three Novels: Molloy, Malone Dies, The Unnamable*. Reprinted. New York: Grove Press, 2009.

Beckett, Samuel. *Worstward Ho*. London: John Calder, 1983.

Bennett, Jonathan. *Events and their Name.* Indianapolis: Haggart, 1988.

Bennington, Geoffrey. *Dudding: Des noms de Rousseau*. Paris: Galilée, 1991.

Bertaud, Jean-Paul. *Choderlos de Laclos: L'auteur des* Liaisons dangereuses. Paris: Fayard, 2003.

Bescherelle aîné, Bescherelle jeune and Litais de Gaux. *Grammaire nationale, ou grammaire de Voltaire, de Racine, de Fénelon [. . .] et de tous les écrivains les plus distingués de France*. 2nd ed. Paris: L. Bourgeois-Maze, 1835–6.

Best, Stephen. *The Fugitive's Properties: Law and the Poetics of Possession*. Chicago and London: The University of Chicago Press, 2004.

Bettelheim, Bruno. *The Uses of Enchantment: The Meaning and Importance of Fairy Tales*. New York: Knopf, 1976.

Biancardi, Elisa, ed. *La Jeune Américaine et les Contes marins (La Belle et la Bête). Les Belles Solitaires. [Suivi de] Magasin des enfants (La Belle et la Bête)*. By Gabrielle-Suzanne de Villeneuve and Jeanne-Marie Leprince de Beaumont. Bibliothèque des génies et des fées 15. Paris: Champion, 2008.

Billardon de Sauvigny, Edme-Louis. *Le Parnasse des dames, ou choix de pièces de quelques femmes célèbres en littérature*. 9 volumes. Paris: Rouault, 1773. *Gallica*. Web. Accessed September 21, 2010.

Blanchot, Maurice. *Le Pas au-delà*. Paris: Editions Gallimard, 1973.

Blay, Philippe. "Chronologie." In *Reynaldo Hahn: Un éclectique en musique*, edited by P. Blay, 44–5. Arles: Acte Sud/Palazzetto Bru Zane, 2015.

Blow, Charles. "The Horrible History of Thanksgiving." *New York Times,* November 27, 2019. www.nytimes.com/2019/11/27/opinion/thanksgiving-history.html.

Boethius. *Consolation of Philosophy*. Translated by Richard Green. New York: Macmillan, 1962.

Bougainville, Louis-Antoine de. *The Pacific Journal of Louis-Antoine de Bougainville, 1767–1768*. Translated by John Dunmore. London: The Hakluyt Society, 2002.

Bougainville, Louis-Antoine de. *Voyage autour du monde*. Paris: Presses de l'Université de Paris-Sorbonne, 2001.

Bougainville, Louis-Antoine de. *A Voyage Round the World by Lewis de Bougainville*. Translated by John Reinhold Forster. London: F.A.S. J. Nourse, bookseller to his Majesty and the Royal Academy, 1772.

Boulard, Stéphanie and Catherine Witt, eds. *Ententes – À partir d'Hélène Cixous*. Paris: Presses Sorbonne Nouvelle, 2018.

Boulez, Pierre. *Points de repère: Regards sur autrui*. Vol. 2. Edited by Jean-Jacques Nattiez and Sophie Galaise. Paris: Christian Bourgois éditeur, 2005.

Bourdin, Jean-Claude. "La rencontre du matérialisme et de l'aléatoire chez Louis Althusser." *Multitudes* 21, no. 2 (2005): 139–47.

Boyer, Pierre-Louis. *Clémence Isaure: Vérités sur une chimère toulousaine*. Biarritz: Atlantica, 2010.

Bracha, Oren. "The Ideology of Authorship Revisited: Authors, Markets, and Liberal Values in Early American Copyright." *Yale Law Journal* 118, no. 2 (2008–2009): 188–271.

Braider, Christopher. *The Matter of Mind: Reason and Experience in the Age of Descartes*. Toronto: University of Toronto Press, 2012.

Briquet, Fortunée B. *Dictionnaire historique, littéraire et bibliographique des Françaises, et des étrangères naturalisées en France*. Paris: Gillé, 1804.

Briquet, Fortunée. *Dictionnaire historique des Françaises connues par leurs écrits*. Edited by Nicole Pellegrin. Strasbourg: Presses universitaires de Strasbourg, 2016.

Brondel, Nicole. "Ussieux, Louis d'." In *Dictionnaire des journalistes, 1600–1789*, edited by Jean Sgard, volume 2, 975–8. Oxford: Voltaire Foundation, 1999.

Brouard-Arends, Isabelle. "Lambert, Anne-Thérèse Marguenat de Courcelles, marquise de (1647–1733)." In *Dictionnaire des femmes des Lumières*, edited by Huguette Krief and Valérie André, 671–75. Paris: Honoré Champion éditeur, 2015.

Broude, Norma. *Gauguin's Challenge: New Perspectives After Postmodernism*. New York: Bloomsbury, 2018.

Bryden, Mary. "Hélène Cixous and Maria Chevska." In *Women and Representation*, edited by Diana Knight and Judith Still, 106–14. University of Nottingham: WLF Publications, 1995.

Buber, Martin. *Between Man and Man*. Translated by Ronald Gregor-Smith. London: Routledge, 2002.

Buber, Martin. *Ich und Du*. Gütersloh: Gütersloher Verlagshaus, 1997.

Le Cabinet des fées. Compiled by Charles-Joseph de Mayer. 41 volumes. *Geneva and Paris: Barde, Manget & Compagnie and Cuchet*, 1785–1789.

Canguilhem, Georges. *Ideology and Rationality in the History of the Life Sciences*. Cambridge: MIT Press, 1988.

Canguilhem, Georges. *Knowledge of Life*. New York: Fordham University Press, 2008.

Cassirer, Ernst. *The Philosophy of Symbolic Forms*. Translated by Ralph Manheim. New Haven: Yale University Press, 1953.

Cauna, Jacques de. *Au temps des isles à sucre: Histoire d'une plantation de Saint-Domingue au XVIIIème siècle*. Paris: Karthala, 2003.

Certeau, Michel de. *L'Écriture de l'histoire*. Paris: Éditions Gallimard, Bibliothèque de l'histoire, 1975; *The Writing of History*. Translated by Tom Conley. New York: Columbia University Press, 1992.

Chappey, Jean-Luc. "Canonisation littéraire et remise en ordre politique et sociale entre révolution et empire." *Revue d'histoire littéraire de la France* 114, no.1 (2014): 13–30.

Charrier-Vozel, Marianne. "Mme. Riccoboni, traductrice de Hugh Kelly." In *La traduction des genres non romanesques au xviii siècle, Centre d'études de la traduction, Université de Metz, 14–15 mars 2003,* edited by Annie Cointre and Annie Rivara, 187–203. Sarreguemines: Pierron, 2003.

Charrière, Isabelle de. *Letters of Mistress Henley Published by her Friend*. Translated by Philip Stewart and Jean Vaché. New York: The Modern Language Association of America, 1993.

Charrière, Isabelle de/Belle de Zuylen. *Œuvres complètes*. 10 volumes. Amsterdam: G. A. Van Oorschot, 1979.
Chater, Kathleen. *Untold Histories: Black People in England and Wales during the Period of the British Slave Trade, c. 1660–1807*. Manchester and New York: Manchester University Press, 2009.
Chaucer, Geoffrey. "General Prologue." In *The Canterbury Tales*. Edited by A. C. Cawley. New York: Everyman's Library, 1958.
Childs, Elizabeth. *Vanishing Paradise: Art and Exoticism in Colonial Tahiti*. Berkeley: University of California Press, 2013.
Chollet, Mathilde, and Huguette Krief, editors. *Une femme d'encre et de papier à l'époque des Lumières: Henriette de Marans (1719–1784)*. Rennes: Presses universitaires de Rennes, 2017.
Chollet, Mathilde. "Une ambition féminine au siècle des Lumières: éducation et culture au château: les journaux de Mme de Marans (1719–1784)." Doctoral Thesis. Université du Maine, 2014.
Chrétien de Troyes. *The Tale of the Grail*. In *Arthurian Romances*. Translated by William Kibler. London: Penguin, 1991.
Cicero. *De Officiis*. Ed. M. Winterbottom (Oxford University Press, Oxford, 2016).
Cixous, Hélène. *Abstracts et Brèves Chroniques du temps. I Chapitre Los*. Paris: Éditions Galilée, 2013.
Cixous, Hélène. *Ayaï ! Le cri de la littérature*. Paris: Éditions Galilée, 2013.
Cixous, Hélène. "First to be Astounded." Translated by Laurent Milesi. In *Alechinsky: À contre-vent*. Paris: Galerie Lelong & Co., 2012.
Cixous, Hélène. "How Not to Speak of Algeria." Translated by Eric Prenowitz. In *Volleys of Humanity: Essays 1972–2009*, edited by Eric Prenowitz, 160–76. Edinburgh: Edinburgh University Press, 2011.
Cixous, Hélène. "L'imagie d'Ernest." In *Face aux murs: Ernest Pignon-Ernest*, 126–9. Paris: Delpire, 2010.
Cixous, Hélène. *Insurrection de la poussière: Adel Abdessemed*, suivi de *A. A. H. C.: Correspondance*. Paris: Éditions Galilée, 2014.
Cixous, Hélène. "Interview with Hélène Cixous." By Catherine Anne Franke and Roger Chazal. *Qui Parle* 3, no. 1 (Spring 1989): 152–79.
Cixous, Hélène. "The Last Painting or the Portrait of God." Translated by Sarah Cornell. In *"Coming to Writing" and Other Essays*, edited by Deborah Jenson with an introductory essay by Susan Rubin Suleiman, 101–31. London and Cambridge: Harvard University Press, 1991.
Cixous, Hélène. "Lettre à Adel." *Études françaises* 51, no. 2 (2015): 37–45.
Cixous, Hélène. *Limonade tout était si infini*. Paris: Des femmes, 1982.
Cixous, Hélène. *Luc Tuymans: Relevé de la mort*. 2 volumes. Paris: La Différence, 2012.
Cixous, Hélène. *Poetry in Painting: Writings on Contemporary Arts and Aesthetics*. Edited by Joana Masó and Marta Segarra. Edinburgh: Edinburgh University Press, 2012.
Cixous, Hélène. "Quand H. C. essaie de s'*excuser*." *Études françaises* 51, no. 2 (2015): 207–12.
Cixous, Hélène. *Les Sans Arche d'Adel Abdessemed et autres coups de balai*. Paris: Gallimard, 2018.
Cixous, Hélène. "The Secret in the Tarp." In *Adel Abdessemed: From Here to Eternity*. Manhattan: Venus, 2015.
Cixous, Hélène. "Seeing with the Tongue: The Lispector Apocalypse," translated by Laurent Milesi. *Matador*, no. 0 (2012): 24–5.
Cixous, Hélène. *Le Tablier de Simon Hantaï: Annagrammes*, suivi de *H. C. et S. H.: Lettres*. Paris: Galilée, 2005.

Cixous, Hélène. "Volées d'humanité." In *Rêver croire penser: Autour d'Hélène Cixous*, edited by Bruno Clément and Marta Segarra. 15–37. Paris: Campagne Première, 2010.
Cixous, Hélène. *Le Voyage de la racine alechinsky*. Paris: Éditions Galilée, 2012.
Cixous, Hélène. "Without End, No, State of Drawingness, No, Rather: The Executioner's Taking Off." Translated by Catherine A. F. MacGillivray. In *Stigmata: Escaping Texts*, 25–40. With a foreword by Jacques Derrida and a new preface by the author. London & New York: Routledge Classics, 2005.
Collection Patricia Mante-Proust. Sotheby's. Paris. May 31, 2016. Lot no. 229, 88–9. www.sothebys.com/en/auctions/ecatalogue/2016/livres-manuscrits-pf1603/lot.229.html.
Copyright Act of 1790, 1 Stat. 124 (1790).
Corrie, Cathleen Eva. 'Sy excellente pasture': Guillaume Briçonnet's Mysticism and the Pseudo-Dionysius." *Renaissance Studies* 20, no. 1 (2006): 35–50.
Cotgrave, Randle. *A Dictionarie of the French & English Tongues*. London: Adam Inslip, 1611.
Couadau, Marie-Louise. "Clémence Isaure ou l'invention d'un mythe méridional." *Midi: revue de sciences humaines et de littérature de la France du Sud* 2 (March 1987): 48–51.
Coulet, Henri, ed. *Nouvelles du XVIIIe siècle*. Paris: Éditions Gallimard, Bibliothèque de la Pléiade, 2002.
Coultrap-McQuin, Susan. *Doing Literary Business: American Women Writers in the Nineteenth Century*. Chapel Hill and London: University of North Carolina Press, 1990.
Courteault, Henri. *Mademoiselle Aïssé, le chevalier d'Aydie et leur fille*. Paris: Société des bibliophiles françois, 1908.
Courtine, Jean-François. "Différence ontologique et analogie de l'être: Le tournant suarézien." *Bulletin de la Société française de philosophie* 83, no. 2 (1989): 163–79.
Courtney, C. P. *Isabelle de Charrière (Belle de Zuylen): A biography*. Oxford: Voltaire Foundation, Taylor Institution, 1993.
Craveri, Benedetta. "Preface." In *Lettres à Madame C*, by [Charlotte-Élisabeth] Aïssé, 5–25. Paris: Payot & Rivages, 2009.
Croft, Marie-Ange. "La réception des *Premières oeuvres poétiques* (1581) de Marie de Romieu sous l'Ancien Régime: de Guillaume Colletet à Louise de Kéralio." In *Sciences et littérature*, suivi de *Fortunes des œuvres d'Ancien Régime*, edited by Solange Lemaitre-Provost et al., 237–52. Paris: Hermann, 2013.
Dacier, André. *La Vie de Pythagore, ses symboles, ses vers dorez et la vie d'Hiéroclès*. Paris: Rigaud, 1706.
Damas, Mme de. *Pensées morales*. [Paris]: Desenne, 1799.
Dante. *The Divine Comedy: 1. Inferno*. Translated by John D. Sinclair. New York: Oxford University Press, 1939.
Darwin, Charles. *Voyage of the Beagle*. 2nd edition. Mineola: Dover, 2002.
Davidson, Donald. *Essays on Action and Events*. Oxford: Oxford University Press, 2001.
DeJean, Joan. "Classical Reeducation: Decanonizing the Feminine." *The Politics of Tradition: Placing Women in French Literature*, edited by Joan DeJean and Nancy K. Miller, special issue of *Yale French Studies* 75 (1988): 26–39. Reprinted in *Displacements: Women, Tradition, Literatures in French*. Edited by Joan DeJean and Nancy K. Miller, 22–36. Baltimore: Johns Hopkins University Press, 1991.
DeJean, Joan E. *Tender Geographies: Women and the Origins of the Novel in France*. New York: Columbia University Press, 1991.
Delesalle-Rowlson, Simone. "'Le Bunibuls de Monsieur Proust' et la philologie." In *Proust et les "Moyen Âge*," edited by Sophie Duval and Miren Lacassagne, 315–32. Paris: Hermann, 2015.

Deleuze, Gilles and Felix Guattari. *A Thousand Plateaus: Capitalism and Schizophrenia.* Translated by Brian Massumi. Minneapolis: University of Minnesota Press, 1987.

Deleuze, Gilles. "Causes et raisons de l'île déserte." In *Desert Island and Other Texts, 1953–74*, edited by David Lapoujade, 9–14. Translated by Michael Taormina. Cambridge: Semiotexte/MIT Press, 2004.

Deleuze, Gilles. *Cinéma 1: L'Image-mouvement.* Paris: Éditions de Minuit, 1983.

Deleuze, Gilles. *Difference and Repetition.* Translated by Paul Patton. London: Bloomsbury, 2006.

Deleuze, Gilles. *Le Pli: Leibniz et le baroque.* Paris: Éditions de Minuit, 1988. *The Fold: Leibniz and the Baroque.* Translated by Tom Conley. Minneapolis: University of Minnesota Press, 1993.

Deleuze, Gilles. *Proust and Signs.* Translated by Richard Howard. Minneapolis: University of Minnesota Press, 2000.

Delmas, André Albert, and Yvette Mialon Delmas. *À la recherche des* Liaisons dangereuses. Paris: Mercure de France, 1964.

Derrida, Jacques and Christie McDonald. "Choreographies: Interview." *Diacritics* 12, no. 2 (Summer 1982): 66–76.

Derrida, Jacques. "Circumfession." In *Jacques Derrida*, with Geoffrey Bennington. Translated by Geoffrey Bennington. Chicago: University of Chicago Press, 1993.

Derrida, Jacques. *De la grammatologie.* Paris: Minuit, 1967.

Derrida, Jacques. *The Gift of Death.* Translated by David Wills. Chicago: University of Chicago Press, 2008.

Derrida, Jacques. *H. C. for Life, That Is to Say . . .* Translated, with additional notes, by Laurent Milesi and Stefan Herbrechter. Stanford, CA: Stanford University Press, 2006.

Derrida, Jacques. "Lignées." In *Mille e tre, cinq/Lignées*, with Micaëla Heinich. Bordeaux: William Blake & Co., 1996.

Derrida, Jacques. "Pas." *Gramma*, no. 3–4 (1975): 111–217. Reprinted in *Parages*. Paris: Éditions Galilée, 1986.

Derrida, Jacques. "Spéculer sur Freud." In *La Carte postale: de Socrate à Freud et au-delà*, 275–437. Paris: Aubier-Flammarion, 1978) suppress).

Derrida, Jacques. *Thinking Out of Sight: Writings on the Arts of the Visible.* Edited by Ginette Michaud, Joana Masó and Javier Bassas. With new translations by Laurent Milesi Chicago: University of Chicago Press, forthcoming 2021.

Descartes, René. "Discourse on the Method." In *Descartes: Selected Philosophical Writings*, edited by John Cottingham, et al. Cambridge: Cambridge University Press, 1988.

Descartes, René. *The Passions of the Soul* [1649]. Translated by Jonathan Bennett. www.earlymoderntexts.com/assets/pdfs/descartes1649.pdf.

Descombes, Vincent. *Proust: Philosophie du Roman.* Paris: Minuit, 1987.

Diamond, Jared M. "Linguistics: Taiwan's Gift to the World." *Nature* 403, no. 6771 (February 2000): 709–10.

Diderot, Denis. *Les bijoux indiscrets.* 2 volumes. [Paris]: [Durand], 1748. http://gallica.bnf.fr/ark:/12148/btv1b8613354b.

Diderot, Denis. *James the Fatalist and his Master: Translated from the French of Diderot*, volume 1. London: printed for G. G. and J. Robinson, 1797. In *Eighteenth Century Collections Online*. Gale. Website. Accessed March 23, 2020.

Diderot, Denis, and Jean le Rond d'Alembert, editors. "Livre [Littérature]." In *Encyclopédie, ou dictionnaire raisonné des sciences, des arts et des métiers, etc.*, 9:602–10. University of Chicago: ARTFL Encyclopédie Project, December 1765. http://encyclopedie.uchicago.edu/.

Diderot, Denis. *Œuvres romanesques.* Edited by Henri Bénac. Paris: Garnier, 1962.
Diderot, Denis. *Rameau's Nephew—Le Neveu de Rameau: A Multi-media Bilingual Edition.* Edited by Marian Hobson. Translated by Kate E. Tunstall and Caroline Warman. Cambridge: Open Book Publishers, 2016.
Diderot, Denis. *Rameau's Nephew and other Works.* Translated by Jacques Barzun and Ralph H. Bowen. Indianapolis: Hackett Publishing Company, Inc. 2001.
Diderot, Denis. *This is not a Story and Other Stories.* Columbia: University of Missouri Press, 1991.
Didi-Huberman, Georges. *Bark.* Translated by Samuel E. Martin. Cambridge: MIT Press, 2017.
Didi-Huberman, Georges. *Essayer voir.* Paris: Minuit, 2014.
Didi-Huberman, Georges. *L'homme qui marchait dans la couleur.* Paris: Minuit, 2001.
Didier, Béatrice. *Choderlos de Laclos, Les Liaisons dangereuses: pastiches et ironie.* Paris: Éditions du Temps, 1998.
Dijk, Suzanna van. *Traces de femmes: présences féminines dans le journalisme français du XVIIIe siècle.* Amsterdam: APA-Holland University Press, 1998.
Dijk, Suzan van, ed. *Women Writers.* Accessed January 5, 2020, http://neww.huygens.knaw.nl/.
Dod, Bernard. "Aristoteles Latinus." In *The Cambridge History of Later Medieval Philosophy*, edited by Norman Kretzman, Anthony Kenny, Jan Pinborg, and Eleonore Stump, 45–79. Cambridge: Cambridge University Press, 1982.
Dorat, Claude-Joseph. "Extrait des Mémoires du comte de Comminges." In *Lettres en vers et oeuvres mêlées,* 29–58. Paris: S. Jorry, 1767. https://gallica.bnf.fr/ark:/12148/btv1b8617174n.
Du Châtelet, Émilie. "Lettre sur les elemens de la philosophie de Newton." *Journal des sçavans,* September 1738: 534–41.
Dupin, Marie Aurore. *La France illustrée par ses femmes.* Paris: Maumus, 1833.
Eagleton, Terry. *After Theory.* New York: Basic Books, 2004.
Épinay, Louise d'. Review of *Les Confidences d'une jolie femme*, by Mademoiselle d'Albert. Edited by Denis Diderot, Friedrich Melchior Grimm, Jules-Antoine Taschereau, and A. Chaudé. *Correspondance littéraire, philosophique et critique* 8 (January 1775): 439–42.
Escoubas, Éliane. "Derrida and the Truth of Drawing: Another Copernican Revolution?" Translated by Paul Milan. *Research in Phenomenology* 36, no. 1 (2006): 201–14.
Esterházy, Péter. *Javított Kiadás: Melléklet a Harmonia Caelestishez.* Budapest: Magvető, 2001.
Evain, Aurore, and Perry Gethner and Henriette Goldwyn, eds. *Théâtre de femmes de l'Ancien Régime.* 4 volumes. Paris: Classiques Garnier, 2011–15.
Falque, Emmanuel. "Jean Scot Érigène: La théophanie comme mode de la phénoménalité." *Revue des sciences philosophiques et théologiques* 86, no. 3 (2002): 387–421.
Flaubert, Gustave. *Correspondance.* Edited by Danielle Girard and Yvan Leclerc. https://flaubert.univ-rouen.fr/correspondance/edition/.
Foucault, Michel. *The History of Sexuality, Volume I: The Will to Knowledge.* Translated by Robert Hurley. New York: Vintage Books, 1988.
Foucault, Michel. *Les Mots et les choses: Une archéologie des sciences humaines.* Paris: Gallimard, 1966; *The Order of Things: An Archeology of the Human Sciences.* New York: Pantheon, 1971.
Fraisse, Luc. *L'Éclectisme philosophique de Marcel Proust.* Paris: Presses de l'université Paris-Sorbonne, 2013.
Fraisse, Luc. *Proust au miroir de sa correspondance.* Liège: SEDES, 1996.

Fréron, Elie-Catherine. Review of *Les Pensées errantes; avec quelques Lettres d'un Indien*, by [Henriette de Marans]. *Année Littéraire*. July 15, 1758.
Fryer, Peter. *Staying Power: The History of Black People in Britain*. London: Pluto Press, 1984.
Gauguin, Paul. *Noa Noa: Gauguin's Tahiti*. Edited by Nicholas Wadley. Translated by Jonathan Griffin. Oxford: Phaidon Oxford, 1985.
Gauguin, Paul. *Oviri: Écrits d'un sauvage*. Paris: Gallimard, Folio, 1974.
Gauguin, Paul. *Paul Gauguin's Intimate Journals*. Translated by Van Wyck Brooks. Bloomington: Indiana University Press, 1958.
Gauguin, Paul. *The Writings of a Savage*. Edited by Daniel Guérin. Translated by Eleanor Levieux. New York: Viking, 1978.
Gavoty, Bernard. *Reynaldo Hahn: Le musicien de la Belle Époque*. Paris: Buchet-Castel, 1976.
Geary, Susan. "Harriet Beecher Stowe, John P. Jewett, and Author-Publisher Relations in 1853." *Studies in the American Renaissance* (1977): 345–67.
Genand, Stéphanie. *Le Libertinage et l'histoire: Politique de la séduction à la fin de l'Ancien Régime*. Studies on Voltaire and the Eighteenth Century 11. Oxford: Voltaire Foundation, 2005.
Genlis, Stéphanie Félicité de. *De l'influence des femmes sur la littérature française, comme protectrices des lettres et comme auteurs; ou précis de l'histoire des femmes françaises les plus célèbres*. Paris: Mardan, 1811.
Genlis, Stéphanie-Félicité de. *Mémoires inédits de Madame la comtesse de Genlis sur le dix-huitième siècle et la Révolution Française*. Volume 1. Paris: Ladvocat, 1825.
Gervai, András. "Egy ügynök azonosítása." *Élet és Irodalom*, January 27, 2006.
Girard, René. *Des choses cachées depuis la fondation du monde*. Paris: Grasset, 1978.
Girard, René. *La Violence et le sacré*. Paris: Grasset, 1972.
Gottman, Felicia. "Du Châtelet, Voltaire, and the Transformation of Mandeville's Fable." *History of European Ideas* 38, no. 2 (2012): 218–32.
Gouges, Olympe de. "Pronostic Sur Maximilien Robespierre, Par Un Animal Amphibie." 1792. 9.4.155. Les archives de la Révolution française. Bibliothèque nationale de France, https://catalogue.bnf.fr/ark:/12148/cb37236069q.
Green, Karen. *A History of Women's Political Thought in Europe, 1700–1800*. Cambridge: Cambridge University Press, 2014.
Grell, Chantal. *L'histoire entre érudition et philosophie: Étude sur la connaissance historique à l'âge des Lumières*. Paris: Presses universitaires de France. 1993.
Grimm, Friedrich Melchior. *1763*, edited by Ulla Kölving. Vol. 10 of *Correspondance littéraire*, edited by Ulla Kölving and Françoise Tilkin. Ferney-Voltaire: Centre International d'étude du XVIIIe siècle, 2016.
Grimm, Friedrich Melchior. Review of *Les Pensées errantes; avec quelques Lettres d'un Indien*, by [Henriette de Marans]. Edited by Henri Duranton. *Correspondance Littéraire* 5 (July 15, 1758): 115.
Groom, Gloria, editor. *Gauguin: Artist as Alchemist*. New Haven: Yale University Press, 2017.
Guattari, Felix. *Chaosmosis: An Ethico-Aesthetic Paradigm*. Translated by Paul Bains and Julian Pefanis. Bloomington: Indiana University Press, 1995.
Guibert, [Élisabeth]. *Pensées détachées de Mme Guibert*. Bruxelles: Couturier fils, 1771.
Hadot, Pierre. *Philosophy as a Way of Life*. Edited by A. Davidson. Translated by M. Chase. Malden: Blackwell, 1995.
Hanslick, Eduard. *The Beautiful in Music*. ed. Morris Weitz, trans. Gustav Cohen. New York: The Liberal Arts Press, 1957.

Hanslick, Eduard. *Vom Musikalisch-Schönen. Ein Beitrag zur Revision der Aesthetik der Tonkunst* [1855]. Edited by Dietmar Strauss. Mayence: Schott, 1990.
Haraway, Donna and Martha Kenney. "Anthropocene, Capitalocene, Chthulhocene." In *Art in the Anthropocene*, edited by Heather Davis and Etienne Turpin, 255–70. London: Open Humanities Press, 2015.
Haraway, Donna. *Staying with the Trouble: Making Kin in the Chthulucene*. Durham: Duke University Press, 2017.
Hayoun, Maurice-Ruben, and Alain de Libera. *Averroès et l'averroïsme*. Que Sais-Je? Paris: Presses Universitaires de France, 1991.
Hébrail, Jacques, and Joseph de Laporte. *Les Académies établies à Paris & dans les différentes villes du royaume*. Vol. 1 of *La France littéraire*. Paris: La Veuve Duchesne, 1769.
Hecht, J. Jean. *The Domestic Servant Class in Eighteenth-Century England*. London: Routledge & Paul, 1956.
Hesse, Carla. "Kant, Foucault, and *Three Women*." In *Foucault and the Writing of History*, edited by Jan Goldstein, 81–98. Cambridge: Blackwell, 1994.
Hesse, Carla. *The Other Enlightenment: How French Women Became Modern*. Princeton: Princeton University Press, 2001.
Hilger, Stephanie M. *Women Write Back: Strategies of Response and the Dynamics of European Literary Culture, 1790–1805*. Amsterdam: Rodopi, 2009.
Histoire universelle depuis le commencement du monde jusqu'à présent, composée en anglois par une société de gens de lettres; nouvellement traduite en françois par une société de gens de lettres . . . enrichie de figures et de cartes, 125 vol. Paris: Moutard, 1779–91.
Hoefer, Jean-Chrétien-Ferdinand, ed. *Nouvelle biographie générale depuis les temps les plus reculés jusqu'à nos jours, avec les renseignements bibliographiques et l'indication des sources à consulter*. Paris: Firmin Didot frères, 1854–77.
Homestead, Melissa. "'When I Can Read My Title Clear': Harriet Beecher Stowe and the *Stowe v. Thomas* Copyright Infringement Case." *Prospects: An Annual of American Cultural Studies* 27 (2002): 201–45.
Howie, Peter C. "Philosophy of Life: J. L. Moreno's Revolutionary Philosophical Underpinnings of Psychodrama and Group Psychotherapy." *Group: Philosophy and Group Psychotherapy* 36, no. 2 (Summer 2012): 135–46.
I***, M. le C. d' [Jules Gay]. *Bibliographie des ouvrages relatifs à l'amour, aux femmes, au mariage, et des livres facétieux, pantagruéliques, scatologiques, satyrique etc.* 2 volumes. 3rd ed. Paris: Bibliothèque Derviche, 1871.
Jacob, François. *The Logic of Life: A History of Heredity*. Translated by Betty E. Spillmann. New York: Pantheon, 1973.
Janik, Linda Gardiner. "Searching for the metaphysics of science: the structure and composition of madame Du Châtelet's *Institutions de physique, 1737–1740.*" *Studies on Voltaire and the Eighteenth Century* 201 (1982): 85–113.
Jaucourt, Louis. "Ouvrage [Arts & Sciences]" (see https://artflsrv03.uchicago.edu/philologic4/encyclopedie1117/navigate/11/3388/). In *Encyclopédie, ou dictionnaire raisonné des sciences, des arts et des métiers, etc.*, edited by Denis Diderot and Jean le Rond d'Alembert, 11:722. University of Chicago: ARTFL Encyclopédie Project, December 1765. http://encyclopedie.uchicago.edu/.
Jeauneau, Edouard. "Néant divin et théophanie (Érigène disciple de Denys)." In *Langages et philosophie: Hommage à Jean Jolivet*, edited A. de Libera, A. Elamrani-Jamal, A. Galonnier, 331–7. Paris: Vrin, 1997.
Jefferson, Thomas. Thomas Jefferson to Isaac McPherson, August 13, 1813. In *The Founder's Constitution*, Volume 3, edited by Philip B. Kurland and Ralph Lerner.

Chicago: The University of Chicago Press, 1986. http://presspubs.uchicago.edu/founders/documents/a1_8_8s12.html.
Joyce, James. *Ulysses*. 1922. Reprint. London: Penguin Books, 2000.
Kafka, Franz. *Letters to Milena*. Translated by Philip Boehm. New York: Schocken Books, 1990.
Kahn, Michèle. *La clandestine du voyage de Bougainville*. Paris: Le Passage, 2014.
Kandt, Kevin E. *Schlüteriana III: Studies in the Art, Life and Milieu of Andreas Schlüter*. Berlin: Lukas Verlag, 2015.
Kavanagh, Julia. *Women in France during the Eighteenth Century*. 2 vols. London: Smith, Elder, and Co., 1850.
Kawashima, Keiko. *Émilie du Châtelet et Marie-Anne Lavoisier: Science et genre au XVIII siècle*. Translated by Ayako Lécaille-Okamura. Paris: Honoré Champion, 2013.
Kawashima, Keiko. "Women's Translations of Scientific Texts in the 18th Century: A Case Study of Marie-Anne Lavoisier." *Historia Scientiarum* 21, no. 2 (2011): 123–37.
Keralio, Louise Félix Guinement de, and Dubois de Fosseux. 7 November 1787. Uncatalogued transcription. Léon Berthe papers, Archives départementales du Pas-de-Calais. Arras.
Keralio, Louise Félix Guinement de. *Collection des meilleurs ouvrages français composés par des femmes, dédiée aux femmes françaises*. 12 volumes. Paris: l'Auteur; Lagrange (vols. 5 and 6: l'Auteur; Maradan), 1786–9.
Keralio, Louise Félix Guinement de. *Histoire d'Élisabeth, reine d'Angleterre, tirée des écrits originaux anglais, d'actes, titres, lettres & d'autres pièces manuscrites qui n'ont pas encore paru*. 5 volumes. Paris: l'Auteur; Lagrange, 1786–8. Google Book Search. Web. Accessed February 18, 2016.
Keralio, Louise Félix Guinement de. Prospectus: *Collection des meilleurs ouvrages français composés par des femmes*. BR-23234. Bibliothèque de l'Arsenal. Paris.
Kilbourne, Edwin D. "Influenza Pandemics of the 20th Century." *Emerging Infectious Diseases* 12, no. 1 (January 2006): 9–14. www.ncbi.nlm.nih.gov/pmc/articles/PMC3291411/. Accessed April 4, 2020.
Korneeva, Tatiana. "Desire and Desirability in Villeneuve and Leprince de Beaumont's 'Beauty and the Beast.'" *Marvels & Tales* 28, no. 2 (2014): 233–51.
Kristeva, Julia. *Time & Sense: Proust and the Experience of Literature*. Translated by Ross Guberman. New York: Columbia University Press, 1996.
Kristoffersen, Børge. "Jacob Levy Moreno's Encounter Term: A Part of a Social Drama." *Zeitschrift für Psychodrama und Soziometrie* 13 (June 2014): 59–71.
La Croix, J.-Fr. de. *Dictionnaire historique portatif des femmes célèbres, contenant l'histoire des femmes savantes, des actrices et généralement des dames qui se sont rendues fameuses dans tous les siècles par leurs aventures, les talents, l'esprit et le courage*. 2 volumes. Paris: L. Cellot, 1769; Nouvelle édition revue et considérablement augmentée. Paris: Belin; Volland, 1788. Gallica. Web. Accessed November 21, 2010.
La Harpe, Jean-François de. *Lycée, ou Cours de littérature ancienne et moderne*. Paris: Didier, 1834.
La Porte, Joseph de [and J.-Fr. de La Croix]. *Histoire littéraire des femmes françaises, ou Lettres historiques et critiques contenant un précis de la vie & une analyse raisonnée des ouvrages des femmes qui se sont distinguées dans la littérature françoise. Par une Société de gens de lettres*. 5 volumes. Paris: Lacombe, 1769.
Landy, Joshua. *Philosophy as Fiction: Self, Deception, and Knowledge in Proust*. New York: Oxford University Press, 2004.

Latour, Bruno and Aït-Touati, "Décor as Protagonist: Bruno Latour and Frédérique Aït-Touati on Theatre and the New Climate Regime." Interview by Sébastien Hendrickx and Kristof van Baarle. *Etcetera*. January 7, 2019. https://e-tcetera.be/decor-is-not-decor-anymore/.

Latour, Bruno. *War of the Worlds: What about Peace?* Edited by John Tresch. Translated by Charlotte Bigg. Chicago: Prickly Paradigm Press, 2002.

Latour, Bruno. *We Have Never Been Modern*. Translated by Catherine Porter. Cambridge: Harvard University Press, 1993.

Lefèvre d'Étaples, Jacques. *Commentarii initiatorii in qvatvor Evangelia. In Euangelium secundum Matthaeum. In Euangelium secundum Marcum. In Euangelium secundum Lucam. In Euangelium secundum Ioannem*. Basileae: A. Cratandri, 1523.

Lefèvre d'Étaples, Jacques. *Contenta: Theologia Damasceni. I. De ineffabili diuinitate. II. De creaturarum genesi ordine Moseos. III. De iis que ab incarnatione vsque ad resurrectionem. IIII. De iis que post resurrectionem vsque ad vniuersalem Resurrectionem*. Paris, Henri Estienne, 1507.

Lefèvre d'Étaples, Jacques. *Theologia vivificans, cibus solidus. Dionysii Celestis hierarchia. Ecclesiastica hierarchia. Divina nomina. Mystica theologia. Undecim epistole. Ignatii Undecim epistole. Polycarpi epostola una*. Paris: Higman and Hopyl, 1499.

Leprince de Beaumont, Jeanne-Marie. *Magasin des enfants*. In *La Jeune Américaine et les contes marins (La Belle et la Bête). Les Belles Solitaires. [Suivi de] Magasin des enfants (La Belle et la Bête)*, edited by Elisa Biancardi. Bibliothèque des génies et des fées 15. Paris: Champion, 2008.

Leprince de Beaumont, Jeanne-Marie. *Magazin des enfans, or the Young Misses Magazine: Containing the Dialogues between a Governess and several Young Ladies of Quality her Scholars*. 4 volumes. London: Printed for S. Field, W. Ware, and T. Johnson, 1765.

Leriche, Françoise. "Lettres inédites du Kolb-Proust Archive." *Bulletin d'informations proustiennes* 26 (1995): 17.

Levinas, Emmanuel. *Proper Names*. Translated by Michael B. Smith. Stanford: Stanford University Press, 1996.

Libera, Alain de. *Archéologie du sujet III.1: La double révolution*. Paris: Vrin, 2014.

Libera, Alain de. *La philosophie médiévale*. 2nd edition. Paris: Presses Universitaires de France, 2014.

Libera, Alain de. *Raison et foi: Archéologie d'une crise d'Albert le Grand à Jean-Paul II*. Paris: Seuil, 2003.

Littré, Émile. *Dictionnaire de la langue française*. 4 volumes. Paris: Hachette, 1863–73. www.littre.org/

Lossky, V. "La notion des 'Analogies' chez Denys le Pseudo-Aréopagite." *Archives d'histoire doctrinale et littéraire du Moyen Âge* 5 (1930): 279–309.

Loti, Pierre. *The Marriage of Loti (Rarahu)* [1880]. Translated by Clara Bell. London: T. Wener Laurie, 1930.

[Louptière, Jean-Charles de la]. Review of *Les Pensées errantes; avec quelques Lettres d'un Indien*, by [Henriette de Marans]. *Journal des Dames* 1 (May 1761): 178–86.

Maliks, Reidar. "Was the French Revolution Really a Revolution?" Oxford University Press Blog. July 14, 2015. https://blog.oup.com/2015/07/french-revolution-bastille/.

Malte Fischer, Jens, ed. *Richard Wagners "Das Judentum in der Musik: Eine kritische Dokumentation als Beitrag zur Geschichte des Antisemitismus."* Frankfurt: Insel Verlag, 2000.

Man, Paul de. *Allegories of Reading: Figural Language in Rousseau, Nietzsche, Rilke and Proust*. New Haven: Yale University Press, 1979.

Manning, Erin and Brian Massumi. *Thought in the Act.* Minneapolis: University of Minnesota Press, 2014.

Manuscrits et autographes. Ader Nordmann. Paris. June 27, 2013. Lot no. 112. www.ader-paris.fr/lot/15316/3105662.

Marans, Henriette de. *Les Pensées errantes; avec quelques Lettres d'un Indien*. [Paris]: Hardy, 1758.

Margolis, Nadia. "Modern Editions: Makers of the Christinian Corpus." In *Christine de Pizan: A Casebook*, edited by Barbara K. Altmann and Deborah L. McGrady, 251–70. New York: Routledge, 2003.

Markey, Lia, editor. *Renaissance Invention: Stradanus' Nova Reperta*. Evanston: Northwestern University Press, 2020.

Markey, Lia. "Stradanus *Nova Reperta* in Renaissance Florence." *Renaissance Quarterly* 65, no. 2 (Summer 2012): 385–422.

Martin, Angus. "Baculard d'Arnaud et la vogue des séries de nouvelles en France au XVIIIe siècle." *Revue d'Histoire littéraire de la France* 73, no. 6 (November–December 1973): 982–3.

Maser, Edward A., ed. Introduction, translations and commentaries. *Cesare Ripa: Baroque and Rococo Pictorial Imagery. The 1758-60 Hertel Edition of Ripa's "Iconologia" with 200 Engraved Illustrations*. New York: Dover, 1971.

Massaut, Jean-Pierre. *Critique et tradition à la veille de la Réforme en France: Étude suivie de textes inédits traduits et annotés*. Paris: Vrin, 1974.

Massumi, Brian. *The Power at the End of the Economy*. Durham: Duke University Press, 2015.

Matsuda, Matt K. *Empire of Love: Histories of France and the Pacific*. Oxford: Oxford University Press, 2005.

Mauriac Dyer, Nathalie. "Composition and publication of *À la recherche du temps perdu*." In *Marcel Proust in Context*, edited by Adam Watt, 34–40. Cambridge: Cambridge University Press, 2013.

McDonald, Christie. *Anne Eisner, an American Artist (1911-1967): Life and Art Across Cultures*. Milan: Officina libraria, 2020.

McDonald, Christie. "Anxiety of Change: Reconfiguring Family Relations in Beaumarchais's Trilogy." In *Eighteenth-century Literary History, an MLQ Reader*, edited by Marshall Brown, 172–203. Durham: Duke University Press, 1999.

McDonald, Christie. "Le dialogue, l'utopie: *Le Supplément au voyage de Bougainville* par Denis Diderot." *Revue canadienne de littérature comparée* 3, no. 1 (1976): 63–74.

McDonald, Christie. *The Dialogue of Writing: Essays in Eighteenth-Century French Literature*. Waterloo: Wilfrid Laurier University Press, 1984.

McDonald, Christie. *Dispositions*. La Salle: Hurtubise, 1986.

McDonald, Christie. "Le dix-huitième siècle: 1715–1793," in *Femmes et littérature: Une histoire culturelle*, vol. 1, *Moyen Âge–XIII siècle*, edited by Martine Reid, 717–944. Paris: Gallimard, 2020.

McDonald, Christie, ed. *The Ear of the Other: Otobiography, Transference, Translation: Texts and Discussions with Jacques Derrida*. Translated by Avital Ronnell and Peggy Kamuf. Lincoln: University of Nebraska Press, 1988.

McDonald, Christie, "On the Ethnographic Imagination in the Eighteenth Century." In *French Global: A New Approach to Literary History*, edited by Christie McDonald and Susan Rubin Suleiman, 223–39. New York: Columbia University Press, 2010.

McDonald, Christie. *The Extravagant Shepherd: A Study of the Pastoral Vision in Rousseau's Nouvelle Héloïse*. Studies on Voltaire and the Eighteenth Century, volume 105. Edited by Theodore Besterman. Banbury: The Voltaire Foundation Thorpe Mandeville House, 1973.

McDonald, Christie, ed. *Images of Congo: Anne Eisner's Art and Ethnography, 1946–58.* Milan: 5 Continents Editions, 2005.

McDonald, Christie, ed. *L'oreille de l'autre: otobiographies, transferts, traductions: textes et débats avec Jacques Derrida.* Montréal: VLB, 1982.

McDonald, Christie, ed. *Painting My World: The Art of Dorothy Eisner.* Suffolk: ACC Editions, 2009.

McDonald, Christie and François Proulx, eds. *Proust and the Arts.* Cambridge: Cambridge University Press, 2015.

McDonald, Christie. *The Proustian Fabric: Associations of Memory.* Lincoln: University of Nebraska Press, 1991.

McDonald, Christie. "Résonnances associatives: La pensée analogique de Denis Diderot." *Ça me fait penser*, edited by Christie McDonald and Ginette Michaud, special issue of *Études françaises* 22, no. 1 (Spring 1986): 9–21.

McGill, Meredith L. "Copyright and Intellectual Property: The State of the Discipline." *Book History* 16 (2013): 387–427.

McGill, Meredith L. "The Matter of the Text: Commerce, Print Culture, and the Authority of the State in American Copyright Law." *American Literary History* 9, no. 1 (1997): 21–59.

Menken, Alan. "Beauty and the Beast." Lyrics by Howard Ashman. Walt Disney Music Company (ASCAP)/Wonderland Music Company Inc. (BMI). Track 9 on *Beauty and the Beast: Original Motion Picture Soundtrack*, 1991, compact disc.

Miernowski, Jan. *Le Dieu néant: Théologies négatives à l'aube des temps modernes.* Leiden; New York: Brill, 1998.

Miernowski, Jan. *Signes dissimilaires: La Quête des noms divins dans la poésie française de la Renaissance.* Genève: Droz, 1997.

Miller, Christopher, *Impostors: Literary Hoaxes and Cultural Authenticity.* Chicago: Chicago University Press, 2018.

Miller, Nancy K. *French Dressing: Women, Men, and Ancien Régime Fiction.* New York: Routledge, 1995.

Millington, Barry. "Nuremberg Trial. Is There Anti-Semitism in *Der Meistersinger*?" *Cambridge Opera Journal* 3, no. 3 (November 1991): 247–60.

Moerenhout, Jacques Antoine. *Voyages aux îles du grand océan.* Paris: A. Maisonneuve, 1959; *Travels to the Islands of the Pacific Ocean.* Translated by Arthur R. Borden. Lanham: University Press of America, 1993.

Montaigne, Michel de. *Œuvres complètes.* Edited by Albert Thibaudet and Maurice Rat. Paris: Gallimard/Pléiade, 1962.

Montaigne, Michel de. *The Complete Works of Montaigne: Essays, Travel Journal, Letters.* Translated by Donald Frame. Stanford: Stanford University Press, 1957.

Moser-Verrey, Monique, guest editor. *Gestes admirable ou la culture visuelle de l'imprimé/ The Visual Culture of Print. Eighteenth-Century Fiction* 23, no. 4 (2011).

Moser-Verrey, Monique. *Isabelle de Charrière: salonnière virtuelle. Un itinéraire d'écriture au XVIIIe siècle.* Paris: Hermann Éditeurs, 2013.

Moser-Verrey, Monique. "Jacques le fataliste et son maître: interdépendances." *Revue canadienne de littérature comparée* 3, no. 1 (1976): 51–62.

Moser-Verrey, Monique. "*Nouvelles espagnoles* (1772) traduites par Louis d'Ussieux." In *Ainsi passe le texte: Mélanges en hommage à Madeleine Jeay*, edited by Véronique Duché, Yen-Maï Tran-Gervat and Daniel Maher, 113–30. Paris: Classique Garnier, Rencontres 360, 2018.

Moser-Verrey, Monique. "Rencontres gravées pour *Hermann und Dorothea* de Goethe et *Trois femmes* d'Isabelle de Charrière." In *Topographie de la rencontre dans le roman européen,* edited by Jean-Pierre Dubost, 363–87. Clermont-Ferrand: Presses Universitaires Blaise Pascal, 2008.

Moser-Verrey, Monique. "Wieland imité par les d'Ussieux ou l'adaptation de productions étrangères à Paris autour de 1770." In *Traduire et illustrer le roman au XVIIIe siècle,* edited by Nathalie Ferrand. *SVEC* 5 (2011): 93–114.

Moser, Walter. "Le recyclage culturel." In *Recyclages: Économie de l'appropriation culturelle,* edited by Claude Dionne, Silvestra Mariniello and Walter Moser, 23–49. Montréal: Les Éditions Balzac, 1996.

Mylne, Vivienne. "The *Bibliothèque Universelle des Dames* (1785-97)." In *Women and Society in Eighteenth-Century France,* edited by Eva Jacobs, et al., 123–36. London: The Athlone Press, 1979.

Naas, Michael. "La nuit du dessin: Foi et savoir dans *Mémoires d'aveugle* de Jacques Derrida." *Cahiers de l'association internationale des études françaises* (*AIEF*) 62 (May 2010): 253–67.

Nader-Esfahani, Sanam, ed. "Works of Fiction and Non-Fiction in French by Women in the Eighteenth Century" (Database). Harvard Dataverse. Last modified December 16, 2019. https://doi.org/10.7910/DVN/DXFSR6.

Nancy, Jean-Luc. *Le partage des voix.* Paris: Galilée, 1982.

Nattiez, Jean-Jacques. *Proust musicien.* Paris: Christian Bourgois éditeur, 1984. 2nd edition 1999; *Proust as Musician.* Translated by Derrick Puffett. Cambridge: Cambridge University Press, 1989.

Nattiez, Jean-Jacques. *Wagner antisémite: Un problème historique, sémiologique et esthétique,* followed by Wagner's texts. Translated by Marie-Hélène Benoit-Otis. Paris: Christian Bourgois éditeur, 2015.

Négrel, Eric, "Politiques du charivari." In *Théâtres et charlatans dans l'Europe moderne,* edited by Beya Dhraïef, Eric Négrel, and Jennifer Ruimi, 301–15. Paris: Presses Sorbonne Nouvelle, 2018.

Newton, Isaac. *Principes mathématiques de la philosophie naturelle, tome I.* Translated by Émilie du Châtelet. Edited by Michel Toulmonde. Centre International d'Étude du XVIIIème Siècle, Ferney-Voltaire. Paris: Amalivre, 2015.

Niklaus, Robert. "Les 'Pensées Philosophiques' de Diderot et les 'Pensées' de Pascal." *Diderot Studies* 20 (1981): 201–17.

Nolte, John. *The Philosophy, Theory and Methods of J. L. Moreno: The Man Who Tried to Become God.* London: Routledge, 2014.

Norton, Marcy. "Tasting Empire: Chocolate and the European Internalization of Mesoamerican Aesthetics." *The American Historical Review* 111, no. 3 (2006): 660–91. https://doi.org/10.1086/ahr.111.3.660.

Nouvelles espagnoles, traduites de différents auteurs par M. D'Ussieux. 2 volumes. Madrid: Ruault, 1772.

Palissot de Montenoy, Charles. *Mémoires pour servir à l'histoire de notre littérature.* Paris: L'Imprimerie de Crapelet, 1803.

Patterson, Lyman Rae. *Copyright in Historical Perspective.* Nashville: Vanderbilt University Press, 1968.

Paul, Kari. "'It's Corona time': TikTok helps teens cope with the coronavirus pandemic." *The Guardian,* March 12, 2020. www.theguardian.com/world/2020/mar/12/coronavirus-outbreak-tik-tok-memes.

Pellegrin, Nicole. "L'histoire et son annotation. La mise en scène des sources par trois historiennes du XVIIIe siècle: Lussan, Thiroux et Kéralio." In *Les Femmes et l'écriture de l'histoire 1400–1800,* edited by Sylvie Steinberg et Jean-Claude Arnould, 269–95. Mont Saint-Aignan: Publications des universités de Rouen et du Havre, 2008.

Perl, Eric. *Theophany: The Neoplatonic Philosophy of Dionysius the Areopagite.* Albany: State University of New York Press, 2008.

Piaget, Jean. *La formation du symbole chez l'enfant.* 6th ed. Neuchâtel-Paris: Delachaux et Niestlé, 1976.

Pollock, Griselda. *Avant-gard Gambits, 1888–1893: Gender and the Color of Art History.* London: Thames and Hudson, 1992.

Pope Francis. *Laudato Si: On Care for our Common Home.* www.vatican.va/content/francesco/en/encyclicals/documents/papa-francesco_20150524_enciclica-laudato-si.html.

Porphyry. *Introduction.* Translated by Jonathan Barnes. Oxford: Oxford University Press, 2003.

Poulet, Georges. "Proust." In *Studies in Human Time,* 291–322. Translated by Elliott Coleman. Baltimore: The Johns Hopkins University Press, 1956.

Prigogine, Ilya and Isabelle Stengers. *La Nouvelle alliance: Métamorphose de la science.* Paris: Gallimard, 1979; *Order out of Chaos: Man's New Dialogue with Nature.* New York: Bantam Books, 1984.

Proulx, François. "Proust's Drawings and the Secret of the 'Solitary House.'" *Modern Language Notes* 133, no. 4 (2018): 865–90.

Proust, Marcel. Cahier 19, fo 29 recto. Paperole. NAF 16726. Bibliothèque nationale de France. Paris. https://gallica.bnf.fr/ark:/12148/btv1b6000680s/f83.

Proust, Marcel. Cahier 2, fo 6 recto. NAF 16642. Bibliothèque nationale de France. Paris. https://gallica.bnf.fr/ark:/12148/btv1b60004692/f8.

Marcel Proust: Collection Marie-Claude Mante, Sotheby's. Paris. May 24, 2018. Lot no. 156. www.sothebys.com/en/auctions/ecatalogue/2018/livres-et-manuscrits-pf1803/lot.156.html.

Proust, Marcel. *Contre Sainte-Beuve.* Edited by Bernard de Fallois. Paris: Gallimard (folio), 1987.

Proust, Marcel. *Correspondance.* Edited by Philip Kolb. Paris: Plon, 1970–93.

Proust, Marcel. *In Search of Lost Time, vol. 1: Swann's Way.* Translated by C. K. Scott Moncrieff and T. Kilmartin. Revised by D. J. Enright. New York: Modern Library, 2003.

Proust, Marcel. *In Search of Lost Time, vol. 2: Within a Budding Grove.* Translated by C. K. Scott Moncrieff and T. Kilmartin. Revised by D. J. Enright. New York: Modern Library, 2003.

Proust, Marcel. *In Search of Lost Time, vol. 4: Sodom and Gomorrah.* Translated by C. K. Scott Moncrieff and T. Kilmartin. Revised by D. J. Enright. New York: Modern Library, 2003.

Proust, Marcel. *In Search of Lost Time, vol. 5: The Fugitive.* Translated by C. K. Scott Moncrieff and T. Kilmartin. Revised by D. J. Enright. New York: Modern Library, 2003.

Proust, Marcel. *In Search of Lost Time, vol. 6: Time Regained.* Translated by A. Mayor and T. Kilmartin. Revised by D. J. Enright. New York: Modern Library, 2003.

Proust, Marcel. *Lettres.* Edited by Françoise Leriche with Virginie Greene. Paris: Plon, 2004.

Proust, Robert. *Les Années perdues de la* Recherche, *1922–1931.* Edited by Nathalie Mauriac Dyer with Alain Rivière and Pierre-Edmond Robert. Paris: Gallimard, 1999.

Pseudo-Dionysius, *The Celestial Hierarchy.* In *The Celestial and Ecclesiastical Hierarchy of Dionysius the Areopagite,* translated by John Parker. London: Skeffington, 1894.

Pseudo-Dionysius, *The Divine Names.* In *Dionysius the Areopagite: On the Divine Names and the Mystical Theology.* Translated by C. E. Rolt. Grand Rapids, MI: Christian Classics Ethereal Library [undated reprint of the 1920 translation].

Pseudo-Dionysius. *Pseudo-Dionysius: The Complete Works*. Edited by Colm Luibhéid and Paul Rorem. Translated by Michael Chase. New York: Paulist Press, 1987.

Quaranta, Jean-Marc. Postface to *Lettres au duc de Valentinois*. By Marcel Proust. Edited by J.-M. Quaranta, 71–3. Paris: Gallimard, 2016.

Rapazzini, Francesco. *Élisabeth de Gramont: Avant-gardiste*. Paris: Fayard, 2004.

Regard, Frédéric. "Un effet de Manche: lecture de 'K. A Notebook' de Maria Chevska et Hélène Cixous." In *Cixous sous X, d'un coup le nom*, edited by Marie-Dominique Garnier and Joana Masó, 97–129. Paris: Presses Universitaires de Vincennes, 2010.

Reid, Jonathan. *King's Sister—Queen of Dissent: Marguerite of Navarre (1492–1549) and Her Evangelical Network*. Leiden; Boston: Brill, 2009.

Reid, Martine. "Introduction." In *Femmes auteurs du dix-huitième siècle*, edited by Ángeles Sirvent Ramos, María Isabel Corbí Sáez, and María Ángeles Llorca Tonda, 9–22. Paris: Honoré Champion, 2016.

Renaudet, Augustin. *Préréforme et humanisme à Paris pendant les premières guerres d'Italie (1494–1517)*. 2nd edition. Genève: Slatkine, 1981.

Rice, Eugene. "The Humanist Idea of Christian Antiquity and the Impact of Greek Patristic Work on Sixteenth-Century Thought." In *Classical Influences on European Culture A.D. 1500–1700*, edited by R. R. Bolgar, 199–203. Cambridge: Cambridge University Press, 1976.

Rice, Eugene. *The Prefatory Epistles of Jacques Lefèvre d'Étaples and Related Texts*. New York: Columbia University Press, 1972.

Richards, Earl Jeffrey. "The Medieval 'femme auteur' as a Provocation to Literary History: Eighteenth-Century Readers of Christine de Pizan." In *The Reception of Christine de Pizan from the Fifteenth through the Nineteenth Centuries: Visitors to the City*, edited by Glenda K. McLeod, 101–26. Lewiston: Edwin Mellen Press, 1991.

Richardson, John. *A Life of Picasso*. New York: Random House, 1991.

Ridley, Glynis. *The Discovery of Jeanne Baret: A Story of Science, the High Seas, and the First Woman to Circumnavigate the Globe*. New York: Crown Publishers, 2010.

Robert, Raymonde. *Le Conte de fées littéraire en France: de la fin du XVIIe à la fin du XVIIIe siècle*. Lumière classique, 40. Paris: Champion, 2002.

Robitaille, Martin. *Proust épistolier*. Montréal: Les Presses de l'Université de Montréal, 2003.

Roques, René. *L'Univers Dionysien: Structure hiérarchique du monde selon le Pseudo-Denys*. Lille: Aubier, 1954.

Rorem, Paul. *Pseudo-Dionysius: A Commentary on the Texts and an Introduction to Their Influence*. Oxford University Press, 1993.

Rosbottom, Ron. *Choderlos de Laclos*. Boston: Twayne Publishers, 1978.

Rosolato, Guy. "L'Inconnu dans l'idéalisation du désir." Reprinted in *La Portée du désir ou la psychanalyse même*, 135–52. Paris: PUF, 1996.

Rosolato, Guy. *La Relation d'inconnu*. Paris: Éditions Gallimard, 1978.

Rothenberg, Stanley. "What if *Don Quixote* Had Been Copyrighted?" *Journal, the Copyright Society of the USA* 50 (2002–2003): 533–46.

Rousseau, Jean-Jacques. *The Confessions and Correspondence, Including Letters to Malesherbes*. Vol. 5 of *The Collected Writings of Rousseau*, edited by Christopher Kelly, Roger D. Masters, and Peter G. Stillman. Translated by Christopher Kelly. Hanover: University Press of New England, 1995.

Rousseau, Jean-Jacques. *Discourse on the Origins of Inequality (second discourse; Polemics; and Political economy)*. Vol. 3 of *The Collected Writings of Rousseau*, edited by Roger D. Master and Christopher Kelly. Translated by Judith R. Bush. Hanover: University Press of New England, 1995.

Rousseau, Jean-Jacques. *Émile, or On Education. Also includes Émile and Sophie, or the Solitaries.* Vol. 13 of *The Collected Writings of Rousseau*, edited by Christopher Kelly. Translated by Christopher Kelly and Allan Bloom. Hanover: University Press of New England, 2009.

Rousseau, Jean-Jacques. *Letter to d'Alembert.* Vol. 10 of *The Collected Writings of Rousseau.* Edited and translated by Allan Bloom, Charles Butterworth, and Christopher Kelly. Hanover: University Press of New England, 2004.

Rousseau, Jean-Jacques. *Les Rêveries du promeneur solitaire.* Vol. 1 of *Œuvres complètes.* Edited by Bernard Gagnebin, Robert Osmont, and Marcel Raymond. Paris: Éditions Gallimard/Pléiade, 1959.

Rousseau, Jean-Jacques. *The Reveries of the Solitary Walker; Botanical Writings; and Letter to Franquières.* Vol. 8 of *The Collected Writings of Rousseau*, edited by Christopher Kelly. Translated and annotated by Charles E. Butterworth, Alexandra Cook, and Terence E. Marshall. Hanover: University Press of New England, 2000.

Rousseau, Jean-Jacques. *Rousseau, Judge of Jean-Jacques.* Vol. 1 of *The Collected Writings of Rousseau*, edited by Roger D. Masters and Christopher Kelly. Translated by Judith R. Bush, Christopher Kelly, and Roger D. Masters. Hanover: University Press of New England, 1990.

Ruelland, Jacques G. "Marie-Anne Pierrette Paulze-Lavoisier, Comtesse de Rumford (1758–1836): Lumière surgie de l'ombre." *Dix-Huitième Siècle* 36 (2004): 99–112.

Ruskin, John. *Fors clavigera.* Vol. 28 of *The Works of John Ruskin.* London: Library Edition, 1907.

Saint-Aubin, Marie-Françoise-Félicité Mauguet de Mézières, Marquise de. *Le Danger des liaisons, ou les mémoires de la baronne de Blémon.* 3 volumes. Geneva: n.p., 1763.

Sainte-Beuve, Charles-Augustin. "Mademoiselle Aïssé." In *Lettres de Mademoiselle Aïssé à Madame Calandrini*, by Charlotte-Élisabeth Aïssé, 3–61. Edited by Jules Ravenel. Paris: Gerdès, 1846.

Salmond, Anne. *Aphrodite's Island: The European Discovery of Tahiti.* Berkeley: University of California Press, 2009.

Sanson, Hervé. "D'apesanteur liés." Review of *Insurrection de la poussière: Adel Abdessemed*, suivi de *A. A. H. C.: Correspondance*, by Hélène Cixous. *Continents manuscrits,* 2015. http://coma.revues.org/610.

Schiller, Friedrich. "Theatre Considered as a Moral Institution." Translated by John Sigerson and John Chambless. The Schiller Institute. https://archive.schillerinstitute.com/transl/schil_theatremoral.html.

Schindler, John R. "Redl—Spy of the Century?" *International Journal of Intelligence and Counterintelligence* 18, no. 3 (2005): 483–507.

Scott, Joan Wallach. *Only Paradoxes to Offer: French Feminists and the Rights of Man.* Cambridge: Harvard UP, 1996.

Segalen, Victor. "Préface." In *Noa-Noa-Séjour à Tahiti.* By Paul Gauguin. Paris: Éditions Complexe, 1989.

Seth, Catriona. "La fortune des 'Liaisons dangereuses,'" in Pierre Choderlos de Laclos, *Les Liaisons dangereuses*, 797–8. Bibliothèque de la Pléiade 6. Paris: Gallimard, 2011.

Seth, Catriona. "Rousseau et ses doubles dans les livres I à VI des *Confessions*." http://ceredi.labos.univ-rouen.fr/public/?rousseau-et-ses-doubles-dans-les.html.

Sgard, Jean. "Collections pour dames." In *La Tradition des romans de femmes: XVIIIe–XIXe siècles,* edited by Catherine Mariette-Clot and Damien Zanone, 19–29. Paris: Champion, 2012.

Shindo, Nahoko, and Sylvie Briand. "Influenza at the beginning of the 21st Century." *Bulletin of the World Health Organization* 90 (2012): 247–247A. www.who.int/bulletin/volumes/90/4/12-104653/en/. Accessed April 4, 2020.

Silvano, Cavazza. "Platonismo e riforma religiosa: La 'Theologia Vivificans' di Jacques Lefèvre d'Étaples." *Rinascimento* 22, no. 2 (1982): 99–149.

Société Internationale pour l'Étude des Femmes de l'Ancien Régime. SIEFAR (website). Accessed January 5, 2020. http://siefar.org/

Sol, Antoinette. "'Se répandre en paroles': Notions of Identity in Mme de Bénouville's *Pensées Errantes*." *Intertexts* 4, no. 2 (Fall 2000): 129–43.

Solomon-Godeau, Abigail. "Going Native: Paul Gauguin and the Invention of the Primitivist Modernism." In *The Expanding Discourse: Feminism and Art History*, edited by Norma Broude and Mary D. Garrad, 312–29. New York: Harper Collins, 1992.

The Song of Roland. Edited and translated by Gerard J. Brault. 2 volumes. University Park: Pennsylvania State University Press, 1978.

Sorkin, David. *The Religious Enlightenment: Protestants, Jews and Catholics from London to Vienna*. Princeton: Princeton University Press, 2008.

Spielberg, Stephen. *Close Encounters of the Third Kind*. New York: Dell, 1977.

Stengers, Isabelle and Frédérique Dolphijn. *Activer les possibles*. Bruxelles: Esperluète, 2018.

Stengers, Isabelle and Bordeleau Eric. "The Care of the Possible: Isabelle Stengers interviewed by Erik Bordeleau." Translated by Kelly Ladd. *Scapegoat: Architecture, Landscape, Political Economy*, no. 01 "Service" (Summer 2011): www.scapegoatjournal.org/docs/01/01_Stengers_Bordeleau_CareOfThePossible.pdf.

Stengers, Isabelle. *In Catastrophic Times, Resisting the Coming Barbarism*. Translated by Andrew Goffey. London: Open Humanities Press, 2015.

Stengers, Isabelle. *Thinking with Whitehead*. Translated by Michael Chase. Cambridge: Harvard University Press, 2011.

Stewart, Joan Hinde. *Gynographs: French Novels by Women of the Late Eighteenth Century*. Lincoln: University of Nebraska Press, 1993.

Still, Judith. "Isabelle de Charrière's *Three Women*—Adopting and Adapting Hospitality After Kant." *German Life and Letters* 64, no. 1 (2011): 19–30.

Stowe v. Thomas 1 Pitts, 82. E.D. Penn, 1853.

Suleiman, Susan Rubin. "The 1.5 Generation: Thinking About Child Survivors and the Holocaust." *American Imago* 59, no. 3 (Fall 2002): 277–95.

Suleiman, Susan Rubin. *Budapest Diary*. Lincoln: University of Nebraska Press, 1996.

Suleiman, Susan Rubin. *Crises of Memory and the Second World War*. Cambridge: Harvard University Press, 2006.

Suleiman, Susan Rubin. "Jewish Assimilation in Hungary, the Holocaust, and Epic Film: Reflections on István Szabó's Sunshine." *Yale Journal of Criticism* 14, no. 1 (Spring 2001): 233–52.

Suleiman, Susan Rubin. "On Exile, Jewish Identity, and Filmmaking in Hungary: A Conversation with István Szabó." In *Kinokultura*, special issue 7 "Hungarian Cinema" (February 2008): www.kinokultura.com/specials/7/hungarian.shtml.

Sweetman, David. *Paul Gauguin: A Life*. New York: Simon and Shuster, 1995.

Szabó, István. "Három kisfilm sikeréröl a rendezővel, Szabó Istvánnal." By Eva Lelkes. *Film, Szinház, Muzsika*, February 15, 1963. In "Personal Folder, 1963–1982" [István Szabó]. Hungarian National Film Archive, Budapest.

Szabó, István. "Ingerelnek a felfuvalkodott, gőgös emberek." By András Szegő. 1987. Reprinted in *Beszélgetések Szabó István Filmrendezővel*, edited by Zsuzsa Radnóti. Budapest: Ferenczy Kiadó, 1995.

Tadié, Jean-Yves. *Marcel Proust*. Paris: Gallimard, 1996.
Tadié, Jean-Yves. "Proust entre la littérature, l'amitié et l'édition." May 17, 2018. Unpublished lecture for *Marcel Proust: Collection Marie-Claude Mante*, Sotheby's, Paris, May 24, 2018.
Teubern, H. E. von. *Dubois und Gioconda, eine korsische Erzählung*. Leipzig: bey der Waysenhaus- und Frommannischen Handlung, 1767.
Thibaut de Champagne. "L'altrier par la matinee." In *Chansons des trouvères: Chanter m'estuet*. Edited and translated by Samuel N. Rosenberg, Hans Tischler and Marie-Geneviève Grossel, 608–9. Paris: Librairie générale française, 1995.
Thicknesse, Ann Ford. *Sketches of the Lives and Writings of the Ladies of France*. 3 volumes. London: Dodsley and W. Brown, 1780–1781.
Torrance, Alexis. "Precedents for Palamas' Essence-Energies Theology in the Cappadocian Fathers." *Vigiliae Christianae* 63, no. 1 (2009): 47–70.
The Trans-Atlantic Slave Trade Database. Accessed September 21, 2018. www.slavevoyages.org/estimates/rIuAF2im.
Tristan, Flora. *Flora Tristan's Journal, 1840: Promenades in London*. Translated by Giselle Pinceti. Charlestown: Charles River Books, 1980.
Tristan, Flora. *Peregrinations of a Pariah* (1838). Translated by Charles de Salis. London: The Folio Society, 1986.
Tristan, Flora. *The Workers' Union* (1843). Translated by Beverly Livingston. Champaign: University of Illinois Press, 2007.
Trousson, Raymond, ed. *Romans de femmes du XVIIIe siècle*. Paris: Robert Laffont, 1996.
Tsing, Anna. *The Mushroom to the End of the World: On the Possibility of Life in Capitalist Ruins*. Princeton: Princeton University Press, 2017.
US Const. art. I., § 8., cl. 1.
Ussieux, Louis d' and Mathieu Chiniac de la Bastide. *Histoire de la littérature françoise depuis les tems les plus reculés jusqu'à nos jours, avec un tableau du progrès des arts dans la monarchie*. 2 volumes. Paris: Edme, 1772.
Ussieux, Louis d' to Benjamin Franklin. [Dated before] January 22, 1782. The National Archives Founders Online. Website. https://founders.archives.gov/documents/Franklin/01-36-02-0318.
Ussieux, Louis d'. *Die Armenischen Prinzen*. Eine Erzählung aus dem Französischen des Herrn d'Ussieux von I. A. E. V. G. Wien: In der Ghelenschen Buchhandlung, 1778.
Ussieux, Louis d'. *Corps législatif. Conseil des Anciens. Opinion de Dussieux, d'Eure-et-Loir, sur la resolution du 24 pluviôse, relative à l'impôt du sel, séance du 9 ventôse*. Paris, Imprimerie nationale, an VII, 1799.
Ussieux, Louis d'. "Dubois et Gioconda. Nouvelle corse." In *Nouvelles françaises*, no. 11, vol. 3, 5–61. Paris: Brunet, 1781.
Ussieux, Louis d'. *Essay sur l'état actuel de la littérature française*. Paris: 1768.
Ussieux, Louis d'. *Les Héros français, ou le Siège de Saint-Jean-de-Lone, drame héroïque en 3 actes et en prose, suivi d'un Précis historique de cet événement*. Amsterdam: chez Lejai libraire, 1774.
Ussieux, Louis d'. *Histoire abrégée de la découverte et de la conquête des Indes par les Portugais*. Bouillon: De l'imprimerie de la Société Typographique, 1770.
Ussieux, Louis d'. "Préface." In *Le Décaméron françois*, vol. 1, i–xii. Paris: Costard, 1772.
Ussieux, Louis d'. "Les princes d'Arménie, nouvelle." In *Le Décaméron françois*, no. 6, vol. 2, 1–66. Paris: Dufour, 1774.

Ussieux, Madame d'. "Lettre du traducteur à Monsieur***." In *Französische Übersetzervorreden des 18. Jahrhunderts*, edited by Wilhelm Graeber, 185. Frankfurt am Main: P. Lang, 1990.

Ussieux, Madame d'. *Le Nouveau Don Quichotte, imité de l'allemand de M. Wieland*. 4 volumes. Bouillon: l'Imprimerie de la Société Typographique, 1770.

Van Dijk, Susan. "Les topoï 'féminins' dans des fictions épistolaires et des correspondances véritables: Mesdames de Graffigny, Riccoboni et Charrière." *L'épistolaire au féminin: Correspondances de femmes*. Caen: Presses Universitaires de Caen, 2006.

Vernet, Jacob. *Traité de la vérité de la religion chrétienne, tiré principalement du Latin de feu Mr. J. Alphonse Turrettin*. Geneva: Henri-Albert Gosse & Comp., 1740.

Versini, Laurent. *Laclos et la tradition: Essai sur les sources et la technique des* Liaisons dangereuses. Paris: Klincksieck, 1968.

Viennot, Eliane. *Et la modernité fut masculine: La France, les femmes et le pouvoir 1789–1904*. Paris: Perrin, 2016.

Villeneuve, Gabrielle-Suzanne de. *La Jeune Américaine et les Contes marins*. In *La Jeune Américaine et les contes marins (La Belle et la Bête). Les Belles Solitaires. [Suivi de] Magasin des enfants (La Belle et la Bête)*, edited by Elisa Biancardi. Bibliothèque des génies et des fées 15. Paris: Champion, 2008.

Virgil. *Aeneid*. Opera, ed. R. A. B. Mynors (Oxford University Press, Oxford, 1969).

Virgil. *Eclogues, Georgics, Aeneid I–VI*. Translated by H. R. Fairclough. Revised by G. P. Goold. Cambridge: Harvard University Press, H. R. Loeb Classical Library, 1999.

Viveiros de Castro, Eduardo. *The Inconsistency of the Indian Soul. Encounters of Catholics and Cannibals in Sixteenth-Century Brazil*. Chicago: Prickly Press, 2011.

Voltaire, Monsieur de. "Gens de lettres." In *Encyclopédie, ou dictionnaire raisonné des sciences, des arts et des métiers, etc.*, edited by Denis Diderot and Jean le Rond d'Alembert, 7:599b. University of Chicago: ARTFL Encyclopédie Project, December 1765. http://encyclopedie.uchicago.edu/.

Voltaire. "Vers à Madame de C.***, auteur du Danger des liaisons." In *Writings of 1763–1764*. Volume 57A of Œuvres *complètes de Voltaire*, edited by Simon Davies, Graham Gargett et al, 319. Oxford: Voltaire Foundation, 2014.

Wagner, Cosima. *Cosima Wagner's Diaries*. Vol. 1. Edited by Martin Gregor-Dellin and Dietrich Mack. Translated by Geoffrey Skelton. New York: Harcourt Brace Jovanovich, 1978.

Wagner, Richard. *Dichtungen und Schriften*. Vol. 10. Edited by Dieter Borchmeyer. Frankfurt: Insel Verlag, 1983.

Wagner, Richard [R. Freigedank, pseud.]. "Das Judenthum in der Musik." *Neue Zeitschrift für Musik* 33, no. 19 (September 3, 1850): 101–7; no. 20 (September 6, 1850): 109–12.

Wagner, Richard. "Judaism in Music." In *Richard Wagner––Stories and Essays*, 24–5. Translated by Charles Osborne. London: Owen, 1973.

Walker, D. P. "The *Prisca Theologia* in France." *Journal of Warburg and Courtauld Institutes* 17, no. 3-4 (1954): 204–59.

Warner, Marina. "Reluctant Brides: Beauty and the Beast I." In *From the Beast to the Blonde: On Fairy Tales and Their Tellers*, 272–97. New York: Noonday Press, 1996.

Weiner, Marc. *Wagner and the Anti-Semitic Imagination*. 2nd ed. Lincoln: University of Nebraska Press, 1997.

West, John B. "The collaboration of Antoine and Marie-Anne Lavoisier and the first measurements of human oxygen consumption." *The American Journal of Physiology, Lung Cellular and Molecular Physiology* 305, no. 11 (2013): L775–L785.

Wheaton v. Peters, 33 US. 8 Pet. 591. 1834.

Whitehead, Alfred. *Adventures of Ideas.* Cambridge: Cambridge University Press, 1933.
Whitehead, Alfred. *The Concept of Nature.* Cambridge: Cambridge University Press, 1971.
Whitehead, Alfred. *Essays in Science and Philosophy.* New York: Philosophical Library, 1947.
Whitehead, Alfred. *Nature and Life.* Cambridge: Cambridge University Press, 1934.
Whitehead, Alfred. *Process and Reality: An Essay in Cosmology.* Cambridge: Cambridge University Press, 1929.
Whitehead, Alfred. *Science and the Modern World.* Cambridge: Cambridge University Press, 1926.
Wieland, C. M. *Les Aventures merveilleuses de Don Silvio de Rosalva, traduites de l'allemand de M. Wieland, par Madame d'Ussieux.* In *Le Cabinet des fées*, vol. 36. Geneva and Paris: Barde, Manget & Compagnie and Cuchet, 1786.
Williams, Linda. *Hard Core: Power, Pleasure, and the "Frenzy of the Visible."* Berkeley: University of California Press, 1989.
Wolfgang, Aurora. *Gender and Voice in the French Novel, 1730–1782.* Aldershot: Ashgate, 2004.
Woodmansee, Martha, and Peter Jaszi. "The Law of Texts: Copyright in the Academy." *College English* 57, no. 7 (1995): 769–87.
Yoshikawa, Kazuyoshi. "The Models for *Miss Sacripant*." In *Proust in Perspectives: Visions and Revisions*, edited by Armine Kotin Mortimer and Katherine Kolb, 248–51. Urbana: University of Illinois Press, 2020.
Yoshikawa, Kazuyoshi. *Proust et l'art pictural.* Paris: Honoré Champion, 2010.
Zayas y Sotomayor, María de. *Nouvelles de Dona Maria de Zayas, traduites de l'Espagnol.* 5 volumes. Paris: G. Quinet, 1680.
Zimmermann, Margarete. "Gedächtnis-Korrekturen: Das literaturgeschichtliche Archiv der Louise-Félicité Guinement de Kéralio." In *Das Schöne im Wirklichen-Das Wirkliche im Schönen*, edited by Anne Amend Söchting et al., 515–28. Heidelberg: Universitätsverlag C. Winter, 2002.
Zink, Michel. *La Pastourelle: Poésie et folklore au moyen âge.* Paris: Bordas, 1972.
Zipes, Jack. *Fairy Tales and the Art of Subversion: The Classical Genre for Children and the Process of Civilization.* 2nd edition. London and New York: Routledge Classics, 2012.

INDEX

Abelard, Peter 1
Academy des Sciences 111
Académie Française 127
accident
    beatitude 41
    discovery 201
    physical 35–6, 39–41
affect 55, 147, 182–4, 196
Ahmed, Sara 60
Aïssé, Charlotte-Élisabeth 87
aleatory 6–7, 82, 84–5, 88–9
Alechinsky, Pierre 169, 173
alienation
    analysis 49
    mimesis 50
    ridicule or *charivari* 52, 57 n.43
Althusser, Louis 6, 84–5, 89, 137
appearance
    a-perception or the inapparent 166
    versus inner character 65–6
Aquinas, Thomas 1

Barbier, Antoine-Alexandre 88
Barchilon, Jacques 59
Baret, Jeanne 206, 211
Barthes, Roland 84, 201–2
Benedictine monks of Saint-Maur 97
Benjamin, Walter 143
Bénouville, Charlotte 88–9
Berlin Wall 193
Bettelheilm, Bruno 59
Biancardi, Elisa 60
Black, Joseph 111
blackness 65–6
Blanchot, Maurice 38
Boethius 2–3
Boulez, Pierre 151–2
Britain *see* Great Britain
Brownscomb, Jeannie Augusta 184
Buber, Martin 8–9
    "The House of Encounter" 9
Bucquet, Jean-Baptiste 110

Budapest 191–5, 197
Byzantine tradition 25, 29

care 9, 15, 182–7
Carter, Angela 59
Catholicism
    Enlightenment 121, 128–9
    Magyrization 196
    Pre-Reformation 21–2, 25
Cavendish, Henry 111
citizenship 108–9
Chaucer 4–5
childhood
    love 197
    memories 193
    of mankind 211
    trauma 191–2, 197
Choderclos de Laclos, Pierre 74
Chollet, Mathilde 88–9
Christianity
    early Greek 22
    dispensations 25, 29
    missionnairies 206–7
    Renaissance 21–9
Cixous, Hélène 168–74
Clairaut, Alexis 110
Clichetove, Josse 21–9
Cocteau, Jean 59
colonialism
    civilizing mission 206–7
    enslaved labor and wealth 63–5
    New World 179–80, 184
    plantations 61, 63
communism
    the Change 194–5
    informers 198
Constant, Benjamin 112
copyright
    definition of "copy" 139
    legal history 136
    philosophy 136–7
    protection 137

Stowe v. Thomas 137–41
Wheaton v. Peters 140
COVID-19 pandemic 14–15, 181
Creative commons 142

Dante 4
decadence 108
deconstruction 165–6
deformity
    as event 42
Deleuze, Gilles
    assemblages 187
    chaos 42, 181
    clinamen 6
    event 41–4
    and Félix Guattari 181, 183, 186
    Leibnitz, Gottfried Wilhelm 41–2
    plane of immanence 186
    prehension and apprehension 42–4
    Proust and Signs 7–8
Derrida, Jacques 118, 165–6, 168–70, 174
desire
    adult 60
    blending with model 49
    clandestine 156
    to control 186
    erotic 2, 50, 53
    for knowledge 87
    lack 167–8
Descartes 5, 109, 155, 181
de Bougainville, Louis
    appropriation of island people 206
    familiarity with Western texts 203–4
    possession of Tahiti 204
    validation of travelogues 204–5
    Voyage autour du monde 204
    voyage to Tahiti 201, 203
de Charrière, Isabelle 76 112–13, 119–22, 128
    see also Belle de Zuylen
de Crenne, Hélisenne 95
d'Épinay, Louise 85
de Genlis, Stéphanie Félicité 74, 76, 108, 121
de Gouges, Olympe 76, 86
de Graffigny, Françoise 82, 108, 118–19
de Gramont, Élisabeth 154
DeJean, Joan 86, 96–7
de Keralio, Louise 93–9

de la Harpe, Jean-François 107
de Laporte, Joseph 74
de Man, Paul 117–18
de Marans, Henriette 88–9
de Navarre, Marguerite 95
de Pizan, Christine 93–6, 98, 105 n.29
de Saussure, Horace Bénédict 111
d'Ussieux, Louis 121–4, 126–9
d'Ussieux, Madame 123–5
de Valois, Marguerite 95, 99
de Villeneuve, Gabrielle-Suzanne 59–64
de Villeneuve, Venture
    attempted seduction 48
    model for Rousseau 49–50, 53–4
    fraudulence and contradiction 50
de Zuylen, Belle 119–22, 128
    see also Isabelle de Charrière
dialectic
    Hegel 118
    Beckett 167
dictionaries 93, 154
didacticism 64
Diderot, Denis
    and d'Alembert's *Encyclopédie* 71, 83, 87, 119, 123, 202
    conditions of communication 117
    Jacques le fataliste et son maître 117–18
    Les Bijoux indiscrets 87–8
    Pensées philosophiques 82–3
    Rameau's Nephew 54–5
    Supplément au voyage de Bougainville 118, 129, 180, 205, 211
    taboos 119
Didi-Huberman 166–8, 173
Dorat, Claude-Joseph 88–9
du Châtelet, Émilie 109–10

Eagleton, Terry 9–10
ecology 183, 187
Eisner, Anne 168, 211
Eisner, Dorothy 168
ekphrasis 166–73
emigration 25, 197
encounter
    according to Augustine 1, 2
    according to Derrida 174 n.1
    aleatory 6–7, 82, 84–5, 88–9
    as becoming 182, 187
    Begegnung 9

as care 183, 187
circumlocution 114
colonial and colonialist 67, 179–82, 185, 206
convergence 3, 72
of the divine 23–4
etymology 3
as everyone and nowhere 180
falling-upon 3, 72
foreign 47
global 66
hermeneutics 9–10
materialism 6–7, 137
missed connections 72
old French 201
of the Other 179–83
in pre-modern literature 2
recognition 7–8
as re-experience 211
reimagined 185
of self 153–5
stranger and subject 60
through image 174, 185
through reading 84
virtual 15
in Western philosophies 11
without precedent 201
enlightenment
age of encounter 109
dialogue between Protestant theologians and *philosophes* 119–20
disciplines 202
Freemasons 128
religious 119, 121; see also Catholicism
values 98 117, 119–22, 126–9
"What is Enlightenment?" 113
women's contribution 96
Esterházy, Peter 198
experience
singularity 44
"Of practice" 43
faith
intellect 21, 24
gnosis 22
feminism
feminist criticism 129, 193, 210
separatist vs. integrationist 93
subtext 99

film
critics 196
and feeling 194
form
epistolary 15, 71, 75, 81–2, 112
renvoi 83
Foucault, Michel 113
France
Annecy 48
imperialism 207
Occupation 193
Revolution 95, 107, 113
Wars of Religion 37–8
see also Paris
friendship
according to Pythagoras and Aristotle 154
with another self 160
between writers 159
female 72, 77
frontispiece 96, 126

Gauguin, Paul
child brides 209–10
influence on Picasso and Matisse 210–11
Noa Noa 208–9
Primitivism 208, 210–11
recreation of Tahiti's idealized past 208
self-conception as maverick 209
gender
as basis of exclusion 76
as moderating encounter 87–9
questions raised by reinterpretation 210
sexual difference 155, 172
"sexuation" of literary field 76
genre
conte philosophique 113
"found letters" 112
nouvelle espagnole 127
unsuitable for women 82–3; see also Philosophy
Génie 86–7, 89, 93–4, 96, 103
Girard, René 50
Grail 2
Great Britain
Enlightenment scientific developments 111

imperialism 65, 207
law 139
travelogues 202
women novelists 99
Grier, Robert (Justice) 139, 141–2
Grimm, Friedrich Melchoir 71, 74–5, 81, 205

Hahn, Reynaldo 153, 156–60
Haiti
    Hispaniola 64
    Saint-Domingue 59–61, 64
Hanslick, Eduard 149
Hébrail, Jacques 74
Héloise 95, 99
Hesse, Carla 93 113
Hinde Stewart, Joan 75
history
    as allegory 96–7
    dialogic 99
    historiography 94
    public versus private life 197, 199
Holocaust 191, 196
humanism
    colonial 179, 184, 187
    early French Christian 21–34
    faith and reason 21

identity
    assimilation 192–3
    self-assessment 38–40
    crisis 55
    trauma 191–2, 199
image 173–4
imposture
    anthropological 49
    counterfeit 56 n.17
    imitation 47
    musical 47, 49
    the other 49–50
interdisciplinarity 201–2
intersubjectivity 118
Isaure, Clémence 97–8, 105 n.25

Jaucourt, Louis 83–5
Jeux floraux 97–8

Kant, Immanuel 108, 112–13
Korneeva, Tatiana 60

kinship 72
Kirwan Richard 111

La Belle et la Bête
    adaptations 59, 67 n.3
    global setting 60, 66–7
    interpretations 59–60
Labé, Louise 95
Landriani, Marsilio 111
Latin 110
Latour, Bruno 181, 184–5
Lavoisier, Antoine 110–11, 113
Lavoisier, Marie-Anne 110–12
Lefèvre d'Étaples, Jacques 21–9
Leibnitz, Gottfried Wilhelm
    dog 43–4
    principles 110
Leprince de Beaumont, Jeanne-Marie 59–60, 64–6
Lepaute, Nicole-Reine 110
Levinas, Emmanuel 160, 203
Lévi-Strauss, Claude 181
Liaison
    chimique 73
    dangerous vs. constructive 74
    Les liaisons dangereuses 74–5
    negative connotation 72
    topos 75, 78 n.22
    vulnerability 73
Loti, Pierre 207

McDonald, Christie
    18th-century women writers database 11–12
    class on Enlightenment 82
    critique of colonial humanism 180–1
    deconstruction 11
    dialogue versus utopia 118
    early career 10
    ethics of care 187
    Femmes et littérature 77, 82, 85
    feminism 10–11
    and Jacques Derrida 10, 143
    music 147, 168
    painting 168, 184
    on Proust 172
    on Rousseau 47, 49
    theory 35, 44, 143
Mallarmé, Stéphane 156

Mandeville, Bernard 109
Massumi, Brian 182–3, 186
medicine
   global pandemic 16
   public dissection 40
Michaud, Ginette 11, 13, 165–78
Mill, Jean Stuart 111
Monkman, Kent 185–6
monster 50–1, 53, 65
   monstrous marriage 59
Montaigne
   Essays 5, 170, 179
   "Of the affection of Fathers for their Children" 183
   "Of practice" 37–40, 43
Montesquieu, Charles-Louis 82, 180
Moreno, Jacob Levy 8–9
Morice, Charles 209
   see also Paul Gauguin
music
   anti-Semitic caricatures 149–50
   concert at the home of M. de Treytorens 51–2
   dissonance 51–2, 54–5
   fiasco 51–2
   magic 49
   Minuet 51
   non-semiotic nature 147
   palimpsest 54
   semantic capacity 149–50
   synagogue imitation 150–1
   The Village Soothsayer 52
mysticism
   vocabulary 26–7
   voyage 41

Nancy, Jean-Luc 184
narrative
   frame 59–64, 72–4, 77
   moral tale 64
   of Frenchness 94, 99
   polyphonic 73
   prefatory 81
   sea tale 61
Newton, John 109–10
other
   constitution of the subject 183
   dissipation of 184
   engagement between the self and 153, 161
   othering 66
   native 179–80, 184–6
   writing for the 161 n.1

Palissot de Montenoy, Charles 107–8, 111–12
Paris
   1889 World Fair 208
   boulevard Haussmann 157
   Café de la Régence 54
   Tuileries 156
Pascal, Blaise 82–3, 109
Pastorella 2
Patristics 22–3, 25
Philosophy
   as allegory 2–3
   conte philosophique 113
   death 37
   event 35, 41, 182
   inherent to the novel 83
   pensées as philosophical genre 82
   phenomenality 165–6
   Platonic and Aristotelian 23–5
   positive or rational 24
   pre- and early-modern 1–3
   spiritual practice 28
   void 7
Pollock, Griselda 210
prehension 42–4, 166, 182
   see also Gilles Deleuze
Pre-Reformation 22
Prigogine, Ilya 181, 187 n.4
progress
   scientific and artistic 94, 96, 117, 137, 141, 143
   spiritual 26
   technological 202
property
   definition of literary 139–42
   intangible 135–6, 138, 140, 143
   intellectual 135–8, 143
prostitution 208–9
Proust, Marcel
   French literature 11
   illness 157
   influence of John Ruskin 158
   nicknames 156, 159, 162 n.25

queerness 154, 156
  role of Racine in writing 154, 161
  solipsistic style 153
Pseudo-Dionysius the Areopagite
  legend 22–3
  thought 23–6, 30 n.10, 31 n.12 and n.14
  works 23–5
psychoanalysis 59–60

Rameau, Jean-François 54, 71
Rameau, Jean-Philippe 54
Reid, Martine 13, 76, 79 n.25
renaissance
  Apolistic thought 29
  rediscovery of classical and medieval theories 21
Riccoboni, Marie Jeanne 71, 113–14
Richardson, Samuel 71
Ripa, Cesare 96, 104 n.17
Robert, Raymonde 59
Roman de la Rose 98
Rousseau, Jean-Jacques
  alterity 180
  composer 51–4
  condemnation of culture 202–3
  Confessions 6, 35, 47–54, 208
  de Villeneuve, Vaussore 49
  Dialogues 51
  Discourse on the Origins of Inequality 6, 202–3
  duplicity 49, 51
  Émile 6
  infatuation 48
  nature 36–7, 202
  plagiarism 51, 53
  Reveries of the Solitary Walker 10, 35–7, 40–1
  relationship with Madame de Warens 48
  religion 119
  sensation and language 36
  Social Contract 203
  views on women 111–12, 119

sacrifice 62–3, 65
Saint-Aubin, Madame de 71–2
  Le Courier de la nouveauté 72
  Le Danger des liaisons 71–4

Mémoires, en forme de lettres, de deux jeunes personnes de qualité 72
  posterity 74, 76
Saint John of Damascus 22, 24
Saint Paul 22
Sgard, Jean 98
sharing
  as encounter 9
  intellectual 87
  sharing-out 172
  voices 184 186
sight
  blindness 168, 170–1
  ends of language 167–8
slavery
  American 138–9, 185
  French 66, 87
  power struggle 116; *see also* Dialectic
  Tahitian 205–6
  see also colonialism
Société Internationale pour l'Étude des Femmes de l'Ancien Régime (SIEFAR) 76
Sol, Antoinette 86
Song of Roland, The 4
Starobinski, Jean 49
Stengers, Isabelle 181–3, 186–7, 187 n.4
Stowe, Harriet Beecher 135, 138, 142
stranger
  Bel Inconnu 62
  constitution alongside subject 60, 66
Suard, Jean-Baptiste Antoine 122
Switzerland 112
  Geneva 119–20, 49
  Lausanne 49, 52–3, 120
  French Protestant 119
symbol
  of hope 14
  as reference 147
Szabó, István 191
  Colonel Redl 192
  formal interview 197
  Meeting Venus 193–4
  Mephisto 192
  personal scandal 198
  Sunshine 195–6
  Sweet Emma, dear Böbe 195

Tadié, Jean-Yves 157
Tahiti
    "discovery" 201–2
    native name 204
    sexual mores 204–6
    as Utopia 204–5, 207–8
    welcome of people 203
Thanksgiving 184
theophany 23, 25–7
    divine vestiges or analogies 27–8
    hierarchy 25–7
    spiritual cognition 27–8
theory
    lyrical vs. melodic 55
    memory boom 193
    musical 47, 52
    literary 141
thinking
    binary 183, 186
    processual 181
    rhizomatic 181
    tribe mentality 198
trade
    book 117, 128, 136
    chocolate 62, 65, 68 n.18
    dangers 61, 63
    sugar 62, 68 n.18
    transatlantic Caribbean 60–2
    transpacific 206
translation
    as enhancement 141
    international purview 113
    public good 139–40
    as reworking 107
    unauthorized 135
    unfaithful 111, 123

US Copyright Act 135–6

Van der Straet, Jan (or Stradanus) 179–81, 184
Vernet, Jacob 119–20
Vespucci, Amerigo 179–82, 185
violence
    confrontation 88
    possession versus passion 207
    sexual 62, 64
    Wallis, Samuel 203
Virgil 4, 203–4
Voltaire 73, 109–10, 118–20, 180
Voyeurism 87

Wagner, Richard
    anti-Semitic texts 148–9
    on Jewish composers 148
    opera 147, 149–51, 193
Wagner, Cosima 150
Warner, Marina 60
Western
    beliefs 202
    knowledge 16, 184
    lack of care 186
    philosophy 1, 12, 28
    traditions 203, 206
    viewers 196
Whitehead, Alfred North 181–2
women writers 72, 76, 85–6
    anthologies of literature 94, 96
    autobiography 194–5
    capacity for genius 85
    countertactics 81–3, 112
    economic condition 75–6
    exclusion from canon 75–6
    as intermediaries 109, 111
    names and pseudonyms 85–7
    natural sciences 110
    as translators 108–9
    worthies 93–4, 96
World War I 192
World War II
    1.5 generation 191
    "Variations on a Theme" 192
    see also Paris
writing
    elusive 171–2
    to oneself 160–1
    and painting 169–70, 173
    self-espionage 38–40
    unknown 171
    versus reading 83–4

Zipes, Jack 60

www.ingramcontent.com/pod-product-compliance
Lightning Source LLC
Chambersburg PA
CBHW072139290426
44111CB00012B/1924